Praise for

PONZI'S SCHEME

"Zuckoff . . . tells Ponzi's story amicably and briskly, and keeps the complicated financial intricacies understandable. . . . Even from his pauper's grave, it seems Charles Ponzi is still working his charms."

—*The New York Times Book Review*

"[Zuckoff] recounts Ponzi's wild cat-and-mouse game with banking and legal authorities with verve and authority."

—*Chicago Tribune*

"Ponzi . . . has now been given his due by Mitchell Zuckoff. . . . This beautifully researched book . . . is a rollicking tale of a man with irresistible charm and moxie."

—*The Washington Times*

"Zuckoff does more than simply explain how the scam . . . was supposed to work. . . . Even minor players in the story—a crooked lawyer, the banking regulator, a publishing scion—get a full biographical treatment . . . Ponzi's story is compelling."

—*The Philadelphia Inquirer*

"Zuckoff turns this giddy phase into an American comedy worthy of Preston Sturges."

—*Orlando Sentinel*

Also by Mitchell Zuckoff

JUDGMENT RIDGE:
THE TRUE STORY BEHIND THE
DARTMOUTH MURDERS
with Dick Lehr

CHOOSING NAIA:
A FAMILY'S JOURNEY

PONZI'S SCHEME

PONZI'S SCHEME

The True Story
of a Financial Legend

Mitchell Zuckoff

RANDOM HOUSE TRADE PAPERBACKS
NEW YORK

2006 Random House Trade Paperback Edition

Published in the United States by Random House Trade
Paperbacks, an imprint of The Random House Publishing
Group, a division of Random House, Inc., New York.

RANDOM HOUSE TRADE PAPERBACKS and colophon are
trademarks of Random House, Inc.

Originally published in hardcover in the United States
by Random House, an imprint of The Random House
Publishing Group, a division of Random House, Inc.,
in 2005.

LIBRARY OF CONGRESS CATALOGING-IN-PUBLICATION DATA

Zuckoff, Mitchell
    Ponzi's scheme: the true story of a financial legend /
Mitchell Zuckoff.
        p. cm.
    Includes index.
    ISBN 0-8129-6836-0
    1. Ponzi, Charles. 2. Swindlers and swindling—
Biography. 3. Swindlers and swindling—United States—
Biography. 4. Ponzi schemes—United States—History.
5. Commercial crimes—United States—Case studies. I. Title.

HV 6692.P66Z83 2005   364.16'3—dc22   [B]
2004046770

Printed in the United States of America

www.atrandom.com

9 8 7 6 5 4 3 2

Text design by Laurie Jewell

For my father

Contents

PROLOGUE   xi

PART ONE

CHAPTER ONE
"I'm the man."   3

CHAPTER TWO
"I'm guilty."   19

CHAPTER THREE
"Newspaper genius"   33

CHAPTER FOUR
"A long circle of bad breaks"   45

CHAPTER FIVE
"As restless as the sea"   59

CHAPTER SIX
"An American beauty"   73

PART TWO

CHAPTER SEVEN
"The almighty dollar"   93

Chapter Eight
"A small snowball downhill"   111

Chapter Nine
"Always reaching for the moon"   127

Chapter Ten
"I never bluff."   143

Chapter Eleven
"Like stealing candy from a baby"   159

Part Three

Chapter Twelve
"Money madness"   179

Chapter Thirteen
"Master of the situation"   197

Chapter Fourteen
"Even his cows couldn't give milk."   215

Chapter Fifteen
"You discovered the money!"   231

Chapter Sixteen
"I feel the strain—inside."   251

Chapter Seventeen
"I'm not the man."   269

Epilogue   293
Acknowledgments   315
A Note on Sources   319
Notes   321
Select Bibliography   373
Index   377

PROLOGUE

On June 9, 1920, a smooth-talking salesman named Martin Kolega went door-to-
door in South Boston, Massachusetts, demon-
strating a double-your-money machine small
enough to fit on a sewing table. When Kolega
knocked at the modest home of Mrs. Blanche
Crasco, she welcomed him inside. But Mrs.
Crasco was no fool. She wanted proof that
the marvelous appliance worked. Kolega happily obliged.

No one could deny that the machine was
a wonder. Encased in an enameled metal box,
it sported flashing lights and a revolving
board dotted with what looked like type-
writer keys. In a darkened room, Kolega in-
serted into the box a hundred-dollar bill and
a blank sheet of paper cut to the same size.
Lights flickered, gears turned, and the box
emitted a mysterious whirring sound. After a
long minute of anticipation, Kolega pressed
a button and, miraculously, two genuine
hundred-dollar bills emerged.

Mrs. Crasco was sold.

Kolega pocketed her money—the $540 was enough for Mrs. Crasco to buy a car, but it seemed worth it for the endless stream of hundred-dollar bills the machine was sure to produce. In exchange, Kolega handed Mrs. Crasco a package wrapped in brown paper. Allowing for time to escape, Kolega warned her not to open it until nightfall, to be certain she did not expose the special duplicating paper to light. He left. She waited.

When Mrs. Crasco opened the bundle, she found a plain wooden box. Realizing that she had been duped, she called the police.

Oddly enough, a gullible newspaper reporter writing about the arrest of Kolega and an accomplice seemed to believe that Mrs. Crasco had been sold a fake version of a truly wondrous device. "It is alleged," the reporter wrote, "that the men reserved one machine for demonstration and sold their customers dummy affairs."

In other words, had Kolega only been kind enough to sell Mrs. Crasco a working copy of the splendid contraption, everyone would be happy and he would not be in jail.

In 1920, anything seemed possible. Especially when it came to money.

A new ethos was emerging, one that would reshape what it meant to be an American. No more pennies saved and pennies earned. Money was best when it arrived fast, easy, and in large quantities. Newspapers fueled dreams of prosperity with stories of poor girls marrying rich men, inherited fortunes from long-lost relatives, and fearless entrepreneurs who'd hit it big. The message was clear: No longer was prosperity the preserve of the well-born; even the laborer and the charwoman could aspire to the manor. All it took was the right break, the right knock at the door. And if wealth did not come knocking, go get it yourself. Plunge into dark waters in pursuit of sunken treasure. Never mind the shallow bottoms.

For promoters of instant assets, it was a time when it paid to think big. Kolega was a small-timer, quickly behind bars, his name soon forgotten. But at the same time, in the same city, a smiling, cane-twirling banty rooster of a man had a better idea for doubling money—a secret formula for financial alchemy that could transform penny stamps into millions of dollars. Admirers hailed him as a wizard, critics branded him a fraud. Either way, he arrived on the scene at the perfect moment. His amazing run would mark the first roar of the 1920s, and his name would live on forever.

PART ONE

Ponzi displays his fancy walking stick in a pose fit for a drum major.

Boston Public Library, Print Department

"I'M THE MAN."

The huge blue car moved slowly through the crooked streets of the old city, its owner sitting on the wide rear seat, his bottom comforted by deep, horsehair-filled cushions that absorbed the bumps from the uneven cobblestones. Heat and sunlight bounced off the brick and granite buildings, baking the Locomobile limousine and broiling its passengers. The morning air bristled with the hint of a developing thunderstorm. When the skies broke loose it would be a welcome relief from the weeks of summer heat that had made downtown Boston ripe with the smells of horses, fish, fruit, fresh-cut leather, and tight-wound rope, all seasoned by salt from the nearby harbor.

At the wheel of the hand-polished Locomobile was a young Irish immigrant named John Collins, wearing the hat and brass-buttoned uniform of a newly created job: motorcar chauffeur. His boss an Italian immigrant, had taken delivery of the dazzling vehicle only three weeks earlier, paying a thousand dollars in cash above the $12,600 list price to spirit it away from the New York financier for whom it had been custom-built. For the same price a man could own twenty Model T's, with enough change to buy a modest house. But what was the point of that? In 1920, the Locomobile was the most expensive car in America, dripping with luxury, from its sterling-silver trim to its crystal bud vases. Purring, glistening Locomobiles filled the garages of Carnegies and Vanderbilts, and General John J. "Black Jack" Pershing, commander of American forces in the Great War, had shipped his to France for use as a staff car. The executives at the Locomobile Company of America understood that exclusivity appealed to the elites. They had positioned their automobile in direct opposition to Henry Ford's backfiring rattletrap of the masses. The company's ads, with the look of engraved invitations, stated that Locomobiles were built by hand "in strictly limited quantities because the making of any pre-eminently fine article is impossible on a large scale."

In the short time he had been driving the car, Collins had learned well the daily twelve-mile route that began at his boss's gracious home in the historic suburb of Lexington, less than a mile from the site of the first skirmish of the Revolutionary War. From there, they rolled east through working-class Arlington and Somerville, into tony Cambridge, across the Charles River, then down Tremont Street to a nondescript building on School Street, less than a block from Boston City Hall. Occasionally there would be detours, most often to a bank, and the boss would use the one-way intercom from the back seat to relay the new directions to Collins. But on this day—July 24, 1920—it was straight from home to office.

Collins slowed as he turned down School Street and saw what awaited them: a mob of several hundred men and women, crowded together hip to hip, chest to back. Viewed from above, it looked like an abstract mosaic of straw boaters and colorful felt cloche hats, punctuated by the dark crowns of a few bowlers. Some in the throng had brought bewildered children, who cried or whined as they struggled to avoid being trampled underfoot. The street was alive with electricity unrelated to the gathering thunderclouds. It came from the horde itself. Each member was a charged electron jittering in a magnetic field created by the man in the back seat of the Locomobile.

The street normally would have been all but deserted on a sultry Saturday in late July. But this was no ordinary day. When the crowd saw the limousine turn down the street they pressed toward it, half in reverence and half in mindless desire. They parted to allow Collins to steer toward the curb in front of the Niles Building, at 27 School Street, the modest home of his boss's extravagantly immodest firm, the impressively named Securities Exchange Company.

From his perch in the back seat, Collins's boss could see that some men in the street were holding copies of that morning's *Boston Post*. The banner headline trumpeted a victory in one of the America's Cup races by the American yacht *Resolute* over its British challenger, *Shamrock IV.* At a time when anything seemed possible except a legal drink of whiskey, elite sports like yachting and golf had captured the public imagination.

If one subject interested Bostonians more than rich men's sports, it was the prospect of becoming rich themselves. Undeniable evidence could be found in that morning's *Post,* just below the yacht race story. On the left side of the front page, in bold black letters, was the headline that had filled School Street to bursting:

DOUBLES THE
MONEY WITHIN
THREE MONTHS

A *Post* reporter had visited 27 School Street a day earlier and acquired a basic understanding of how the Securities Exchange Company claimed to create spectacular profits for its investors. The unbylined story even described the Locomobile limousine and the boss's Lexington home, which was "furnished with the best" and "does not give the impression of *nouveau riche* either, for the fine Italian tastes of the owner fixed that."

The man who owned the fine home, the flashy car, the Securities Exchange Company, the adoration of the people on School Street, and anything else he cared to buy was named Charles Ponzi.

Reading the *Post* story that morning, Ponzi could chuckle with appreciation of his good judgment in granting the reporter access to his office and home. He had handled the interview himself, but from now on he would rely on advice from a publicity man he had just hired, an ex-reporter named William McMasters. At first, Ponzi had been skeptical about publicity—he had not needed much to achieve success that approached his wildest dreams—but his gentle treatment by the *Post* made it seem as though every card he turned would be an ace.

The front-page *Post* story eclipsed two previous stories Boston papers had printed about him and his business. The first, six weeks earlier in the *Boston Traveler,* had described his company in flattering terms but never mentioned it or him by name. Still, word had spread as to the identity and location of Ponzi's operation, and hundreds of thousands of dollars had poured in during the weeks that followed. The second story, three weeks earlier in the *Post,* had been a brief item about a million-dollar lawsuit filed against Ponzi by a furniture dealer. That, too, had helped. The fact that he was rich enough to be sued for a million dollars had attracted swarms of new investors.

The brief account of the enormous lawsuit had piqued the interest of the *Post*'s young acting editor and publisher, who had ordered the follow-up feature story that appeared this day. In it, the *Post* reporter printed Ponzi's comments at length and without challenge, as though Ponzi had delivered them with his hand on a Bible. During the course of several hours of discourse, the thirty-eight-year-old entrepreneur had offered a condensed, sanitized version of the seventeen years since he had emigrated from Italy. Then Ponzi had explained his business in broad, confident terms, telling how it was built on a modest and unlikely medium: International Reply Coupons, slips of paper that could be redeemed for postage stamps. He'd described his company's growth—from pennies to millions of dollars in seven months—and had boasted of the opening of branch offices from Maine to New Jersey. The reporter had filled a notebook with Ponzi's comments and played the notes back to *Post* readers as clear and sweet as a song from a Victrola.

Ponzi had capped the interview with a priceless assertion, and again the reporter had obliged him by printing it: "I get no pleasure out of spending money on myself, but a great deal in doing some good with it. Always I have said to myself, if I can get one million dollars, I can live with all the comfort I want for the rest of my life. If I get more than one million dollars, I will spend all over and above the one million trying to do good in the world. Now I have the million. That I have put aside. If my business closed tomorrow I am sure that I will have that amount on which to make myself and family comfortable for the rest of our days." If anyone doubted how secure Ponzi felt, the story continued: "Ponzi estimates his wealth in excess of $8.5 million."

With a maestro's touch, Ponzi had struck a perfect balance among the forces competing to control the new American identity: altruism and avarice. Now that he was all set, he insisted, he had no need for more investors. But he would continue accepting their money out of the goodness of his heart, so they could join him and his family in savoring the finer things in life.

If there was any reason for the people of Boston to be suspicious of Ponzi, they would not find it in the morning *Post*. The story read with all the confidence of the advertisements the paper ran that promised disappearing dandruff to wise buyers of Petrole hair tonic, or "sunshiny" stomachs courtesy of Goldenglo tablets, or relief from chronic constipation in a tin of Fruit-a-Tives.

The closest the story came to skepticism was to mention that federal and state authorities had looked into Ponzi's extraordinary investment plan. But the reporter defused that land mine in a single sentence, writing, "The authorities have not been able to discover a single illegal thing about it." Ponzi could not have hoped for a more sterling endorsement.

Adding to Ponzi's delight, below the front-page story was an ad for a prominent local bank, the Cosmopolitan Trust Company. The bank was trying to drum up new deposits by guaranteeing a generous interest rate: 5 percent a year, compounded monthly. To Ponzi, the ad was a divine gift. For months he had been comparing his promised rate of return—50 percent in forty-five days—to the paltry sum paid by banks. Here was the same comparison on the front page of the *Post*, the self-proclaimed "Great Breakfast Table Paper of New England."

A working man with one hundred dollars to invest, reading that day's *Post* over a bowl of Grape-Nuts, faced two choices of seemingly equal reliability but vastly different outcomes. Even in the margins of his newspaper, he could calculate that depositing his hundred dollars in the Cosmopolitan Trust Company would yield him an annual profit of five dollars and change. That was assuming the bank did not fail in these days when federal insurance for deposits was barely a whisper of an idea. Or he could entrust his hundred dollars to this Charles Ponzi fellow and watch it multiply over and again during the same year.

If he reinvested his hundred dollars plus interest after each forty-five-day period, he would walk away with more than twenty-five hundred dollars after a year. If he let it ride for a second year, he would pocket more than sixty-five thousand dollars. It was an unimaginable sum at a time when the average U.S. income was about two thousand dollars, the president of Harvard University was paid six thousand dollars, a Men's Ventilated Raincoat could be ordered from the Sears catalog for less than twelve dollars, a can of codfish cakes for a family of three cost twenty-five cents, and the newspaper he held in his hands cost two cents. Only a fool would choose the bank's interest over Ponzi's.

Having read the *Post* and done the math, would-be investors had begun assembling on School Street long before the Locomobile had even started the trip from Lexington. They came from all corners of

Boston and beyond, a miniature League of Nations, with immigrants brushing shoulders with Brahmins, Italians mingling with Spaniards, Irish alongside English, Greeks chatting with Poles. Among them were Swedes, Frenchmen, Jews, blacks, and Portuguese, new and old Americans. Kitchen maids stood alongside businessmen, office boys squeezed against society matrons. It was the one place in the tribal city where the only denomination that mattered was engraved on the bills clutched in investors' hands.

Bookbinder Arthur Case of the city's Dorchester neighborhood was ready to invest a whopping three thousand dollars, just a week after his wife, Clara, had put in one thousand. Their neighbor, candy-factory worker William Hoff, emptied his wallet and came up with seventy-eight dollars. Boston florist Philip Feinstein was ready to place eleven hundred dollars in Ponzi's hands, while Patrick Horan had stuffed sixteen hundred dollars into his billfold. Benjamin Brown intended to add six hundred dollars to the six hundred he had deposited just four days earlier. Stable worker Timothy Donovan of suburban Somerville and Alfred Authoir of nearby Cambridge each expected their fifty-dollar investments to grow into seventy-five dollars by the first week of September. Print shop foreman Percy Stott of Methuen had made the thirty-mile trip to Boston for the third straight day, this time to add one hundred dollars to the two hundred he had already invested.

Luggage shop owner Joseph Pearlstein came bearing not cash but a note signed by Ponzi that would allow him to collect fifteen hundred dollars. He had heard about the Securities Exchange Company from none other than the lovely Rose Gnecco Ponzi, who had stopped at his Dorchester store the first week in June. She had come by to purchase new bags for a trip she and her husband, Charles, were planning to Italy, to visit his mother. Rose Ponzi had proudly described her husband's remarkable financial skills to the luggage vendor, and Pearlstein had been so impressed he had invested one thousand dollars. Now his note was due, so Pearlstein was in line to collect his original stake plus his five-hundred-dollar profit. But he would not invest again. Reluctant to press his luck, Pearlstein was satisfied with one spin of the wheel.

The crowd also included a fourteen-year-old boy in short pants named Frank Thomas. He earned $7.20 a week running errands, and he was eager to invest ten dollars with Ponzi. Charlie Gnecco of Medford, six miles away across the Mystic River, was there for his fourth and largest investment of the month, one thousand dollars. And why not? His baby sister, Rose, was happily married to the man in charge of the whole operation. If she had faith in Ponzi, well then, Charlie Gnecco did, too. Carmela Ottavi of nearby Chelsea brought two thousand dollars to add to the six hundred she had invested twelve days earlier. Ponzi's chauffeur, John Collins, had already thrown in five hundred. Watching the crowd from the front seat of the Locomobile, he resolved to add seven hundred more.

While some had come because of the *Post* story, others had heard from friends and relatives of the profits to be found on School Street. Although the *Post* seemed to have only just discovered the Securities Exchange Company, the streets of Boston had been buzzing about it and Ponzi for months. Some people had heard testimonials from men like Fiori Bevilacqua of Roslindale, whose friends knew him by his anglicized name, Frank Drinkwater. In a lifetime of hard work as a laborer and a real estate investor, Bevilacqua had painstakingly amassed the small fortune of ten thousand dollars. In June he had entrusted the entire amount to Ponzi, then spent the next few weeks sharing the news of his impending good fortune. His friends listened, and they came, too. When the *Post* story hit the streets, the Securities Exchange Company was already averaging more than a million dollars a week in new investments. If the pace held, it would soon be a million dollars a day.

But potential investors were not the only ones focused on Ponzi. The *Post* story aroused the interest and concern of some of the most powerful men in Massachusetts. Several of them had already begun asking questions. The newspaper's inexperienced acting publisher, Richard Grozier, who had ordered the feature story after reading about the million-dollar lawsuit, directed his staff to dig deeper into Ponzi's rise from poverty to prosperity. Similar orders issued from Boston's federal prosecutor, Daniel J. Gallagher, and Massachusetts Attorney General J. Weston Allen, whom the *Post* reporter had tracked down vacationing on Cape Cod. The attorney general, as priggish as he was ambitious, answered vaguely that one of his assistants, a young prosecutor named Albert Hurwitz, was dutifully investigating Ponzi. Two other public officials also took note of the *Post* story: Boston's corrupt district attorney, Joseph Pelletier, and the state's incorruptible new bank commissioner, Joseph C. Allen, who had only recently been named to the job by Governor Calvin Coolidge.

Collins eased the Locomobile to a stop, hopped out, and hustled to the back door. It swung open and the man himself alighted from the car, stepping onto the wide running board, then planting his feet on the sidewalk. If the crowd had expected a large man, it would have been sorely disappointed. Ponzi was five foot two, shorter than some of the arm-weary newsboys selling their papers in the crowd. He weighed just 130 pounds fully clothed after a heavy meal.

But what he lacked in size he made up for in style.

Ponzi was a human dynamo, handsome in his own way, with a regal nose, a dimpled chin, and full lips that curved upward in a barely suppressed grin. Usually he did not suppress it, and the resulting smile seemed almost too big for his face, as though painted on by a child. On his head was a jaunty golfing cap—a smart weekend fashion statement, more casual than his usual straw boater. Under the hat was a crown of brown hair flecked with gray, slicked down and razor-parted on the left side, with a low pompadour in front. The only signs of age were starbursts of wrinkles around his lively brown-black eyes, seemingly etched not by worries but by a lifetime of laughter. He wore a new Palm Beach suit, impossibly crisp given the sultry weather, with a silk handkerchief peeking from the coat pocket like a fresh-cut daffodil. His polished shoes clicked and clacked on the stone sidewalk. A starched white collar was held in place by the knot of his dark moiré silk tie, which sported a dazzling diamond-topped pin. His right hand gripped a gold-handled malacca walking stick, similar to one favored by a showman of an earlier age, P. T. Barnum. His left fist held the handle of a leather satchel that would prove too small for the bushels of cash awaiting him this day.

Looking around, Ponzi could not help but beam. Much later, when writing his memoirs, he would remember the street looking as though "the two million inhabitants of Greater Boston were all there!" All to see him. In fact, Ponzi overstated the region's population by a half million people, but inflation of numbers was something of a habit with him. Emerging with Ponzi from the car was a stern-faced, heavily armed bodyguard from the Pinkerton National Detective Agency, which rented out its agents when they were not busting "Red menace" unionists or chasing bank robbers.

Security had lately become a concern for Ponzi, whose business was generating so much cash it made him fear that he was a ripe target for thieves. To reinforce the Pinkertons, Ponzi had obtained a gun permit three months earlier from the police department in Somerville, where he'd lived before moving to Lexington. A small, blue steel pistol, a .25-caliber Colt automatic, rested snugly inside a vest pocket. Another pocket held contents he was much more eager to wave in public: a bank statement, in his name, for $1.5 million.

"There's Ponzi!" someone shouted when he stepped from the car. On that cue the masses moved as one. They surrounded him and his guard, some pleading for a moment of his time, others content to pat him on the back, and some thrilled simply to lay eyes on the Merlin of money. A few skeptics mingled among the believers. One was loudly labeling the Securities Exchange Company a bogus get-rich-quick scheme when Ponzi arrived.

"I'd like to see the man who could do it—" the doubter shouted.

Faced with the challenge, Ponzi called out, "Well, I'm doing it! I'm the man!"

The words emerged in a mellifluous tone, accented only slightly by his native Italian. Ponzi sometimes spoke in staccato bursts, but more often he had a pleasing, charismatic voice—women heard a mildly insistent suitor; men, a trusted friend. It was a voice that would have fit rising movie star Rudolph Valentino, if only his films had sound.

Ponzi kept moving—past two uniformed policemen at the doors of the Niles Building and up the narrow flight of stairs to his cramped second-floor offices. Along the way he had to push into the stairwell past people who formed what one observer called "a swirling, seething, gesticulating, jabbering throng." Some kind of commotion was happening down the hall from his office, but Ponzi paid it no mind. He stepped through a glass-paneled door into a small anteroom his company used as a waiting area. There, each investor was met by one of the sixteen clerks and assistants, many of them added to the payroll in recent weeks to handle the torrents of cash.

Moving deeper into the office, prospective investors would be turned over to a team of agents led by one John A. Dondero, a distant relative of Ponzi's by marriage. After making sure the investors had cash on hand or endorsed money orders, Dondero would lead them to a second, larger room, divided roughly in half by a four-foot wooden barrier topped by iron bars. Between the bars and the counter were slim openings for three tellers.

Investors slid their cash to one of the young tellers. Often they were three particular girls: Angela Locarno, her sister Marie Locarno, and their friend Bessie Langone. In return for cash, the investors received promissory notes, receipts really, that guaranteed the original investment plus 50 percent interest in forty-five days. The receipts bore Ponzi's ink-stamped signature, which led many to call them simply "Ponzi notes." Lately the waves of cash had come crashing over the counter so quickly that the bills were dumped into wire baskets, to be sorted when the tide rolled out. At slower times the cash was funneled from the clerks directly to a man named Louis Cassullo, an unpleasant acquaintance from Ponzi's past whom Ponzi neither liked nor trusted. Where Cassullo was concerned, Ponzi applied the old adage about keeping friends close and enemies closer. From Cassullo, the cash was counted, bundled, and deposited into one of Ponzi's fast-growing bank accounts. That is, minus any stray bills Cassullo siphoned off.

The other half of the room, a space perhaps eight by fourteen feet, was partitioned off for an office shared by Ponzi and a pretty, dark-haired girl named Lucy Meli, his eighteen-year-old chief bookkeeper, secretary, and gal Friday. The walls of the office were bare, and the furniture consisted of three chairs and a single flattop desk, at which Ponzi and his young assistant sat on opposite sides, facing each other. Visitors were surprised to see no adding machines or file cabinets. Despite the enormous sums of money pouring in, the offices of the Securities Exchange Company were dark and dingy, with a few scuffed, mismatched pieces of furniture and the lingering smell of the Turkish cigarettes Ponzi smoked in a five-inch, ivory-and-gold holder.

As soon as Ponzi arrived, his overwhelmed workers rushed to greet him with word of trouble. The fuss that he had passed in the hallway was the opening of a competing, copycat investment plan that called itself the Old Colony Foreign Exchange Company. Its owners had had the temerity to rent an office on the same floor of the Niles Building as Ponzi's Securities Exchange Company. Old Colony was promising the same 50 percent in forty-five days, and its organizers were more than happy to steal away the overflow of would-be Ponzi investors who grew tired of waiting in line. The Old Colony promoters had even printed up promissory notes that strongly resembled Ponzi's.

Ponzi understood instantly that some investors might be confused into thinking that the two companies were one and the same. He also quickly surmised that his rivals had rented the rooms down the hall from a man named Frederick J. McCuen, who ran a struggling business selling and repairing electrical appliances. Weeks earlier, when the mobs had begun to overrun the Niles Building, McCuen had briefly worked for Ponzi in a minor capacity. With Old Colony, McCuen had seen an opportunity to get in on the ground floor.

Outside the offices of this upstart Ponzi imitator, a large man in a Stetson hat was beckoning investors who had come to see Ponzi.

"Right this way!" cried the ballyhoo man. "A new million-dollar company!"

As Ponzi's employees described the scene down the hall to him, Ponzi emptied his pockets, searching for a key to a strongbox that held receipts from the previous day. Large sums of ready cash might be needed to handle this Old Colony threat. Out of Ponzi's pocket came loose cigarettes, several bunches of keys, and a roll of bills so fat it "would have made anyone but a bank teller gasp," as one witness described it. After finding the strongbox key, Ponzi took a moment to consider the news of his competition.

As a mother bear knows its young by scent, Ponzi knew that the Old Colony operators were frauds and scam artists—though he could never say how he knew. Privately, Ponzi assessed the situation and reached a troubling conclusion: "They had me by the small of the neck, and the best that I could do was squirm." Though he could not denounce them directly, he would sic his Pinkerton agents on them to dig up whatever dirt they could find. But that would take time.

In the meantime, he could at least scare them. Ponzi grabbed the black, candlestick-style telephone on his desk and asked the operator to connect him with the headquarters of the Boston Police Department. In recent months, Ponzi had made many friends on the force; by some estimates, nearly three-quarters of the department had invested with him. Low pay had long been a nettlesome issue among Boston police officers, and Ponzi's investment offer was a welcome supplement to their paltry incomes. Indeed, the department was filled with newly hired officers, replacements for eleven hundred veteran policemen—more than two-thirds of the force—who were fired nine months earlier by Governor Coolidge for striking over wages and working conditions. Several patrolmen even moonlighted as agents for Ponzi, collecting investments from others for a cut of the take.

Ponzi could have called Captain Jeremiah Sullivan at Police Station No. 2, located around the corner from the Niles Building on City Hall Avenue. But instead he called headquarters to seek help from a fellow immigrant, Inspector Joseph Cavagnaro. The inspector had no trouble finding 27 School Street. He had invested nine hundred dollars on June 16, and then over the next four weeks had added $1,750 more. Providing for his wife and four daughters, aged eleven to eighteen, would be much easier when his notes began coming due in eight days.

Ponzi explained the situation, strongly suggesting that Old Colony was deceiving the public by making investors think they were trusting their money to a firm associated with Ponzi. That could be bad for business, and anything bad for business would be bad for investors like Cavagnaro. The inspector got the message. Ponzi hung up, turned on his heel, and headed out of his office and into the hallway. His anger rising, Ponzi steeled his resolve for a nose-to-chest confrontation with the oversized ballyhoo man.

Halfway down the hall, he caught sight of a tired-looking woman with a baby in her arms. Ponzi's rage vanished. He brought his quick march to a halt. "Here, let me help you," he said in Italian, their shared native tongue.

She explained that she had grown exhausted while waiting to collect $150 on a Ponzi note that had just come due. Ponzi took the note and gently asked her to wait a moment. He returned to the offices of the Securities Exchange Company and emerged a few minutes later, money in hand.

"*Buona fortuna!*" he told her as she walked away. "Good luck."

She was swallowed up in the crowd just as the ballyhoo man resumed his chants. When he saw Ponzi, the big man turned his come-on into a taunt.

"Ah, Mr. Ponzi!" the man called. "Want to put in two thousand?"

"Mister," Ponzi shot back, "if you've got two thousand you'd better hang on to it for bail. There'll be a couple of police inspectors down to see you in a few moments."

Not waiting for a reply, Ponzi whirled around and returned to his office. Soon, Inspector Cavagnaro strode through the door. He wanted to help, but he explained to Ponzi that he had no evidence of wrongdoing by the Old Colony gang. He had no cause for arrest. Still, Ponzi could be pleased that Cavagnaro's presence had put the

"I'm the man." 17

Old Colony crowd on notice that they were being watched and that Ponzi had friends in high places. That would have to do until the Pinkertons could get busy with their investigation. All Ponzi needed was a little time. He had figured out how to turn this soon-to-be-exhausted gold mine into a permanent mint, one that would make him as rich and respected as the Brahmins who ran this town. At least that was the plan. In the meantime, he could not let anything derail him.

Investors kept pouring into the office the rest of the day, and by the time Ponzi locked the doors after six that night he had taken in more than $200,000. That did not include the receipts from his two dozen similarly overwhelmed branches. It was his best day since he had birthed his brainstorm the previous summer.

As Ponzi sat back in the Locomobile for the ride home to Lexington, the basement-level presses of the *Post* began rumbling to life once more. By coincidence, the newspaper's offices were only a hundred yards away from the Securities Exchange Company, around the corner on Washington Street, a Colonial-era cow path known as Newspaper Row. If he had stayed in the city a few more hours, Ponzi could have picked up a copy of the *Boston Sunday Post* still warm and inky. This time the story about him would be at the very top of the front page, with a headline set in bold type. It would have photos, too, not only of him but also of his wife, his mother, the scene outside 27 School Street, and his fabulous Lexington home.

But the glorious tide that had carried him so far, so fast, was threatening to overwhelm him. The *Post*'s Sunday story would not be as flattering as the one that had appeared this morning. It would signal the *Post*'s rising doubts about his honesty and rally authorities to intensify their sluggish investigations. Ponzi was about to get a run for his money.

Postcard of S.S. Vancouver, *the ship that brought Ponzi from Italy to America in 1903.*

CHAPTER TWO

"I'M GUILTY."

Ponzi's moment of success had been decades in the making. The thirty-eight years that preceded that Saturday in July 1920 were notable mostly for setbacks, misadventures, and persistent failures in pursuit of riches.

He was born March 3, 1882, in Lugo, Italy, an ancient crossroads town populated by merchants and farmers, in a fertile plain sandwiched between Bologna and the Adriatic Sea. Ponzi's parents were living with his widowed maternal grandmother in an apartment at No. 950 Via Codalunga, a curving road lined with three-story stone buildings. It was a decidedly working-class neighborhood; down the street was the ghetto where Lugo's large Jewish population had been required to live since the 1700s. At the other end of the street was the Church of Pio Suffragio, a gloomy sanctuary filled with baroque stuccos of cherubs and frescoes depicting the deaths of saints. Stained-glass windows high on the walls allowed only dim shards of light to fall

on the narrow wooden pews. Ponzi's parents, Oreste and Imelde
Ponzi, brought him there to be baptized, anointing him with names
chosen to honor his maternal and paternal grandfathers: Carlo Pietro
Giovanni Guglielmo Tebaldo Ponzi.

The family was comfortable but far from wealthy, richer in name
and reputation than in savings. Ponzi's father was descended from
middle-class tradesmen and hoteliers but he was employed in Lugo as
a postman. The work of delivering mail and selling stamps was steady
if not glamorous, and the post office was only a short walk from the
family's apartment. Ponzi's mother came from significantly more
prominent stock—Imelde Ponzi's father was an official of the Civil
and Criminal Court of Parma. More notably in the class-conscious
world of nineteenth-century Italy, her father, mother, and grandparents all bore the titles *Don* or *Donna*—Don Giovanni, Donna Teresa,
Don Antonio, and so on—which placed them among the aristocracy
in the duchy of Parma.

Imelde Ponzi doted on her only child, staking her family's future
on the little boy who resembled her so strongly, hoping he would restore the family to its former social and financial rank. Throughout
Carlo's childhood she dreamed aloud about the illustrious future she
wanted for him, building what he called "castles in the air" in her stories of the glory she hoped he would achieve. A favorite notion was
that her smart, pampered boy would follow the example of one of her
grandfathers and become a lawyer and perhaps even a judge.

When Carlo was a few months old, the family moved south to
Rome, but then returned to the north and settled in Parma, a prosperous city halfway between Milan and Bologna, where both Oreste
and Imelde were born. Carlo entered Parma's public schools at age
five, but when he was ten his parents decided it was time to begin
preparing him for the professional life they had mapped out. Oreste
and Imelde sent young Carlo to a prestigious private boarding school
founded under the auspices of Napoleon's second wife, Princess
Marie-Louise, who had ruled the province for thirty years in the early
nineteenth century. Ponzi impressed the nuns who taught him, learn-

ing to speak fluent French and generally winning good grades. His chief regret was that although the school was not far from his home, he could visit his parents only on occasional weekends and holidays. His loneliness increased when his father died while he was away.

A modest inheritance from his father, supplemented by some money left to him by an aunt, allowed Ponzi to chase his mother's dreams and attend college. If he invested carefully and budgeted wisely, his inheritance would be just enough to cover tuition and living expenses. To his mother's delight, he earned acceptance to the University of Rome, the city's oldest university, founded six centuries earlier in the name of "La Sapienza," or wisdom. But five hundred miles from home, free from the control of boarding school nuns, Ponzi had other pursuits in mind. He identified with the stories his mother had told of their aristocratic blood, and he gravitated toward a group of wealthy students who lived *la dolce vita*. Ponzi did everything he could to emulate them, adopting their manners and especially their spending habits. Their funds seemed limitless, so he dug ever deeper into his fast-dwindling inheritance to dress in the latest European fashions and pick up restaurant tabs for his friends and the pretty girls they met.

His rich friends considered the university a four-year vacation, and so Ponzi acted as though he could, too. He skipped classes, preferring to sleep away his days. At dusk he roused himself from his boarding-house bed and roamed the city's fashionable neighborhoods, carousing in cafés, attending the theater, and refining his taste for opera. At midnight he joined the gamblers and thieves in the casinos of Rome's underground. Young, naive, half-drunk, and reckless with money, Ponzi made an appealing mark. At dawn he would trudge to his rooms to sleep, and then the cycle would begin again. Throughout, he assured his mother he was hard at work, making her proud. But the good times could not last. The combination of an exhausted bank account and a thorough disregard for classes killed any chance he had for a degree. Ponzi looked himself over and made a brutally honest self-assessment: He had become a fop. Worse, an impoverished fop. The easy accessibility of money had spoiled him. He had no choice but to leave Rome.

Before he died, Oreste Ponzi had enlisted one of young Carlo's uncles to watch over him. Now, the uncle suggested that the twenty-one-year-old college washout find a job, perhaps as an entry-level clerk. Carlo flatly refused. He considered himself a gentleman, a member of the elite class of his Roman friends. Taking a mundane job would be beneath him. Humiliating, even. The thought of physical labor was not even discussed. Ponzi considered himself a mollycoddle, and no one disagreed. The uncle tried a different tack: "Poor, uneducated Italian boys go to America and make lots of money," the uncle said. "You have a good education, you are refined and of a good family. You should be able to make a fortune in America easily." Then Ponzi's uncle spoke the magic words that were luring millions of Europeans across the ocean: "In the United States," he said, "the streets are actually paved with gold. All you have to do is stoop and pick it up."

Ponzi knew his mother was disappointed by his Roman holiday. He was ashamed that he had misled her and ignored her advice. Going to America and coming home a rich man would make her proud. Even better, it would satisfy his thirst for a life of leisure and hers for a prominent son. Confident that he would soon be the toast of the New World, after which he would return triumphant to Italy, Ponzi accepted his uncle's suggestion and packed his best clothes. As a send-off, his family provided him with a steamship ticket and two hundred dollars to get established in America and begin collecting his gold. With a blessing from his mother still ringing in his ears, Ponzi went south to Naples. There, on November 3, 1903, he climbed the gangplank of the S.S. *Vancouver,* bound for Boston.

At 430 feet and five thousand tons, the *Vancouver* could carry nearly two thousand immigrants on each two-week transatlantic crossing. Most spent about twenty-five dollars for tickets that entitled them to the crowded misery of steerage—an area deep within the bowels of the *Vancouver,* perhaps seven feet high, as wide as the ship, and about one-third its length. Iron pipes formed small sleeping berths with narrow aisles between them. Most steerage passengers spent the entire journey lying on their berths—outside space for them was severely limited and inevitably located on the worst part of the deck, where the rolling of the ship was most pronounced and the dirt from the smokestack most likely to fall. The food was barely edible, the water often salty, and the only places to eat were shelves or benches alongside the sleeping areas. Toilets were nearby, overused, and poorly ventilated. Within a few days at sea the air in steerage reeked of vomit and waste. Passengers lolled in a seasick stupor on mattresses made from burlap bags filled with seaweed, using life preservers as pillows.

Most of the *Vancouver*'s passengers were from the south of Italy, which had withered economically since the country's unification in 1861. They were young laborers like Giuseppe Venditto, who had twelve dollars in his pocket and the address of a cousin in Ohio, and domestic servants like the widow Lauretta Zarella, who boarded the ship with her two teenage daughters, nine dollars, and a plan to join her son in Providence. A few were from Greece, others from Austria and Russia. Several dozen Portuguese boarded when the ship stopped in the Azores. To pass the empty days at sea, they traded rumors of America, thought of their families back home, and wondered what awaited them.

Ponzi had almost nothing to do with them. Not only was he from the ostensibly more cultured north of Italy, he was among the more privileged travelers. He and sixty-four other passengers had paid an extra twenty dollars for more comfortable berths in the *Vancouver*'s second-class cabins, though he would forever claim he had traveled to America first-class. While the human sardines in steerage suffered, Ponzi spent the passage continuing his college ways, buying drinks and gallantly tipping waiters. Ponzi's biggest expense was gambling. A cardsharp caught sight of the bushy-tailed young fellow with the ready billfold and invited him for a friendly game. By the time they were through, Ponzi's two-hundred-dollar stake had been reduced to two dollars and fifty cents, even less than most of the unfortunates in steerage.

The ship entered Boston Harbor on November 17, greeted by a steady drizzle and an icy east wind that whipped the dirty waters into a liquid mountain of whitecaps. The *Vancouver*'s captain eased the ship to the Dominion Line's dock in East Boston, where the nearby Splendor Macaroni Company and a fish-glue plant provided the immigrants with their first smells of the new land. Before disembarking, the first- and second-class passengers underwent immigration inspections— only the steerage passengers would be held in quarantine. Ponzi stretched the truth and identified himself to the inspector as a student, but he admitted that he was down to his last few dollars. To gain legal entry into America, he vowed that he was not a polygamist, a cripple, or otherwise infirm, and that he had never been held in prison or a poorhouse.

Having satisfied the inspector, Ponzi strolled jelly-legged down the gangplank wearing his best suit, with spats fastened to his shoes. Despite his nearly empty pockets and his rain-soaked clothes, Ponzi thought he looked "like a million dollars just out of the mint." He imagined that he cut the figure of a young gentleman from a fine family, perhaps the son of wealthy parents visiting Boston on a pleasure tour before taking his rightful place in Roman society. His excitement ebbed the moment he stepped onto U.S. soil. No gold awaited him. On the ground from the pier to Marginal Street in the distance was sticky, black mud, an inch deep wherever he stood, stretching as far as he could see. It was certain to ruin his spats.

Having anticipated the possibility that young Carlo would leave the ship broke—he had been stranded before, on much shorter trips—his mother and uncle had provided him with prepaid train fare to Pittsburgh. There he could spend a few days with a distant relative—"some fifth cousin of some third cousin of ours," Ponzi called him. But even before he reached Pittsburgh two days after landing, Ponzi was feeling tricked. He was hungry to the point of starving, alone, and down to a few coins. He began wishing he had never heard of America. He spoke no English, had no marketable skills, and considered it a source of pride that he had never worked a day in his life.

America did not seem terribly welcoming, either. The trip to Pittsburgh took him through New York, and when he bolted off the train in search of a meal during a stopover he ran smack into the arms of an Irish policeman. Ponzi lacked the language to explain that he was running because he was hungry, not because he had stolen something, and it was only through the intervention of an Italian bootblack that Ponzi avoided a night in jail. Once in Pittsburgh, Ponzi spent only a short time with his relative before finding a bed in an Italian rooming house and beginning a life of hand-to-mouth hardship. He considered writing home for help, but he could not bear the thought of disappointing his mother again. So he set off in the footsteps of millions of immigrants before him.

For the next four years, Ponzi worked as a grocery clerk, a road drummer, a factory hand, and a dishwasher. He repaired sewing machines, pressed shirts, painted signs, sold insurance, and waited tables. He rarely lasted long—sometimes he was fired, sometimes he quit in disgust, and other times he quit to avoid being fired. He rambled up and down the East Coast, staying close to the ocean to ease his homesickness. He cadged meals and slept in parks when he could not afford a bed. One time in New York he saved a bit of money but blew it all on a two-week spree at Coney Island, the beachside amusement park where a young immigrant could forget his troubles on the Steeplechase ride, roam the "Electric Eden" of Luna Park, or chase girls in the dance hall at Stauch's restaurant. But that was a brief respite. His silken clothes fell to shreds and his years of the good life became a receding memory.

In America, Carlo became Charles, and at times he found it useful to adopt a new last name: Bianchi, or "white," which fit his fair complexion. English spellings of Italian names were not yet standardized, and he was also known as "Ponsi," "Ponci," and "Ponse." He grew a mustache that sat on his upper lip like a bottlebrush. With the new names and new look came a new language. Soon he was as fluent in

English as he was in Italian and French, and with his new tongue he began seeking jobs more suited to his dreams.

In July 1907, he scraped together a few dollars for a train ticket to Montreal, arriving at the magnificent Gare Bonaventure with no baggage and a single dollar in his pocket. Ponzi walked up Rue Saint Jacques, Canada's Wall Street, past ornate eight- and ten-story bank and insurance buildings that were the skyscrapers of their day. Not two blocks from the train station he saw the sign of an Italian bank, Banco Zarossi. Calling himself Charles Bianchi, he made himself as presentable as possible and walked confidently through the door. Five minutes later he was hired as a clerk. Ponzi/Bianchi was delighted. After four years of menial labor, he finally had a job that complemented his skills and fit his self-image. Never mind that it was just the sort of job he had rejected as beneath him in Italy.

Canada was in the midst of an immigration wave of Italians, many of them brawny young men from the south of Italy who sought jobs in the coal mines of Nova Scotia and clearing forests for the Canada Pacific Railway. Nominally based in Montreal, they would be away from the city for months at a time. They needed a safe place to send their paychecks, but their business held little appeal for the British and Scottish financiers who lorded over Rue Saint Jacques. Banco Zarossi was one of several Montreal banks that had sprung up to fill the void.

The bank's owner, a jolly man named Luigi "Louis" Zarossi, had formerly been in the cigar business. But as soon as he'd entered the world of finance he'd been intent on beating his competitors. It was a daunting task, largely because another Italian bank, located almost directly across the street, was owned by the notorious Antonio Cordasco, the city's richest and most powerful padrone. The padrone system of labor bosses was in full flower at the turn of the century in North American cities with large Italian immigrant populations. At its center were native Italians who formed relationships with companies seeking unskilled laborers, then established themselves, sometimes through force, as the men to see for jobs, housing, loans, travel papers, and everything else they could control. Cordasco was that man in

Montreal. He ruled an extensive network of agents and subagents in his native country and Canada who kept business humming, workers coming, and cash flowing. At a parade three years before Ponzi's arrival in Canada, Cordasco had himself fitted with a crown and declared the "King of Montreal's Italian Workers."

But Zarossi had an idea. Cordasco's bank and others catering to immigrants paid depositors 2 percent interest on their accounts. It was a simple system: the banks invested in Italian securities that paid 3 percent, then gave 2 percent to depositors and kept 1 percent for costs and profits. Zarossi announced that he would pay depositors the full 3 percent, plus another 3 percent as a bonus, for an unheard-of 6 percent. Asked how he could do it, Zarossi tapped into the public's widespread suspicions that greedy bankers paid pennies on the dollar while keeping huge profits for themselves. His largesse was possible, he claimed, because he would share his bank's earnings more fairly with his depositors. Cordasco was furious. Dubious, too. Cordasco considered it impossible to pay such returns. He kept quiet, but he suspected that Zarossi would be paying one man with another man's money, an age-old fraud known as "robbing Peter to pay Paul."

As months passed and business boomed at Banco Zarossi, Ponzi impressed his boss with his intelligence, his easy smile, and his smooth way with customers. Ponzi was especially solicitous of the bank's female customers, flirting with them and basking in their attention. Even more than the customers, Ponzi liked Zarossi's pretty seventeen-year-old daughter, Angelina. Soon Ponzi was promoted to bank manager, and it looked as though he was finally making something of himself.

As the promised interest came due, Zarossi needed to find ways to make the relatively exorbitant payments. If he paid his depositors 6 percent through traditional means, he would soon be bankrupt. An alternative, albeit illegal, was staring him in the face: the money immigrant workers sent to their families via the bank. Zarossi began dipping into those funds, knowing it would be weeks or months before word got back to Montreal that the money had never arrived. He would buy more time by claiming he had sent the money and the fault rested with the mails or whoever received the money in Italy. If a depositor raised a stink, the bank would send money from its fresh deposits. Zarossi figured the cycle of finger-pointing and late payments could keep the scheme afloat long enough for him to come up with another way to pay. If that failed, he would have enough time to gather his profits and his family, and flee.

But events moved more quickly than Zarossi had anticipated. Depositors wanted their interest, immigrants demanded to know what had become of the money they'd sent home, and authorities began investigating the bank for embezzlement. In mid-1908, less than a year after Ponzi came to work for him, Zarossi packed a bag full of cash and fled alone to Mexico City. In the aftermath, one employee killed himself, and another, Antonio Salviati, disappeared when authorities accused him of stealing $944.85 from a customer named Francesco Charpaleggio, who had come to the bank to send money to his family in Italy. The suicide and Salviati's disappearance raised suspicions that the fraud went deeper than Zarossi. Eventually the bank collapsed, costing depositors even more. It was unclear how much Ponzi knew, but as bank manager he made a clear target for investigators.

Yet unlike Salviati, who ran, Ponzi stayed put in Montreal. For several months, though jobless, he watched over Zarossi's family, which included not just Angelina but three other daughters and Zarossi's wife. But by August 1908, Ponzi grew tired of domestic life and feared that he might face arrest, deportation, or both. It was time to hit the road. As usual, though, he had spent whatever money he had earned. The twenty-six-year-old Ponzi made a decision he would long regret.

On Saturday morning, August 29, 1908, he went to the offices of a shipping firm called the Canadian Warehousing Company, a client of Banco Zarossi. Ponzi had been there many times before to collect receipts and to handle other business matters. He raised no suspicions when he walked into the empty office of the manager, Damien Fournier. While no one was looking, Ponzi went to Fournier's desk and

found a checkbook from another bank where the company had an account, the French-owned Bank of Hochelaga. Ponzi tore a blank check
from the back of the checkbook and left as quickly as he had come.

That afternoon, Ponzi filled out the check in the legitimate-
seeming amount of $423.58. He signed it "D. Fournier" and presented
it at a branch of the Bank of Hochelaga. He asked the teller for four
one-hundred-dollar bills in American currency, but the teller told him
that would not be possible. Agitated, Ponzi accepted forty-two ten-
dollar bills, three singles, and the rest in coins. Cash in hand, Ponzi left
the bank and began outfitting himself for his return to the United
States. He went from store to store, buying two suits, an overcoat, a
pair of boots, and a watch and chain. He completed the spree with
thirty-two dollars' worth of shirts, collars, cuffs, ties, and suspenders
from a men's clothing store called R. J. Tooke.

Before Ponzi could leave town, officials at the Bank of Hochelaga
began having serious doubts about the signature on the check. At
noon the following Monday, Montreal Detective John McCall headed
over to Ponzi's boardinghouse, across town from the bank on Rue
Saint Denis. When McCall first confronted Ponzi, the detective asked
if his name was Bianchi. Ponzi said no, his name was Clement. Mc-
Call then identified himself as a detective. Before McCall could say
anything more, Ponzi sighed, "I'm guilty."

The detective and a partner searched Ponzi and found the receipt
from the forged check. They also counted out what was left of the
money: $218.12. McCall placed Ponzi under arrest and brought him to
the city's vermin-infested jail.

Ponzi's years as a sojourner had taught him a few things, and he
quickly began calculating a way to improve his accommodations. Pretending to be catatonic, he curled up in a corner, stared at the wall,
and chewed a towel to shreds. A guard brought him to the jail infirmary, where Ponzi emerged from his trance and began whooping and
climbing a wall to get to a barred window. After a few hours in a
straitjacket, he acted as though he were recovering from a bout of

epilepsy. It was a crude ruse, but it worked. His jailers kept him in the relative comforts of the infirmary until his November trial.

Ponzi pleaded innocent before the court, but it was a hopeless cause. The testimony of Detective McCall and the bank teller, not to mention Ponzi's sudden shopping spree, made quick work of the trial. Ponzi was found guilty of forgery and sentenced to three years in prison under the name Charles Ponsi, alias Bianchi.

Ponzi served his sentence three miles from Montreal, inside the looming gray stone walls of Saint Vincent de Paul Penitentiary, a prison with all the charm of the Bastille. Like a passenger in steerage, he slept on a mattress made from a sack of corncobs and husks. His cellmate was a fellow Italian immigrant, a swindler named Louis Cassullo who was serving a three-year stretch. Ponzi sized up Cassullo as a man who would steal the poor box in a church or pick a drunkard's pocket—"one of those prowling, petty, sneaky thieves whose counterparts in the animal kingdom are the hyenas and the jackals." Their days were spent in an unheated shed where they pounded rock into gravel. In time, Ponzi joked that he had crushed enough stone to pave Yellowstone National Park. Within a few months, Ponzi put his banking experience to work by winning a job as a clerk in the jail blacksmith's shop, after which he won a promotion to the chief engineer's office, and finally to the warden's office.

Despite the softer working conditions, Ponzi stewed endlessly over his situation. He wrote several pleading letters to Cordasco, but the padrone turned a deaf ear. Cordasco suspected that Ponzi was the mastermind of the Zarossi scheme, and he was not about to help. Over time, Ponzi earned the warden's trust as a model prisoner, and his sentence was shortened to twenty months for good behavior.

On July 13, 1910, Ponzi was doing his clerk duties when the warden came to him with a paper to type: his own parole form. Elated, Ponzi was released with five dollars in his pocket and an ill-fitting suit from the prison tailor shop. Longing for the fine Italian garments of his youth, Ponzi considered the suit grotesque. Not that it mattered where he was headed.

Edwin Atkins Grozier, editor and publisher of The Boston Post.

CHAPTER THREE

"NEWSPAPER GENIUS"

Like Ponzi, Richard Grozier was a bright, handsome young man with a taste for fine clothes. Also like Ponzi, he was approaching the midpoint of his life with little to show for himself. Unlike Ponzi, however, Grozier had every possible advantage—he was descended from *Mayflower* Pilgrims and had spent his life bathed in wealth and privilege.

Yet in 1917 Grozier was thirty years old, single, and living in his parents' house. He worked, without distinction, for his father's company after nearly flunking out of college and washing out of law school. As the only male heir, Grozier was destined to inherit his family's business and the money and power that went with it. But it looked as though his inheritance would drop in value the moment he took possession.

Richard's father was Edwin Atkins Grozier, editor, publisher, and owner of the *Boston Post,* the largest-circulation newspaper in Boston and one of the largest in the na-

tion. Through relentless work and rare gifts, Edwin Grozier had engi-
neered the *Post*'s rise from the brink of bankruptcy to the top of the
pig pile of Boston newspapers. By the time he was Richard's age,
Edwin had already been one of the most respected newspapermen in
the country. Without him, the *Post* would have been long dead, can-
nibalized by competitors on Newspaper Row.

Some thought the paper might still end up that way, once it passed
to his son.

The first edition of Boston's *Daily Morning Post* hit the streets November 9, 1831, under the ownership and editorial direction of
Colonel Charles G. Greene, whose military title was honorary but
whose journalism was sound. The *Post* appeared at a time when
Boston newspapers seemed to be opening and closing every few
months; fifteen printed their first and last editions between 1830 and
1840. But under Greene's steady hand, the *Post* survived and grew
steadily for four decades, establishing itself as a well-written, reliable
Democratic voice in an age of partisan newspapers.

Then came November 9, 1872. A fast-moving fire consumed an
empty hoopskirt factory on the edge of Boston's financial district,
then leapt from one building to the next. Many of the horses that were
used to pull the city's fire equipment had recently succumbed to an
equine epidemic, so the Great Boston Fire burned for more than two
days, consuming 776 buildings and leveling sixty-five acres downtown. The City upon a Hill was a smoldering ruin. Sullenly surveying
the damage, Oliver Wendell Holmes was moved to verse: "On roof
and wall, on dome and spire, flashed the false jewels of the fire." The
Post's offices escaped the flames, but the oceans of water used to protect it ruined almost everything inside. Greene and his son, Nathaniel,
reopened the paper in a new location, but it was never the same.
When the nation fell into economic depression during the presidency
of Ulysses S. Grant, the Greenes decided to sell.

The eager buyer was the Reverend Ezra D. Winslow, a Methodist minister, staunch prohibitionist, and member of the state Senate. He was also a forger and a swindler. In a scheme that would anticipate stock manipulators of a later day, Winslow sold twice as many shares of the Boston Post Company as allowed by the incorporating papers. He also forged the signatures of more than a dozen prominent men on banknotes for nearly a half million dollars, and pocketed thousands more loaned to him. He exchanged much of his stolen cash for gold, fled to Holland, and by some accounts ended up in Argentina, enjoying his ill-gotten gains in Buenos Aires and working as a reporter for a local newspaper.

The story of Winslow's scam became part of *Post* lore, passed down year after year, deeply ingrained in the memories of its employees. Winslow had ruined the finances and shattered the credibility of the once-proud newspaper. For the next fifteen years the *Post* floundered under transient ownership. By 1891 it was hobbling along with fewer than three thousand subscribers. It had an antiquated printing plant, only a handful of advertisers, and a debt of $150,000. But where creditors saw a newspaper in its death throes, Edwin Grozier saw the opportunity of a lifetime.

Edwin Grozier was born September 12, 1859, aboard a clipper ship within sight of the Golden Gate in San Francisco harbor. It was a fitting arrival; Grozier men were storied mariners, and the ship's master was Edwin's father, Joshua, who routinely captained voyages from Boston around Cape Horn to California and back. When Edwin was six, his parents brought him and his two brothers to live on the far tip of Cape Cod, in Provincetown, the home of generations of sea captains and their families.

A sickly boy and an avid reader who dreamed of becoming a poet or a novelist, Edwin Grozier attended public schools and graduated from high school at age fifteen. In keeping with family tradition, and to improve his health, he spent the next two years sailing around the world. The teenage wanderer wrote detailed descriptions of the exotic ports he visited and sent them to Greene's *Boston Post,* which was impressed enough to publish them as a series. In 1877, he returned home, spent some time at prep school, then entered Brown University in Providence, Rhode Island. After a year he transferred to Boston University, drawn to Boston by the lure of Newspaper Row.

After graduating he landed a job at the *Boston Globe,* where he worked under the tutelage of the editor and publisher, General Charles H. Taylor, a gregarious Civil War veteran. Grozier was paid ten dollars a week, which he at first considered an enormous sum. Then his ambition took hold. "It was soon raised to twelve, to fifteen, to eighteen dollars," he recalled. "I wanted more money—because I needed it!" Despite his fondness for Taylor, an offer of twenty-five dollars a week sent Grozier across Newspaper Row to the *Boston Herald* to cover politics. He distinguished himself quickly, in part because he was able to accurately record the long-winded speeches of the day with his uncommon skill at shorthand. During the 1883 campaign for Massachusetts governor, Grozier so impressed the Republican candidate, George D. Robinson, that as soon as Robinson was elected he hired the young reporter as his personal secretary.

But the pull of newspapering was strong. Eighteen months later, Grozier moved to New York and became personal secretary to Joseph Pulitzer, the Hungarian-born editor of the New York *World* and a journalism legend in the making. Pulitzer pioneered a formula of compelling human-interest stories, social justice crusades, and sensational battles with William Randolph Hearst and the New York *Journal.* Under Pulitzer, the *World* became the most profitable and most copied newspaper in the nation. Edwin Grozier had a front-row seat, and he was in thrall to Pulitzer: "I never saw anyone to equal him. His mind was like a flash of lightning, illuminating the dark places."

For six exhausting years, Edwin Grozier routinely worked eighteen- and twenty-hour days learning the newspaper business top to bottom. Pulitzer recognized and rewarded Grozier's brains and drive with some of the most difficult jobs in New York newspapers. By twenty-eight, Grozier was city editor of the *World,* and six months later he was editor in chief and business manager of the *Evening World* and the *Sunday World.* He did so well boosting circulation that Pulitzer once handed him a bonus of one thousand dollars in gold coins. But Grozier wanted to captain his own ship. His fondest wish was to buy a newspaper in New York, but he did not want to break his bond with Pulitzer by competing against the *World.*

While vacationing in Boston in 1891, Grozier heard from friends that the *Post* was on the verge of collapse. It was everything he wanted, in a city he knew and loved, and just right for his meager price range. First, he sought out the *Globe*'s Taylor, who was second only to Pulitzer as a newspaper mentor. Grozier came to Taylor's office seeking absolution.

"If you have even the slightest objection, General," Grozier told him, "I won't consider purchasing the paper."

Taylor placed a hand on Grozier's shoulder. "Go ahead, Mr. Grozier. I don't mind in the least." Smiling, Taylor added, "If you can gather up any of the crumbs that fall from the *Globe*'s table, you're welcome to them."

"Thank you, General," Grozier replied. "But I want to warn you that I shan't be satisfied with crumbs. If I can, I shall go after the cake, too!"

At first, even crumbs would have seemed a feast. Boston was crowded with newspapers. In addition to the *Post* and *Globe,* there were the *Daily Advertiser,* the *Evening Record,* the *Herald,* the *Journal,* the *Telegraph,* the *Transcript,* and the *Traveler.* Soon the *Boston American* would join the scene. While the *Post* had hemorrhaged money and readers, its competitors had grown entrenched with various constituencies—the Brahmins who ruled the city relied on the *Transcript,* for instance.

Grozier was in danger of folding almost from the first edition. To purchase the paper, he had exhausted his life savings and plunged deep into debt. When he took the keys to the *Post*'s tired offices he was left with only one hundred dollars in cash. In the meantime, the thirty-two-year-old newspaper owner had a growing family to feed. In 1885, while working for Pulitzer, he had married Alice Goodell, the daughter of a prominent Salem, Massachusetts couple. When they returned from New York to Boston they had a four-year-old son and a two-year-old daughter.

In the days of larger-than-life newspapermen, Edwin Grozier seemed physically unfit for the job. One day, a young leather worker walked upstairs to the publisher's second-floor office overlooking Washington Street. The leather worker stepped inside, hoping to be hired as a reporter despite his complete lack of qualifications for the job. He immediately thought he had entered the wrong office. He found the editor and publisher of the *Post* to be "a small, brownish man who sat at a large desk . . . just another undersized party, rather delicate and plaintive-looking, perhaps because he wore a straggly moustache, had a rug over his knees, and peered benevolently at me over the tops of his glasses." The job applicant also might have noted that Grozier had close-set eyes, curtained by heavy lids.

Yet Grozier would not have minded the unflattering description; he was modest by nature and had no interest in provoking awe, particularly among the reporters he sent scouring the city for scoops. Something about the young man appealed to Grozier, and he offered him a job at eighteen dollars a week. It was the start of a remarkable writing career for Kenneth Roberts, who became a star at the *Post* and the best-selling author of the historical novels *Arundel* and *Northwest Passage*.

Edwin Grozier compensated for his lack of physical presence with what Roberts called "newspaper genius." From the moment he took control of the paper, Grozier operated under a few guiding principles he once articulated: "Of first importance is the securing of the confidence, respect, and affection of your readers—by deserving them. Study the census. Know your field. Build scientifically. Print a little better newspaper than you think the public wants. Do not try to rise by pulling your contemporaries down. Attend to your own business. Do not believe your kind friends if they assure you that you are a genius. But work, work, work."

He issued a public call to arms in his debut editorial: "By performance rather than promise the new *Post* seeks to be judged. By deed rather than words its record will be made." He declared that the *Post* "aspires to guard the public interests, to be a bulwark against political corruption, an ally of justice and a scourge to crime; to defend the oppressed, to help the poor, to further the still grander development of the glorious civilization of New England."

Grand sentiments were one thing, but Grozier knew he had to meet a payroll and the demands of creditors. His first actions on those fronts were counterintuitive: He dropped the paper's price from three cents to a penny—a technique he had learned from Pulitzer to boost circulation—and lowered the cost of advertising. He also called a meeting of his creditors and asked their forbearance; he would pay them in full, he promised, but he needed time and more credit to keep afloat. Impressed by his sincerity, and hoping to avoid the pennies-on-the-dollar payoff that would result from Grozier's failure, the creditors agreed. Still, the early years remained lean, and paydays were sometimes anxious. Grozier never missed a payroll, but more than once his staff gathered at the cashier's window waiting to be paid from last-minute advertising receipts and the pennies turned in by newsboys. Sometimes even that was not enough, and Grozier borrowed to pay his staff.

"Most of the time, figuratively speaking, there was an 'angel' in one room and the sheriff in another," Grozier once recalled. "An angel, you know, is someone who may possibly put up money to back you. But I was generally much more certain of the sheriff than I was of the angel." What he needed most were readers, lots of them, so he tapped the techniques he had learned from Pulitzer and added new flavors all his own. Soon they paid off handsomely.

To capture public interest and build circulation, Grozier was not above employing carnival tactics, organizing a stream of inspired and slightly wacky promotions. He heard that an Englishman and his wife wanted to rid themselves of three trained elephants named Mollie, Waddy, and Tony. Grozier thought they would make ideal residents at the city's Franklin Park Zoo. He was making enough money by this point that he could have paid for them himself and reaped all sorts of praise, but instead the *Post* called upon the children of Boston to become part owners of the pachyderms. The newspaper began collecting contributions toward the $15,000 purchase price. Grozier promised to print the names of every one of the contributors, even those who could spare only a cent or two. Thousands of children responded, and seventy thousand people turned out to welcome the elephants at a ceremony in Fenway Park, built two years earlier by the *Globe*'s Taylor as the new home of the Red Sox. From a simple profit-loss standpoint, it was a disaster. It cost the *Post* thirty cents, based on its advertising rate, to print the name of a child who had contributed a penny, and the newspaper still had to cough up several thousand dollars to close the deal. But Grozier knew it was a huge success.

"Every child who had given even one cent wanted to see his name in the paper, and was thrilled by the thought that he owned part of an elephant," Grozier told a reporter. "Of course, it added thousands to the circulation of the *Post,* but it was a gain that was based not on appealing to the worst elements in human nature but to the best: to civic pride, to generosity, to interest in animals, to the affection of parents for their children. And so it helped us to win liking and affection."

Later, the *Post* announced a giveaway of a free car for the best human-interest story: A FORD A DAY GIVEN AWAY! the paper screamed. Thousands of suggestions poured in, and scores of Model T's were delivered. The paper printed photos of women only from the neck down, then offered ten dollars in gold to any woman who could identify herself and prove it by wearing the same outfit to the *Post* offices. They came in droves, and thousands more grabbed the paper each day hoping to recognize their headless selves. Another time, Grozier hired a movie scout named Bijou Fernandez to search for girls who wanted to be in the movies. Fernandez would spot a pretty girl in a small town

and a *Post* reporter would write a story that would be printed alongside the girl's picture. Circulation shot up by ten thousand the first
week, though actual movie offers were scarce. Tapping into the same
vein, the paper ran a feature called "The Prettiest Women in History,"
featuring luminaries including Cleopatra and Helen of Troy.

Barely a day went by without some kind of promotion or gimmick.
Once, Grozier announced that he was sending a reporter incognito to
a certain part of the city. The paper would give one hundred dollars in
cash to the first person who spoke these words to the reporter: "Good
morning, have you read the *Post* today?" Suddenly those were the first
words out of Bostonians' mouths whenever they happened upon a
stranger.

Then there was the "primitive man" stunt. The *Post* sent a man
named Joe Knowles into the Maine woods, naked and empty-handed,
to live completely alone for sixty days. During the two-month adventure, the paper printed dispatches and drawings Knowles made with
charcoal on birch bark and left at a prearranged drop point. When
Knowles emerged from the woods, wearing deer skins and carrying the
tools of a caveman, some 400,000 people crammed the length of Washington Street to greet him. The paper's circulation doubled that year.

When Grozier learned that letters addressed to Santa Claus were
dumped in the dead-letter office, he began thinking about the unmet
needs of the city's poor children. He created the *Post* Santa Claus
Fund to raise and distribute money and toys to Boston's needy during
the holidays. Grozier measured the fund's success less by the number
of newspapers it sold than by the number of toys it handed out. His
soft spot for children showed just as clearly when the *Post* received letters about lost pets. "I see that this little girl has lost her dog," he told
a young editor one day. The editor knew what was coming next: "Do
you think one of our men could find it for her?" A reporter was
quickly dispatched.

The most enduring promotion was Grozier's 1909 brainstorm to
honor the oldest man in every town in the *Post*'s circulation area. He
imported hundreds of the finest ebony canes from Africa and fitted

them with polished fourteen-karat-gold heads, on which was inscribed: "Presented by *The Boston Post* to the oldest citizen of," followed by the name of the resident's town. Below that, to make clear
that the cane should pass to the next oldest man upon the holder's
death, were the words "To be transmitted." Grozier wrote to select-
men throughout much of New England asking them to locate the deserving recipients and present the canes, then inform the *Post* of the
selection, ideally with a photo. Eventually, 431 canes were handed out,
often with great pomp and ceremony followed by fawning stories in
the *Post*. Holders of the canes variously attributed their longevity to
abstinence from, or daily devotion to, alcohol and tobacco. The death
of a *Post* cane holder was cause for another story, as was the token's
passage to the town's next oldest man. To Grozier, the appeal was obvious: "In many small towns and villages the general store was a place
where many men gathered to talk and swap stories. One of the most
conspicuous figures in the group was the 'oldest man.' Age is a subject
of universal interest, no matter whether it is among city folks or country folks. A man who has succeeded in cheating death longer than
most of us manage to do it is always an interesting figure."

Edwin Grozier knew he needed more than fun and games to win
readers. He loved a good murder case. Lizzie Borden's father and step-
mother turned up dead less than a year after he bought the *Post,* and
the early years of the new century provided an endless stream of other
celebrated killings. Circulation always rose when murders involved the
rich, the pious, an attractive woman, or a spurned lover. A case involving a minister with two beautiful young fiancées, one of whom
turned up dead from poison in what looked like suicide, kept Grozier
in gravy for weeks. A *Post* reporter cracked the case when he tracked
down the minister's purchase of cyanide. A close second was when a
diver hired by Grozier found the severed head of a beautiful showgirl
at the bottom of Boston Harbor. "Missing Head Found by the *Post*'s
Diver," the headline blared.

When not covering crime, the paper kept its promise to be a friend
to the little guy. Grozier supported the labor movement and shorter

work weeks, and fought for lower gas and telephone rates. The paper leaned to the Democratic Party, and Grozier worked to stay in touch with the needs of the common man. It was an approach he had pioneered in New York: "I used to go over among the swarming millions of the East and the West sides of the city; because it was there that we must build up our circulation if it was to be a large one; there, among the masses, not in the narrow strip of millionaires along Fifth Avenue." In Boston, Grozier was a careful reader of the census, and he recognized that Boston's surging Irish population would support the Irish nationalist movement. The *Post* was the first prominent American paper to show solidarity with Sinn Fein, and Grozier personally made large contributions to the nationalist cause.

At a time when "No Irish Need Apply" remained the practice in certain Brahmin quarters, Grozier supported the candidacy of David I. Walsh in his successful effort to become Massachusetts' first Irish Catholic governor. Grozier further ingratiated the *Post* with Irish Bostonians by treating interviews with the city's Catholic cardinal as front-page news.

Though Grozier calculated his positions carefully in terms of circulation, he also took unpopular positions based on his sense of fairness. Boston's Irish and blacks were often at odds, competing for scarce resources, but the *Post* refused to favor one group over the other. William Monroe Trotter, editor of the *Boston Guardian,* a black newspaper, once said that Grozier ran his newspaper under a policy of "identical justice, freedom, and civil rights for all, regardless of race, creed, or color."

The combination of aggressive news coverage, community appeal, and dedication to fair play, along with a healthy dose of razzle-dazzle, worked beyond all expectations. In time, Edwin Grozier's *Post* outsold the *Globe.* And in a much smaller city, its circulation exceeded that of Pulitzer's New York *World.* But the *Post*'s status as Boston's premier newspaper would soon be tested as never before.

Mug shots of young Carlo Ponzi from his 1908 arrest in Montreal.

The Boston Globe

CHAPTER FOUR

"A LONG CIRCLE OF BAD BREAKS"

Back on the bumpy streets of Montreal, Ponzi learned that his reputation was worse than his prison-issued suit. Not only was he a convicted forger and an ex-con, but his name remained linked to the fleecing of depositors and the collapse of Banco Zarossi. Hardly an impressive résumé for a would-be financier. Cordasco the padrone had taken to calling him "Bianchi the Snake." He slept at a friend's home and earned a few dollars working odd jobs, but his future in Montreal was ruined. He gathered his belongings and began planning a return to the United States.

Seventeen days after his release from prison, Ponzi boarded a southbound train with five other Italians, young men newly arrived from the old country, none of whom had proper papers and none of whom spoke English. As the train approached the New York border, a United States Customs inspector named W. H. Stevenson came aboard and questioned Ponzi about his companions. Ponzi insisted they were strangers to him. He told Stevenson that he had run into an old schoolmate at the depot, and the schoolmate had asked him to look after these men. Ponzi mentioned nothing about whether money had changed hands, telling Stevenson merely that he had generously, innocently agreed to his old chum's request. Ponzi did not mention that the old friend was Antonio Salviati, his fugitive former colleague at the Zarossi bank, who was still wanted for allegedly pocketing money a customer intended to send home to Italy. Regardless, the customs man did not believe Ponzi's story. Stevenson called an immigration inspector, who ordered all six men taken into custody as suspected illegal immigrants. Ponzi faced the most serious charge: smuggling aliens into the United States.

Ponzi was back behind bars. His thousand-dollar bail might as well have been a million, and he languished for two months in the Plattsburgh, New York, jail before being brought to trial. He insisted he was innocent, telling whoever would listen that he had done what any decent person would have done in his situation. After a heart-to-heart talk with a prosecutor, Ponzi got the impression that a guilty plea would cost him no more than a fifty-dollar fine or a month in jail. Fearing that an innocent plea and a guilty verdict would result in serious time, Ponzi bought the deal and pleaded guilty. But his luck turned from bad to worse. The judge stunned Ponzi by sentencing him to two years in a federal prison and fining him five hundred dollars. The five undocumented Italian immigrants testified as witnesses at Ponzi's trial and afterward were set free.

Ponzi was soon back on a train, this time headed for the United States federal penitentiary in Atlanta.

To his surprise, Ponzi traveled to Atlanta in style, more like a chief executive than a felon. With deputy U.S. marshals as his escorts, Ponzi went south with a berth in a Pullman sleeping car. He enjoyed his meals in a dining car and lounged in the plush seats as farms and cities rolled past the windows. His small entourage stopped in Washington and enjoyed lunch at a restaurant that Ponzi considered pretentious, then took an afternoon constitutional on the grounds of the Capitol. By the time they reached Atlanta, the marshals had grown fond of the charming convict. They brought him to a bar for a last bracing drink before prison, but to Ponzi's disappointment the only libation was flat, sour-tasting near beer.

Still, the trip was oddly appropriate considering their destination. The Atlanta Federal Penitentiary was considered the cushiest prison in the land, more like the Willard Hotel than a medieval dungeon. Built a decade before Ponzi's arrival, it sat proudly on a hill, looking to the world like a fine southern college. Ponzi reasoned that the men who ran the country wanted a haven for themselves in case they ever ended up in prison. "Since it had to be a cage," Ponzi figured, "it might as well be a gilded cage."

Ponzi was given a job as a clerk in the prison laundry, but his linguistic skills soon won him a transfer to the mail clerk's office. He impressed his boss, prison record keeper A. C. Aderhold, as smooth, smart, and congenial, a clever young man with a gift for figures who kept error-free books without complaint. The only peculiarity Aderhold noticed was what he called Ponzi's "obsession for planning financial coups." Aderhold thought his assistant took so much pleasure from plotting elaborate moneymaking schemes that he might someday put one into play simply to see if it would work.

Ponzi's least favorite part of the job was translating for Warden F. G. Zerpt the incoming and outgoing letters of a dough-faced Sicilian mobster named Ignazio "the Wolf" Lupo. Lupo represented a new kind of criminal turning up in prisons like the Atlanta penitentiary. He had landed in New York twelve years earlier, in 1898, having fled Italy to avoid arrest for the murder of a customer of his dry goods store. He'd continued to mix fine food and major crime in the United States, opening an importing business while moonlighting in murder and extortion as a boss of the fearsome Mafia group known as the Black Hand. Lupo was suspected of ordering or taking part in numerous killings, most notoriously the 1909 murder of legendary New

York police lieutenant Giuseppe Petrosino. Petrosino's relentless pursuit of mafiosi had made him the scourge of the Italian underworld, whose leaders ordered him shot to death when he was in Italy pursuing leads against the Black Hand. Prosecutors had lacked the evidence to pin the murder on Lupo, so instead they'd nailed him with a thirty-year prison sentence on two counts of counterfeiting. Printing funny money was seldom punished so severely, so the sentence was understood as payback for the violent crimes authorities suspected him of but could not prove.

Adopting the code of prisoners everywhere, Ponzi took the health-conscious position that any unproven allegations against his fellow inmates were between them and their Maker. Yet, with time to kill, Ponzi found himself feeling a certain kinship with his countryman Lupo. Not only did they share a native tongue; Ponzi believed that they had both been treated unfairly by overzealous, duplicitous authorities, and were both serving excessive sentences for nonviolent offenses. Lupo the Wolf must have sensed Ponzi's comradeship.

After being housed with a string of prisoners he suspected were informants, Lupo approached Ponzi one day after a ball game in the prison yard. He was sick of stool pigeons, Lupo said. Would Ponzi become his cellmate? Ponzi agreed—it was always wise to say yes to Lupo—and prison officials approved the transfer, apparently thinking the skinny young mail clerk would make an ideal stoolie. They were wrong.

Ponzi was wary of Lupo, but he liked his new cellmate. The optimist in Ponzi found Lupo to be good-hearted and straightforward. What Ponzi liked most was Lupo's stoicism. Even after Ponzi had survived almost a decade of tough living and prison time far from home and family, deep down he was still the soft college boy of his youth. Lupo was tough and fearless, and Ponzi admired him for it. Yet there was little practical that Ponzi could learn from Lupo—the schemes Ponzi conjured in his mind had nothing to do with threats of violence. But another prisoner was an endless source of fascination for Ponzi.

Charles W. Morse was a dark model of American prosperity at the turn of the century: physically ugly, amoral, rich beyond reason. Born in Maine to an affluent family, Morse established a shipping company with his father after graduating from Bowdoin College in 1877. The business boomed, and so did Morse's rapacity and his capacity for shady deals. In 1897 he expanded to New York, where he felt right at home amid the corrupt politicians of Tammany Hall. After lining the pockets of Mayor Robert Van Wyck and Tammany boss Richard Croker, Morse set out to win complete control of New York's ice business, which, in the days before electric refrigeration, was a multimillion-dollar utility. He formed the Consolidated Ice Company, merged it with the American Ice Company, then sharply boosted the price of ice. Morse was unfamiliar with the scent of food rotting for want of cold, and so he underestimated the intense public reaction to his gambit. An investigation disclosed his bribes to political patrons and ended his brief run as the "Ice King." But not before he siphoned off a cool $12 million in profit.

Morse returned to his shipping roots, establishing a virtual East Coast monopoly. Then he bought a dozen or so New York banks and attempted to corner the copper market with a small group of like-minded monopolists. The collapse of that effort contributed to the nation's 1907 financial panic, which would be remembered as a crisis caused by the soon-to-be familiar demons of irresponsible speculation, widespread financial mismanagement, and inadequate regulation. Morse's high public profile made him an appealing target for authorities who had slept through the run-up, and he was soon indicted. Convicted of misappropriating bank funds, in January 1910 Morse was sentenced to fifteen years in the Atlanta prison.

Like his prison mates Ponzi and Lupo, Morse considered himself a victim of overzealous prosecutors, calling his sentence "the most brutal . . . ever pronounced against a citizen in a civilized country." More convincingly, he added: "There is no one in Wall Street who is not doing daily as I have done." Morse had no intention of serving out his sentence; he hired lawyers who would help him press his case all the way to the White House. As part of the campaign, he won support from luminaries such as Clarence W. Barron, owner of the *Wall Street Journal* and hailed as the father of financial journalism. Barron appealed directly to President William Taft for leniency. On a parallel track, Morse suddenly displayed signs of a mysterious illness that his lawyers claimed left him only days from death. Morse's condition was confirmed by doctors at an army hospital, and his retinue whipped up public support for a presidential pardon on humanitarian grounds. In January 1912, thirteen years before the court-imposed end of Morse's sentence, Taft granted him an unconditional release.

Morse left immediately for a European vacation, having regained his robust health almost within moments of Taft's pen stroke. Later it was disclosed that Morse had poisoned himself by eating soap shavings before each medical exam. The toxins left his system as quickly as the doctors left his bedside.

From his post as a prison clerk, Ponzi watched with astonishment and admiration as the Morse episode unfolded before him. Even before he knew the details of the death's-door medical ruse, Ponzi suspected Morse was gaming the system. When Morse was freed, Ponzi learned a lesson he would never forget: The American legal system is kinder and gentler to men with money. If a man is rich, powerful, and well-connected, he can escape prison through the front gate.

At the moment, though, Ponzi was in no position to put that knowledge into practice. He was too broke to buy his way out of anything. The summer after Morse was freed, Ponzi completed his two-year term, plus an extra month tacked on for his inability to pay his five-hundred-dollar fine.

Ponzi had had enough of Atlanta, so he headed west to Birmingham, Alabama, for no other reason than it was a city where he had yet to try his luck. Not long after arriving in Birmingham, Ponzi met up with a fellow he had known years earlier during his travels. The man was making a killing by filing false medical claims against coal-mining companies. He had agents in mining camps throughout the region, and whenever a miner got hurt an agent would coax and coach him to exaggerate the injury. A small lump of coal falling on a miner's shoulder could be turned into a near-death cave-in. If the miner was game, he would eventually end up at a Birmingham infirmary run by Ponzi's acquaintance. There, the miner would remain laid up for weeks or months, however long it took to document all kinds of imaginary ailments. Eventually the miner would win a large settlement from the mining company, which would of course include medical costs and a generous share for Ponzi's pal. The infirmary was doing land-office business.

Ponzi considered joining his old acquaintance but hesitated. He was as eager to get rich as he had ever been, but he believed he could do it legitimately with one of the many plans he had cooked up in prison. Another reason he turned down his old friend's offer was a suspicion that taking part in such a crude operation would land him on an Alabama chain gang. Ponzi was thirty. He had just lost four years to prison and he was determined never to go back.

Ponzi hit the rails again, heading fifty miles southwest to Blocton, Alabama, an Appalachian mining town founded after the Civil War by a New Yorker named Truman H. Aldrich. By the 1880s, Aldrich had made a fortune by establishing the Cahaba Coal Mining Company, which owned eight mines and blasted thousands of tons of high-grade coal from the earth to help power the newly industrialized country. By the time Ponzi arrived, coal was better than gold in Alabama, and boomtowns like Blocton, Scratch Ankle, Coalena, and Marvel were peopled with coal-dusted miners and their families, a growing number of them Italian immigrants.

For several months Ponzi scraped together a living as a translator, a part-time bookkeeper, and, occasionally, a nurse to injured miners. The Italian camp in Blocton reminded him of small-town life back home, always celebrating a christening, a marriage, or a holiday, and he felt embraced by "a brotherhood of common interests and endeavors and neighborly love." But conditions were only a step above prim-

itive. The camp's ramshackle wooden houses had no electricity or
running water. Still dreaming of riches, Ponzi began laying plans to
make himself the local czar of light and water. Imagining himself a
Charles W. Morse in miniature, Ponzi outlined for his neighbors a vision of a corporation in which community members would purchase
stock to finance a small power plant that would supply electricity and
pump water from a nearby creek. Ponzi, of course, would retain a
controlling share to compensate him for his work and leadership.
Water and power rates would be set based on Ponzi's cost estimates,
and he promised he would take no more than "a reasonable margin of
profit." He would effectively be owner, supplier, and rate setter of two
essential utilities. If it worked, Ponzi would no doubt attempt to du-
plicate those monopolies in other isolated mining camps.

Early support from his neighbors was strong, and Ponzi was certain
he had come upon his first chance to make real money legitimately.
But it was not to be. "Something always happens!" he lamented.
"Something so entirely unexpected that it always catches me unaware. Like a flower-pot that lands on a man's head from a three-
story window."

The flowerpot in this case was a young woman named Pearl Gossett.

Gossett was a nurse at the mining company's hospital. In October
1912 she was cooking a patient's meal when the gasoline stove burst
into flames, leaving her with severe burns on the left arm, shoulder,
and breast. Ponzi's occasional work as a nurse brought him into con-
tact with the hospital staff, and he had grown friendly with a physi-
cian, one Dr. Thomas. On a visit to the miners' camp a few days after
Gossett's accident, the doctor stopped by to share a beer with Ponzi.

"How's Pearl?" Ponzi asked.

"Her condition is very serious," Dr. Thomas answered. "Almost
desperate. Gangrene is setting in."

Ponzi asked if anything could be done to help her.

"Skin grafting, perhaps," the doctor said. "I wanted to try it. But I can't find anybody who will give up as little as an inch of his skin for her."

Ponzi did not know Gossett well, but others had told him how caring she was. Hearing the doctor say she might die or, at the minimum, lose her arm, "made my blood sizzle," Ponzi said. "It did not seem fair that a young girl like Pearl should be permitted to die such a horrible death. That girl had been so kind to her patients that it seemed inconceivable that she should meet with such ingratitude."

It angered him, Ponzi said, "to think that any person could be so selfish, so cowardly, as to refuse a mere inch of his own skin to save a human life."

"How many inches of skin do you need altogether?" he asked the doctor.

"Forty or fifty, I guess," Dr. Thomas said. "But I can't find even ten in a community of two thousand or more people."

"You're all wrong, Doctor," said Ponzi. "You have found them. I will give all the skin you need."

"You? You will give the whole of it?"

"Yes, Doctor, I will. When do you want me?" Ponzi asked.

"We cannot put the thing off for very long," the doctor answered. "But I don't want to hurry you, either. You might want to prepare for it. Sort of brace up. When can you be ready?"

"I am ready now," Ponzi said.

Dr. Thomas looked hard at Ponzi, making certain he would not flinch. "Evidently," Ponzi said later, "what he saw in my eyes decided him."

"All right, then," Dr. Thomas said. "Come along."

That night, doctors removed seventy-two square inches of skin from his thighs. Ponzi spent the next few weeks in the hospital, bandaged from hip to knee. When he had nearly recuperated, Ponzi got another visit from Dr. Thomas. The nurse needed more skin.

"Go as far as you like," Ponzi answered.

On November 5, another fifty square inches were taken from his back. He spent most of the next three months in the hospital, battling pain and pleurisy. The donations would leave him with broad white patches of scar tissue on his back and legs. Gossett remained scarred as well, but she recovered.

An account of Ponzi's giving the skin off his back and legs to help a nurse made the local newspaper. Ponzi proudly sent a copy of the clipping to his old boss at the Atlanta prison, A. C. Aderhold, who would keep it tucked away for years. The newspaper story spurred talk among prominent Blocton citizens about recommending Ponzi for a medal and a reward from the Carnegie Hero Fund, established eight years earlier, in 1904, by industrialist Andrew Carnegie to honor acts of civilian heroism. But the effort never got off the ground, and Ponzi received no formal recognition.

By the time he was released from the hospital, other plans were being made to supply the mining camp with water and light. Another opportunity lost, Ponzi returned to the drawing board.

Ponzi left Blocton a few months later, meandering south to Florida, where he moved from town to town painting signs, houses, and anything else that paid. He signed on to paint an iron-hulled freight and passenger steamer named the S.S. *Tarpon* as it cruised from port to port along the northern Gulf Coast. But he quarreled over pay with the *Tarpon*'s fierce captain, William Barrows, and Ponzi found himself stranded in Mobile, Alabama. He took up painting again, but when work slowed he looked for jobs in a newspaper's help wanted ads. One read: "Librarian Wanted at the Medical College." He got the job for a meager thirty dollars a month.

Ponzi took his meals at the home of the college caretaker and spent nights in a room on the first floor of the medical school. His on-campus lodgings made him easy prey for the pranks of medical students. One night when a storm knocked out the lights, they carried an embalmed corpse from a classroom to Ponzi's room and tucked it in his bed. "I laid him on the floor of my room," Ponzi recalled. "We both slept peacefully, but I woke up first."

He moved to a rooming house owned by Mrs. T. C. White, who grew fond of him as she listened to his endless fantasies about becoming rich. He spent nights locked in his room, Mrs. White said, "and when we asked him what he was doing he would say that he was figuring and not to worry him." One time he made an arrangement with a local automobile dealer to raffle off a new car. But Mrs. White drew the line when he began inviting young women to the house—not for dates, but for a jewelry sales business. When she told him he could not make the house an office, he abandoned his plan but told her that he would someday have a fine office downtown.

He found new rooms at the home of the college's caretaker, Gus Carlson, and once he boasted to Carlson's daughter-in-law that his picture would be in all the newspapers. She joked that it would be when he was hanged.

"Either that or I will be a millionaire!" Ponzi answered.

He grew friendly with Carlson's son, Gus Junior, who watched as Ponzi routinely spent whatever money he made on girls or friends. Ponzi especially delighted in buying ice cream for the children who gathered during the afternoon to play on the college lawn. "He would never let you spend your money," Carlson said after Ponzi left town, "no matter if he was spending his last cent on you."

Through his work in the library, Ponzi learned that doctors in Birmingham were lobbying to uproot the medical school from Mobile. Doctors in Mobile were fighting to keep the school, and Ponzi sided with his new friends in Mobile. He became upset when he discovered that a member of the school's faculty was secretly scheming in favor of the Birmingham move while publicly opposing it. Motivated by loyalty to his adopted home and new friends, Ponzi intercepted a letter the two-faced faculty member was sending to a leader of the

Birmingham contingent. He steamed it open, "and there before me was the evidence that he had been double-crossing the college right along. He was working hand-in-hand with the Birmingham bunch."

Ponzi brought the letter to the acting dean, who demanded the resignation of the duplicitous faculty member. But it did not end there. The college president, who sided with the Birmingham forces, did not appreciate a Mobile librarian tampering with mail. The president crossed out the budget line for Ponzi's job. Ponzi was disappointed— he liked the school and its students, he enjoyed the steamy weather in Mobile, and he cherished the friends he had made. "I should have known it wouldn't last," Ponzi said afterward. "If it had, it would have interrupted a long circle of bad breaks."

He left Mobile in ragged clothes, with empty pockets. He headed for New Orleans just in time for the hurricane of September 1915. The storm made plenty of business for a sign painter, and he kept busy through Mardi Gras the following spring. From there he moved farther west, to Wichita Falls, Texas, a straitlaced cotton and cattle town halfway between Dallas and Oklahoma City. The town was pretty much owned by two brothers-in-law, Joseph Kemp and Frank Kell, who controlled the banks, the dry goods business, the grain elevators, much of the land, and the railroad lines. Soon they would grow richer with the discovery of oil.

As a sideline, in 1910 Kemp and Kell had formed the Wichita Falls Motor Company, whose rugged flatbed trucks were soon turning up throughout North and South America and everywhere else from Europe and India to China and the South Sea Islands. Ponzi found work as a sixteen-dollar-a-week clerk in the foreign sales department, helping the company live up to its motto: "The Sun Never Sets on a Wichita Truck."

The company's extensive foreign business was done by mail and cable, transacted in a half dozen or so languages that Ponzi knew either fluently or passably. In addition, Ponzi had to school himself in the esoteric business areas of foreign currencies and exchange rates, shipping routes, customs tariffs, and postal and telegraph fees. It was the kind of knowledge he realized he could use to make a name for himself.

First, though, he had to get out of sleepy Wichita Falls. His chance came in December 1916, when he got word that Italy was seeking emigrants as reservists to reinforce its armies for the Great War. Ponzi was prepared to fight for his homeland, so he went to New York and boarded a steamer bound for Italy. But he never made it out of the harbor.

Before the ship weighed anchor, he learned from the local consul's office that the Italian government would not pay reservists' fares or expenses for the trip home. Fighting was one thing; paying for it was another. Incensed, Ponzi left the ship, though not in time to remove some of his luggage, which went on to Italy without him. By some accounts, he was so eager to avoid paying the fare he jumped overboard and swam the short distance to the pier.

Stuck in New York, Ponzi again scoured the help wanted ads. One seemed written just for him. The J. R. Poole Company needed a clerk for its import-export business. The salary was only fair, about sixteen dollars a week, but Ponzi liked the location. After thirteen years of roughing it through North America, Ponzi was returning to the city where he had first landed in search of gold: Boston.

Richard Grozier during his difficult years at Harvard.

Mary Grozier

CHAPTER FIVE

"AS RESTLESS AS THE SEA"

Edwin Grozier's devotion to the *Post* did not leave much time for family. As he put it, "There were many times when I worked twenty-four hours a day for several days in succession." Even when he was not on Newspaper Row, work followed him home. A frequent guest at his dinner table was the *Globe*'s General Taylor. One observer wrote of Grozier, "The bulk of the work in every department of the paper—business, circulation, editorial—all fell on his shoulders. He did not know what it was to rest. . . . All his work was for the *Post* and there his heart was—with the paper, its employees, and its readers."

With his heart at the *Post,* the job of rearing his children fell to his wife, Alice, a serious woman who oversaw the care of their son, Richard, and daughter, Helen. Edwin Grozier was at once distant from and demanding of his children. One of the few pastimes father and son shared was chess. Thanks to Edwin's success, the family lived increasingly well, taking lavish vacations when he could be pried away from the *Post* and hiring servants at their home in a bowfront town house on Boston's fashionable Newbury Street. A friend of Edwin's recalled visiting the family there and seeing young Richard dreamily drawing tiny boats and ships on a painted ocean.

The family summered at an elegant home on Commercial Street in Provincetown, on Cape Cod, with a park and a beach across the street. But Edwin often remained in Boston, missing the chance to see his slender son, Richard, join the other boys diving off a dock for pennies tossed to the bottom of the cool harbor waters. He also found little time to discover that his son had an inventive, if restless, mind, with a gift for math and science.

When Richard was twelve, his parents sent him north to bucolic Exeter, New Hampshire, to attend one of the most prestigious boarding schools in the country, Phillips Exeter Academy. For tuition and expenses of about $325 a year, a young man at Exeter could be reasonably certain of winning entry into an Ivy League college. But Richard lasted barely three months, earning D's in math and English, and a failing grade in history. He returned home after one term, in time for Christmas.

A year later, his parents insisted he try again. He returned to Exeter, this time maintaining a C-minus average over the next four years, with an occasional A in math or physics, and a few failing grades in Latin and history. He seemed comfortable, though, winning election as president of his dorm and as captain of the chess team, and warming his father's heart by becoming secretary of the school newspaper, the *Exonian*.

As planned, Richard was accepted at Harvard in the class of 1909, a collection of 434 pedigreed young men who had every reasonable expectation that they would rule the world. Half were from Massachusetts, and more than half, including Richard, were Protestants, with twenty-six Catholics, sixteen Jews, five Christian Scientists, three Free Thinkers, and two atheists thrown in for diversity. Fifty-four were the sons of men who had attended Harvard, and three-quarters declared themselves Republicans. One of those was Theodore Roosevelt Jr., whose father was president of the United States at the time. Classmates also included T. S. Eliot, Walter Lippmann, and scores of other young men destined for fortune and various levels of renown.

Whether he was intimidated or just uninterested, it was not long before Richard began following a path almost identical to Ponzi's at the University of Rome. He developed a taste for fine wine and champagne, ate sumptuous meals at fashionable restaurants, smoked cigarettes in a rakish holder, and put his gentle voice and handsome face to use wooing older women. He had chestnut-brown hair and sensitive dark eyes, and his finely tailored clothes hung perfectly on his trim five-foot-ten frame. With the world at his feet, he found little time for classes. Richard Grozier seemed especially determined to fail freshman English composition, a galling prospect for his newspaper editor father.

In November 1905, not three months after his arrival at Harvard, Richard received a letter from the freshman dean, Edgar H. Wells: "I am very sorry to tell you that the Administrative Board at its meeting last night voted to put you on probation for your unsatisfactory record. Probation means that you are in serious danger of separation from College, and unless from now on your record both in attendance and grades is thoroughly satisfactory you may be sent away without further warning." Wells wrote a similar, though somewhat more polite, letter to Edwin Grozier.

There was a cachet to laxity among certain Harvard students. This was especially true among the "club men," who thought a grade above a C was a waste of effort. They dressed in expensive but casual disarray, disdained rah-rah school spirit, and refused to date the brainy women at Radcliffe. Outwardly, Richard fit the profile. His only nonacademic activity was his membership in the Exeter Club. He played no sports, joined no groups, and despite his newspaper heritage spent no time at the school paper, the *Crimson*. He lived like a prince in Dana Chambers on Dunster Street, a private dormitory in an area near the college known as the "Gold Coast," where students of means escaped the drafty, dingy housing provided by the college. A flattering description of the club men of that era would be "cool"; a less-generous one would be "feckless." Richard resembled them in many ways, but in one important respect he differed: arrogance. Richard had none. He was charming and gracious, with a gentle voice and an aversion to limelight. Women adored him. He might have been a loafer and a lothario, but he was not a lout.

Upon receiving the dean's letter, Edwin Grozier began a campaign to save his son from the ignominy of being exiled from Harvard. He took a piece of *Post* stationery and wrote a careful reply to Wells: "Richard is a boy of more than average ability, and there is no good reason he should not stand well in his class. Unfortunately he seems to have a habit of acquiring a great deal of information about everything except the studies he is actually pursuing. It is, of course, a great disappointment to his parents that he should not attend properly to the business in hand." Edwin Grozier vowed to do everything possible toward "obtaining the desired result."

As if to purposely break his father's promise, Richard did even worse. His professors took notice. "My dear Mr. Wells," literature Professor W. G. Howard wrote the dean. "So far as I know R. Grozier I am inclined to think that temporary separation from College would be the most wholesome medicine that could be administered to him." After receiving that letter, Wells wrote Richard's father another warning. Edwin Grozier answered with a father's lament.

"I . . . very much regret that my son, Richard, did so poorly in his midyear examinations," he wrote. "I am much puzzled by the young man's failure to do well in his college studies. He is naturally bright; his fund of general information is unusually good; he has no bad habits that I know of. We see a great deal of him at our home, and he devotes a good deal of time to study. Why he fails to do, at least, fairly well is an enigma to me."

The letter traffic continued through spring 1906, the end of Richard's freshman year. For the year, he received a B in physics, D's in French, philosophy, and math, and a failing grade in English composition. Already on probation, Richard was, in Harvard parlance, "separated" from his class. He was entitled to petition for reinstatement, but Dean Wells suggested that it was not worth the bother. Some men just were not cut out for Harvard. Edwin Grozier was not ready to hear that.

At his father's insistence, Richard attended a Harvard summer school program and did well enough to seek readmission. With more assurances to the dean from Edwin and warnings from Wells about staying on track, Richard was readmitted as a sophomore. But soon the pattern repeated itself, and by the following spring Richard was back on probation. No longer a freshman, Richard now came under the purview of the dean of Harvard College, a well-fed man named Byron Satterlee Hurlbut. He invited Richard to his office.

"I beg to thank you very much indeed for your kind and inspiring talk with my son, Richard," Edwin Grozier wrote Hurlbut afterward. "Needless to say I am very fond of Richard. He is my only son, and I believe he has fine natural capacities. But he has sadly neglected opportunities, despite many urgent talks on my part. He seems much impressed by the timely advice which you gave him."

"I think we can get the boy on his feet all right," Hurlbut answered. "There is no reason why he should not win relief from probation at the final examinations. What he needs most is to realize that it is time to look at things as a man does."

More letters followed between Hurlbut and Edwin Grozier, but Richard's schoolwork continued to lag. His father's letters to the dean became increasingly apologetic: "I am extremely sorry that despite the utmost efforts of his parents the young man has made no better showing."

At the end of his sophomore year, Richard's probation led again to separation—he had earned D's in four of the eight classes he had taken since entering Harvard, and he had failed English again. That failure, Hurlbut told Edwin Grozier, was due to simple neglect. It was back to summer school, after which, in September 1907, Richard petitioned to be readmitted, this time not as a member of his own class but as a second-time sophomore. The request was granted, and he returned to Harvard.

Two months later, in November 1907, the *Boston Globe* ran a brief news item that went a long way toward explaining why Richard Grozier was not focused on his studies. The headline read: ROMANCE DISCLOSED; NEWTON HIGH SCHOOL GIRL TO WED HARVARD MAN. Below it was a photograph of an attractive, serious-looking woman with a fashionable choker necklace and her hair swept high on her head. Her name was Vera Rumery and, despite the headline, she was no high school girl. She was twenty-three, the daughter of a former alderman, a young woman two years older than Richard. The story began: "The pretty romance of one of Newton High School's most popular young women athletes and a Harvard junior was revealed today by the engagement announcement of Miss Vera E. Rumery of Newtonville and Richard Grozier of Cambridge." Richard was not technically a junior, but an engagement announcement was no place to air his academic failings. The next three paragraphs described the bride-to-be's prowess at field hockey and her devotion to snowshoeing. It mentioned her family and Richard's father, though it neglected to note that Edwin Grozier was editor and publisher of the rival *Post*. The last line of the story struck the only odd note: "Because of the illness of Mr. Grozier's mother the date for the wedding has not been fixed."

In the immediate afterglow of the engagement, Richard pulled up his grades enough to rejoin his class as a junior in February 1908. But by spring Richard was back to his old habits and in danger of again failing freshman English composition. Once more, he became a topic of discussion for Harvard's academic masters.

"I am sick in bed," Richard wrote Hurlbut in April while he was suffering from an ear infection. "Can you put off action on my case until I am able to see you?" The dean granted his request, and also agreed to hold off writing another letter to Richard's father. Two weeks later, though, the board stopped waiting and placed Richard on probation for his third time in three years at Harvard. He was failing three of his five classes, and Hurlbut wrote again to Edwin Grozier. This time the dean injected a touch of melancholy not found in their earlier exchanges.

"It is unnecessary for me to write you about the meaning of probation, for Richard has been on probation before," Hurlbut wrote. "I hope that his final record will justify his relief from probation, so that it will be unnecessary to close his connection with the College. I wish that you would let me know of anything I can do to help the boy. Personally, he is a very attractive fellow, but I judge him to be as restless as the sea, or anything else that is a comparison for great restlessness."

Hurlbut's sympathy was answered by Edwin Grozier's rising frustration.

"I do not see what you could do to help the young man, as you kindly offer," the elder Grozier wrote. "It is up to him to help himself. That is what I am earnestly urging him to do, and hope to succeed. I am confident that he has his full share of natural ability, but to keep him down to the actual work in hand is the difficulty."

A month later, in June 1908, at the end of Richard's junior year, his third probation turned into his third separation. Hurlbut suggested that it was the last time.

"You are, I am sorry to say, dropped for two reasons; first, because of your unsatisfactory work for the year, and secondly, because of your failure to secure the necessary total of grades requisite for promotion to the Senior Class," Hurlbut wrote to Richard. A special vote of the Administrative Board would be required for readmission, but Hurlbut thought that unlikely. "Personally I feel that experience out in the world would be better for you than a further attempt to succeed here at Cambridge."

To Edwin Grozier, Hurlbut wrote: "I believe that it would be best to put the boy at work." After some pleasantries and sympathies, he reinforced his point: "Were he my son I should put him at work."

The wrought-iron gates to Harvard were closing. But Edwin Grozier, for whom a relentless work ethic was a defining trait, was determined to keep them open. And, as editor and publisher of the *Post,*

he undoubtedly knew that his voice would carry weight, even among
the dons of Harvard. "I am much disappointed and grieved that my
son Richard should continue to do so poorly in his college studies,"
he wrote Hurlbut. "Without doubt your advice to put him to work is
sound, but, while there is any chance remaining of his completing his
college course, I hesitate to abandon the effort." He sent Richard to
Harvard's summer engineering camp, exiling the cosmopolitan young
man to a world of trees and blackflies at Squam Lake, in New Hampshire. His orders were to return home with passing grades.

"Good work at camp will certainly be an important consideration
with the Board," Hurlbut wrote Edwin Grozier when he heard of the
plan. Reluctant to shrug off the editor and publisher of the *Post,* he
offered a glimmer of hope and a cautionary note. "I should like to
have Richard get a degree; at the same time I question whether his
being allowed so many chances would not in the long run be bad for
him."

"While the young man has not shown it in his studies," Edwin
Grozier answered, "I still cling to a father's fond confidence that he
possesses rather unusual natural abilities, and I trust that he may have a
final chance to demonstrate that in connection with his college
work. . . . I will urge him to put his best foot forward this summer,
and trust he may yet make a creditable record."

Halfway through the summer, when Richard had earned a B in his
first course, Edwin Grozier grew cautiously optimistic. He began
seeking Richard's readmission from Hurlbut: "The young man has put
in a lot of hard, earnest work this summer, evincing some of his natural capacity, and I trust that he may yet graduate and in after years
prove to be a credit to his University."

Hurlbut answered in kind, though with a hint of sarcasm: "I hope
that he will keep up his good work in college. He certainly has allowed things to slide right along so far."

After passing his second summer course, Richard was rewarded
with a trip to Denver with his father. But with reinstatement still
pending, Edwin Grozier was not ready to rest. Fearing they would

miss an important deadline, he sent a Western Union telegram to Hurlbut: "Please wire me collect [at] Hotel Metropole just what date it is necessary for him to be in Cambridge."

Two days later, September 29, 1908, Hurlbut told Richard he had been readmitted as a junior on probation, a condition that would remain in force at least through the middle of the term. "This is to insure that you do not again, as you have done in the past, work hard at first, and then slump."

Despite the warnings, the cajoling, and the outrage caused by the three separations and reinstatements, Richard soon returned to form. He ignored his studies and seemed to be daring Harvard to ignore his father's campaign and finally be rid of him. Then fate and friendship intervened.

Richard's roommate, Joseph W. Ross, a baby-faced engineering student from Ipswich, Massachusetts, saw his friend heading for a fall. Privately, Ross approached Dean Hurlbut at a college event on November 10, 1908, and then followed up with a letter: "I am writing to the effect that I should like to have the case of Richard Grozier handed over to me in case that his hour exam marks do not warrant a continuance of his probation," Ross wrote. "I want to make plain that I am doing this absolutely without his knowledge. . . . I am very sure that I can bring around the required attention to his duties." He asked the Administrative Board to formally approve his standing as Richard's anonymous taskmaster.

With Ross's guarantee, the board voted a week later to give Richard yet another chance. Dean Hurlbut wrote to Ross explaining that this was done only after "accepting your offer that if he were put in your charge you promised to have him keep up his work." Hurlbut added one more condition: The deal could not be kept secret; both Richard and his father would be informed of Ross's new role.

Ross answered with a "promise that my part of the agreement, meaning Richard's part, will be faithfully lived up to." He tacitly accepted that Richard would be informed, but begged Hurlbut not to tell Richard's father. Ross must have known from Richard how angry

Edwin Grozier had become about the situation. Learning that another student had been made caretaker for his son would only have enraged him further, making life harder on his friend Richard. Hurlbut briefly protested, but there was no indication that Edwin Grozier ever learned of the guardian angel on his son's shoulder.

Hurlbut kept tabs on Richard the rest of the year. With Ross's help, Richard fulfilled all his requirements and passed all his classes, including English comp, in which he got a C.

At the Class Day exercises near the end of June, one of Richard's classmates may have unwittingly explained why the heir to a newspaper fortune had so much trouble with that particular class. That is, aside from his own halfhearted effort. Delivering an address entitled "The College and the Press," Richard's classmate told the crowd, "One of our teachers of English composition here at Harvard concludes his classroom work each year with a little advice to his young friends with regard to journalism. The gist of it is that newspaper work, like some medicines, is beneficial only when the dose is small."

Official word that Richard would graduate with his class came at the very last minute on June 29, 1909, a day before commencement. It was too late for his photograph to appear in the treasured *Class Album*. Richard had made it through Harvard, but he would not make it down the aisle. He and Vera Rumery broke off their engagement and went their separate ways.

After graduation, Richard's friend and savior Joseph Ross found an engineering job and moved home to Ipswich for what he later called "a very routine life, interrupted by a few Caribbean cruises." In 1912, three years after graduating from Harvard, Ross received his reward for rescuing his roommate: He married Vera Rumery.

After college, Richard packed his belongings and moved from his private dormitory to his parents' new house, less than a mile from Harvard Square, in the most prestigious part of Cambridge. Flush with profits from the *Post*'s success, in October 1907 Edwin and Alice

Grozier bought the enormous Queen Anne–style home at 168 Brattle Street. Alice had found the house by scouring the classified ads in the *Post* before the paper was printed; she furnished it much the same way, finding ads for estate sales and offering to buy items before the rest of the city knew they were available. Built two decades earlier, the house befit a powerful publisher, with gleaming woodwork, a teak-paneled ballroom designed to hold two hundred people, and a grand staircase. Christened "Riverview" by its original owner, the house allowed the son and grandson of sailing captains to look out over a sweeping lawn to the green-gray waters of the Charles River.

After scraping through college, Richard was uninterested in the routine of a job. He enrolled in Harvard Law School, but he wilted under the rigors of legal scholarship. Within a year he was finished with school and working at the *Post*. For the next decade, Richard followed the well-worn path of the newspaper heir, working his way through the various departments—reporter, editorial writer, printshop apprentice—to learn the business he would someday own. For some months he even served as a pressman, laboring amid the clatter of the largest printing plant in New England, which Edwin Grozier had built with much fanfare on five floors directly beneath the *Post* offices on Washington Street. It was an ideal fit: Richard was a man of mechanical bent, unimpressed by the fancy scrollwork on the face of a watch but awed by its metal intestines, the screws and gears and springs that made the thing tick.

By 1920, Richard was the *Post*'s general manager, assistant publisher, and assistant editor. But the paper was still firmly in his father's control, and the titles carried little power. Richard devoted himself to his work, but his performance at Harvard lingered in Edwin Grozier's mind. Richard was given few chances to prove himself, and nothing he had done during the past decade seemed to win his father's confidence or approval.

Yet during those years, Richard Grozier had quietly studied his father's stunts—the elephants, the headless photos, the primitive man, the free cars, the canes. He understood them for what they were:

flashes of fireworks that caught the eye and relieved the reader of his two cents before he knew what hit him. Richard also recognized that the gimmicks were a means to an end, a way to foot the bills for solid journalism. Now if only he had some way to prove how much he had learned.

Photograph of an oil portrait of a teenage Rose Gnecco.

CHAPTER SIX

"An American Beauty"

In 1915, two years before Ponzi's return to Boston, construction began on a mansion that came to symbolize the spoils within the reach of poor men who were bursting with ambition, gifted with charisma, and unburdened by scruples.

The Georgian Revival manor would be the home of Boston's mayor, James Michael Curley, an up-from-the-slums force of nature who viewed politics as a sure path to wealth and power. Clad in brick and roofed in slate, the house sat on a two-acre lot facing a park that was part of Frederick Law Olmsted's "emerald necklace" around Boston. Past the park was Jamaica Pond, where hand-holding couples and raucous families skated in winter and picnicked in summer. The location was within the borders of Boston yet seemed light-years from the inner city.

Even more magnificent than the site was the house itself: more than twenty-one rooms, including an oval dining room paneled in mahogany, fireplaces framed in white Italian marble, fixtures plated with gold, and a curving staircase lit by a two-story chandelier bought from the Austro-Hungarian embassy in Washington. The only signs of the owner's humble beginnings were the festive shamrock cutouts in all thirty of the white shutters, placed there as much to annoy the Yankee neighbors as to display Hibernian pride.

Curley was born in 1874 in Boston's poor Roxbury section. Fatherless by age ten, imbued with resentment of the Brahmins, and blessed with prodigious energy, Curley devoted himself to the punch-in-the-nose, pat-on-the-back world of Boston Irish politics. At twenty-six he won election to the Boston Common Council, a raucous body that was the stepping-stone for every young would-be Democratic politico in the city. He soon became boss of Roxbury's Ward 17, which along with his council seat gave him the power to barter jobs and other goodies for loyalty and votes. He launched a political organization called the Tammany Club, defiantly named for the New York machine. Curley insisted it was a tribute not to the New Yorkers' corruption but to their commitment to constituents in the absence of government aid programs. But the Boston Tammany Club soon emulated its New York cousin in graft and scandal, with Curley larding the public payroll and dipping his fingers in every slice of municipal pie. The club's mascot was a crouching tiger. The public treasury was its prey.

To raise money for its activities, the Tammany Club sponsored all sorts of promotions at its summer festivals, known as "powwows." Men would struggle to catch greased pigs for a prize, vie for the title of "ugliest man," and pay ten cents to take an ax to a piano, with a five-dollar reward to the man with the mightiest swing. Only a few years had passed since Massachusetts was atwitter over the trial of Fall River's Lizzie Borden, so the ax-swinging spectacle was certain to send shivers down spines. Speakers at the powwows included local celebrities, including Curley's pal John L. Sullivan, the former heavyweight champion known as "the Boston Strong Boy." In spirit, Curley borrowed Sullivan's familiar cry, "I can lick any man!"

From the Common Council, Curley rose to a seat in the Massachusetts legislature. But in 1903 his rise was nearly derailed when he
became the first member of that body arrested for a crime. He and a
fellow leader of the Tammany Club had taken civil service exams for
two Irish immigrants who wanted jobs as letter carriers. Curley and his
cohort were charged with "combining, conspiring, confederating and
agreeing together to defraud the United States." The maximum
penalty for each was two years in prison and a ten-thousand-dollar fine.
Curley admitted to the scheme in the face of overwhelming evidence.
He was convicted of the charges and sentenced to two months in jail.

Refusing to slink away quietly, he appealed the conviction and
sought a seat on the Boston Board of Aldermen, a step up from the
state legislature in the pecking order of Massachusetts politics. Incredibly, he won. The state supreme court ultimately declined to hear his
appeal, and Curley was sent to the Charles Street Jail, where his friend
the warden made sure he had an extra-large cell, good food, salt baths,
a steady stream of visitors, and a ready supply of books.

Instead of destroying his career, the jail term invigorated it. He was
renominated as the Democratic candidate for alderman while still behind bars, then boasted of his criminal record in a campaign slogan
that appealed to the us-against-authority culture of the famine Irish:
"He did it for a friend!" Soon he was back to his old tricks—a few
months after his release Curley was accused of selling his aldermanic
vote to a shipping company that wanted to build a rail line through the
streets of East Boston. A grand jury refused to issue indictments, but
that luck would not hold. In 1907 Curley was indicted for pressuring
New England Telephone and Telegraph to hire phantom workers as
an apparent cover for the payment of bribes. Fearing that his ambitions would not survive a second conviction, Curley hired lawyer
Daniel Coakley, a thoroughly unscrupulous ex-reporter and boxing
referee who relied more heavily on blackmail than legal briefs. Coakley worked his magic, and the indictments were dropped.

In 1909 Curley rose to the newly formed Boston City Council,
which replaced the Board of Aldermen as well as the Common

Council. From that perch he won a seat in the U.S. Congress in 1910, was reelected two years later, and set his sights on the plum job of Boston mayor. His main obstacle was a fellow Irish-American: John "Honey Fitz" Fitzgerald, who was enjoying his second term as mayor and considering running for a third. Fitzgerald had come up in a fashion similar to Curley's, from ward politics to the Boston Common Council to the Massachusetts senate to Congress, where he'd served three terms and won a reputation as a staunch supporter of immigrants. His nickname was a tribute to his honeyed rendition of "Sweet Adeline" at every public event save wakes. Fitzgerald's diminutive stature and acquisitive nature earned him another sobriquet, "the Little Napoleon."

By 1913, Curley was eager to become mayor—the job paid better than being a congressman, and there were more opportunities for pocket lining. But he loathed the idea of having to face a sitting incumbent Democrat with a similar following. Once again the lawyer Dan Coakley proved useful. Coakley shared with Curley a scandalous piece of information about Fitzgerald: The mayor had made a spectacle of himself with a buxom roadhouse gal named Elizabeth "Toodles" Ryan. Curley had just what he needed to squeeze the family man Fitzgerald from the race. A letter soon arrived at Fitzgerald's house threatening exposure of his public flirtation with Toodles. Fearing for his reputation, Fitzgerald ended his candidacy, giving Curley the opening he needed to take control of Boston City Hall. The episode was eventually memorialized in a classic bit of Boston doggerel: "A whisky glass and Toodles' ass made a horse's ass out of Honey Fitz." Fitzgerald's only consolation was the wedding soon after of his beloved eldest daughter, Rose, to Joseph P. Kennedy, the son of an Irish politico-cum-saloon-keeper-cum-rumrunner. Rose would pay special tribute to her father by naming her second son after him: John Fitzgerald Kennedy.

Curley claimed the mayor's office in the name of honest government, ironically suggesting that he was just the man to clean up the mess of graft, patronage, and incompetence that Fitzgerald had left behind. At first, he seemed true to his word, but soon he returned to form: ethnic warfare, intimidation, and a level of graft unparalleled in Boston history. The nadir was the palace he was building on the parkway.

The big question was how he could possibly afford such a mansion. Curley had no declared savings, yet he had also recently purchased a seaside summer home in Hull. His mayoral salary of ten thousand dollars was not enough to pay for the land, much less the building and its sumptuous furnishings.

An investigation by the city Finance Commission led to a recommendation that Curley face prosecution for an array of criminal charges. But action depended on the local district attorney, Joseph C. Pelletier, a political ally of Curley's who, years earlier, had rejected calls to prosecute him for the New England Telephone and Telegraph bribe allegations. Beyond their political ties, Curley shared with Pelletier a link to Dan Coakley: Coakley had served as Pelletier's campaign manager, and Pelletier and Coakley were in league on a sexual blackmail game. At Coakley's urging, Pelletier rejected the call for prosecution. That was how it worked. Once again Curley had caught a break.

Still, Curley had to answer to voters if he wanted to win a second term in 1917. When graft was doled out in small doses or tucked in secret bank accounts, it could be hidden, denied, or downplayed. It surprised no one in Boston when a man with a hand on the tiller of government had his other hand in the government till. But the mansion was too much, a ten-thousand-square-foot gorilla climbing to the roof of Curley's City Hall with his future in its grasp.

The newspapers had a field day. Edwin Grozier's *Post* was especially disgusted with Curley, despite the paper's Democratic leanings and the fact that Grozier actually agreed with the mayor on a number of key issues. In his race for reelection, Curley ran not only against his opponents but against the *Post,* at one point holding a rally on Washington Street across from the offices of "that foul sheet." Pretending to be a David among Goliaths, he shouted, "With every corrupt boss and rotten newspaper against me, with all of these powers of rotten-ness and corruption against me, they can't beat Jim Curley."

Awash in scandal and distrust, and with old enemies like Honey Fitz working behind the scenes against him, Curley persevered in his bid for a second mayoral term. The *Post* endorsed Congressman James A. Gallivan of South Boston for mayor, enabling Gallivan to take a big enough chunk of Curley's core constituency to deny him reelection. With Gallivan and Curley splitting the Irish vote, the winner was An-drew J. Peters, a thoroughly forgettable Yankee. Peters's only lasting mark on the city would be a dark one: his debauchery with an eleven-year-old girl who had been placed in his care.

From the moment Curley lost the 1917 election, no one doubted he would engineer a return to the political stage. But the lesson was clear, and it applied to every ambitious man in the city: Boston would toler-ate, even celebrate, a rogue who made his own rules and lined his own pockets, as long as he knew the limits. If he grew too bold or too flashy, or if his spoils became too big to ignore, he would be made to pay.

Ponzi arrived in Boston just in time to watch the Curley house scan-dal play itself out in the newspapers and the streets. Ponzi found him-self rooting for Curley, whom he admired for his moxie and sense of style, and whom he considered a "likeable chap."

While the mayor was fighting for his political life, Ponzi went duti-fully to work as a clerk and stenographer at the J. R. Poole Company, named for its owner, John R. Poole. Ponzi's workplace was on South Market Street, in the shadow of the new Custom House Tower, a thirty-story, peaked-roof wonder of Italian renaissance architecture that was Boston's first skyscraper. All around the area were bright col-ors and the wafting smells from the stalls of produce vendors, dairy merchants, and fishmongers. On his way to work Ponzi could hear the screams of gulls and see the masts of ships along Central and Long Wharfs. If he listened hard enough, he might hear his mother tongue carried on the wind from T Wharf, where the Italian fishermen congregated. A few steps away was Faneuil Hall, the Revolutionary War meeting place where Sam Adams had inflamed his compatriots upstairs and merchants sold their wares in a marketplace downstairs.

For months Ponzi toiled to keep track of Poole's extensive foreign businesses, only to be disappointed by his pay of sixteen dollars a week. At first, Ponzi considered the job a gamble in the futures market—the company was doing well and lavished its employees with promises of eventual rewards. He won a raise to twenty-five dollars a week, but still he struggled. "By starving one day and eating a little less the next one," he complained, "we employees always managed, more or less, to keep handsomely in debt."

His only consolation was his certainty that he had established a firm foothold on the ladder up from manual labor. He had painted his last sign, washed his last dish, begged his last bowl of macaroni. Never again would he seek a menial job. But he was far from satisfied. It remained a long, unsteady climb to the top rung, and at thirty-five Ponzi was impatient about getting there. His impatience grew exponentially at the end of May 1917.

On Memorial Day weekend, Ponzi accompanied his landlady, Myrtle Lombard, to a Boston Pops concert. Ponzi played mandolin and considered himself an aficionado of fine music, and Mrs. Lombard taught piano to neighborhood children. Afterward, music still in their ears, they made their way to the Boylston Street station to catch an electric streetcar to Mrs. Lombard's house on Highland Avenue in nearby Somerville, home to a growing colony of Italian immigrants.

As midnight approached, they stood on the platform waiting for the train. Looking around at the postconcert crowd, Ponzi noticed a lovely young woman. She was tiny, at four foot eleven just the right size for him, with rounded curves that defied the stick-figure fashions of the day. She had luxurious brown hair, lively dark eyes, and skin as smooth as Gianduja cream. An oil portrait painted of her as a teenager portrayed her in Mona Lisa–like pose, with a faint smile and a billowing silk blouse pushed low on her shoulders. In the eyes of the painter, a Somerville neighbor, Rose bore a striking resemblance to Lillian Gish, the ethereal beauty of silent film.

Ponzi watched her intently, ignoring the young man who was her escort. Eventually Mrs. Lombard noticed that her normally talkative tenant had dropped his end of the conversation. She searched for the source of Ponzi's distraction.

"Why, there is Rose!" Mrs. Lombard said, spotting the young woman. "I want you to meet her, Mr. Ponzi. She is one of my pupils."

Mrs. Lombard led a delighted Ponzi down the platform and made the introductions. Rose Gnecco was twenty-one, the youngest of six children of a fruit merchant and a homemaker who had emigrated from Genoa. Born in Boston, she had spent two years in high school but dropped out to take a job as a stenographer and bookkeeper for a Somerville contractor. Rose liked the work, but her fondest dream was to fill a small, happy home with a husband and children.

"How do you do?" she asked Ponzi in a voice he found as sweet as her looks.

An accomplished flirt, normally quick with a quip, Ponzi could do little more than repeat the phrase back to her. The streetcar arrived, and Rose and her escort took a seat a few rows ahead of Ponzi and his landlady. As the trolley clacked and rattled along the steel rails embedded in the street, Ponzi stared at the back of Rose's head. He spent the entire twenty-minute ride that way, his eyes locked on her curls. He would remember the moment his entire life: "Time, space, the world, and everything else around me, except that girl, had ceased to exist."

When they got home, Mrs. Lombard asked Ponzi what he thought of Rose.

"I think she is wonderful," he replied. "I am going to marry her."

"Why, Mr. Ponzi!" Mrs. Lombard said. "You must be crazy!"

A few days later, Ponzi telephoned Rose to invite her to a moving-picture show. His failure to ask her father's permission was a breach of accepted courting etiquette, but she had a mind of her own, and she was attracted to the older, worldly suitor. Rose accepted. That night, they sat side by side in the darkened theater, and Ponzi knew he never wanted to be farther apart. He told her he wanted to marry her. She laughed.

But Ponzi was serious. After so many rootless years, he was ready to settle down. Rose fit his every dream of a loving, beautiful wife, and he pursued her as ardently as he had money and success. Nearly every day he sent sodas or flowers to her office, and whenever she accepted his invitations he would treat her to a night at the movies or the symphony. If she begged off by saying she was taking her nephews and nieces to the beach at Nantasket, Ponzi would show up unannounced on the ferry. He was relentless, and she relented. He told her about his boyhood in Italy and his adventures in the United States, though he left out his years in prison. Whenever he described his activities during that period, he said only that he had been involved in "investigations." At times he would suggest mysteriously that he had been working on behalf of the Italian government.

Not long after, Ponzi's immediate supervisor died and he was promoted to a position that doubled his salary to fifty dollars a week. Flush with his new job, he felt ready to make good on the vow he'd made the night he'd met Rose. A glistening, full-carat stone in a Tiffany setting would have cost perhaps three hundred dollars, but that was out of his league. So he bought what amounted to a diamond chip. This time when he told Rose he wanted to marry her, she did not laugh. She accepted the ring.

During their engagement, Rose received a letter from Ponzi's mother, welcoming her to the family and sharing some difficult news. Imelde Ponzi suspected her son would not tell his bride-to-be all the stories of his past, and Imelde wanted to be sure Rose knew that her betrothed had spent time in prison. The letter explained the cases in the same innocent light that Ponzi had used when describing them to his mother—he took blame for the forgery to spare the Zarossi family, and he was duped into pleading guilty to the immigrant-smuggling charge. Rose accepted her mother-in-law's explanations and admired Ponzi even more for his chivalry toward Zarossi and the Italian immigrants. It fit perfectly in her mind with his donation of skin to Pearl

Gossett, a story she had heard from Ponzi himself. At Imelde's suggestion, Rose did not tell Ponzi that she knew of his prison past. Both women believed it would damage his ego if he thought Rose viewed him as an ex-convict.

On February 4, 1918, Rose Maria Gnecco and Charles Ponzi—he had dropped Carlo altogether—stood before the marble tabernacle inside the basement sanctuary of Saint Anthony's Church on Vine Street, in the heart of Somerville's Italian district. As rays of winter sunlight angled through ground-level stained-glass windows, the Reverend Nazareno Properzi pronounced them husband and wife. Rose's sister Theresa was her maid of honor, and Ponzi's friend Lawrence Avanzino, a grocer, stood as best man. The wooden church pews were filled with Gneccos, extended family members, and friends. Ponzi's joy was tinged only by his mother's absence: He could not afford to bring her over from Italy.

The newlyweds moved into a tidy five-room apartment a few miles from the church, near Tufts College, on tree-lined Powder House Boulevard. Their apartment was the upstairs half of a two-family house owned by Anders Larsen, a Danish immigrant factory worker and his wife, Karen, who lived on the first floor. Ponzi leapt happily into married life—the devil-may-care boy who'd gambled and drunk away his nights in Rome had matured into a devoted husband who hurried home after work at J. R. Poole. He made certain he and Rose were never apart for even a single night. Rose stopped working to care for their home, so there was little money for extras. They went to dinner and the theater once a week—it thrilled Rose to have a night out with no cooking—but most often they stayed home, ate a meal Rose prepared, and listened to music. Sometimes Ponzi would serenade his young wife by strumming a song on the mandolin. Afterward, Rose would gingerly put away her few prized belongings. One, a sterling silver ladle that was a wedding present from a coworker, was tucked into its chamois bag after every use.

Not for Rose the ways of the flapper girls who smoked cigarettes and haunted speakeasies. She believed in old-fashioned domesticity.

All she wanted was a husband who loved her, children to love, and a home she could keep to her immaculate standards. She would be happy to stay in Somerville, near her parents, John and Maria Gnecco, and her large extended family of two sisters, three brothers, and assorted cousins, in-laws, nieces, and nephews. With Ponzi, she figured she was well on the way to fulfilling that modest dream.

The new Mr. and Mrs. Charles Ponzi rarely quarreled, but there was occasional tension over their different approaches to money and his endless puzzling over how to obtain it. Rose wanted them to be economical, living carefully within their means "in a cozy little place where we can pay our bills." Ponzi, she despaired, "had the air and the tastes of the millionaire."

Rose craved his attention, and grew peeved at times over her husband's dedication to a stamp collection he had kept throughout his years of travel. For some men it would be an idle hobby, but it seemed more for Ponzi. He would pore for hours over the colorful little pieces of paper he had lovingly pressed into several books, as though the different denominations printed on their faces held a secret he was desperate to unlock. It was a fitting hobby for the son of a postman who had died young.

Ponzi's uncommon interest in the foreign stamps might have had something to do with a recent conversation he had had with Roberto de Masellis, manager of the foreign banking department at the Fidelity Trust Company, where Ponzi kept an account. Ponzi had met de Masellis when he'd strolled into the bank one day to exchange some dollars for Italian lire. De Masellis, who had been deputy Italian consul to the United States in Naples before immigrating to Boston, was a loquacious authority on foreign exchange. Unprompted, he launched into a tutorial about fluctuations in the values of European currencies after the Great War. Looking at Ponzi through pince-nez glasses, his banker's paunch restrained by his suit coat, de Masellis explained that Italian lire, once worth five to the dollar, had been so devalued that lately it took eighteen or twenty to equal one dollar. The wild fluctuations created the possibility of hugely profitable speculation for anyone smart, daring, and lucky enough to figure out a way to buy one currency for a low price and sell it when its value increased.

Rose, meanwhile, considered his persistent focus on the stamp books unwanted competition. "Charlie, for heaven's sake drop it and talk to me," Rose implored him. "What do you think I want to do after I've worked all day? Darn socks?"

Sometimes Ponzi would smile and put down the book, but more often he would gently tease her: "Well, why don't you get hold of something that's worth spending your own time with?"

"Oh well," she would answer coyly, "if you don't think my husband is important enough to spend some time with . . ." And they would laugh.

To anyone who would listen, Rose would boast about her good fortune in finding him. "When a man is always a gentleman to his wife," she would say, "behind closed doors as well as in front of them, he's absolutely certain to be, at heart, a good man." Ponzi, she was sure, was just such a man.

Ponzi was equally delighted by his wife—"An American beauty. My Rose!" he called her. But the rest of his life left him unsatisfied. Ponzi wanted to drape Rose in finery, lavish her with servants, own a home big enough to get lost in. How could they start a family without financial security? "I want you to be able to throw away a hundred dollars," he told Rose, though he must have known she could never be so extravagant. As they sat together at the small table in their kitchen, Ponzi outlined one intricate moneymaking scheme after another. Once she took a photograph of him sitting there, his feet up on the stove as though he already owned the world. He turned the camera on her and captured a more modest image, of Rose sitting demurely in her nightgown.

When he spun his web of dollar dreams, Rose listened politely. Then she would remind him again that she did not need money to be happy. He went on dreaming. But it was not only about the money, Rose knew. Her husband wanted the world to take notice of him, to celebrate his ingenuity and be dazzled by his charm.

Six months after they married, Ponzi got a chance to prove his financial acumen at Gnecco Brothers, the wholesale fruit business Rose's father and uncle ran near Faneuil Hall. The company was failing, and John Gnecco turned to his bright new son-in-law for help. In September 1918, Ponzi quit J. R. Poole to work full-time on an effort to save Gnecco Brothers. He took the titles of president and treasurer and threw himself into the work, but his efforts proved fruitless. An end-of-the-year accounting showed that the company's assets were worth about six thousand dollars and its liabilities were about eleven thousand. No one faulted Ponzi—the company had been in a hole before he'd gotten involved. But at the very end, Ponzi thought he could wrangle a dramatic way out. He appealed to the company's lawyers to allow him to borrow the six thousand dollars in assets, promising he would use his knowledge of exporting to repay the money plus all the debt within a year. The lawyers said no, and on January 4, 1919, Gnecco Brothers went into bankruptcy.

The same month Ponzi quit J. R. Poole to join Gnecco Brothers, his home life came under stress when Rose's mother died. As much as she loved her husband, Rose's one question when they'd married had been whether she could love him as much as she did her mother. Rose went deep into mourning. Ponzi was pure patience. He lavished her with kindness. He gave her gifts and offered to buy whatever she wanted, though she asked for nothing. She already had what she wanted. Her love for him deepened.

After the collapse of Gnecco Brothers, Ponzi found himself without a job. He had no interest in going back to J. R. Poole or seeking similar work. He was "tired of working for expectations that didn't pay either my rent or my grocery bills, tired of making money for my employers in general and none for myself." He and Rose had saved enough to carry them for a while, and she had inherited some money from her mother, so Ponzi figured this was his chance to put his dreams into action.

He rented a windowless, one-room office over the Puritan Trust Company on Court Street at the edge of Scollay Square, the heart of

Boston's commercial district and home to risqué entertainment at the Old Howard Theater. Ponzi was hungry for the former and ignored the latter. Since his marriage, Ponzi had become immune to all temptations except those with dollar signs. He sat in the office's lone armchair for hours on end, hunched over the rolltop desk scribbling figures on pads of paper. As hard as he tried, his endless reams of calculations did not add up to profits. So Ponzi tried to become something of a commodities broker. His chief mistake was trying to do so with someone else's commodities.

On May 10, 1919, Ponzi was served with a warrant charging him with stealing 5,387 pounds of cheese valued at forty-five cents a pound. Two days later, he pleaded innocent in Boston Municipal Court. Then he received a rare stroke of good luck. The clerk who wrote out the warrant misspelled his surname, substituting a *u* for the *n,* listing the defendant as "Charles Pouzi." The mistake frustrated efforts by authorities to follow up on the purloined cheese, and the case was continued several times before finally being dismissed for lack of prosecution. Ponzi never told his side of the story—he surely would have claimed it was an innocent misunderstanding.

Best of all, the collapse of the case meant it would not be revealed that he had already served two prison terms, a circumstance that might have triggered deportation proceedings. He had never moved to become an American citizen, knowing that his felony convictions might make him an undesirable alien. Also fortunate for Ponzi, the misspelling would make the cheese incident almost undetectable in the future if anyone tried to check into his background.

That same month, the Court Street office building changed hands, coming under ownership of the Tremont Trust Company, known throughout the city as "Simon Swig's bank." Swig was a leader of Boston's Jewish community who treated Tremont Trust as a personal piggy bank. Swig fancied himself a political player, doing business with kingmaker and blackmailer Dan Coakley. To Ponzi, though, Swig was simply a landlord who wanted him out; Swig planned to renovate the building and charge higher rents.

Ponzi moved around the corner to a couple of dingy rooms on the fifth floor of 27 School Street, the Niles Building. It was unfurnished, so he went to Daniels & Wilson Furniture Company in the city's increasingly Italian North End. Ponzi picked out $350 worth of used desks, chairs, a typewriter, filing cabinets, and a small rotary printing press called a Multigraph. He could not afford the full cost, so he struck a deal with the store's owner, Joseph Daniels, a deceitful man who had anglicized his name from Giuseppe Danieli. Under their agreement, Ponzi would pay fifty dollars down and five dollars a month. Once the furnishings were in place, Ponzi had an optimistic sign painted on his office door: CHARLES PONZI, EXPORT & IMPORT. The world took no notice.

Ponzi's original plan was to work on commission as an import-export agent, acting as a broker for domestic and international companies hoping to trade across borders. He thought he would be especially attractive to companies too small to hire such agents outright. Unfortunately, he had no contacts of his own at companies that might need his services. To attract business, Ponzi thought about printing circulars and sending blanket mailings to potential clients. But that would cost him a nickel per circular for domestic companies and eight cents each for international firms. Ponzi realized he would be wiped out by mailing fees before he collected his first commission. Instead, he decided to advertise in foreign trade magazines, but again he was stymied by the cost. That led to a new plan: He would start his own foreign trade publication, one whose huge circulation would allow him to charge lower advertising rates for budding entrepreneurs like him. Inspired, he had a new sign painted on his door—THE BOSTONIAN ADVERTISING & PUBLISHING COMPANY—and set about launching a publication he called the *Trader's Guide.*

Ponzi devised an elaborate, impossibly ambitious business plan that envisioned his guide as a permanent reference book. He would distribute it in loose-leaf binders, to allow additional pages to be added as years passed and new editions were printed. To increase the guide's reach, he intended to print it in English, French, Italian, German,

Spanish, and Portuguese. The most audacious aspect of his plan was his imagined method for doubling circulation on a regular basis. First, he would mail 100,000 free copies of the *Trader's Guide* to companies whose names he found in directories from the U.S. Bureau of Foreign and Domestic Commerce and the U.S. Consular Service. Six months later, he would mail those same companies an updated edition of the guide, while also sending the original mailing and the update to another 100,000 companies, also for free. Ponzi thought he could do this indefinitely, or at least until his mailing lists were exhausted. By then, he was sure, he would be rich.

The initial mailing, he thought, would cost him thirty-five cents a copy, or $35,000. To meet that cost, he would lard a two-hundred-page guide with 150 pages of advertising. The ads would cost $500 a page, with a $5,000 premium for the cover page, for a total imagined advertising income of $80,000. After expenses, he figured on a profit of at least $15,000 in the first six months. He expected his profits would double as many times as he doubled circulation.

Certain of success, he took larger quarters on the building's second floor, Room 227, and hired two stenographers and a messenger boy. In his excitement, he began writing letters to acquaintances abroad, making wonderful claims for his soon-to-be-published guide and seeking to interest them in buying or selling ads and writing articles.

Beyond the mountainous logistical challenges of selling so much advertising and producing fifty pages of editorial content of interest to exporters and importers, Ponzi was fast exhausting his limited money supply. He tried to interest investors in purchasing a half interest in the guide for five thousand dollars—a steal if it were possible to yield even a fraction of his anticipated profits—but found no takers. By summer 1919 he was running low on cash and options. Certain he was on the verge of greatness, Ponzi walked around the corner from his office to the Washington Street branch of the Hanover Trust Company, where for several months he had kept a small checking account that frequently approached a zero balance.

Adopting the nonchalant air of a man certain to be approved for any loan he sought, Ponzi walked smartly through the bank's heavy front door and asked to borrow two thousand dollars. He tried to say the sum "with the same inflection with which I would have asked change for a nickel." But his faux confidence could not overcome his real lack of collateral. The application never made it to the loan committee. It was dealt with immediately by the bank's president, Henry Chmielinski.

"Sorry," he told Ponzi, "but I cannot approve the loan. While it is our policy to accommodate our depositors whenever we can, your account is more of a bother than a benefit to us. Good day, sir."

Ponzi seethed as he watched Chmielinski turn on his heel and return to his private office. Bile rose in his throat—"I could have spat poison," he said afterward—as he made the short walk back to the Niles Building. Anger turned to despair as he opened the door to his office. With a heavy heart, he laid off his small staff and pronounced the *Trader's Guide* dead before its first edition.

He swallowed his pride and placed a small newspaper ad offering office space to sublet. His new tenants would help cover the rent, but the added names painted on the door below his own were blows to his dignity. "Another house of cards had collapsed," he said afterward. But he remained undaunted: "I was getting accustomed to chasing rainbows. As one would fade away, I would pursue another."

Sitting alone in the office one day in August 1919, Ponzi began idly leafing through his mail. He opened a letter from Spain inquiring about the *Trader's Guide*. Unaware that the guide had been permanently mothballed, the letter writer asked to be sent a copy. To pay the postage, the Spaniard had pinned to the corner of his letter a strange piece of paper. It was roughly the size of a dollar bill but nearly square, with intricate watermarks and a fanciful drawing of a woman dressed in flowing robes delivering a piece of mail from one part of the globe to another.

Ponzi held the note in his soft hands. In a spark of inspiration he saw a glittering future spread out before him. Everything up to this point in his life, from major events to chance encounters, from his never-quit persistence to his unquenched thirst for wealth, had led to this moment. It had its roots in his upbringing and his spendthrift youth, his dashed expectations of gold in American streets, and his jobs in banking and exporting. It could be traced to his stretches in prison and the men he'd met there, his acts of generosity, his return to Boston, his passion for stamp collecting, his memories of his father the postman, his chance meeting with foreign exchange expert Roberto de Masellis. All of this made it possible for him to see what no one else could, to dream what no one else dared.

PART TWO

A Ponzi note, issued to Boston Post *reporter Principio Santosuosso.*

CHAPTER SEVEN

"THE ALMIGHTY DOLLAR"

The paper in Ponzi's hand was an International Reply Coupon. A more mundane and obscure financial instrument is hard to imagine.

In April 1906, representatives of the United States and sixty-two other countries gathered in Rome with the goal of making it easier to send mail across national borders. All were members of one of the world's first international governmental organizations: the Universal Postal Union, founded in 1874 to reduce the maze of postal regulations that made mailing a letter overseas a high-risk, high-cost proposition. A key item on the Rome agenda was to create a way for a person in one country to essentially send a stamped, self-addressed envelope to someone in another.

The lack of such a mechanism posed a problem to anyone with an overseas family member or business associate. Consider, for instance, a lawyer in New York who wanted a Paris accountant to send him an important document. The lawyer would reasonably be expected to enclose with his request an envelope with his return address and the necessary postage. But at the turn of the twentieth century, there was no way to do that. The New York lawyer's stamps would be United States issue. If the French accountant tried to use them, he would be turned away by any self-respecting, law-abiding Parisian postal clerk. The accountant would have to pay the postage himself, in French postage stamps, to send the document. Of course, it was possible that the American lawyer could enclose a few dollars to cover the return postage, but then the French accountant would need to exchange the dollars for francs before buying the stamps—hardly an efficient system. The same problem arose when young immigrants tried to correspond with parents or grandparents in the old country. The young émigrés wanted to hear back from their faraway family members, often as soon as possible, and so were happy to include postage for a return letter.

As a solution, the Rome treaty writers created a system of international postal currency, paper that held a fixed value from one country to the next and could be redeemed for stamps in any post office of a country belonging to the Universal Postal Union. They called the currency they created International Reply Coupons. But they were not finished. The treaty writers wanted to make sure no one tried to profit from the purchase and redemption of their coupons. They created regulations that set the rate of exchange between countries' currency and postal reply coupons, so coupons purchased for one American dollar in New York yielded the equivalent of one dollar's worth of French stamps in Paris, minus a small processing fee.

All that was fine in 1906, but the Rome treaty negotiators did not foresee a world war a decade later. The Great War left some countries' currency deeply devalued. Governments were too busy dealing with massive human and economic losses to worry about recalibrating postal exchange regulations. The result was an opportunity to profit. The Spaniard who'd sent Ponzi the coupon considered it nothing more than an act of proper business etiquette. He was, after all, asking to be sent a copy of the *Trader's Guide*. But in a flash of insight, some might even say genius, Ponzi saw something more, a global currency whose value fluctuated wildly depending on where it was used. He took out a pencil and a pad of paper and began calculating the possibilities.

The coupon had cost the Spaniard thirty centavos, or roughly six cents. After a penny processing fee, it could be exchanged in the United States for a stamp worth five cents. Ponzi knew that the Spanish monetary unit, the peseta, had been devalued after the war, so he began figuring how many pesetas he could buy for a dollar. Using exchange rates published in Boston newspapers, Ponzi concluded that a dollar was worth six and two-thirds pesetas. Because there were one hundred centavos to a peseta, Ponzi calculated that a dollar was worth 666 centavos. If each International Reply Coupon cost thirty centavos, a dollar could buy twenty-two of the coupons in Spain. If Ponzi brought them to the United States, those twenty-two coupons would be worth five cents each, or a total of a dollar and ten cents. By redeeming them in Boston rather than Barcelona, Ponzi would earn a profit before expenses of ten cents, or 10 percent, on each dollar's worth of coupons he bought in Spain and redeemed in the United States.

Ponzi knew from his conversation with currency expert Roberto de Masellis at Fidelity Trust Company that few world currencies had suffered as much as the Italian lira. Once valued at five to the dollar, the lira had fallen after the war to twenty to a dollar. With the lower value, Ponzi calculated, a dollar could purchase sixty-six International Reply Coupons in Italy—three times as many as in Spain. Ponzi could scarcely believe it. The same dollar that could buy twenty coupons for five cents each in the United States could buy more than three times as many of the same coupons in Italy. Sixty-six coupons purchased in Rome for a dollar would be worth $3.30 in Boston. Ponzi's mind reeled at the thought—he was looking at profits of $2.30 on every dollar spent, or 230 percent, before expenses. Other countries might have even more devalued currencies, and the profits would be even more astronomical. One example was Austria. After the war, the Austrian krone had fallen from the equivalent of twenty cents to less than a penny. A thousand dollars would buy 140,000 kronen, which theoretically could purchase more than a half million International Reply Coupons. If redeemed in the United States, Ponzi's initial thousand-dollar investment would yield stamps worth more than twenty-five thousand dollars.

The hitch, Ponzi understood, would be getting cash for the stamps he bought with the coupons. One possibility would be to sell the stamps at a slight discount to businesses that used large amounts of postage, giving them a bargain on a necessary item while still maintaining huge profits for Ponzi. Another hurdle would be figuring out how to buy and transport the enormous numbers of coupons necessary to turn a significant profit. But these crucial details would wait for another day.

Sitting at his desk, Ponzi could hardly contain himself. The whole calculation had taken him less than five minutes, but he was certain of the conclusion. If he bought coupons in bulk in countries with weak currencies, converted them into stamps, and cashed them in the United States or other countries with strong currencies, he would soon be richer than Rockefeller. All he needed was a small pile of money to get him started with his first stack of coupons. But that was no small hurdle. As the summer of 1919 turned to autumn, Ponzi was deep in the hole.

His first thought was to borrow the money in large sums from a few sources, but his options were limited. Banks were out. He was struggling to make payments on fifteen hundred dollars in loans from Fidelity Trust, and his rejection at the Hanover Trust when he'd sought seed money for the *Trader's Guide* gave him a good idea about how Boston's banks would receive his new idea. Also, he feared that if he thoroughly explained his plan to bankers, they might steal it and leave him cold. He would need private investors, but first he needed proof that his epiphany was more than a pipe dream.

In the weeks after his brainstorm, Ponzi mailed a dollar to each of three acquaintances, one in Spain, one in Italy, and one in France, with instructions to exchange the dollars for the local currency, go to a post office, buy as many reply coupons as possible, and then send them to him in Boston. A few weeks later Ponzi had his answer. His calculations were correct. The Spanish and French deals were a wash, a small profit from Spain and a small loss from France, but the Italian effort was a big moneymaker. In the meantime, while waiting for his European correspondents, Ponzi went to a Boston post office and confirmed that coupons could be exchanged there for stamps. He also began collecting newspaper columns with quotations on foreign exchange rates, to demonstrate the fluctuations to potential investors.

The more Ponzi thought about his idea, the more he liked it. He would effectively be operating under the umbrella of one of the most trusted institutions in the world: the postal service. Anyone with money and a mailbox was a potential customer. Even better, he reasoned, the supply of coupons was potentially limitless, like postage stamps. No matter how many a person bought, more would always be available. If they ran out, the issuer would print more until the demand was met. "They could not limit the number of coupons I wanted either to buy or redeem," Ponzi concluded. "In other words, the burden of living up to the terms of the contract was entirely on the government's side and not on mine. All I could be expected to do was to tender cash in payment of coupons. Coupons in exchange for stamps. But what I did with the stamps afterwards was nobody else's business but my own."

Best of all, Ponzi was certain it was legal. The coupons were, in effect, legal tender used to buy stamps anywhere in the developed world. If a coupon bought more stamps in Romania than Rhode Island, that was not his fault. He was merely the first person smart enough to figure out how to take advantage of it. On the other hand, he acknowledged, some people might say exploiting exchange rates by trafficking in postal coupons might not be entirely ethical. But his experiences during the sixteen years since he'd arrived in America made that a secondary consideration: "Environment had made me rather callous on the subject of ethics. . . . Then, as now, nobody gave a rap for ethics. The almighty dollar was the only goal. And its possession placed a person beyond criticism for any breach of ethics incidental to the acquisition of it."

In the weeks after devising his plan, Ponzi appealed to anyone he thought might have significant amounts of available cash. But everyone he knew in that position declined his offer, at least in part because Ponzi refused to provide many details about his idea, lest would-be investors try it themselves. Also working against him was his lack of a track record to justify being entrusted with serious sums. He was close enough to touch success, but with one rejection after another he began worrying that once again wealth would escape his grasp.

With his debts rising along with his frustration, on December 1, 1919, Ponzi swallowed his pride and walked across town to Northampton Street, in Boston's South End. There he found a little storefront with a sign displaying a cluster of three gilded balls—the universal symbol for a pawnshop. Ponzi stepped inside Uncle Ned's Loan Company and fished four items from his pocket: three diamond rings that belonged to Rose and his own gold, open-faced pocket watch. If ever Ponzi were looking for confirmation of Rose's devotion, he needed to look no further than her willingness to let him pawn her rings.

Ponzi placed the valuables on the counter and told the pawnbroker, a Russian immigrant named Max Rosenberg, that he was hocking them to start a business. He outlined his coupon idea in the hope of enticing Rosenberg to invest. Rosenberg listened to his pitch, but pawnbrokers as a rule do not invest with men who hock their family jewels. Rosenberg appraised Ponzi's belongings and handed him five hundred dollars for the rings and twenty for the watch. Ponzi stuffed the cash into his wallet and left.

His debts approached three thousand dollars and, as Ponzi liked to say, his only assets were his hopes. So the money from Uncle Ned's did not last long. Just over a week later, Ponzi's wallet was empty again when furniture dealer Joseph Daniels walked through the narrow,

glass-paneled door of Room 227 in the Niles Building. Ponzi was behind on his five-dollars-a-month payments, and Daniels was threatening to haul the desks and chairs back to his store in the North End.
Seeing the angry look on Daniels's face, Ponzi was glad he and
Daniels were the same height.

"For the love of Mike, sit down," Ponzi told him. "That chair is
still yours, and [sitting in it] won't place you under any obligations."

Ponzi had no money for Daniels—"I did not have it, and that settled it, and he couldn't draw blood out of a turnip," Ponzi explained
later. But he hated the idea of Daniels seizing the furniture and leaving him with nowhere to sit but the floor or the windowsill. Ponzi
began talking as fast as he could think. He came up with a deal that
would delay the day of reckoning for at least two months.

Ponzi offered to give Daniels a promissory note for two hundred
dollars. Daniels could cash it, using the furniture dealer's own credit at
the First State Bank. Daniels scoffed—Ponzi was already in debt to
him for the furniture. Why should he add two hundred dollars in
cash? Anticipating that reaction, Ponzi parried with an appeal to
Daniels's greed. Ponzi told Daniels to keep half of the cash for himself—a hundred dollars—as a payment toward Ponzi's furniture.
Daniels would pay the remaining hundred dollars to Ponzi in twenty-
dollar increments, and in sixty days Ponzi would pay back the full two
hundred dollars, plus interest. If Ponzi defaulted, Daniels would be
out only a small sum of money, and the bank where he cashed the
promissory note would help him pursue Ponzi to make good.

The deal remained a risk for Daniels—there was no guarantee
Ponzi would be in any better shape two months hence, and even with
the bank on Daniels's side Ponzi might stiff him. On the other hand,
Daniels would be giving Ponzi only a relatively small loan, and the alternative of repossessing the furniture held no upside for him.

Still, Daniels was skeptical. He wanted to know how Ponzi intended to pay the note at maturity. Ponzi expected that question, so
he outlined his plan to build a financial empire based on International
Reply Coupons. He spoke of the meeting in Rome, showed Daniels

a coupon, and read a passage from page 37 of the *United States Official Postal Guide* that described how the coupons could be redeemed for stamps in any country that was a member of the Universal Postal Union. Feeling the fish nibbling on the bait, Ponzi let out more line, expounding on foreign exchange rates and fluctuating currencies. He went in for the kill by describing the crux of his business plan: to pay investors 50 percent interest on any amount invested within ninety days, or forty-five days if everything went as smoothly as anticipated.

Daniels listened to the rapid-fire delivery and found himself swept up in Ponzi's excitement. Daniels accepted Ponzi's note and gave him a check for twenty dollars, the first installment of Ponzi's half of the two-hundred-dollar loan. Emboldened, Ponzi pressed his luck by asking if Daniels wanted to invest in the coupon business. Daniels declined—first he wanted to drop by the post office down the street from his store to inquire about postal coupons. Still, for Ponzi it remained a pivotal moment.

Until then, everyone to whom Ponzi had explained the plan had brushed him off—it was impossible, impractical, and anyway, who was this pint-sized immigrant to imagine himself a financial giant? The only person who had believed Ponzi was Rose, and even she had trouble understanding the coupons-for-stamps-for-cash machinations. Although she did not tell her husband, Rose suspected it would turn out to be another of his short-lived inspirations, soon to be replaced by another. But now, by winning Daniels's meager support, Ponzi sensed the possibility of success. And after so many years of failure, he was intoxicated by it. He had convinced a hard-nosed, if not terribly bright businessman that he was onto something. With some polish, he was certain his sales pitch would draw investors in droves.

Just as important, the experience made Ponzi realize that he should launch his company by seeking small sums from large numbers of people. The few big-money types he knew had shunned him, but almost anyone could spare ten dollars, or fifty, or maybe even a hundred, on the promise of a 50 percent gain. Even if they did not grasp the details of how he would do it, or even if they had doubts about him, the possibility of huge returns in such a short time would be too tempting to pass up. If they gambled a small amount and lost, oh well, no great harm. But if the gamble paid off, they might invest more, believing they were on the verge of fulfilling the financial promise of the American Dream: great riches, easily obtained, swiftly delivered.

Put another way, Ponzi had chanced upon what he was certain was a legitimate, foolproof formula to Get Rich Quick.

In contrast to con artists who use stealth and subterfuge to target individual marks for big scores, Get Rich Quick promoters generally take a wholesale approach to generating wealth. When critical masses of people have ostensibly prospered, their friends and neighbors come running, setting off a financial frenzy. By the time Ponzi appeared on the scene, the people of Boston and New England had had plenty of experience with Get Rich Quick operators. Unlike Ponzi, however, most promoters paid no attention to the boundaries of legality, focusing only on the greed and gullibility of their audience.

Fast-talking salesmen had promised fortunes from silver fox–fur farming and from engines that supposedly used water for fuel. Some had claimed divine intervention or inspiration. Many had told tales based on high finance—offering stocks, bonds, insurance, and complex loan deals with fraudulent underpinnings. Some had combined elements of several approaches to turn themselves into money magnets. What they'd all had in common was a three-step playbook: splash, cash, and dash. That is, make a big impression, grab as much money as possible, and disappear before being exposed.

In the late 1890s, a handsome Baptist minister named Prescott Ford Jernegan, the scion of a well-known whaling family from Martha's Vineyard, declared that a "heavenly vision" had delivered unto him the secret of extracting gold from seawater. He shared this revelation with several prosperous members of his former congregation in Middletown, Connecticut, who agreed to provide financing to test his discovery. Among them was Arthur B. Ryan, a former city alderman and

partner in a successful jewelry company. Less publicly, Jernegan enlisted his boyhood friend, one Charles E. Fisher, a burly confidence
man and professional diver from Cape Cod. Minister Jernegan once
displayed his true nature in a letter to Fisher: "Money and lust," he
wrote, "have been the two most vexing problems in my life."

Jernegan needed proof of his "discovery" to attract big money, so
one winter night he sent Ryan to a deserted resort on Narragansett
Bay in Rhode Island. Swathed in fur coats to fight the chill, Ryan and
an associate went out to a pier, cut a hole through the ice, and
dropped into the water a box with iron bars and a secret catalyst that
Jernegan called an "accumulator." Jernegan claimed that a current of
electricity, carried by platinum wires attached to the accumulator,
would attract noticeable amounts of gold within twenty-four hours.
While the experimenters waited, Jernegan's accomplice, Fisher, took
a back route to the resort on horseback. He slipped into a diving suit
and followed the wires through the icy water to the box. He dropped
nuggets of gold into the accumulator box and vanished without being
seen. When the box was pulled to the surface the next day, Ryan
tested the nuggets with tools of the jewelry trade. The gold was real.
Ryan believed it had truly been sucked from seawater. He declared the
test a rousing success.

Word spread quickly, and soon Jernegan and Fisher began planning
the Electrolytic Marine Salts Company in the remote fishing village of
North Lubec, Maine. Jernegan said he chose the site because it
boasted a daily twenty-foot rise and fall of the tides, which would send
an enormous volume of seawater through the huge accumulating
equipment he intended to build. He incorporated the company in
November 1897 with $10 million worth of stock for sale at a dollar per
share. Gold similar to the nuggets pulled from Narragansett Bay were
displayed in Boston and elsewhere. Already primed by recent news of
the Alaska Gold Rush, investors threw money at the idea. Newspapers
throughout the region could barely contain themselves: "The amount
of gold in all the oceans is estimated at seventy billion tons, forty-eight
trillion dollars," the *Hartford Courant* breathlessly announced.

After several thousand investors bought stock, Fisher took the familiar path of fast-money magicians. In July 1898, he disappeared with about $100,000 in cash. Jernegan followed soon after, with perhaps twice as much. When a newspaper reporter caught up to him, Jernegan claimed he had left town in search of Fisher, who had stolen his secret formula. Fisher was never found, but Jernegan was struck by an apparent attack of conscience. Two years later, he returned a large amount of money to his dupes—as much as $175,000—and then lived most of the rest of his days in the Philippines.

The gold-from-seawater trick fell into the category of Get Rich Quick stock schemes based on miracles of science, a particularly popular approach for scammers at a time of medical breakthroughs and mechanical sensations like flying machines and Marconi's wireless. Another form of Get Rich Quick stock scheme could be called the exotic-products variety. Several years after Jernegan's scheme, a smooth talker named Ferdinand Borges came to Boston with just such an idea.

For several months Borges lived in obscurity, taking rooms in lodging houses and eating meals at the counters of low-cost lunchrooms. He knew no one would invest with a man living hand to mouth, so he pooled his resources and moved into a suite of offices that he filled with mahogany furniture, oil paintings, and expensive rugs. It was an elaborate stage on which Borges offered to sell bonds of a corporation he called the Consolidated Ubero Plantation Company. The bonds, he said, would allow investors to share in the enormous profits expected from "the four-hundred-thousand rubber trees, the million pineapple trees, and the million coffee trees now under cultivation."

More than $2 million flowed into the company's coffers, much of it from poor people who appreciated Borges's offer to sell them bonds on the installment plan, investing as little as two dollars a month on the promise that when their account reached five hundred dollars they would be presented with a bond. Unlike Jernegan's gold ruse, Borges's company actually owned some plantation land. But that was never the point. Borges spent only a fraction of the money on the business. He kept the rest for himself, a few close associates, and a cadre of agents hired to sell bonds in exchange for commissions of 5 to 15 percent of whatever they brought in. It took authorities several years to catch up with Borges, but in 1906 he was convicted of conspiracy and seventy-three counts of larceny. Of course, by then most of the money was gone.

A variation of Get Rich Quick schemes was robbing Peter to pay Paul, or benefiting one person at the expense of others. The origin of the phrase is open to dispute, but one account traces it to the 1500s in England, when the lands of Saint Peter's Church at Westminster were sold to fund repairs at Saint Paul's Cathedral in London.

One example came to public notice in Boston on January 3, 1880, when an ad appeared in the *Boston Herald* under the headline: HOW'S THIS FOR HIGH? EIGHT PERCENT A MONTH PAID TO DEPOSITORS BY A SOUTH END BANK "FOR WOMEN ONLY."

Below that was a further explanation:

> **The Ladies Deposit is a Charitable Institution for Single Ladies, Old and Young. No Deposit Received for less than $200 nor more than $1,000. Interest at the Rate of $8 per hundred per month is Paid every Three Months in Advance. The Principal Can be Withdrawn upon Call any day except Sunday. No Deposit Received from Anybody Owning a House.**

The ad had been placed by Sarah Howe, a nearly illiterate former fortune-teller with a long history of petty crime and a standing reservation at the State Lunatic Asylum in Taunton. Her past notwithstanding, Howe's "bank" briefly made her the darling of apartment-dwelling Boston spinsters. More than a thousand women made deposits, trusting her with more than a half million dollars. Howe spent lavishly on herself, with a particular fondness for expensive real estate.

Doubts eventually led to a run on the Ladies Deposit, and when the money was gone Howe missed her chance to flee and was arrested. She went to prison as a thief and an insolvent debtor. As the *Herald* later explained, Howe "simply took the money that one set of patrons paid in to meet her obligations to another set. She never invested a penny of income. She took Miss Mary Jane Smith's money to pay off Miss Abigail Brown's claim, and so on to the end of the chapter."

Howe was a small-timer compared to William Franklin Miller, for years the reigning king of the Peter-Paul scam. In 1899 he was thirty-six, with nothing to show for himself except a five-dollar-a-week job as a brokerage-house clerk. Eager to satisfy his expensive tastes, he devised a Peter-Paul scheme so simple and yet so audacious that it succeeded fabulously, though briefly.

Miller opened for business as the Franklin Syndicate in Brooklyn, New York, with an eye-popping promise: 10 percent a week interest paid on any investment. He soon acquired the nickname "520 Percent Miller," based on expectations of what investors would receive over the course of a year. Asked how he could possibly pay such unheard-of interest, Miller talked of tapping into the methods of Wall Street barons who hoarded their wealth. He spoke loosely of "inside tips" about mining companies, stocks, and other businesses that supposedly churned out large profits.

A trickle of investors turned into a flood when word spread that Miller was paying the interest every week as promised. Unbeknownst to his customers, Miller was using his new investors' money to pay the interest on the old. Soon a majority of customers were leaving their principal untouched and "reinvesting" their interest, reducing Miller's expenses and increasing his personal bankroll. He used his low-rent office as a selling ploy: "Your money buys neither mahogany desks nor oil paintings. It is put to work for you at 10 percent a week. Our running expenses are small, our profits enormous and sure."

The New York office proved so successful that Miller opened a Boston branch, operating out of the Hotel Harvard on Main Street of the city's Charlestown neighborhood. Mail from around the country poured into the hotel office with sums for Miller to "invest." The Franklin Syndicate took in more than a million dollars before Miller was exposed as a fraud by the *New York Herald*. He fled to Montreal but was captured there, returned to New York for trial, and sentenced to ten years in Sing Sing. His creditors ultimately received about twenty-eight cents on the dollar. Miller won a pardon halfway through his term and opened a grocery store on Long Island, eventually earning the moniker "Honest Bill."

Despite Miller's fall, there was no shortage of other scammers eager to pick up where he left off. Around the same time as Miller's release from prison, an imitator named C. D. Sheldon, alias Wilson, alias Hoyt, alias O. D. Washburn, went to work using the same Peter-to-Paul scheme in Canada. Sheldon's run was brought to a halt shortly before Ponzi arrived in Montreal, though it was still the talk of the town when Ponzi went to work at the Zarossi Bank.

But for every story of a Jernegan or a Borges, every account of a Howe, a Miller, or a Sheldon, there were a hundred tales of up-from-nothing men who had given birth to innovative ideas that legitimately made them rich. Some were inventors, others monopolists, still others financiers. Some worked tirelessly; others got lucky. Those stories, as much a staple of early-twentieth-century newspapers as photos of oddly shaped vegetables, kept alive two dreams in the hearts of millions of working Americans: Let such an idea come my way or, failing that, let such a man cross my path on a day he feels generous.

With the small loan from Daniels, Ponzi began getting organized. Three days later, on December 13, 1919, he pulled on his threadbare coat to ward off the winter chill, left his cubbyhole office, and strolled around the corner to Boston City Hall. More chipper than he had been in months, Ponzi walked past the pigeon-splattered courtyard statues of Benjamin Franklin and the city's second mayor, Josiah Quincy, whose likeness was dressed incongruously in classical Greek attire. Ponzi entered the granite wedding cake of a building through massive wooden doors inlaid with marble circles.

With the help of Boston's assistant city clerk, Ponzi filled out paperwork declaring that he would do business as the International Security Company, with him as sole proprietor. He was pleased that the transaction set him back only fifty cents, little more than the cost of three boxes of his favorite Murad Turkish cigarettes. But Ponzi soon cooled to the name he had chosen for his company. He returned to City Hall the day after Christmas, determined to get it just right. He paid another fifty cents to register a more descriptive and less exotic-sounding name: the Securities Exchange Company. With the new name painted on his office door, he ordered a stack of printed certificates to give to investors. Inside a decorative border, in a style reminiscent of the International Reply Coupons on which the business was based, the certificates read:

No. _____   Boston, Mass. __(date)__

The Securities Exchange Company, for and in consideration of the sum of (*amount invested*) dollars, receipt of which is hereby acknowledged, agrees to pay to the order of (*investor's name*), upon presentation of this voucher at ninety days from date, the sum of (*invested amount plus 50 percent*) at the Company's office, 27 School Street, Room 227, or at any bank.

$ (amount due).   The Securities Exchange Company
                                           Per Charles Ponzi

Although the certificates said that the 50 percent would be paid in ninety days, almost from the first Ponzi told investors he would shorten the payoff period to half that. As soon as he was ready for business, Ponzi began his hunt for investors who had as little as ten dollars to spare. He instinctively knew he would find them: "We are all gamblers," he believed. "We all crave easy money. And plenty of it. If we didn't, no get-rich-quick scheme could be successful." Ponzi called around town, visiting people he knew and people who knew people he knew, talking about his company and describing the coupons-stamps-cash continuum in enticing terms. He made a point of never directly soliciting investments, preferring to whet his listeners' appetites and make sure they knew where to find the offices of the Securities Exchange Company.

A few days after he began spreading his gospel, Ponzi was sitting alone in his office, waiting for the seeds he had planted to take root. Someone knocked on the door, and Ponzi invited him inside.

Customers line up at 27 School Street to invest money with Ponzi's Securities Exchange Company.

The Boston Globe

CHAPTER EIGHT

"A SMALL SNOWBALL
DOWNHILL"

Ponzi's visitor was an acquaintance named
Ettore Giberti, a grocer in the northern suburb of Revere. During the dozen years since
he had come to America, Giberti had followed a sedate path, working steadily and
painstakingly to build his business. Married
for two years, the thirty-two-year-old Giberti and his eighteen-year-old wife, Edith, a
fellow Italian immigrant, had recently welcomed the arrival of a son they'd named
Frederick. When he climbed the stairs to
Ponzi's office, Giberti's net worth was perhaps twelve hundred dollars. But with a
growing family to support, he hoped that
would soon change. People were talking
about this Ponzi fellow and his investment
idea, and Giberti wanted to learn about it
firsthand.

Ponzi poured it on thick, just as he had
done with Daniels, talking about the Rome
treaty writers, fluctuating currencies, and the
incredible potential for a visionary like him-

self who knew the secret of how to turn International Reply Coupons into piles of cash. The one thing he did not explain, the one thing he would never tell anyone, was precisely how he exchanged the coupons for greenbacks. But like a magician who focuses his audience's attention on one hand while performing feats of prestidigitation with the other, Ponzi knew that the details of the transactions were less interesting than the promised results. Indeed, Giberti listened attentively but impassively until Ponzi mentioned the 50 percent return on investments. Ponzi could tell from the expression on Giberti's face that his countryman was doing some mental calculations, pyramiding some imaginary investment over and over again to figure out how much he might have in three months, or six, or a year. Yet the numbers flashing through Giberti's mind were still not enough—or perhaps they were too much—to make him a believer. He told Ponzi he could not afford to invest and got ready to leave.

A shiver of panic raced down Ponzi's spine. He was about to lose his first sale, and with it, he feared, a measure of confidence in himself and his plan. He could not let that happen. Giberti had to be sold. Impulsively, Ponzi came up with an idea that harked back to his time in Montreal during the heyday of the padrone. A man could grow rich and powerful not only by his own hard work but by putting others to work for him. Ponzi made Giberti an offer: Become the first sales agent for the Securities Exchange Company. Surely lots of people came into Giberti's store, and if they trusted his choice in vegetables they might also trust his choice in investments. Ponzi urged the grocer to tell his customers and friends about the Securities Exchange Company and collect investments on Ponzi's behalf. Giberti would be entitled to 10 percent of whatever money he brought in. Giberti accepted.

Before his new agent left, Ponzi gave Giberti a tutorial on what he called "salesmanship and psychology." He insisted that Giberti never use pressure tactics—"Never crowd a prospect," he said. "I was selling my dollars at about sixty-six cents," Ponzi explained. "That's all there was to it. And they were good dollars. Any attempt to force them on a prospective investor would have been to create suspicion rather than confidence."

Giberti absorbed the lesson and went to work. Winter had just begun, and Ponzi considered Giberti his first snowball of the season; pushed in the right direction it would get bigger and bigger. By early January 1920, Giberti had tempted eighteen people to give the Securities Exchange Company a try, returning several times to the Niles Building to hand Ponzi a total of $1,770. Though the average investment was a hundred dollars, individual amounts varied widely. Giberti put up only ten dollars—just enough to allow him to tell prospective clients that he was an investor.

The day Giberti laid the first wad of cash across Ponzi's outstretched palm marked a pivotal moment in the career of the would-be financier. An angel sat on one shoulder and a demon on the other. The angel's approach was straightforward. Ponzi had the money necessary to determine if his theory about legally exploiting fluctuations in foreign currencies could be put into practice. With the money from his initial investors, he could test whether he could clear the major logistical hurdles facing his enterprise: Who would exchange his dollars for foreign currencies and buy the reply coupons overseas? Would enough be available to operate on a large scale? If so, and if he could get the coupons back to Boston, how would he turn them into cash? If any of the obstacles proved fatal within the ninety-day window Ponzi's notes gave him before the payment was due, Ponzi could admit partial defeat, refund whatever money remained, and hand out IOUs for the rest. Then he could retool his idea, try another approach altogether, or follow Rose's advice to be satisfied with a typical job and a typical life.

The demon's alternative was to secretly abandon any pretense that this was a legitimate business and follow the notorious example of 520 Percent Miller. When Ponzi's first investors came looking for their 50 percent, he would pay them with money from later investors. Those investors might well be enticed to take another spin, bringing friends along with them, to multiply their winnings and keep Ponzi's perpetual-motion machine whirring. When the time was ripe and his wallet was bursting, he would take Rose to Italy, where he remained a citizen. His cash and his home country's fluid extradition practices might allow him to get away scot-free.

Both approaches held a certain appeal. From the moment he'd landed in America, Ponzi had been looking for a legitimate way to get rich and remove the shame he felt over disappointing his mother. Never much of a churchgoer, he believed that the words printed on International Reply Coupons were the gospels that would lead him to financial, and perhaps even spiritual, salvation. Yet as he approached his thirty-eighth birthday, he was bound to wonder how many more chances he might have if this elegant idea failed. He wanted the moon for Rose, wanted to start a family they could raise in comfort, wanted to prove to his elderly mother that he could accomplish everything she had dreamed for him when he was a boy.

Torn, he plotted a middle route: Allow the business to keep growing and enjoy the fruits immediately, while continuing to iron out kinks in the system. Not quite as dangerous, illegal, or immoral as the demon's path, it was nevertheless riskier, less honest, and more unethical than the angel's. If it worked, no one would be the wiser. If it did not, Ponzi would have to come up with a new idea to meet his obligations, or he would have to run. Either way, there was no rush. With Giberti's help, business would grow slowly and steadily, Ponzi thought, giving him plenty of time to test, refine, and perfect his cash-for-coupons transfers.

Ponzi took his first step down the path between cautious and reckless abandon within days of Giberti's first cash delivery. On January 3, he returned to Uncle Ned's pawnshop, not to borrow but to claim what was his. He went to the counter and waited for Max Rosenberg to notice him. With a flourish, Ponzi pulled out a wad of cash and asked only for his gold pocket watch. When Rosenberg produced it, Ponzi repaid the twenty-dollar loan, plus a few singles for a month's interest.

Ponzi might have had enough money to also claim Rose's diamond rings, but they would have to wait a while longer.

First he needed to keep his other creditors at bay while figuring out how to pay his investors $885 in interest, plus the principal for those who would not let their money ride. Based on current exchange rates, Ponzi thought he could use just four hundred dollars from his initial investors to yield a 50 percent return for all of them, leaving him more than thirteen hundred dollars in "profit." A more conservative man would have waited to claim even his watch until he'd actually produced that profit, while a more devious man might have immediately claimed the rings as well.

Giberti made himself scarce during the first weeks of 1920, and Ponzi soon realized why: Giberti's friends had trusted him with their money, and he thought it would be wise to lie low until Ponzi made good. In the meantime, word of Ponzi's business plan reached a Massachusetts bureaucrat named Frank Pope, whose job as state supervisor of small loans was to protect the public against lenders who charged obscene rates of interest. Pope dropped by 27 School Street. Ponzi easily weathered his first official inquiry. His investors were effectively lending him money at a rate of 50 percent for anywhere from forty-five to ninety days. Pope's only authority would have been to protect Ponzi from his own investors! Realizing that Ponzi was more than willing to "borrow" money at high rates, Pope returned to his State House cubbyhole. His only action was to call the Boston police, to suggest that they keep an eye on Ponzi and the Securities Exchange Company.

Forty-five days passed and Ponzi somehow began paying his initial investors. When asked how he did it, Ponzi eventually said that he had given the money to a man named Lionello Sarti who worked aboard a transatlantic liner. Ponzi said he'd instructed Sarti to buy as many coupons as possible in Italy and bring them to School Street when his ship returned to Boston. Ponzi insisted that Sarti had showed up in early February with the happy news that coupons were readily obtainable in even the smallest post offices. With advance notice, and perhaps a few well-placed bribes, Ponzi claimed, Italian postal officials could be persuaded to supply them in large quantities.

Over time, skeptics would doubt Sarti's existence, suspecting that Ponzi had borrowed from Peter to pay Paul. They would point out that most of his initial investors did not collect their winnings, preferring instead to reinvest and reap bigger profits. Adding to skeptics' reservations was Ponzi's steadfast refusal to say how he had turned the coupons into cash. Stamps, perhaps. But United States post offices were not in the business of currency exchange using coupons and stamps as mediums. Even if it were possible, it certainly would have caused a stir. Ponzi needed $2,655 to repay his investors with interest. If each International Reply Coupon could be traded in the United States for a stamp worth five cents, it would have taken more than fifty-three thousand coupons to satisfy the first eighteen investors. A stack of two hundred coupons measured about one inch high. Fifty-three thousand coupons would make seven three-foot-high stacks, or enough to fill a steamer trunk.

However he did it, by pleasing his original investors Ponzi sent the first pebble tumbling off a cliff. From that moment on, "Each satisfied customer became a self-appointed salesman. It was their combined salesmanship, and not my own, that put the thing over. I admit that I started a small snowball downhill. But it developed into an avalanche by itself."

As Ponzi expected, most of his initial investors returned. In February, the Securities Exchange Company recorded $5,290 in new investments, from seventeen investors. The biggest sum came from the life savings of John S. Dondero, at forty-four a trim, square-jawed man with a well-tended mustache and a fondness for three-piece suits. Married to Rose Ponzi's aunt Jennie, Dondero was therefore Ponzi's uncle by marriage. On February 24, he handed Ponzi two thousand dollars, a year's wages. Dondero had earned the money in a North End liquor business that had dried up with Prohibition. A few weeks later, Dondero's cousin John A. Dondero entered Ponzi's good graces by investing the same amount.

Ponzi claimed that after John S. Dondero's two-thousand-dollar investment, he gave Sarti money for another trip to Italian post offices—though no one had ever seen Sarti except for Ponzi. If Ponzi did hand money to Sarti, he made sure he kept plenty on hand for himself. Three days after John S. Dondero trusted his money to the Securities Exchange Company, Ponzi returned to Uncle Ned's. This time, Max Rosenberg noticed something different about his customer. Long eager to relive the sartorial splendor of his college days, Ponzi had decked himself out in a sharp new suit at the height of fashion. Rosenberg thought the undersized financier looked like a prosperous businessman straight from State Street, the heart of Boston's financial district. Ponzi flashed a wad of big bills and peeled off a few to redeem Rose's diamond rings, again urging Rosenberg to invest in his coupon business. But appearances meant little to Rosenberg. His world was concrete—loans made against collateral he could literally hold in his hand—while Ponzi dealt in the abstract. Once again the pawnbroker declined. Ponzi walked out of Uncle Ned's door for the last time.

As pleased as she was to see her husband prospering, and as happy as she must have been to have her rings back, Rose was distracted from Ponzi's growing success by the death of her father. After suffering in brief succession the losses of his wife and his business, John Gnecco had no fight left in him. He died on February 13, 1920, leaving Rose heartbroken but binding her even more closely to her husband of two years.

In the weeks that followed, Ponzi kept busy, talking about his business and taking care of himself and Rose. The death of Rose's father also made him focus more on his own mother. On March 9 he wired ten thousand lire, worth about five hundred dollars, from the Tremont Trust bank to Imelde Ponzi in Italy. Five days later he sent the same amount in his own name to an account in an Italian bank. He began regularly sending similar small sums to his mother and his own accounts in Italy.

Word was spreading and business was growing—in March, 110 investors turned over nearly twenty-five thousand dollars to the Securities Exchange Company. It was more money than Ponzi would have seen in almost a decade of working for J. R. Poole. Ponzi made his uncle John S. Dondero an agent, paying him 10 percent of whatever he brought in. He assigned John A. Dondero to manage the office when he was out and to greet customers when he was in. John A. Dondero was paid thirty-five dollars a week, double what he was earning at the Faneuil Hall markets, plus 5 to 10 percent of investments made when he was working the door.

Things were going so well that Ponzi began to worry that something might go wrong. He began paying off old debts whenever possible, including the two-hundred-dollar loan the furniture dealer Joseph Daniels had given him the previous December. To further satisfy Daniels, in March Ponzi bought more office furniture for his growing business.

Yet Ponzi still had some outstanding debts, and he feared his creditors might try to horn in on his business. He was especially afraid that the Fidelity Trust Company might file an attachment against him that would freeze his bank accounts and other assets. To shield himself, on March 12 Ponzi filed new papers at City Hall declaring that he was the manager of the Securities Exchange Company, in partnership with his uncle John S. Dondero and a second man, Guglielmo Bertollotti of Parma, Italy. Neither Dondero nor Bertollotti knew anything about the supposed partnership. Ponzi chose Dondero for his early confidence and family ties. Bertollotti had been Ponzi's landlord at one time in Italy. Bertollotti was at least seventy when Ponzi last saw him, so Ponzi figured he must be long dead, which made him an ideal silent partner. Ponzi's fears were well-founded. Three days after he filed his new corporation papers, Fidelity Trust brought a lawsuit against him seeking repayment of his debts.

Ponzi took other precautions as well. One afternoon he walked a few blocks from his office and trotted up the granite stairs of Boston police headquarters in Pemberton Square. He stopped outside the office of Commissioner Edwin Curtis.

"Does anyone accept funds for the relief of the widows and orphans of the members of the police force?" Ponzi asked Captain Thomas Ryan, the commissioner's aide.

"There is a Boston Police Relief Association," Ryan answered, "and that association has a fund and frequently accepts contributions for the benefit of the heirs of its members."

"Well," said Ponzi, "you have an excellent police force in Boston, and there are some fine men among them. I desire to make a small contribution to the fund for their relief." He placed $250 in crisp new banknotes on the counter, alongside his card. "This is my contribution—for the present."

Ponzi's comment about the "fine men" of the Boston police was grounded in firsthand knowledge. Inspectors from the detective bureau had been dropping by 27 School Street ever since Frank Pope, the state's supervisor of small loans, had urged the police to keep a lookout. Mostly, though, they kept watch on their own investments. Two detectives sent to talk to Ponzi about his operation had been so impressed that they'd pulled out their wallets and invested on the spot. In time, five Boston police inspectors and a lieutenant would hold certificates of the Securities Exchange Company, along with hundreds of rank-and-file officers. Several policemen even worked for Ponzi as agents, collecting the usual 10 percent and, even better as far as Ponzi was concerned, lending his enterprise the respectability of their badges.

Yet the more successful he became, the more perilous Ponzi's life grew. Each dollar he accepted put him deeper into debt. Unless he could figure out a way to carry out his idea on a large scale, or come up with some other way to pay 50 percent interest on short-term investments, he would drown in red ink. He shared his concerns with no one, outwardly maintaining his chipper appearance. If anything, his apparent success seemed to exaggerate his savoir faire. But inwardly the pressure was beginning to take a toll. His guts were churning. Acid was drilling an ulcer in his stomach lining. Yet he was unshakable in his belief that he would find a way out.

On March 24, three months into the operation of the Securities Exchange Company, Ponzi wrote a letter to postal officials asking a few questions it might have been more prudent to pose back in December. Would it be possible, Ponzi inquired, to redeem International Reply Coupons for cash instead of stamps?

The question was effectively an admission by Ponzi that, even if he could obtain the coupons in enormous quantities at depressed prices, he was stumped after that. He knew of no way to turn them into the dollars he needed to pay his investors. At one point, Ponzi had imagined he could reap huge returns by selling the stamps at a discount to businesses that relied on the mails, but that had proved unworkable. In his letter, Ponzi also wondered whether coupons bought in America, rather than overseas, could be redeemed for cash at United States post offices. The reason for that question was less clear. A coupon bought in America, with dollars, redeemed in America for dollars, would be the equivalent of moving a dollar from one pocket to another.

The letter triggered a visit to Ponzi's office by postal inspectors, who informed Ponzi of the obvious: International Reply Coupons were not intended for financial speculation. No, they could not be redeemed for cash. Ponzi shrugged off the news and went on with his business. A solution to that problem would have to wait.

A more authoritative response came on April 19, when Ponzi received an official and officious response from Washington, signed by W. J. Barrows, a man with the unwieldy title of acting third assistant postmaster-general: "You are advised that International Reply Coupons are issued . . . for use in pre-paying international reply postage. To effect that purpose they must be exchanged for stamps of foreign countries, and I know of no necessity for redeeming American reply coupons in this country. Post office inspectors have reported their interview with you concerning a proposed speculation in International Reply Coupons issued by foreign governments. They are not intended as a medium of speculation, and the department cannot sanction their use for that purpose."

During the weeks between Ponzi's letter and the postmaster's reply, the Securities Exchange Company experienced explosive growth.

Word of the easy money spread like a financial version of the Spanish flu. It moved from police officers to trolley drivers, from trolley drivers to their passengers, from shopkeepers to waiters, to diners, to their families. Fruit peddlers polished their apples while telling stories of the riches they were expecting. Newsboys in knickerbockers passed the word on street corners, though the newspapers under their arms told no story of the amazing financier. Kitchen girls heard from their fishermen husbands, then passed the news to their upstairs employers. News incubated in the Italian enclaves, then moved among the tribes of Boston, from the Irish to the Jews, the Armenians to the Poles, the Swedes to the Brahmins. Some still had doubts, but human nature was asserting itself; in the absence of hard evidence, too good to miss trumps too good to be true.

Clementi Viscarello ran into cook Antonio de Agostino at Henry Fravega's provision store and mentioned all the money to be had on School Street. So de Agostino invested a hundred dollars and Fravega bet the bank, putting eighteen hundred dollars on Ponzi for himself, plus a hundred dollars each for his son and daughter. Canal Street butcher Amarco Cataldo told customer John Badaracco, who promptly invested five hundred dollars.

South End bricklayer Ricardo Bogni heard about it on the job and brought his wife, Rose, to 27 School Street. Ponzi sensed that Mrs. Bogni was the skeptical one, so he focused his charm on her, displaying sample International Reply Coupons as he spoke. To make her laugh, he told Rose Bogni that the deal was so safe she could sell her shoes and invest the money. Ponzi told Ricardo Bogni that if he took sick or otherwise needed his money, it would be returned no questions asked, though without the 50 percent interest if withdrawn before the due date. When Ponzi was finished, Rose Bogni reached into her purse and pulled out fifteen dollars. Ricardo ran down to their bank and withdrew four hundred dollars, a world of money for them. Soon he went to work for Ponzi as an agent.

Just for show, Ponzi himself took out a few notes, and his own Rose came by the office for a visit on April 17 and proudly deposited her pin money, seventy dollars. A twenty-seven-year-old English immigrant named Abe Rhodes outdid her, investing fifteen hundred dollars the same day. But even he fell short of the North End's Antonio D'Avanzo, who bet two thousand. All three would be back to collect their winnings on June 1.

More than ten thousand dollars a week was surging into 27 School Street. By mid-April Ponzi needed help handling it all. He had been keeping the accounts himself, and sloppily, at that. He had barely any idea how much money he had taken in. When he wanted to check his cash assets, he simply added his bank deposit slips. He had less interest in counting his liabilities. He knew they would exceed his assets.

John A. Dondero was proving a more able salesman than he was an office manager, so Ponzi called an employment agency seeking a young woman with experience—but not too much experience—as a bookkeeper and stenographer. The agency sent him a doe-eyed eighteen-year-old. Lucy Meli was a native of Sicily who had immigrated with her family a decade earlier and still spoke Italian. After high school in Revere, she'd graduated from business school less than a year before coming to work for Ponzi, giving her the ideal combination of youthful enthusiasm and unquestioning trust in Ponzi's word. He promptly put her in charge of the office. With her thick brown hair pulled back in a bun, Lucy Meli set about trying to get the company organized by the principles she had learned in school.

She and Ponzi occupied opposite sides of the same desk, and she looked across at him with respect bordering on adoration. He enjoyed the attention but offered only avuncular friendship in return. Rose was at home in Somerville, expecting him home for dinner, and Ponzi would do nothing to upset that. Meli expressed her confidence by investing her paychecks and her parents' money with her boss, and the Meli family eventually owned nearly two thousand dollars in Securities Exchange Company notes.

Other new faces began turning up regularly at 27 School Street, as Ponzi hired more salesmen. April receipts would exceed $140,000, an average of three hundred dollars each from 471 customers. One of the new salesmen was Percy Lamb.

Lamb, a thirty-three-year-old English immigrant, had been laid off from his job as a foreman in a textile factory in the mill city of Lawrence, near the New Hampshire border. He'd moved to Boston and found a job earning fifty-five dollars a week as a sorter in a wool house on Summer Street, a mile from Ponzi's office. One day an Italian coworker began talking about the money to be made with the Securities Exchange Company. Lamb and his wife went to see for themselves and were so convinced by Ponzi's patter that they placed their life savings—six hundred dollars—in his hands. On April 17, Ponzi offered Lamb a job, matching his sorter's salary and adding the promise of 15 percent commissions. Lamb grabbed it, agreeing to open the Securities Exchange Company's first branch office, to serve the millworkers of Lawrence. Ponzi was expanding beyond his Italian base, using Lamb to reach other immigrant groups and native-born Americans who might be tempted by easy money.

Ponzi was glad to have salesmen like Lamb aboard, but not all his employees were so welcome. Months earlier, Ponzi had run into his old Montreal cellmate, the chronic thief and con man Louis Cassullo. Like Ponzi, Cassullo had bounced around after his release from prison, landed in Boston, and gotten married. Since learning Ponzi was in town, Cassullo had kept tabs on his comings and goings, looking for an angle to exploit. When he heard about the Securities Exchange Company, he wasted no time before heading to 27 School Street, where he made it clear he wanted a piece of Ponzi's action. Ponzi was in a bind. If word slipped out about his prison record, particularly on a charge of bank forgery, his financial empire would come crashing down. "I was in his power," Ponzi concluded. "And he was my most dreaded enemy. . . . I was going straight. He was still going crooked. Under the circumstance, I had to capitulate." Ponzi gave Cassullo a job.

Ponzi sent Cassullo on an endless number of fool's errands and wild-goose chases. One was to the wharves of New York to buy a few bottles of Ponzi's favorite after-dinner drink, Hennessy Three Stars cognac, from a French ship in port. Secretly he hoped that Prohibition agents would catch Cassullo with the contraband liquor and take him to jail, but Cassullo returned with the bottles as ordered. When that did not work, Ponzi kept him away from School Street by making Cassullo an advance man, scouting out locations for branches in cities around New England. Ponzi did not particularly want a string of offices, but he wanted Cassullo hanging around even less.

Soon Ponzi had Massachusetts branch offices not only in Lawrence but also in Brockton, Clinton, Fall River, Framingham, Lynn, Plymouth, Quincy, and Worcester. He opened a second Boston branch in the North End, at 196 Hanover Street, next door to the Daniels & Wilson Furniture Company. Then came Manchester and Portsmouth, New Hampshire; Barre and Burlington, Vermont; Hartford, Bridgeport, and New Haven, Connecticut; Bangor and Portland, Maine; Pawtucket, Providence, and Woonsocket, Rhode Island; and Bayonne and Clifton, New Jersey. Agents in Boston and the ever-expanding branches—some little more than a traveling salesman, others modeled after 27 School Street—began doing so much business that they hired subagents, splitting with them the 10 percent commissions that became Ponzi's going rate. And the money kept coming.

The bigger Ponzi got, the more threats he faced. Inquiries by the postal inspectors had not slowed his ascent, but they had sent shock waves through the cobwebbed corridors of the Universal Postal Union. The possibility that a Boston man was growing rich by trafficking in International Reply Coupons was too much to bear. Questions needed to be asked. Regulations needed to be tightened. During his meeting with the Boston postal inspectors, Ponzi had mentioned trading in coupons imported from Italy. They could not prove he was doing it, but they could not be sure that he was not. Either way, action needed to be taken. In April, Italian postal officials abruptly suspended sales of reply coupons. Their counterparts in France and Romania quickly followed suit.

The moves were technically not a problem for Ponzi, who had at least temporarily abandoned efforts to purchase coupons, having failed to overcome the practical and logistical obstacles. But looked at from another perspective, it meant his operation was attracting unwelcome notice. A net was slowly being woven to ensnare him.

The Ponzi family's new home on Slocum Road in Lexington.

CHAPTER NINE

"ALWAYS REACHING
FOR THE MOON"

By early spring, Ponzi's operation was becoming the talk of Boston, exceeding thirty thousand dollars a week in new investments and attracting increased attention from police and postal officials. Yet despite the location of the Securities Exchange Company on the edge of Newspaper Row, the city's newspapers had been completely silent about it.

One reason might have been reporters' and editors' deeply ingrained aversion to providing free publicity—"Let 'em buy an ad" was a common newsroom refrain. For his part, Ponzi saw no reason to spend money on advertising; money was coming in as fast as he and Lucy Meli could count it. Another reason for the newspapers' silence might have been the absence of any official action against Ponzi. Newspapers tended to be reactive rather than proactive, and until someone with standing either accused Ponzi of wrongdoing or declared him a genius, he failed to meet the most basic definition of news. It was easy to expend ink on a shady politician, a disgraced sports figure, or an accused murderer. But editors and reporters understood that it was dangerous to go out on a limb to challenge a seemingly successful private businessman. It was no secret that the Supreme Court took a narrow view of the First Amendment. Only a year earlier, the court had unanimously ruled that the First Amendment, in the words of Justice Oliver Wendell Holmes Jr., does not "protect a man in falsely shouting fire in a theater." Though that decision upheld the Espionage Act, journalists could imagine how the same court might respond to a libel case in which a businessman was mistakenly branded a fraud. Someone like Ponzi, with access to money and lawyers, might end up owning any newspaper that attacked him without hard evidence.

Another reason Ponzi escaped reporters' attention was the extraordinary number of major stories occupying Edwin Grozier's *Post* and the city's other newspapers during the first months of 1920. The national news pages were filled with stories about the Eighteenth and Nineteenth Amendments to the Constitution: Prohibition and women's suffrage. The liquor ban took effect in January, and the state-by-state battle to ratify women's voting rights raged into the summer.

Boston was overflowing with local news as well. The city was still recovering from the police strike the previous fall. Reporters were paying close attention to the abundance of rookies on the reconstituted force. Political reporters were taking the measure of Governor Calvin Coolidge, who had made a national name for himself by breaking the strike. Now he was being talked about as a vice presidential candidate.

Roundups of suspected radicals had the city on edge, as shackled foreigners were being held for interrogation and deportation at the emigration station on Deer Island in Boston Harbor. Crime reporters were keeping track of the usual mayhem, devoting an abundance of ink to the April 15 murders of a paymaster and a guard during a robbery in South Braintree, followed by the arrests of two Italian anarchists, Nicola Sacco and Bartolomeo Vanzetti. Sports pages followed Babe Ruth's first season pounding home runs for the New York Yan-

kees after his stunning sale the previous winter by the Boston Red
Sox. The Babe's move fueled the question of whether New York City
might eclipse Boston as the "Hub of the Universe." Most Bostonians
doubted it.

The *Post* kept its readers abreast of all those stories, while preoccu-
pied by yet another, one that would take a heavy toll.

James Michael Curley was anxious to mount a political comeback.
After losing the mayor's office, he ran for Congress in 1918 but lost
again. With another mayoral election approaching, Curley was determined to regain City Hall and its spoils. As he looked around the city
to count friends and enemies, he knew the *Post* would surely be
among the latter. Edwin Grozier and his managing editor, Clifton B.
Carberry, Boston's premier political commentator, considered Curley
and his machine throwbacks to a corrupt past. They were ready to
throw the full weight of the paper against him.

In the spring of 1920, Curley went on the offensive. He publicly
and repeatedly accused Grozier of secretly taking money from England to oppose Irish independence. Such a charge, if true, would certainly alienate the *Post*'s large Irish immigrant readership, which
Grozier had assiduously and sincerely courted for decades. Curley
took the stage at the St. Patrick's Day celebration on Boston Common and claimed that he had learned of Grozier's alleged perfidy several years earlier. In 1917, Curley claimed, he'd discovered that Grozier
had purchased a quarter million dollars in city bonds. Curley said the
city treasurer had informed him that money for the bonds had come
from a draft on a London bank and that the money was "part of an
immense propaganda campaign fund spent in this country . . . to influence the American mind in favor of Great Britain." The money
had supposedly come from Lord Northcliffe, a British newspaper
baron. In short, Curley was accusing Edwin Grozier of prostituting
himself and the *Boston Post* to betray the cause of Irish independence.
Curley's timing was incendiary: The feared British irregulars, known
as the Black and Tans, were just arriving in Ireland to battle the rebels.

Grozier was outraged. The claim was a bald-faced lie from a politi-

cian with only a casual regard for the truth, but the publisher feared
that his years of support for the Irish would be undermined without
an equally fierce response. He sat down in his cubbyhole office on
Washington Street and wrote an extraordinary challenge that he published on the front page of his newspaper, headlined in bold type:

A CORDIAL INVITATION TO EX-MAYOR CURLEY

Here Is an Opportunity for Him to Prove His Interesting Charges Against the Boston Post and Edwin A. Grozier, Its Editor

Below that, Grozier recounted Curley's scurrilous charges, then
made his offer: "If Mr. Curley has a scintilla of evidence to back up his
charges of improper conduct, I hereby ask him to produce it for free
and conspicuous publication in these columns. If he or anyone else
can produce proof to show that Edwin A. Grozier or *The Boston Post,*
as conducted by Edwin A. Grozier, ever received at any time, anywhere, anyhow, from Lord Northcliffe or his representative $250,000
or $1, or any sum or other consideration, directly or indirectly, to in-
fluence its attitude . . . Edwin A. Grozier will take pleasure in presenting to James M. Curley his entire interest in *The Boston Post.*"
Grozier was betting his fortune, his legacy, everything he had spent
three decades building. All to defend the honor of his name and his
beloved paper.

Curley had no evidence; but that was never the point. The wily
politician had borrowed a strategy from his friend the pugilist John L.
Sullivan: Lead with wild punches to keep a dangerous opponent from
delivering an early knockout. Knowing he could not provide proof of
his charge, Curley tried to turn Grozier's invitation to his advantage.
He offered to debate the *Post* publisher at any time or place of
Grozier's choosing on the question of whether Grozier was a paid
agent of the British government. Grozier ignored the proposal. It was
as if Curley had proposed a debate on whether Grozier beat his wife.
No matter what he said, Grozier could not win. Even if he was

tempted to try, he was no public speaker, certainly not in Curley's league.

Grozier could take satisfaction in knowing that all but the most rabid Curley fans would recognize that the *Post* had carried the day. Curley would surely have produced evidence, humiliated Grozier, and seized the newspaper if he could have. His diversionary tactic of a debate challenge could only be seen as a concession.

Though Grozier won the round on points, the timing of the episode suggests it was a costly victory. Never blessed with robust health, the sixty-year-old *Post* publisher had spent his entire adult life trying to emulate the dawn-to-midnight work ethic of his newspaper mentor Joseph Pulitzer. In late spring 1920, in the weeks that followed his face-off with Curley, Edwin Grozier suffered a complete physical collapse. He was hospitalized in intensive care, fighting for his life, unable to play any role at the *Post*. At the same time, the *Post*'s managing editor was away for the summer. Their roles needed to be filled, and the job fell to the man who held the titles of assistant publisher and assistant editor.

For the first time in his life, at thirty-two, Richard Grozier had a chance to escape his father's shadow. He was in charge.

As spring gained confidence, so did Ponzi's investors. By May, the twenty-dollar guppies were still welcome, but more often they were dwarfed by thousand-dollar whales who saw 27 School Street as prime feeding grounds.

Louis and Charlotte Blass had met Ponzi a year earlier, when he was a poor clerk, and had watched from a safe distance as he parlayed his big idea into a moneymaking machine. Knowing that his friends the Blasses had money in the bank, and hoping to separate them from some of it, Ponzi dropped by their home in the Jamaica Plain neighborhood in March. Louis Blass was forty-five, a traveling salesman of cotton waste products who had formerly run a mill in New York. He and his forty-two-year-old wife had emigrated from France seventeen years earlier, and now they were raising two sons and two daughters. The eldest planned to start classes at the Massachusetts Agricultural College in the fall. Ponzi showed them a few reply coupons and described his business, watching as always for the moment their eyes lit up at the sound of 50 percent interest in forty-five days. The Blasses spent weeks thinking about Ponzi's proposal before plunging in with both feet.

On May 10, the couple showed up at Ponzi's office with eleven thousand dollars in certified checks, from two emptied bank accounts, plus ten thousand dollars in Liberty bonds. Ponzi accepted the bonds as the equivalent of nine thousand dollars in cash and wrote out the biggest single certificate to date from the Securities Exchange Company: twenty thousand dollars, with thirty thousand dollars due in forty-five days. Louis Blass was so certain of the windfall he began urging his bosses and his customers to follow his lead and invest all they could. His boss, textile merchant Sam Finkel, was intrigued enough to inquire about speculation in postal reply coupons during a trip to Washington. He was told it was implausible. He declined to invest and shared that information with Blass, who nevertheless remained confident in his pal Ponzi.

With more investors came more salesmen. Ponzi brought in his brother-in-law Rinaldo Boselli, who was married to Rose's sister Mary; and his friends Harry Mahoney and Henry Neilson, among others, and by the end of the month the Securities Exchange Company had more than three dozen employees. Neilson's route to a job with Ponzi was typical. A Danish immigrant who worked as a forty-five-dollar-a-week meat cutter in Somerville, he had met the finance wizard socially the previous year at the home of a friend of his, Ponzi's landlord, Anders Larsen. They stayed in touch, and when Larsen and his wife, Karen, invested five thousand dollars with Ponzi, Neilson and his wife, Hilda, took a chance with two thousand. The Neilsons made their first investment on May 18, then got so excited by the expected profits that they returned twice more within the next week, adding another thirty-four hundred dollars. Ponzi appreciated Henry Neilson's confidence, not to mention the thirty-six-year-old Dane's dashing looks and smooth manner. Ponzi knew a natural salesman when he saw one. So Ponzi hired Neilson to work in the office, explaining the system to would-be investors. Ponzi knew that customers were comforted when they heard salesmen honestly utter the words "Why, I have several thousand dollars of my family's own money invested here."

Another new salesman was Charles Ritucci, who ran the Plymouth office for Ponzi. He learned quickly from his boss's enterprising nature, printing flyers in English, Italian, and Portuguese, then pasting them on store windows. They read:

**Securities Exchange Company, No. 27,
School Street, Boston, Mass.**

NOTICE

Do you want to get rich quick? See our agent, Charles Ritucci, 301$^{1}/_{2}$ Court Street, Upstairs in Plymouth Theatre Building, who will explain how you can get fifty percent profit on your investment, payable forty-five days from date of investment. Our bank office in Plymouth opens every night from 6 to 8. Yours truly, Securities Exchange Company.

Investors could not help but throw money at such a sure thing. Ponzi began opening new bank accounts, including one at the North End branch of the Hanover Trust Company, where he deposited sixty thousand dollars on May 24 at the urging of the bank's manager, an ambitious young man named Charles Pizzi. Pizzi was tired of seeing his depositors withdraw their money to invest with Ponzi.

Meanwhile, Lucy Meli had begun an index-card system so the company could, for the first time, keep track of the names and addresses of investors, the number of the certificate each was given, the amounts invested, and the due dates of payments. As a courtesy and a confidence builder, she followed up by sending postcards to investors a few days before their notes came due, to let them know the company stood behind its promises. The card file was soon overflowing. In May alone, 1,525 investors placed more than $440,000 in Ponzi's care. They all wanted to see how, as Ponzi put it, "A little dollar could start on a journey across the ocean and return home in six weeks, married and with a couple of kids."

As May drew to a close and his bubble kept expanding, Ponzi faced a decision: Admit defeat and return what money he could; flee with Rose and a small fortune of a few hundred thousand dollars; or plant his feet and keep the ball rolling.

If flight or surrender crossed his mind, Ponzi refused to acknowledge it. His ambition to succeed was blinding, his superficial success intoxicating. "The average man is never satisfied with what he has," Ponzi reflected. "He does not realize when he is well off. If he has a shirt, he wants two. If he is single, he wants a wife. If he is married, he wants a harem. . . . He is always reaching for the moon and stepping off into space."

Publicly admitting that he had not been able to perfect the alchemy of coupons for cash would have carried too heavy a cost for him to bear. At the moment, authorities were only vaguely focused on him. But the large number of police who were Ponzi investors would surely lead to swift and severe punishment the moment they learned that some or all of their money was gone. He would suffer, too, a crushing loss of faith among his in-laws and perhaps even his wife. The Gneccos and the Donderos had poured their life savings and inheritances into the Securities Exchange Company—the depositor lists included eight Gneccos and ten Donderos. After the recent losses of Rose's parents and the failure of Gnecco Brothers, it looked as though Ponzi would be their deliverance. He took what might be viewed as a tentative step toward flight by making plans to sail with Rose to Italy on July 1 to visit his mother, whom he had not seen for seventeen years. But there was little chance he would not return, if he took the trip at all.

"What was I going to do? Proclaim my insolvency and face prosecution, or keep up the bluff and trust to luck?" he wondered rhetorically. "I kept up the bluff, hoping that I might eventually hit upon some workable plan to pay all of my creditors in full." Privately, he abandoned the self-sustaining fiction that postal reply coupons might yield millions and accepted the fact that he was redeeming his certificates with money derived from new investors. Robbing Peter to pay Paul. "Not only couldn't I pay the promised 50 percent return," he lamented, "but I couldn't even refund the principal at more than seventy-five cents on the dollar."

He consoled himself with a story of a spectacular failure by a fellow Italian that had turned into unparalleled success: "Four centuries before, Columbus had started out from Spain on what he thought was the western route to Asia and the East Indies. On the way over he had discovered America. He didn't know it was there, and nobody else knew it, except the Indians. Yet, he ran smack right into it." With characteristic self-aggrandizement, Ponzi assessed his attributes—determination, luck, and unlimited confidence in his ability to exploit both—and concluded that he was a spiritual heir to Columbus.

Once he decided to stick it out, Ponzi began making the most of his newfound status. A rented apartment in a two-family house in Somerville was no place for a budding Rockefeller and his lovely wife. So Ponzi began searching for a grand house to buy, ideally in a moneyed suburb like the society enclave of Cambridge or the bankers' colony of Winchester. He had already bought himself a car, a cream-colored Hudson coupe, so the commute would be no bother. But he and Rose disagreed about what kind of house to buy. He wanted a mansion, but she wanted a home, not "a big place with great rooms and secret passages."

Eventually they were steered to Lexington, a dozen miles northwest as the crow flies from 27 School Street. The town prided itself on the two-and-a-half-acre Lexington Battle Green, where the war for independence began with the "shot heard round the world" on April 19, 1775. Since then, Lexington had matured into understated affluence, a home for literary luminaries and comfortable business owners, dotted with stately homes on swaths of land.

Their focus swiftly became a vacant house on Slocum Road, a half mile from the town center. Built seven years earlier, the yellow stucco house had little in common with the white clapboard Colonials popular in town. Situated close to the quiet street, impressive without being overwhelming, the house featured a columned portico and wooden porch at the front entrance, flanked on one side by a round sunroom and on the other by an archway leading to a carport, beyond which was a quaint carriage house. Above the portico was a balcony with a low railing and a flagpole poking out like a ship's prow. Dormers sat atop the slate roof, and the windows in the sunroom and the second-floor bedrooms were shielded by striped awnings that snapped and flapped in the spring breeze. The two-acre grounds had grown unruly from lack of care, but through an arbor to the left of the house were a tennis court and a stone fountain in fine shape.

When he first saw the house, Ponzi was unimpressed. "Oh, this won't do," he sniffed, preferring something more in keeping with his new status. But Rose was smitten. It had the makings of a real home, not a cloistered mansion. Ponzi relented and began negotiating the sale. The home had been built by Richard Engstrom and his wife, Anne, Swedish immigrants who had run into money troubles and had moved out the previous October. The Engstroms had spent between forty and fifty thousand dollars on the house, but the best offer they had received to date was twenty-five thousand, which they had flatly rejected. The Engstroms had never heard of Ponzi—not surprising, considering the absence of publicity for his business and the lack of branches in affluent towns like Lexington. But their lawyer, J. C. Thompson, told the Engstroms that the new bidder for the house was a good prospect who had made "barrels of money."

Ponzi craved acceptance as much as he loved making deals. He tried to do both with the purchase of the house. He twice invited Richard Engstrom and his lawyer to dinner at the Copley Plaza Hotel and the Boston City Club. Engstrom was not interested. Rebuffed, Ponzi began playing hardball, offering twenty-five thousand dollars, the same amount Engstrom had already rejected. When Engstrom said no, Ponzi raised his offer to twenty-nine thousand. Knowing how much Rose wanted the place, he allowed himself to be pushed up to thirty-nine thousand, but on one condition: the seller would have to become an investor in the Securities Exchange Company.

When they passed the papers on May 28, Ponzi paid for the house with nine thousand dollars in cash plus an orange-colored Securities Exchange Company certificate for twenty thousand dollars, payable as thirty thousand dollars on July 12. Engstrom's lawyer was worried. For security, he persuaded Ponzi to put up a thirty-thousand-dollar certificate of deposit at the Tremont Trust Company, payable to Engstrom in case of a problem with the Securities Exchange Company certificate.

The Ponzis moved into the Copley Plaza for several weeks while Rose and a decorator went gaily and expensively to work making the house a showplace. Visitors walking up the front path might see gardener Cornelius Palmer trimming the hedges and turning the lawn into an expanse of green velvet. Inside, Palmer's wife, Teresa, the Ponzi family cook, would be busily preparing Italian delicacies. A tall, proper butler would open the heavy mahogany door, leading the way into a large foyer with hardwood floors covered by thick Persian and Oriental rugs. To the left was a long living room with damask-covered walls in old blue, a grand piano at one end and a bearskin rug laid out before a marble fireplace at the other. In the center of the room sat a mahogany table, hand-carved in Italy, surrounded by chairs upholstered in velour and damask. In a corner of the room was a tiger-skin rug beneath a Victrola, on which the Ponzis would play "Dardanella," the hit song whose lyrics Ponzi might have sung to Rose: "There'll be one girl in my harem, when you're mine . . . my star of love divine." The room's only wall hanging was the Mona Lisa–like portrait of a teenage Rose.

Beyond the grand piano was the entrance to the light-filled sun parlor, a circular room filled with wicker chairs and a round wicker table, with three wire birdcages for decoration. On the other side of the foyer was another small parlor leading to the large dining room, with light gray walls and a walnut table and chairs upholstered in black cloth. At the center of the table stood an impressive cut-glass vase filled with fresh flowers. A butler's pantry at the far end of the entrance hall led to a modern kitchen, which Ponzi had equipped with gas. That alone had cost five thousand dollars, and Rose's purchases at Paine Furniture set him back another fifteen thousand.

Halfway up a curving staircase an alcove housed a tall French clock. At the top of the stairs was a sitting area with a window seat looking out to the street. Four comfortable bedrooms were filled with fine enamel furniture and beds covered by hand-embroidered bedspreads. One room was outfitted with a desk for when Ponzi brought work home at night. Two more bedrooms on the third floor were servants' quarters. It was not as grand as Curley's mansion, but it was close enough. The Ponzi family had arrived.

The Slocum Road house provided Ponzi with a respite from the cataracts of cash and the emergence of new threats raining down on him at 27 School Street.

The money spigot opened wider starting on June 9, when Ponzi received his first notice of sorts in a Boston newspaper. The story on the front page of the *Boston Traveler* was headlined DEAR OLD 'GET RICH QUICK' POPS OUT OF POSTAL GUIDE.

"You pay us your money, any amount does the trick," the story quoted an unidentified "salesman" as saying. The paper said he appeared at the door of the office with a postal guide under his arm and proceeded with a quick explanation of International Reply Coupons and monetary exchange rates, then outlined how a globe-hopping agent could buy coupons in Romania, exchange them in Switzerland, and capitalize further on the strength of the United States dollar to spin profits from stamps. Then, printed in all capital letters, was the salesman's claim: "WE GUARANTEE YOU 50 PERCENT PROFIT IN 45 DAYS!"

The *Traveler* reporter inquired about the company to a ranking postal inspector, whose answers further excited potential investors. "We, of course, investigated the thing—for months—but there seems to be no violation of law here," the inspector said. "We haven't figured out how they make their enormous profit, but they seem confident of their ability to do so. And I guess they can keep on so far as the law goes."

Overall, the story provided a vague but fair representation of what Ponzi and the Securities Exchange Company promised. But in a remarkable feat of flawed journalism, the story did not name Ponzi or his business, and it failed to tell readers where they might go to share in the good fortune. Still, enough Bostonians tracked Ponzi's agents down to swell his income exponentially.

On the other side of the ledger, Cassullo remained as constant a pain as Ponzi's festering ulcer. Ponzi's purchase of a new home only whetted his ex-cellmate's greed. Ponzi mollified Cassullo, at least momentarily, by buying him and his wife, Theodoria, a fine home in the coastal town of Winthrop, directly opposite the Winthrop Arms Hotel. Ponzi paid fourteen thousand dollars for the newly renovated Dutch Colonial, whose best feature was a glassed-in sun parlor and sleeping porch with unobstructed views of the ocean. Still, Cassullo was not satisfied, and he soon took to stealing cash from the Securities Exchange Company, one time stuffing a thousand-dollar bill into his pocket in front of John A. Dondero and declaring, "Charge it to Ponzi." Dondero could not prove it, but he suspected that this sort of thing happened often. He knew nothing of Ponzi's past relationship with Cassullo, so he could not know why Ponzi was so tolerant.

Ponzi chalked up Cassullo's extortionate demands as the cost of doing business, and he was too busy to worry about a few thousand dollars when millions were at stake. With help from word-of-mouth testimonials by satisfied customers and the *Boston Traveler* story, June was on track to be nearly five times better than the previous months combined. One of the biggest sums of the month came from Daniel Desmond, whose investment of ten thousand dollars was made all the more sweet for Ponzi by the fact that the fifty-year-old Desmond was the treasurer of the Lawrence Trust Company. Ponzi was so eager to gild his books with such a large investment from a banker that he made a personal loan to Desmond in the full amount. But Desmond's investment was dwarfed by one made by Louis and Charlotte Blass, who returned to Ponzi's office when their twenty-thousand-dollar note reached maturity on June 24. Rather than collect the thirty thousand dollars they were due, the Blasses spun the wheel of fortune again, betting it all on a new note that promised to yield forty-five thousand dollars in forty-five days.

Ponzi's loyal bookkeeper, Lucy Meli, in their School Street office.

The Boston Globe

CHAPTER TEN

"I NEVER BLUFF."

With his bank accounts bulging and no postal coupons to buy, Ponzi went on a shopping spree. He resolved that the only way to become a latter-day Columbus was to sail on, all sheets to the wind, until he somehow bumped into a continent of profits. His investments fell into four categories: businesses that were already profitable, real estate, unsecured loans to friends, and, most significantly, attempts to gain control of one or more banks. Then there were a few personal items for himself and Rose.

As summer approached, Ponzi spent sixty-one thousand dollars to buy a thousand shares of the Napoli Macaroni Manufacturing Company, joking that he did so to make sure he "wouldn't run out of spaghetti at home." He wrote a check for thirty thousand dollars to buy three hundred shares and a controlling interest in the C & R Construction Company. Then one day he wandered past Faneuil Hall and into the offices of his old employer the J. R. Poole Company. After catching up with his former office mates, Ponzi walked unannounced into John Poole's private office for a meeting that Ponzi never grew tired of recounting.

"Have a seat, Charlie," Poole said. "They tell me that you're in business. Dealing in some sort of foreign securities."

"That's right," Ponzi answered.

"How are you making out?" his former boss asked.

"Fairly good," he replied. "That's what brought me here. To get your advice. I have a few dollars I would like to invest."

"Why don't you buy a few shares of my preferred stock? It pays 7 percent."

"I would rather have some common."

"I'll tell you what I'll do," Poole said. "I will give you twenty-five shares of each."

"Is that all?" Ponzi asked coyly. "It hardly seems enough to bother with it."

Poole wondered if his former clerk was joking. "How much more stock do you want?" he asked.

"I'll take all you have," Ponzi said casually.

Poole laughed, and then, like a teacher addressing a not terribly bright child, told Ponzi: "Listen, Charlie, it takes a lot of money to buy this company."

"I figured it would," Ponzi said. "That's why I waited this long to call on you. I was afraid I wouldn't have enough."

"And you may still be short of the mark," Poole said, beginning to wonder.

They dickered a bit over the price Ponzi would have to pay for a directorship, and Ponzi brought out his checkbook.

"I didn't think you meant it," Poole said.

"J.R., I never bluff."

Over the next few days Ponzi paid Poole $240,000 for control of the company. He gave Poole five loans totaling $155,000 to launch a major expansion that included opening branches in several foreign countries. In addition to the import-export business, Poole's holdings included a sardine factory in Maine and a meatpacking plant in Kansas City, which Ponzi thought went nicely with the Napoli Macaroni Manufacturing Company. All he needed was some contraband Italian red wine and he could make a meal from his own holdings.

Next he expanded his real estate holdings. He bought a small tenement house in the city's West End that cost him six thousand dollars. He issued loans secured by mortgages ranging from fifteen hundred dollars to thirty-five thousand dollars on homes in East Boston, Brookline, and the city's Roslindale section.

Ponzi also made a series of unsecured loans, given mostly under the same terms as the one he had given Daniel Desmond, the treasurer of the Lawrence Trust Company—money provided to friends or acquaintances to help them buy certificates from the Securities Exchange Company. The biggest was for forty thousand dollars to Charles Pizzi, the young Hanover Trust banker who had landed Ponzi's deposits. The smallest, for five hundred dollars, went to James McTiernan, police chief in the suburb of Sharon. Ponzi did not like McTiernan, who he thought had "more gall than a brass monkey." But with postal inspectors still dropping by on a regular basis, Ponzi wanted as many friends with badges as possible.

When Ponzi turned his attention to the banks, he started by spreading his money around. He bought fifty shares of Fidelity Trust for six thousand dollars, five shares of Tremont Trust for five hundred dollars, and one hundred shares of Old South Trust for $12,500 dollars. But little pieces of large institutions did him no good. He certainly was not going to earn his way out of the hole he was in by collecting dividend checks on his relatively small investments. A plan began to form in his mind. If he could gain control of a bank, he might weather any storms that came his way. Given enough time, the plan might allow him to transform his unsustainable business into something more permanently profitable.

He set his sights on Hanover Trust, a bank with about $5 million in assets, small enough for him to have a shot at taking over, yet large enough for it to be worth his while. An added incentive was the chance to settle an old score. Ponzi had not forgotten that when he'd been in dire straits the previous summer and had needed two thousand dollars to keep alive his *Trader's Guide* idea, he'd been shown the door by the bank's president, Henry Chmielinski.

Ponzi began putting his plan into motion with a two-pronged strategy of buying stock and increasing his deposits. On the stock side, he first bought small blocks of shares, seventy-five in all—not enough to gain control but enough for a foothold. At the same time, he endeared himself to several of the bank's Italian stockholders the way he knew best: financially. The largest mortgage loan Ponzi made was to one of those stockholders, Enrico DiPietro, who turned around and invested in the Securities Exchange Company.

By making friends with other Hanover Trust stockholders, Ponzi might eventually control the votes that came with the shares they owned. By Ponzi's count, between his own seventy-five shares and the stock owned by his friends, he controlled about six hundred of the two thousand shares of Hanover Trust stock. At the beginning of June, the bank intended to issue another two thousand shares. If Ponzi could buy fifteen hundred, he would have about twenty-one hundred, a majority of the stock.

At the same time that he was eyeing Hanover Trust stock, Ponzi was depositing more and more money into the bank. Though he kept accounts at more than a dozen other banks as well, he focused his money on Hanover—eventually keeping $2.7 million there, making him easily the bank's biggest depositor. Ponzi knew that the larger his deposits, the greater his leverage over the bank's officers. A bank with $5 million in assets might have access to only one-tenth that amount at any given time. The reason is that money accepted as deposits—which are liabilities on a bank's books because the bank has to pay interest on them and the principal on demand—is not kept in vaults but is put to work making money as loans. Banking in 1920 was not a lot more complicated than that. Some bankers joked about how easy it was, describing their work as governed by the "rule of threes": Pay 3 percent interest on deposits, charge 6 percent interest on loans, pocket the 3 percent difference as profit, and be on the golf course by 3:00 P.M. But that apple cart would be upset, perhaps irreparably, if a large depositor like Ponzi suddenly closed his account and withdrew his money without advance notice. At the moment, none of that was on anyone's mind at Hanover Trust. Chmielinski and the bank's other officers—none of whom remembered the poverty-stricken Ponzi who had come to them barely a year earlier—were plainly thrilled to have such a prosperous new depositor. And Ponzi knew it.

One afternoon in early June, he walked around the corner from his office and into Hanover Trust's main branch on Washington Street. This time, Ponzi was ushered into Chmielinski's private office, where bank officials buzzed around him like yellow jackets at a honeysuckle shrub. Chmielinski was a bull of a man, with a large head mounted on a thick neck. At thirty-seven he was almost the same age as Ponzi but twice his size. Chmielinski had emigrated from Poland in 1898. He'd run a Polish-language newspaper, the *Daily Courier,* before getting started in the banking business several years earlier by his brother, a Catholic priest. Father John Chmielinski headed the Polish Industrial Association, a combination bank, steamship agency, and all-purpose service center for Boston's Poles in the North End.

With little preamble, Ponzi promptly offered to buy all two thousand shares of the bank's soon-to-be issued stock. As eager as they were to please, the Hanover Trust officials recognized the danger.

"We cannot do that," said one, "because we would be selling you the control of the bank."

"That's just what I want," said Ponzi.

"We are sorry, but we cannot consider anything like that."

They went back and forth awhile, but neither side would budge. Ponzi had expected as much, so he played his trump card.

"It seems to me that our differences cannot be bridged," Ponzi said.

"Let's drop the subject. Keep your bank and I'll look for another one." He slid his checkbook out from his jacket pocket. "Can you tell me what my balance is today?"

Blood drained from the bankers' faces. Fearing the sudden loss of Ponzi's account and the havoc it would play with their books, the bankers hastily offered a compromise.

"We will sell you one thousand shares of the new stock," one said.

"Nothing doing," answered Ponzi. With some more prodding, he got the bank's officers to acknowledge what he already knew: Collectively, they controlled roughly fourteen hundred shares. If the votes attached to those shares were added to the votes of the Italian shareholders, who had until then always supported the bank's officers, the current Hanover Trust regime would continue to control a majority. Thinking their reign was safe, the bank officers made another proposal: "We will sell you fifteen hundred shares." They also agreed to make him a director of the bank, in the belief that he could do no harm. But Chmielinski was unaware that Ponzi had already courted the Italian stockholders. With fifteen hundred shares of his own, Ponzi would effectively control the majority he needed.

"Fine," said Ponzi, swallowing his excitement to avoid tipping his hand. "I'll take the fifteen hundred shares."

At the bank's annual meeting of stockholders on June 8, Ponzi was elected a director of Hanover Trust. The next day, at a meeting of the directors, he won election to the bank's powerful executive committee. A week later, Ponzi paid $187,500 for fifteen hundred shares of the bank's newly issued stock. The Hanover Trust Company, which less than a year earlier had denied him a loan for two thousand dollars, had effectively become the Bank of Charles Ponzi.

After so many years of scraping by, Ponzi found he liked the feeling of money passing through his manicured fingers in exchange for a bauble or a building. The more he bought, the more he wanted to buy. As Bostonians became enmeshed in the mania of smashing piggy banks to invest in postal coupons, Ponzi became caught up in the mania of spending their money and making himself the man he had always dreamed of becoming.

He imagined himself a latter-day Count of Monte Cristo, reveling in the parallels he found between his life and the fictional experiences of Edmond Dantès, the title character in Alexandre Dumas's classic. After fourteen years of false imprisonment, Dantès escaped and found a hidden treasure. He appeared mysteriously to benefit the good, wreak vengeance on his betrayers, and expose the ills of society. In Ponzi's version, his fourteen-year ordeal spanned the difficult period from his 1903 immigration to his 1917 return to Boston. It included his two prison terms, both of which he considered as unjust as the trumped-up treason sentence suffered by Dantès. But now, if everything went as planned, he envisioned borrowing a page from Dumas's book. He would use his money, his bank, his businesses, and his savoir faire to upset Boston's caste system.

The money itself, he averred, was secondary to what it could do. Ponzi declared that he wanted to "test its power. To derive from it the thrill incidental to the accomplishment of things called impossible."

On the other hand, Ponzi's favorite phrase became "Wrap it up, please. I'll take it." He enjoyed saying it regardless of whether the item was a box of cigars or a building. He grew disappointed if a day passed without a big purchase, and he was feeling that way in mid-June when a car salesman dropped by the School Street office.

"I have a car," Ponzi told him, testing his visitor's salesmanship.

"A good car?" the man asked with a hint of sarcasm.

"What do you think? Do you think I drive around in a wheelbarrow?"

Shifting his tack, the salesman said, "I have been told that you own a Hudson."

"It's very true."

"But you need a much larger and more expensive car."

"What, for instance?" asked Ponzi. "What are you selling, anyway?"

"Locomobiles," the salesman answered proudly, spreading out a brochure like a magician fanning a deck of cards. Ponzi saw a photo of a dark blue limousine and jumped to the bait. "How much for that?"

"Twelve thousand, six hundred dollars, delivered," the salesman answered.

"All right," Ponzi answered, "send it right over."

The salesman blanched. The car Ponzi had picked was two weeks away from completion, he explained. Like all Locomobiles it was a custom job, in this case for a New York millionaire. That made Ponzi want it all the more.

"Fine!" he said. "Have it downstairs, in front of the door, by July first."

"But that car is already sold."

"Listen, young man, I want that car," Ponzi said. "And when I want something, I am prepared to pay for it. Have that car here by not later than one o'clock on July first, and I will give you a thousand dollars more for it."

Done deal.

The person least interested in Ponzi's money was Rose. Though she loved their new home, she missed the simple joys of life in their little apartment in Somerville. Not long out of her teens, she was uncomfortable overseeing a staff as the lady of the house. "The more servants, the less freedom," she would say. "I like a house where you can talk and not be overheard, where you can say what you like at all times." And no matter how clean her maid kept things, deep down Rose believed she would have kept them cleaner.

One day Ponzi came home with a glittering diamond bracelet while Rose was entertaining her friend Lillian Mahoney, the wife of Ponzi's agent Harry Mahoney. Embarrassed by his extravagance, Rose insisted that he return the thousand-dollar bracelet for a refund. Another time, Ponzi brought home a string of lustrous pearls. Again she demurred, but Ponzi thought he could outwit his thrifty wife. He agreed to tell her the price, but then tossed out a number that was only a fraction of the necklace's true cost. Rose accepted the necklace, and Ponzi thought he'd carried the day. But Rose had the last laugh. Not long after, she quietly returned them for a full refund. Ponzi had better luck with a much different gift: To keep Rose company during his long days at work, Ponzi surprised her with a Boston terrier puppy they named Beauty.

Ponzi's regular trips to a North End jewelry store led to a friendship with jeweler Alphonso Ciullo. It came in handy one morning when Ponzi was dealing with yet another visit from a pair of postal inspectors. Postal authorities had remained frustrated in their attempts to prove that Ponzi was doing something illegal, but they continued to examine his claims, including the recent statements printed in the *Traveler* about building his business by trading in reply coupons.

"Where do you buy them?" one inspector inquired.

"I am not telling that," Ponzi answered. "I will merely say that they can be profitably bought in any country having a depreciated paper currency."

"For instance?" the inspector wanted to know, setting a trap.

"For instance," Ponzi answered, "Italy, France, Rumania, Greece, and so forth."

"Exactly," the inspector said, thinking he had caught Ponzi in a lie. "Now we have information that Italy, France, and Rumania have withdrawn from the postal agreement and stopped the sale of coupons . . ."

Ponzi parried as best he could, but the inspectors seemed to be gaining the upper hand. Just then Ciullo walked up the stairs at 27 School Street with a fat envelope.

"Charlie," Ciullo said, "I have just received this package of coupons from Italy." Ciullo wanted to know if Ponzi could transform them into cash. Scarcely believing his luck, Ponzi took the envelope and dumped out three hundred International Reply Coupons. He smiled. The inspectors pounced.

"Where did you get them?" one demanded of Ciullo.

"I got them from my uncle in Italy," the jeweler answered, not knowing what was going on.

"Who is he?" the inspector asked.

"He is a postmaster in a small town," Ciullo said.

"When did you receive them?"

"This morning."

"How?"

"By mail," Ciullo said.

The inspector examined the envelope and saw that it had been mailed from Italy in May and had only just arrived.

"Well," Ponzi said, his voice tinged with sarcasm. "I hope you are satisfied now that somebody else beside myself can buy coupons in Italy."

The inspectors turned tail and left.

And all the while, larger waves of investors kept crashing on Ponzi's shores.

John Elbye of Everett bought a certificate for fifty dollars on June 10, and then his wife put up the same amount the next day. That gave John confidence, so he came back five days later with one hundred dollars. Five days after that he got up his real nerve and plunged in for a thousand dollars. Ernesto Giovino of Boston topped that with eleven hundred dollars on June 11. Giuseppe Albano of Boston deposited two hundred dollars on June 14 and came back two days later to add two hundred more. Catherine Callahan of Cambridge brought in a hundred dollars on June 18, and Samuel Goldstein of Charlestown put in double that the same day. Fred Drener of New Bedford could spare only fifty dollars on June 19. Harry Ash of Roxbury invested four hundred dollars on June 21, while Michael Kennedy of Somerville came in to collect his 50 percent interest on the $175 he had invested forty-five days earlier. He then took the whole $262.50 and bought another Ponzi note.

That same day, the first day of the hot summer of 1920, an unassuming man with a prominent nose and marquee-sized forehead came to 27 School Street from his office around the corner. With two hundred dollars in cash, he bought the 9,641st certificate issued by the Securities Exchange Company. A clerk wrote the man's name on the certificate in graceful script: Principio A. Santosuosso. But nobody called him that. To his friends and colleagues at the *Boston Post,* where he worked as a reporter, he was simply "P.A."

Post employees from newsboys to pressmen had been lining up in recent weeks to buy Ponzi notes. There was little doubt that word would spread to a well-liked reporter like Santosuosso. But his visit to 27 School Street was personal, not professional. He was twenty-nine, unmarried, the sole supporter of his widowed mother and his unmarried younger sister, both of whom lived with him in East Boston. The three hundred dollars he was due on August 5 would be a welcome addition to their household finances. If he thought the stream of people hoping to strike it rich at 27 School Street might make a good story for the *Post,* he mentally filed it away and returned to work.

The soaring number of new investments made Ponzi rethink his plan to take Rose on a second honeymoon to meet his mother in Italy. Although he fancied himself Boston's Count of Monte Cristo, Ponzi knew that his sudden success made some people wonder if he modeled himself after a more recent literary character, J. Rufus Wallingford, the creation of author George Randolph Chester.

Chester's 1908 novel *Get-Rich-Quick Wallingford: The Cheerful Account of the Rise and Fall of an American Business Buccaneer,* had become embedded in popular culture with help from a long-running 1910 Broadway play written by George M. Cohan. Wallingford is a consummate con artist who fleeces investors with a scheme based on items even more mundane than postal coupons: carpet tacks. Wallingford is ultimately undone by a small oversight and sent to jail, but he is rescued at the last minute by his devoted wife and a businessman whom Wallingford had swindled. The businessman forgives Wallingford because "you're only the logical development of the American tendency to 'get there' no matter how. It is the national weakness, the national menace, and you're only an exaggerated molecule in it." The businessman then hires Wallingford as an executive.

Ponzi had already decided that he would not take the money and run, but he wanted to be certain that no one had any reason to suspect him. Leaving the country was something Wallingford would do. So Ponzi canceled his and Rose's trip to Italy and wired more than five thousand dollars to his mother with instructions that she sail to Boston, first class, as soon as possible. Her only child had struck it rich, and he wanted her to come live with him and his wife. Rose worried that Imelde Ponzi might not like America or, worse, her daughter-in-law. But having lost her parents, and knowing how badly Ponzi missed his mother, Rose accepted the change in plans and began preparing for the arrival of the elder Mrs. Ponzi.

With money rolling in, and the pace increasing from week to week, Ponzi knew that he and his staff of amateur money minders needed professional help. He looked no further than his old acquaintance Roberto de Masellis, manager of the foreign banking department at the Fidelity Trust Company, who two years earlier had planted the seed in Ponzi's mind about fluctuating currency values. Ponzi took de Masellis to dinner at the Copley Plaza, where he described the business of buying postal reply coupons and redeeming them in countries with favorable exchange rates. De Masellis thought Ponzi seemed an honest man with a logical business plan. Practical, even. De Masellis knew nothing about reply coupons, but he had always believed profits could be found in rising and falling currency rates with the right medium of exchange and the money to pull it off in a big way. Based on how well Ponzi dressed, it seemed to de Masellis that his dinner companion had discovered the magic formula.

Ponzi told de Masellis that he should come to work at the Securities Exchange Company as a financial "efficiency expert" who would create a system more comprehensive, or at least less primitive, than the index-card file. To seal the deal, Ponzi agreed to pay de Masellis the princely salary of a thousand dollars a month. In addition, he would deposit ten thousand dollars in de Masellis's name at the International Trust Company, "in case the business stopped or if the rate of exchange became normal and spoiled the investments." De Masellis was delighted. He agreed to begin work July 1.

De Masellis was hardly the only business expert Ponzi convinced. On June 30, Ponzi invited into his office a representative from the respected credit reporting firm the Bradstreet Company. A stamp of approval from Bradstreet would be a huge boon to Ponzi, and he got it. After hearing Ponzi's account of his enormous success, the company issued a report that outlined the business and concluded authoritatively, "Mr. Ponzi bears a favorable personal reputation."

Despite talking a good game with de Masellis and the Bradstreet Company, Ponzi was searching more desperately than ever for a way to turn a profit. And he still had not completely given up on International Reply Coupons. As a last-ditch effort, he tried to enlist Henry Chmielinski, president of Hanover Trust, in an effort to obtain coupons from Poland, where Chmielinski maintained ties with government officials. Ponzi promised that they would both reap profits from the deal.

"Henry," Ponzi told him, "this is your chance of a lifetime to clean up some real dough."

Chmielinski tried to do as Ponzi instructed, but the deal—implausible to begin with—fell through. With it went Ponzi's last hope of turning postal coupons into cash. "I was left high and dry," he reflected, "with no coupons and no profits in sight, and no way of meeting my notes, except by the time-honored custom of robbing Peter to pay Paul. It was a case of either sink or swim, and . . . I didn't want to sink. Not just yet, in any event."

In the meantime, Ponzi's popularity kept soaring. When Ponzi and Lucy Meli tallied the investments from June, they could scarcely believe their eyes. Ponzi knew that deposits had been coming in so fast that his clerks had filled wastebaskets with greenbacks when the cash drawers had overflowed. But no one could have predicted the astonishing total: In June alone, the Securities Exchange Company had taken in more than $2.5 million from seventy-eight hundred customers.

Just as Ponzi was giving up on reply coupons, postal authorities in Washington were finally awakening from their torpor. They prepared an order, to be issued July 2, prohibiting post offices from redeeming more than fifty cents' worth of International Reply Coupons per person at one time. The order made no mention of Ponzi, but it was a clear sign that postal officials still believed he was somehow trafficking in postal coupons. In that sense, postal officials were on a par with Ponzi's investors, who fervently believed that Ponzi had a secret method of turning coupons into cash.

In the meantime, Ponzi continued playing the role of wealthy benefactor. On June 30, he gave a ten-thousand-dollar loan to his brother-in-law George Bertoldi, who was married to Rose's sister Theresa, to buy a note that would be worth fifteen thousand dollars by mid-August. Ponzi also decided to square old debts. The failure of his late father-in-law's wholesale fruit business eighteen months earlier had resulted in losses of about eight thousand dollars to creditors. At the time, that had been a world of money to Ponzi. But now, he collected more in an hour. He paid all Gnecco Brothers' creditors, in full, with a smile.

But Ponzi's grin was about to be sorely tested by another old creditor, one who had already been repaid but who wanted to collect far more.

*Richard Grozier, after taking over for his father as
the* Post's *acting editor and publisher.*

Mary Grozier

CHAPTER ELEVEN

"LIKE STEALING CANDY FROM A BABY"

Day after day throughout June, furniture dealer Joseph Daniels had watched streams of people troop down Hanover Street, walk past his store, and climb the stairs next door to the North End branch of the Securities Exchange Company. Several months had passed since Daniels had last spoken with Ponzi, who had repaid Daniels's two-hundred-dollar loan in full and who had no interest in seeing him again. At their last encounter, Ponzi had told Daniels that his plan to wring profits from postal coupons had been a dud, which was technically true. But Daniels did not trust Ponzi. If the Securities Exchange Company was a bust, why would Ponzi open a second Boston office, and why would happy investors be lining up to trade cash for Ponzi notes?

A plan formed in Daniels's mind. He reasoned that the small loan he had given Ponzi the previous December must have been the seed money for a successful enterprise. Surely he was entitled to more than simple repayment of principal and interest. So, at the end of June, he dropped by 27 School Street to see Ponzi, ostensibly to offer to sell him more furniture. But Ponzi saw through Daniels's ruse and delivered a curt message: I am still not making any money. Even if I were, you would not be entitled to any.

An honest man would have let it drop there. Daniels hired a lawyer, Isaac Harris.

On July 2, Harris filed a million-dollar lawsuit claiming that Daniels was entitled to half ownership of the Securities Exchange Company. The claim had no merit, so it did not worry Ponzi. But Daniels's lawyer also filed an attachment against five of Ponzi's bank accounts, effectively freezing about $700,000 in cash, a legal maneuver designed to squeeze a settlement out of Ponzi.

A million-dollar lawsuit was no everyday occurrence, so it caused enough of a stir in the halls of the Suffolk County Courthouse to reach the ears of a *Boston Post* reporter. On page 1 of the paper on Sunday, July 4, the headline over the brief, unbylined story read: BOSTON MAN IS SUED FOR $1,000,000.

The reporter could not locate Daniels, who was in Vermont for the Fourth of July weekend, but he found a confident, talkative Ponzi on School Street. First the reporter wrote a vague explanation of the business: "The company, which was started in December 1919, claims to be able to pay 50 percent profits out of dealings in foreign exchange through international postal agreements." Then he turned the story over to Ponzi, whose name was appearing for the first time in a Boston newspaper.

"I haven't the slightest idea why Mr. Daniels brought the suit. So far as I know, he has no claim against me," Ponzi told the reporter. "The only reason I can see for the suit is a desire to get some money out of me. If Mr. Daniels has a just claim he will have no difficulty in getting it satisfied because I have got two million dollars over and above all claims of investors against me in this country. This does not include funds in foreign lands."

He rebuffed a suggestion that the lawsuit might hurt his business, turning the question to his advantage. "Anybody who withdraws funds to his credit only increases my profits. At the beginning, when I was trying to establish foreign connections and working out my idea, I needed capital and was forced to depend upon the public for assistance. Happily, my own private fortune is now sufficient to meet all demands upon the business for ready money."

Privately, though, Ponzi knew he needed to take the lawsuit seriously. For one thing, it was sure to trigger additional scrutiny from postal officials and, quite possibly, law-enforcement authorities. Ponzi needed a good lawyer, and he looked no further than the investor list of the Securities Exchange Company. Frank Leveroni had arrived in Boston from Genoa at age four and had graduated from Harvard and Boston University Law School. A handsome man, forty years old, with an aquiline nose and a high forehead, Leveroni ran his own law firm and served as the first Italian-born judge in Massachusetts, sitting part-time on the bench in juvenile court. What really impressed Ponzi was that Leveroni had invested five thousand dollars during two weeks in June. With a wife and five young daughters to support, Leveroni believed he had found a sure thing.

Although confident he could beat Daniels in court if the suit came to trial, Ponzi instructed Leveroni to open settlement talks with the furniture dealer. Ponzi could not afford to let it distract him from the business at hand, nor could he allow his bank accounts to remain frozen indefinitely. He might need that money to carry out one of his planned switches to a legitimate business. Paying Daniels to go away might be worth it. At first they were miles apart; Daniels was holding out for a bigger payday than Ponzi could stomach. But they kept talking.

In the meantime, Ponzi took the precaution of opening bank accounts in other people's names, to keep them out of reach of Daniels or anyone else. Sometimes the names were fictitious, such as his Lucy Martelli account at Hanover Trust, a name created by combining Lucy Meli's first name with her mother's maiden surname. As a further precaution before Daniels's attachment took effect, Ponzi emptied his account at the Cosmopolitan Trust Company, taking home $283,710.62.

He could rebuild the account later; at the moment, he wanted piles of cash on hand.

Ponzi knew the *Post* story would prompt some depositors to demand refunds out of fear that the lawsuit would destroy the Securities Exchange Company and swallow their investments with it. Indeed, the story ignited a two-day "run," as several thousand nervous investors asked for their original deposits back, forfeiting the 50 percent interest. Ponzi gladly obliged; the result was addition by subtraction. Each refund demonstrated that he was a man of his word, prompting even more investors in the days that followed. By mid-July, Ponzi was taking in more than a million dollars in new investments a week. Each day was better than the one before.

The story about Daniels's suit piqued the interest of Richard Grozier. He was especially troubled when he learned that Ponzi's investors included scores of *Post* employees, most notably the low-wage workers in the pressroom. On one of his regular tours through the building, Grozier stopped at the desk of his city editor, Edward J. Dunn, whose soft features and sun-deprived skin masked the steel spine of a no-nonsense newsman. A Boston native, Dunn had joined the *Post* eighteen years earlier, in 1902, and had served as a City Hall and State House reporter, a war correspondent, and a political editor before being named city editor in 1917.

Just as Richard Grozier had abruptly taken over for his stricken father, the forty-year-old Dunn was newly in control of the day-to-day news operations, having stepped in during the summertime absence of managing editor Clifton Carberry. Grozier told Dunn he was intrigued by the story of the lawsuit against this Ponzi fellow. How could anyone promise 50 percent profits in forty-five days? If Grozier was correct in his doubts, *Post* readers and employees were headed for a painful fall. He instructed Dunn to deploy a couple of reporters to look more closely at Ponzi.

Grozier and Dunn both knew they needed to be careful. Four

months earlier, when Edwin Grozier had bet the paper against Curley, he had done so with confidence, knowing that no proof existed showing he had sold out the cause of Irish independence. Now, with Edwin Grozier still hospitalized and unable to speak, his son, the untested young acting publisher, was taking a far greater risk. Richard Grozier had just told his city editor to investigate a private businessman, one with seemingly limitless resources and a thriving company to protect. If the paper damaged his reputation with unsupported charges, Ponzi might replace the Grozier family as owner of the *Boston Post*.

Recognizing the danger, Grozier had one more message for Dunn: Don't worry about the consequences. I'll take full responsibility if anything goes wrong.

Daniels's lawsuit made Ponzi realize he could wait no longer to transform the Securities Exchange Company into a legitimately profitable business. He was supremely confident he could do just that, having spent untold hours hatching moneymaking ideas. Now he had the distinct advantage of wheelbarrowloads of cash lined up behind him, and one thing Ponzi believed above all else was that money made money.

One approach might have been to sell the Securities Exchange Company to one of the many suitors who had begun showing up at 27 School Street. Once the deal was done, he could disappear to Italy with the money. But that was never Ponzi's style. Much more creative ideas were percolating, all of them seemingly grounded in reality yet each more fantastic than the next.

Over their initial dinner at the Copley Plaza, Ponzi's new financial manager, Roberto de Masellis, had suggested that Ponzi consider going into the banking business. Ponzi had taken a step in that direction with his investment in the Hanover Trust Company, but now he hoped to go further. He imagined turning Hanover Trust from a sleepy, midsized bank into a financial powerhouse, which in turn would make his nearly 40 percent ownership of the bank soar in value. The first step, he thought, would be to sap the deposits of other banks and draw them to Hanover Trust. Once the bank had more deposits, it could make more and larger loans, which would burnish its balance sheet and ratchet up the stock price.

First, Ponzi planned a contest with a monthly prize of one thousand dollars to the person who brought the most new business to the bank. To determine a winner, Ponzi would print up thousands of what he called "introduction cards," each one with spaces for the signatures of a contestant and a new depositor. A card would be turned in whenever a new account was opened, and the contestant with the most cards at the end of each month would win the prize. To get the ball rolling, Ponzi hung a sign outlining the contest on a wall at the Securities Exchange Company office. At about the same time, he quietly paid his debt to Fidelity Trust, settling the lawsuit the bank had filed against him in March and for the moment putting himself on good terms with Boston's banking community.

A second piece of his plan involved increasing Hanover's attractiveness to depositors and shareholders by creating a power- and profit-sharing program. It was a radical notion, one that Ponzi knew would be branded a Socialist plot by Brahmin bankers and their supporters.

The third element of Ponzi's plan was to monitor which banks lost the most depositors and, as a result, suffered the steepest decline in stock price. Ponzi would then buy large blocks of those banks' stock at a rock-bottom price, replenish the banks' vaults with deposits of his own, and reap the benefits when the stock price rose again.

As usual, Ponzi ignored or understated the obstacles. "There was absolutely nothing to it. It was a cinch," he believed with his trademark optimism. In his mind, his quick-and-easy realignment of Boston's entire banking structure represented "an opportunity to switch, gradually, from the coupons venture into a more conservative line of business. . . . To get out from under all together, and retire a multimillionaire, in a non-distant future."

An even more elaborate scheme sprang to Ponzi's mind when he saw an announcement that the United States government was seeking bidders for several thousand mothballed freight and passenger ships that had been built during the Great War and declared surplus afterward. By Ponzi's calculations, the ships were worth $2 billion but could be had for the bargain price of $200 million. Ponzi figured he could raise the money within a month simply by expanding the Securities Exchange Company from the Northeast to the entire nation.

The bigger challenge, he thought, was figuring out how to make a profit from a fleet of three thousand ships. He lay awake for several nights before latching onto an ingenious, if impossibly impractical idea. Ponzi figured the ships would actually cost him $320 million— the $200 million price tag, plus $100 million for the 50 percent interest on the money he was "borrowing" from investors, plus $20 million in commissions to the agents who collected the initial $200 million.

To repay that sum, he would form two companies, the Charles Ponzi Steamship Company, which would own the fleet, and the International Shipping & Mercantile Company, which would lease and operate the ships. He envisioned a complicated series of stock sales, bond offerings, equity swaps, and lease deals that would take a team of accountants years to untangle. The immediate result would be the paying off of all debts of the Securities Exchange Company, at which point Ponzi would abandon the postal coupon business forever. He would then spend a decade as an unimaginably rich shipping magnate with a decidedly patriotic bent. The passenger ships, he declared, would double as "floating sample rooms for American products." They would travel from port to port, their holds brimming with huge cargoes of made-in-America goods. Each time the ships dropped anchor, teams of salesmen would burst forth onto foreign soil and drag local merchants aboard. The salesmen would expertly display their wares and offer immediate delivery of goods from the below-decks warehouse.

As unlikely as it might have seemed, Ponzi was certain he could pull it off, as long as he had enough time.

Rerouting his financial path could wait, though, as Ponzi spent the morning of July 9 anxiously anticipating the arrival of his mother. After canceling his trip with Rose to Italy, Ponzi had wired Imelde Ponzi money to buy two first-class tickets aboard the S.S. *Cretic,* an immense White Star liner previously known as the *Mayflower.* One ticket was for his sixty-nine-year-old mother and the other was for Elena Omati, her twenty-nine-year-old maid. The ship had left Naples for Boston on June 25, and the elder Mrs. Ponzi and her helper were in good company for the two-week trip; merchants, a painter, and an Italian diplomat to Venezuela were among their fellow first-class passengers.

When he arrived at the Boston pier, Ponzi was as giddy as a child on his birthday. He bubbled with unrestrained joy when he caught sight of the black-hulled ship, as long as two football fields end to end, with four soaring masts and a single funnel jutting into the blue summer sky. During his rootless years in America and Canada he had often wondered whether he would see his mother again, whether he would overcome the shame of his dissolute college days and live up to her dreams of "castles in the air." Now he had done it. He was rich and she was steaming into Boston. Ponzi could not wait a minute more than necessary to see her.

Spreading cash and charm, Ponzi enlisted the help of an immigration official named Joseph Merenda, a fellow Italian immigrant who happened to be a small investor in the Securities Exchange Company. Together they boarded a tugboat that Ponzi hired on the spot to motor him across Boston Harbor to the quarantine building where *Cretic* passengers were undergoing immigration inspections. While waiting to see his mother, Ponzi learned that the ship's steerage passengers were suffering terribly from the summer fortnight at sea. Adding to their troubles, some had arrived penniless. Remembering his own landing with little more than two dollars and a gnawing hunger, Ponzi opened his wallet, handed out cash to help as many as he could, and sent for sandwiches and drinks.

Then he caught sight of Imelde Ponzi, a tiny, regal woman with a halo of white hair and an Italian widow's black wardrobe. Ponzi rushed to embrace her. Tears streamed down his face. He held his mother tight in his arms. Merenda's heart swelled as he witnessed the reunion.

"It is seventeen years since I have seen you," the old woman told her son.

"Yes," Ponzi answered through his tears, "but we shall never part again." He rushed his mother and her maid home to Lexington, to meet Rose and to coddle the elder Mrs. Ponzi with comforts in their new house.

At that moment, Merenda set aside lingering doubts about the promise of 50 percent profits in forty-five days. He had invested only two hundred dollars to date, but now he resolved to deposit as much as he could with Ponzi. As he later told the financier: "I made up my mind that a man doing a criminal business could not bring his mother over from Italy after seventeen years with the possibility of his going to jail. And when I saw you with tears in your eyes and heard the things you planned for her, that put the lock on my belief that your business was all right."

Merenda not only invested for himself, he bought a Ponzi note for his mother.

Others remained dubious.

After quashing the police strike in the fall of 1919, Massachusetts Governor Calvin Coolidge had turned his attention to what he believed was a rot undermining the roots of the state's financial system. Coolidge had grown concerned that a cozy relationship between state banking officials and the bankers they were supposed to regulate was inviting a crisis. Moreover, Coolidge thought his banking commis-

sioner, the estimable Augustus L. Thorndike, the scion of an old
Brahmin family, was more comfortable dining with bankers than
overseeing them. When Thorndike's term ended in March 1920,
Coolidge decided to fill the five-thousand-dollar-a-year job with a
candidate far from the cloistered world of Boston finance and politics.
He chose a rural Republican in his own image: Joseph C. Allen.

At forty-two, Allen was tall and trim, with pince-nez glasses
perched on a handsome nose, a downturned mouth, and stiff, high
collars poking from pinstriped suits. Newly wed to a Smith College
graduate fourteen years his junior, Allen was a prominent banker and
civic leader in Springfield, ninety miles west of Boston. Born in New
York, he had moved to western Massachusetts as a boy and had begun
his banking career as a messenger for the Second National Bank of
Springfield. He'd risen through the ranks of several banks to become
vice president of the Union Trust Company, the job he held when
Coolidge tapped him. Allen also served on the Springfield City
Council and had run for mayor of the small city in 1912. But he was a
banker, not a politician, and the glad-handing necessary to win votes
was not his style. In the messy world of Massachusetts politics, Allen
was a misfit, a man one reporter described as "quiet, dignified, immaculate, kind." He liked nothing more than a perfectly clean office
with "never a speck of dust on his desk; never a piece of paper mis-
placed," the reporter found. The closest thing Allen had to a vice was
a lousy golf game. To no one's surprise, he failed to win the Republican mayoral nomination and returned to the more quantifiable world
of profit and loss. Which made him all the more attractive to
Coolidge. The governor was looking for a banking commissioner
without baggage, someone with a pillar-of-the-community résumé
and physical and psychological distance from Boston. Joseph Allen fit
the bill.

Early in his tenure as bank commissioner, Allen realized that whatever good work he did might be undermined without a cordial relationship with the newspapers covering his agency. He knew he would
never be one of the fast-talking, tip-dropping, back-slapping political

animals who stalked the marble corridors of the gold-domed State House atop Beacon Hill. So he took the opposite tack. He opened his office to the newspapermen who covered the business world and told them plainly, "I am new to this game. I am not used to being interviewed and quoted. You all can probably take advantage of me. I am asking you to help me in my job, and not hinder me. I am asking you to help the public. What I give the press will be first carefully prepared in my office. I shall then read it to you experienced men and ask whether you think it is best to publish." It was a frank admission, one that might have opened the out-of-towner to criticism or doubt among hard-bitten Boston reporters. Instead, his candor endeared him to them, and for the most part they gave him a chance to prove whether he could rein in mismanaged banks and protect depositors in the process.

Just as he was getting comfortable in office, Allen began to hear word of the Securities Exchange Company. Ponzi's enterprise was not a bank, but the *Post* story about Daniels's million-dollar lawsuit mentioned that the business was based on currency speculation. Allen wondered whether the public or the banks he regulated might be at risk from a fast-money operator. Not certain of his boundaries, Allen called for an opinion from the state's chief law-enforcement officer, Attorney General J. Weston Allen.

The two Allens were unrelated. The attorney general had a classic Boston pedigree that the bank commissioner lacked. J. Weston Allen was descended from two *Mayflower* passengers, was the son of a former editor of the *Boston Advertiser,* and held degrees from Yale University and Harvard Law School. For more than a decade he had headed a prominent Boston law firm; then he'd served two terms in the Massachusetts legislature before becoming attorney general. He considered the job a stepping-stone to the governor's office and perhaps beyond. At forty-eight he was grim-faced and balding, with a wary eye toward anyone stepping onto his political or prosecutorial turf. He answered the bank commissioner's inquiry about Ponzi with a curt reply: Keep out.

Joseph Allen backed off, but only briefly. On July 15, Hanover Trust officials reported, as required, that they had completed their sale of new stock. Checking around, Joseph Allen learned that most of the new shares had gone to Ponzi, and that was unquestionably within his realm. He called the attorney general's office a second time, this time not to ask permission but, as a courtesy, to announce his plans to investigate Charles Ponzi, his Securities Exchange Company, and his ties to Hanover Trust. The two Allens agreed that the attorney general's office should remain involved, and J. Weston Allen assigned two assistant attorneys general, Albert Hurwitz and Edwin Abbott Jr., to work with the bank commissioner. Their first step was to meet Ponzi.

An invitation was sent to 27 School Street asking Ponzi to attend a meeting at the State House with Bank Commissioner Joseph Allen, the two assistant attorneys general, and a vice president of a Boston bank brought in as an expert on foreign exchange and currency transactions. Ponzi knew that Allen could not compel him to attend, but his pride got the better of him. "I couldn't very well stay away and let him think that I was afraid," he said later. "After all, his questions were not apt to embarrass me. What he didn't know about coupons and foreign exchange would have filled a good-sized library."

Ponzi walked into Allen's well-appointed State House office, exchanged cordial greetings, and was thoroughly unimpressed. He thought the bank commissioner underestimated him, viewing him the way "a cannibal greets a missionary." Ponzi imagined Allen smacking his lips in anticipation of serving him on a platter to Boston's established financial and political powers.

Ponzi sat down and calmly gave his standard speech about International Reply Coupons. He wheedled the foreign exchange expert into endorsing the feasibility of exploiting fluctuating exchange rates with fixed-price coupons. The only questions Ponzi declined to discuss were the identities of his foreign agents and the countries where they bought and exchanged coupons. "I was almost ashamed to match wits with them," he said later. "It was like stealing candy from a baby.

But they were the challengers. And I couldn't very well let them get away with their lollypops."

Hurwitz, the assistant attorney general, found himself enjoying Ponzi's company. Like Ponzi, Hurwitz was an immigrant and an outsider, a Russian Jew who had arrived in the United States in 1892, when he was eight years old. Not much taller than Ponzi, with a long face, prominent nose and jaw, and deep-set eyes, he had years earlier made a brief foray into Boston's Brahmin- and Irish-dominated world of politics. In 1905, he'd run for the Common Council when he was a twenty-one-year-old law student at Boston University. He had run as a Republican and been thoroughly trounced.

Sitting in the bank commissioner's office, Hurwitz respected the confidence and ease with which Ponzi carried himself, the touches of humor in his answers. He took note of Ponzi's impeccable fashion sense, admiring his custom-tailored suit, the sparkling jeweled pin in his tie, and the soft gray spats on his glossy shoes. Ponzi completed the look of success with a gold-tipped cane in one hand and soft gloves in the other. The assistant attorney general was especially drawn to Ponzi's dark eyes, the way they danced as he spoke, seducing his listeners with what Hurwitz considered "a romantic look."

Yet by the end of their talk, Hurwitz detected a note of condescension in Ponzi, a bit of cockiness he found less becoming. At one point, Hurwitz mildly challenged Ponzi, expressing doubt that it was possible to turn large-scale profits from postal coupons. Ponzi retorted that Boston police officers who had held similar doubts had grown so confident that they'd become frequent and successful investors. Ponzi then urged Hurwitz to deposit some of his own money, even offering a loan to get the assistant attorney general started in the business of 50 percent profits. Hurwitz declined, telling Ponzi he was investigating, not investing.

After Ponzi left, the three state officials and the banker agreed that Ponzi's business certainly sounded plausible, though Albert Hurwitz and Joseph Allen remained skeptical. By contrast, the banker and Abbott, the other assistant attorney general, declared they were satisfied that Ponzi was a legitimate businessman, solvent, and on the level. Abbott was so persuaded that he proposed a bet: If their investigation showed that Ponzi was a fraud, Abbott would buy Hurwitz dinner. If Ponzi lived up to his claims, the meal was on Hurwitz. Unknown to Hurwitz, Abbott expressed his confidence to Ponzi, privately mentioning that he might drop by School Street with some money to invest.

A heat wave settled over Boston during the days after the State House meeting, but the sweltering temperatures did nothing to thin the ranks of men in suits and women in long dresses who lined up outside 27 School Street. Now that the Securities Exchange Company had passed the million-dollar-a-week mark, the only question seemed to be how long it would take for Ponzi to surpass two million a week.

Rising along with the mercury was the intensity of the bank commissioner's investigation. Allen's staff of bank examiners focused first on the banks where Ponzi maintained large accounts, particularly Tremont Trust and Hanover Trust. The two were also natural targets because in recent weeks Ponzi had often mentioned them as references to potential investors who questioned his solvency.

Ponzi had never gotten along well with Simon Swig, who ran Tremont Trust as its vice president and had installed his son as treasurer. Swig looked like a dour European aristocrat, with a thick mustache and a dimple in his square chin. He lived like one, too, in a palatial home on Humboldt Avenue in the city's Roxbury section, with a live-in Irish maid and a chauffeur. Since arriving in Boston from Lithuania as a teenager in 1880, the fifty-four-year-old Swig had risen from a peddler to a wealthy bank officer. Along the way, he had alienated a large portion of the financial establishment by persuading state lawmakers to pass legislation that helped midsized banks like his compete with the entrenched financial powerhouses run by the Brahmins. At the same time, Swig had tended to ignore laws he did not like, for years making loans that were improper or downright illegal, running misleading advertisements in the newspapers, and issuing more than a half million dollars in loans, many of them dubious, to his own family. Swig's house was a prime example. In December 1919, he took a twenty-five-thousand-dollar mortgage from Tremont, repaid ten thousand dollars from the bank's own profits, and then never bothered to make payments on the remaining balance.

Ponzi thought Swig looked down on him because he was Italian, just as the Brahmins snubbed Swig because he was Jewish. "He was of the opinion that a Jew was better than a wop," Ponzi said. "I could not agree with him. In my own mind, nothing could be better than a wop. Except two wops." Some class-conscious Bostonians made no such distinctions, lumping Italians and Jews together as untouchables. "Whenever I gave the name of the Tremont Trust Company as a reference to some supercilious investor," Ponzi said, "I could read a message on his countenance: 'Birds of a feather.' And I would wince."

Swig winced, too, when state bank examiners inquired about his relationship with Ponzi, who, by mid-July, had more than $400,000 on deposit at Tremont Trust. Always dubious about Ponzi's claims, and increasingly uncomfortable with the added scrutiny from regulators, Swig wrote Ponzi a caustic letter on July 21. "If what we have heard about your plan of business is true, then certainly we do not care to accept your deposits, no matter how large they may be," Swig wrote. "And even if reports are untrue, we do not care to accept your future deposits because you have taken unfair advantage in using our name as you have. We therefore advise you that henceforth your deposits will not be accepted, and you will favor us by closing your account." Ponzi did as Swig asked, but he refused to take a Tremont bank check. He demanded the money in cash, just to give Swig a taste of his own medicine. Though Ponzi's account was closed, another $185,000 of his money remained at Tremont Trust, stuck there by the attachment filed by Daniels with his lawsuit.

With Ponzi the owner of so much stock in Hanover Trust, that bank's officers could not follow Swig's example even if they had wanted to. But Hanover president Henry Chmielinski and treasurer

William McNary, a former congressman who served as chairman of
the bank's board of directors, felt it essential to take precautions. Only
a month earlier, Ponzi had threatened to withdraw his deposits immediately, a potentially catastrophic event, and now the risk was far
greater. Lately, Ponzi's account at Hanover Trust had been rapidly rising, falling, and rising again. It fell when investors in the Securities
Exchange Company redeemed their Ponzi notes at 27 School Street,
then walked to the bank with checks written against Ponzi's Hanover
Trust account. It rose again when Ponzi deposited piles of cash from
his latest depositors. The cycle took place almost daily. But Hanover
Trust officials recognized that if Ponzi's income were interrupted, the
danger existed that withdrawals would greatly exceed deposits, and
Ponzi's account would be hugely overdrawn. Unless his account were
quickly replenished, Hanover Trust would likely collapse, putting the
bank's officers and depositors at risk of ruin.

On July 22, with bank examiners breathing down their necks,
Chmielinski and McNary insisted that Ponzi provide Hanover with
enough security to hold the regulators at bay and guard the bank
against the roller-coaster shifts in his account. Ponzi agreed to put $1.5
million in a thirty-day certificate of deposit, enough to withstand any
anticipated run of withdrawals on his account. Although it satisfied
the bankers, Ponzi realized it put him in a tight spot, tying up a large
amount of cash for a minimum of thirty days at the same time the lawsuit by Daniels had frozen some of his other bank accounts. It was
more impetus for him to hasten his plan to get out of the faux-coupon
business and into something more tangible and sustainable.

Ponzi took the first step on July 23 by hiring publicity man William
McMasters, a former *Boston Post* reporter who had come recom-
mended by Ponzi's lawyer, Frank Leveroni. McMasters had earned his
stripes by handling publicity for the mayoral campaigns of John
"Honey Fitz" Fitzgerald and James Michael Curley, as well as the 1918
governor's race for Calvin Coolidge. McMasters's first job for Ponzi
was to promote the financier's dream of becoming a banking magnate,
the next J. P. Morgan. At a starting salary of a hundred dollars a

week—fifty less than he had asked for—McMasters's first move was to place advertisements promoting Ponzi's contest to increase business at Hanover Trust and his idea to launch a string of banks that would share profits with depositors.

But Ponzi, and by extension McMasters, was quickly swept up in more urgent business. That same day, a *Boston Post* reporter dropped by to follow up on the story about Daniels's lawsuit. He spent the day at 27 School Street, and then Ponzi invited him home to Lexington. The remarkable result appeared in the paper the next day, July 24, 1920:

DOUBLES THE MONEY WITHIN THREE MONTHS

50 Per Cent Interest Paid in 45 Days by Ponzi— Has Thousands of Investors

Deals in International Coupons Taking Advantage of Low Rates of Exchange

A proposition fathered by Charles Ponzi, as head of the Securities Exchange Company at 27 School Street, where one may get 50 per cent in 45 days, 100 percent in 90 days, on any amount invested, is causing interest throughout Boston.

Yesterday his offices were crowded with people trying to loan him money on his personal note.

The proposition has been in operation for nine or ten months, rolling up great wealth for the man behind it and rolling up much money for the thousands of men and women who are tumbling over themselves to entrust him with their money on no other security than his personal note, and the authorities have not been able to discover a single illegal thing about it.

Ponzi, starting last October or November with hardly a "shoestring," so to speak, is today rated as worth $8,500,000— purchaser of business blocks, trust companies, estates, and motor cars.

His investors—and they run the gamut of society, rich men
and women, poor men and women, unknown and prominent—have seen their money doubled, trebled, quadrupled.

The story went on merrily from there, liberally and generously quoting Ponzi recounting the Horatio Alger version of his life, describing
the vague outlines and enormous success of his business, marveling at
his Lexington home, and detailing the acquiescence to date of federal,
state, and local prosecutors. Unaware of the bank commissioner's interest, the *Post* made no mention of Joseph C. Allen.

Everything in Ponzi's life changed the moment the first newsboy
tucked a stack of fresh-printed papers under his arm, stepped onto
Washington Street, and yelled with his Boston accent, "*Post* heah!"

PART THREE

Bank Commissioner
Joseph C. Allen
The Boston Globe

Attorney General
J. Weston Allen
The Boston Globe

Financial journalist
Clarence Barron
The Boston Globe

United States
District Attorney
Daniel J. Gallagher
The Boston Globe

Suffolk County
District Attorney
Joseph Pelletier
The Boston Globe

CHAPTER TWELVE

"MONEY MADNESS"

When the crowd drawn to 27 School Street by the *Post* story had gone home, Ponzi returned to Lexington to share the news of the day with Rose. There was plenty to tell. The phone was ringing ceaselessly with well-wishers and would-be investors hoping for a moment of the great man's time.

Meanwhile, the reporters and editors at the *Post* were working well into the night preparing a story to run the next day, Sunday, July 25. The magnitude of what was happening around the corner from the newspaper's offices had caught Grozier, Dunn, and their reporters off guard. For a journalist, the only things worse than being surprised are being scooped and being wrong, and the *Post* might soon experience both. The city's other papers might be preparing follow-up stories of their own, and one might develop information significant enough about Ponzi's operations, negative or positive, to wrest front-runner status from the *Post*. The clear goal for Grozier and Dunn was to remain in control of the Ponzi story without over-reaching.

To strike that balance, the story in the *Boston Sunday Post* was built around a straightforward account of the excitement at the Securities Exchange Company on Saturday. It recounted the opening of the rival business down the hall that claimed to match Ponzi's rate of return; the ballyhoo man trying to lure away Ponzi's customers; Ponzi's anger at his competitors; and the excitement of his investors. The headline, in the lead position on the top right side of the page, was more than twice the size of the one on Saturday:

PONZI HAS A RIVAL NEXT DOOR TO HIM

The headline spanned five of the eight columns across the top of page 1 and was accompanied by five photographs: a portrait of Rose and Imelde Ponzi outside the Lexington home on page 1, and on an inside page photos of the home itself, Ponzi alighting from his Locomobile with an armed guard, a "head shot" of Ponzi, and the scene at 27 School Street.

Beyond the report of what had happened a day earlier, from the crowds to Ponzi's summoning of police against the rival Old Colony Foreign Exchange Company, the Sunday story dripped with skepticism. Ominously for Ponzi, it began with the report that a federal investigation "is being pushed with vigor." The story added no specifics but breathlessly told readers that Boston's federal prosecutor, United States District Attorney Daniel J. Gallagher, "has set in motion all the government machinery to learn whether Ponzi is telling the truth when he asserts that he is able to pay such enormous profits by juggling of International Reply Coupons in Europe."

But if the *Post* wanted its readers to doubt claims that seemed to be too good to be true, the paper was sending a very mixed message. A few pages past the report on Ponzi's business appeared the headline TO MAKE OLD WOMEN YOUNG. The story described the amazing work of Dr. Serge Veronoff and his wife and assistant, Madame Evelyn

Veronoff, who had recently arrived in America from Paris to promote the good doctor's success in implanting young chimpanzee glands in aged humans "to make them vigorous and hale again." The reporter, Marguerite Mooers Marshall, guilelessly asked, "Will women be made young in the sense of recovering the beauty and charm of youth, of banishing their wrinkles and gray hair?" Madame Veronoff answered: "It is not inconceivable that fresh, lovely facial tissues should take the place of those that are worn and lined—that even the color of the hair should be changed." Marshall was sold. "It will be a wonderful thing for women!" she wrote.

Meanwhile, the other Boston papers were silent about Ponzi on Sunday. The closest any of them came was an item buried in the *Boston Sunday Herald* about the finances of Lawrence millworkers that blandly mentioned how some put their money "in various other forms of 'get-rich-quick' speculation that promises a maximum of return in a minimum of days." The *Herald,* the *Globe,* and Boston's other papers were paying more attention to an attempt to raise bail for Bartolomeo Vanzetti and the sensational murder trial of dashing undertaker Byron M. Pettibone, accused of poisoning his wife with strychnine so that he could marry a beautiful nurse.

Even though Ponzi remained overlooked by the other papers, the combined effect of back-to-back page 1 stories in the *Post* was to instantly make him the most talked-about, sought-after man in New England. People began calling Ponzi "a wizard of finance." Like most overnight sensations, he had spent decades laying the groundwork for his triumph, and now he wanted to milk it for all it was worth. He would get no rest this Sunday, and that was fine with him.

The telephone began ringing at daybreak. Western Union delivery boys—"Telegram for Mr. Ponzi!"—soon followed. Ponzi basked in the attention: "Every one of them anxious to get on the right side of me. Because I was a multimillionaire. I received more congratulations than a president-elect!" The *Post* photo of Ponzi's house was accompanied by a caption placing it on Slocum Road, so the quiet lane became a destination for a steady stream of motorists taking Sunday drives in the country.

A *Post* reporter dropped by the house and ran into Ponzi's lawyer, Judge Frank Leveroni.

"As a judge of the Juvenile Court," the reporter asked, "do you think it a proper thing for a concern of that kind to accept loans from fourteen-year-old boys?" It was a clear reference to Frank Thomas, the errand boy in short pants who had praised Ponzi to a *Post* reporter a day earlier on his way to invest ten dollars.

"Mr. Ponzi," Leveroni replied, "has given me assurance that his promises to pay are good. I believe him, and on that score I consider it perfectly proper for him to accept loans tendered by anyone."

Two men came to the house with a plea: "Will you pose for us?" They were movie men certain that the public would clamor to see newsreel footage of the elegant financier, his family, and their gracious home. Ponzi was only too happy to oblige. He, Rose, and his mother, dressed in their Sunday best, ambled back and forth in front of the house while the cameraman shot several hundred feet of film.

Out of view of the camera, Ponzi and Leveroni strategized on how best to respond to the threat posed by Ponzi's imitator, the Old Colony Foreign Exchange Company. Stealing Ponzi's customers by opening an office down the hall at 27 School Street was bad enough, but Ponzi's real fear was that his rival would bring additional heat down upon him just as he was racing to go legitimate. And if government officials took a hard look at the men behind Old Colony, "none of them had either the courage or the ability to hold their own in a match of wits. They would have been exposed in no time." Ponzi could not tell Leveroni or anyone else how he knew, but he was certain the outfit was a rob-Peter-to-pay-Paul scam. That meant Old Colony "constituted for me a greater menace than all of the government agencies put together."

To himself, Ponzi rationalized the difference between his Securities Exchange Company and copycat upstarts: "Perhaps my activities were not entirely within the law," he allowed. "But my intent was honest. I was in a critical position and I had fallen into it without any intention to do wrong. Now that I was in it, I was trying my hardest to pull myself out of it, without hurting my investors. The means I was resorting to, in order to swim out of the hole, might not have been sound and might not have been entirely legitimate. But I felt that the end justified the means, and the end, my purpose, was not dishonest."

He had been paying agents of the Pinkerton National Detective Agency to provide security for himself and his business. Now he had a new job for the agency's Boston manager: Find out all you can about every man and woman associated with Old Colony. "Follow them everywhere—to China, if necessary," he ordered. "Spare no expense. I want you to land those people in jail." He instructed the agents to send one copy of their findings to him and another to the county prosecutor, District Attorney Joseph Pelletier. Ponzi was angling for a two-bank shot to eliminate the threat: quickly knocking Old Colony out of business while positioning himself as a friend of justice.

Ponzi also spent part of the day making plans to open a new Boston office. The hordes on Saturday convinced him that he had outgrown 27 School Street, so he made arrangements to move to a second-floor office next door to Hanover Trust on Washington Street, even closer to the *Post* building.

When he crawled into bed alongside Rose that night, Ponzi was exhausted. Afterward, he remarked: "That Sunday was the busiest day in all my life I ever put in doing nothing!"

While one *Post* reporter spent part of Sunday in Lexington watching Ponzi soak up the limelight, other *Post* reporters were working overtime trying to nail him. Boston's other newspapers were still ignoring the story, so Richard Grozier and city editor Eddie Dunn sought to press their paper's advantage—but carefully. One step was to shore up the Ponzi reporting staff. Joining P. A. Santosuosso was Herbert L. Baldwin, a bookish Harvard graduate selected for his knack with financial stories and features. The previous Saturday, Baldwin had written a lively profile of one Lucius Dodge, a man who had meticulously recorded nearly every penny he had spent during the previous thirty years.

The next step was to advance the story. But it was Sunday, and nothing much was happening beyond the commotion at Ponzi's house. The Securities Exchange office was closed, as were the government offices managing the investigations. Not wanting to lose momentum, the *Post* staff engaged in the time-honored journalism practice of consulting an outside expert. They did not have to look far.

Clarence Walker Barron was a Bostonian who, as the *Post* put it, was "recognized internationally as among the foremost financial authorities of the world." At sixty-five, Barron was called "the father of American financial journalism." Abundantly bearded, with bright blue eyes, and carrying 330 pounds on a five-foot-five frame, Barron looked like a cross between a sea captain and Saint Nicholas. Born in the city's North End in a stone house covered with vines and overrun with cats, he was the son of "Honest Henry Barron," a teamster who worked at the wharves and warehouses of Commercial Street. Some of his earliest memories were of tugging at the dress of his mother, Elana, as she stood at the door of their house talking to peddlers and tradesmen about President Abraham Lincoln, slavery, and the latest news. By fifteen, he had resolved to become a newspaperman and had taught himself stenography, which he put to use with a temporary job on the *Boston Daily News.* By twenty-one he had found work at the *Evening Transcript,* where he gravitated to financial reporting and soon inaugurated the paper's financial section, which he boasted was responsible for increasing circulation by 15 percent.

In 1887, at thirty-two, he founded the *Boston News Bureau,* having concluded that Boston's State Street, at the time a rival to New York's Wall Street, needed financial news delivered more often than once with the morning papers and once with the evening papers. For the exorbitant sum of a dollar a day, Barron promised the city's business elite that he would provide them with news as fast as he could report it, printing his stories himself on a hand-fed press in a basement office, then dispatching two messenger boys to deliver the goods. Barron was a gifted writer and an intrepid reporter. His rough-printed handbills were soon essential reading for the bankers, brokers, and business leaders of Boston. In 1902 he expanded to New York by buying control of the *Wall Street Journal* and its parent, Dow Jones & Company.

His success allowed him to keep a permanently reserved suite at the Ritz-Carlton in New York and to buy a grand town house on Beacon Street with views of the Charles River, a yacht named the *Hourless,* and a huge, seaside country home he called "The Oaks" in the South Shore town of Cohasset. He also was a gentleman farmer, raising prized Guernsey cows on a perfect swath of pasture and willingly selling their milk at a loss to nourish Boston's sick children.

A demanding taskmaster, thorough in his reporting, he was unafraid to wade into unpopular territory if he considered something unjust. This was the same Barron who had successfully pleaded the case of Ponzi's old Atlanta prison mate Charles Morse, the "Ice King." Nevertheless, Barron would caution his reporters, "If you must fight, pick only worthy adversaries." He instantly placed Ponzi in that category: Invited by the *Post* to give his opinion of Ponzi's business, Barron emptied both barrels.

"No man of wide financial or investment experience would look twice at a proposition to take his money upon a simple promise to pay it back with a 50 percent increase in three months," Barron said. He zeroed in on *Post* stories from that morning and the day before that said Ponzi had placed his profits from the enterprise in bank stocks, real estate, government bonds, and other conventional investments.

"If Mr. Rockefeller, the richest man in the world, should offer even 50 percent for money and be found to be putting his own money into 5 percent bonds, there would not be much money offered to him by financial people," Barron scoffed.

Barron understood fluctuating currency rates better than most, and he acknowledged that "there is now probably opportunity for people to deal in a small way under these postal arrangements so as to make money out of the fall in foreign exchange. But it is unreasonable to ask anybody to believe that any large amount of money can be so invested."

Even if it were possible, Barron said, it would be "immoral" because it would be profiting at the expense of a government. "When a man gets money from the government without performing a service," he said, "it is just the same as when a man takes money from an individual without performing a service for that money."

The *Post* printed Barron's attack the next morning, Monday, July 26, as its lead story at the top of the front page, under a headline more cautious than Barron's comments: QUESTIONS THE MOTIVE BEHIND PONZI SCHEME; the subhead added, "Barron Says Reply Coupon Plan Can Be Worked Only in Small Way." Still, the message the *Post* was sending its readers was clear, and the story began with the ominous claim that the foreign countries where Ponzi was supposedly operating were expected to report to United States authorities by the next day. But if Grozier, Dunn, and their staff expected pronouncements from the Zeus of State Street to dissuade Ponzi investors, they were in for a shock.

When Ponzi arrived at work on Monday morning, School Street was teeming with people desperate to trust their money to the Securities Exchange Company. It was as if Barron had endorsed the idea as foolproof. The street was so jammed police closed it to traffic; only two cars were allowed to pass: Ponzi's and Mayor Peters's.

A conga line of would-be investors, four abreast, snaked around the block from the City Hall Annex, up City Hall Avenue, down School Street, and into the Niles Building. Ponzi counted a half dozen mounted policemen in the street, then found more than a dozen others afoot keeping order inside the building. When Ponzi stepped from his Locomobile, he was greeted by three cheers. After the din died down, Ponzi called back, "And three groans for the *Post!*" The crowd answered with laughter and more cheers. Eddie Dunn, the *Post*'s city editor, had walked around the corner from his office to watch the spectacle. "Pigs being led to the slaughter," he said before returning to work.

Ponzi did not entirely disagree with Dunn, but he rhapsodized about what he saw and sensed: "The air was tense with ill-suppressed excitement. Hope and greed could be read in everybody's countenance, [or] guessed from the wads of money nervously clutched and waved by thousands of outstretched fists! Madness, money madness, the worst kind of madness, was reflected in everybody's eyes!"

Ponzi was at once exhilarated yet oddly repulsed. It struck him as an "exhibition of reckless mob psychology, entirely too susceptible to the fatal spell of misguided or perverted leadership!" But the notion that he was solely responsible for the "misguided or perverted leadership" was soon replaced by intense satisfaction.

"I was the realization of their dreams," he exulted, his grandeur growing with each new thought. "The idol. The hero. The master and arbiter of their lives. Of their hopes. Of their fortunes. The discoverer of wealth and happiness. The 'wizard' who would turn a pauper into a millionaire overnight!" He became intoxicated by the sight of the madding crowd and became certain it spelled the success he had always imagined: "Nothing could stand in the way of the most complete achievement of my ambitions. I had won!"

It was difficult to argue. By noon he would take in several hundred thousand dollars from all his branches—in his recollections, he rounded it off to one million. The new office he opened that morning around the corner on Washington Street collected more than ten thousand dollars an hour during its first three hours of operation. All told, in July alone Ponzi had taken in nearly $6.5 million, from more than twenty thousand investors, for an average of $325 each. In the remarkable seven months since it had opened for business, the Securities Exchange Company had amassed thirty thousand investors and $9.6 million. All Ponzi had to do to keep them satisfied was to pay them nearly $15 million in return.

But for all his excitement, all his satisfaction about his success, Ponzi knew it could not continue. That reality became inescapable after he waded through the crowds outside 27 School Street, walked around the corner to the Hanover Trust, and slipped into Henry Chmielinski's private office for a moment of peace. He had been so busy he had yet to read the morning papers. Ponzi picked up a copy of the *Post* and scanned Barron's comments—the first public criticism of him and his company. He was outraged and, although he would not show it, afraid. He knew the disparaging words of a financial legend would goad public officials into immediate action, even overreaction. "The situation was especially dangerous," Ponzi concluded, "because a man in public office generally runs amok the moment he becomes the target of printed criticism. Under the spur of what he believes to be a public opinion, he is apt to do almost anything. Except keep quiet."

"Within the day, within the next hour or so, some proceedings might be instituted against me," Ponzi told himself. "Without any doubt, I had a battle on my hands." His biggest fear was a court injunction that would shut him down immediately, short-circuiting his plans to switch businesses and go straight. With his trademark flair, Ponzi decided to go on the offensive and do what his enemies least expected.

Ponzi reached for the phone in Chmielinski's office and told the operator to call the United States district attorney, the Massachusetts attorney general, and the Suffolk County district attorney—the federal, state, and local authorities Ponzi considered his greatest threats. "Tell them I want to talk to them," Ponzi said. "Give me the calls as they come in."

First to answer was Dan Gallagher, the United States district attorney for Massachusetts. A graduate of Boston College, Gallagher was an undistinguished lawyer and local leader of the Knights of Columbus who had been appointed federal prosecutor by Woodrow Wilson.

He was forty-seven, married with four children, with an impassive, doughy face and wavy light-brown hair parted in the middle.

After exchanging pleasantries and mentioning the *Post* story, Ponzi got down to business. "It occurs to me," he said, "that it is rather unfair for them to criticize public officials for their alleged laxity. Personally, I resent the criticism because of its implications. I am going to demand a showdown. I am going to offer you and the other officials an opportunity to investigate my business. Would you be willing to join the attorney general and district attorney at a conference with me, in order that the details of such an investigation may be arranged?"

Gallagher immediately agreed—a target of inquiry inviting himself to a prosecutor's office was about as common as a mouse chasing a cat. Ponzi got the same positive response from Boston's county prosecutor, Suffolk District Attorney Joseph Pelletier, a friend and political ally of Gallagher's. Judging from his past history, Pelletier's most likely motive for agreeing to see Ponzi was to gauge whether he could squeeze money from the financier.

Pelletier was forty-eight, a lumbering ruin of a man, physically and morally. Like Gallagher, Pelletier was a Boston College grad—Pelletier had won the college debate prize a year before Gallagher did. Though his prosecutorial domain was limited to Boston and its surrounding suburbs, Pelletier occupied a small role on the national stage as supreme advocate of the Knights of Columbus. But Pelletier adhered to none of that organization's high-minded ideals. He had grown thoroughly corrupt during his decade as district attorney. The price he charged to quash an indictment varied by the crime, but his real specialty was blackmail and extortion. His favorite fleece was the sexual entrapment con known as the badger game. A wealthy man, usually married, would be lured into a compromising position with a comely young woman in a hotel room, apartment, or taxicab. Just when things were getting interesting, another man would burst in and claim to be a policeman, the woman's husband, her father, or a Justice Department agent, depending on which variation of the scheme had been decided upon. The wealthy pigeon would be informed that he faced public exposure, an alienation-of-affection suit, and criminal charges. He would be advised to hire a politically connected lawyer. That lawyer was none other than Daniel Coakley, who had proved so useful to former mayor James Michael Curley in blackmailing John "Honey Fitz" Fitzgerald in 1913. Coakley, who had served as Pelletier's campaign manager, also was an intermediary between Pelletier and Curley when the district attorney chose not to prosecute then-councilman Curley.

When the pants-around-the-ankles mark had paid Coakley an exorbitant retainer, Coakley would pretend to use his adroit legal mind and close relationship with District Attorney Pelletier to make all charges, lawsuits, despoiled women, and angry husbands miraculously disappear. Pelletier would take a cut of the money from Coakley, and the game would begin again with a new victim. Pelletier and Coakley had even enlisted Daniel Gallagher in at least one shakedown before Gallagher became a federal prosecutor. Coakley ran the same racket with the district attorney of a neighboring county. Devoted to Rose, Ponzi was immune to sexual shenanigans. But given what Pelletier had read about his millions in the *Post,* Ponzi might be the district attorney's biggest score yet.

While old pals Gallagher and Pelletier welcomed a joint conference, Attorney General J. Weston Allen declined. He preferred to go it alone rather than join forces with two Boston College buddies from the lower social and political classes. Ponzi decided to spend the rest of the day meeting with each one separately, starting with Pelletier and making Allen wait until last.

With his publicity man, William McMasters, in tow, Ponzi made the three-block walk from the bank, past City Hall, to the granite mountain that was the Suffolk County Courthouse on Pemberton Square. En route, Ponzi looked more like a man going to a cotillion than to the gallows, having dressed that morning as sharply as ever in white flannel trousers, silk shirt and socks, white bucks, and a blue coat with a handkerchief poking from the breast pocket. A large diamond pin glinted from the center of his cravat, and a silver-topped walking stick was tucked under his arm. He felt as good as he looked; he believed he was entering the darkness just before dawn. It would take every ounce of his intelligence, creativity, and moxie, not to mention split-second timing and preternatural coolness under fire. But where another man would have seen threats to his livelihood and freedom, Ponzi saw opportunity. This was the moment to begin making his big move.

Ponzi and McMasters entered the courthouse through the Great Hall, walking past marble statues and under a five-story vaulted ceiling adorned by frescoes. They entered Pelletier's office at eleven o'clock and made themselves comfortable. Pelletier began the meeting brusquely, criticizing Ponzi over a false rumor that Pelletier was a Ponzi investor to the tune of twenty thousand dollars. Given his nature, it was entirely possible that, for all his protests, Pelletier mentioned that figure to signal to Ponzi where the bidding for his services should begin. Ponzi made what McMasters considered a cringing apology, then shifted the conversation to say that he was happy to cooperate with authorities despite the fact that no criminal or regulatory complaints had been made against him or his business.

After explaining the postal reply coupon business, overlooking the fact that he was in no such business, Ponzi maneuvered Pelletier into an extraordinary agreement: He would open the books of the Securities Exchange Company to an auditor to be selected by Pelletier and the other authorities. The auditor would establish the extent of his liabilities, after which Ponzi's only requirement would be to prove that he had enough assets to meet them. If Ponzi could do that, he would be declared solvent and all investigations would cease. Ponzi still had not figured out how he would gather enough assets to offset his liabilities, but that would come later. At the moment, what he needed most was to stay in control of his business and buy some time.

Pelletier could see no downside to the deal—it would look as though he had the public interest at heart. He had no proof of wrong-doing by Ponzi, so his leverage was limited. This was probably the best deal Pelletier was going to get, and both he and Ponzi knew it.

Then Ponzi sprang an ingenious trap, a risky but potentially viable way for him to begin his transition out of the postal coupon business for good.

"Mr. District Attorney," Ponzi said, "it occurs to me just now that it might be an impossible task for an auditor to determine my liabili-ties, if I should continue to issue notes every day throughout the in-vestigation."

"I guess it would be, at that," Pelletier agreed, taking the bait. "Couldn't you stop issuing those notes?"

"I could," Ponzi said, as though the thought had never occurred to him. "But I haven't had the time to consider whether it would be ex-pedient for me to do so. However, the suggestion has an appealing fea-ture. Because it offers me the opportunity to spike certain insinuations which are being made by the press, I will do it."

"You will stop issuing notes?" Pelletier asked. "When?"

"Right now," Ponzi said. "May I use your phone?"

Ponzi called his School Street office, and Lucy Meli answered. He told her to post signs inside and outside their office announcing that, effective immediately, the Securities Exchange Company would take no new deposits but would continue redeeming matured notes with the promised 50 percent interest. Worried investors who did not want to wait for their notes to come due could receive refunds of their ini-tial investments, without interest. Ponzi instructed her to wire or phone the same instructions to all their agents and subagents.

From the courthouse Ponzi and McMasters took the short walk to 85 Devonshire Street, the offices of the United States district attorney. They spent the next two hours in Gallagher's ninth-floor office with the federal prosecutor and two postal inspectors who had been mak-ing regular visits to Ponzi's office. The conversation was largely a re-peat of the meeting with Pelletier, and Gallagher agreed to consider

Ponzi's offer to abide by the findings of a single auditor selected by investigators.

At one point, Gallagher asked why Ponzi had continued to invite the public to invest with him when he had already amassed a personal fortune.

"I don't need the money, but eventually I will need the people," Ponzi said.

Gallagher asked why and Ponzi said, "I don't know. It is possible I may want to run for office." Surprised, Gallagher asked Ponzi if he was a citizen. "Almost," Ponzi replied, when in fact he had never taken out naturalization papers, knowing that his past prison terms might well disqualify him.

Ponzi also spun for the federal prosecutor a tale of his plans for a profit-sharing banking system and hinted at his shipping company idea. He told Gallagher that he intended to make Boston the largest import and export center in the country. Ponzi mentioned casually that he anticipated profits of $100 million, though he added magnanimously that he intended to keep only $1 million for himself and to spend the rest on philanthropy.

Next they headed toward the State House to see Attorney General Allen, but on the way Ponzi wanted to look in on what was happening at 27 School Street. Word was just getting out that Ponzi would accept no new deposits. Scores of nervous investors had begun lining up to cash in their notes well before their maturity dates. Ponzi knew the storm of withdrawals would intensify by the next morning, after news of his stoppage was spread by reporters and by a notice he'd agreed to place on the front page of the *Post*. As a precaution, Ponzi called the Pinkertons to provide added crowd control.

The meeting with the attorney general and his staff took nearly three hours, with no resolution. He was not under oath, so Ponzi tossed out a welter of confusing, exaggerated figures and claims, from how he operated his business to which banks he used to move money in and out of the country, all of which a stenographer duly recorded. Through it all, J. Weston Allen remained uninterested in the auditing deal that Ponzi had made with Pelletier and was likely to be accepted by Gallagher. Instead, the attorney general seemed intent on pressing ahead with his own investigation.

When Ponzi left the State House, a clutch of reporters was waiting for him. No longer would the *Post* be alone on the Ponzi story; competition had arrived en masse. Official action had been taken, and now Ponzi and the Securities Exchange Company were fair game. Not only were reporters from several other Boston papers there, the news had also attracted stringers for out-of-town papers, including the *New York Times*. But if the reporters expected their prey to be frightened or flummoxed by his ordeal, they found the opposite. He merrily waved a slip of paper showing his $1.5 million certificate of deposit in the Hanover Trust Company and airily promised that he had more than enough money to meet all obligations.

"He was the same Ponzi of the day before," one reporter marveled, "just as debonair, just as dapper, just as smiling." When the reporters shouted questions to Ponzi, McMasters dragged him away.

"I can't say anything now—I'm hungry," Ponzi called breezily over his shoulder.

Ponzi poses for a newspaper photographer in his School Street office in August 1920.

CHAPTER THIRTEEN

"MASTER OF THE SITUATION"

The next morning, Tuesday, July 27, Ponzi spent the half-hour ride from Lexington to Boston assessing his situation and refining a daring survival plan he had hatched the night before.

Ponzi was certain that his move to suspend deposits and agree to an audit kept him in the driver's seat, "master of the situation," as he put it. Gallagher and Pelletier seemed willing to wait patiently for the results of the audit while congratulating themselves publicly on pressuring Ponzi to suspend his business. Of course, what they did not realize was that Ponzi welcomed the chance to stop taking investments, as each new dollar he accepted put him deeper into debt. Conversely, his debt fell with each early withdrawal: "Every time I refunded the principal," he gloated privately, "I would save the 50 percent interest."

Allen, the attorney general, was a bit of a rogue elephant, but Ponzi was not terribly worried. "He wasn't likely to make any trouble because, with two district attorneys on my side, he didn't have a chance either with the courts or the public." If the attorney general sought information or tried to demand an audit of his own, Ponzi could simply tell him to speak with the local and federal prosecutors. Ponzi gave no thought to the bank commissioner, believing that he had already allayed Joseph Allen's concerns.

The biggest problem on his mind was what to do when an independent auditor tallied his liabilities and he needed to prove he had enough assets to cover them. At the moment he was well short—Ponzi was dependent on new investors to pay old. When the music stopped, there would be no chair on which to sit.

Ponzi did some rough calculations. He had issued promissory notes for about $15 million. He was not quite sure, but he believed he had about $8 million at his disposal, which meant he was $7 million short. But that was not the whole story. He anticipated massive withdrawals in the coming days by frightened note holders, and he optimistically predicted that those withdrawals would wipe out as much as $4 million of liabilities. Better, but still $3 million in the red.

It was a high-stakes poker match, with millions more at stake than the card games he'd consistently lost during his college years in Rome and aboard the ship that had carried him to America. He was sunk, he reasoned, "unless I happened to have a couple of wild deuces up my sleeve." Irrepressible as always, Ponzi believed he did. The only thing was, he would have to rob a bank to get them.

Ponzi's wild cards were in the vaults of the Hanover Trust Company. He estimated that the bank had at least $5 million in negotiable securities plus significant reserves of cash. As a major stockholder and the bank's single biggest depositor, he believed he might be able to gain brief access to the vault, remove the cash and securities, and pass them off as his own. After using them to prove that he had more than enough assets to pay his debts, he would stealthily return them to their rightful place with no one the wiser. It was, admittedly, a far-fetched

scheme fraught with pitfalls, not the least of which was its utter ille-
gality. But it was his only hope, so Ponzi even mapped out a route and
a sequence for the big heist.

Hanover Trust was on the corner of Washington and Water Streets.
Gallagher's office was only a half block away, at the corner of Devonshire
and Water. Ponzi would press for the showdown with the auditor to take
place at Gallagher's office, a reasonable expectation, considering that the
federal prosecutor outranked Pelletier and the attorney general had not
even signed on to the idea of a winner-take-all audit. When the auditor
was ready to disclose the total of Ponzi's liabilities, Ponzi would gather
all his bank books and other assets. But he would not go directly from 27
School Street to Gallagher's office at 85 Devonshire. He would stop on
the way at Hanover Trust and make a highly unauthorized withdrawal of
enough cash and securities to cover any shortfall. Ponzi expected the
showdown to last only an hour, after which he would casually drop by
Hanover Trust once again to redeposit his borrowed assets.

"The investigation would have ended right there and then. The authorities would have to certify as to my solvency," Ponzi figured. He
would go into a new business with an official stamp of approval. "All
considered," he thought, "I was far from licked yet."

When Ponzi arrived at 27 School Street, the adoring crowd he'd
found a day earlier had been replaced by a larger, edgier horde, their
bodies drenched in sweat, their eyes alive with dread and anger. Some
carried the morning *Post,* its lead headline triumphantly predicting
Ponzi's demise and feeding investors' fears: PONZI CLOSES; NOT LIKELY
TO RESUME.

The story knocked into also-ran status the latest news of the America's Cup races and a report that Pancho Villa was holding an American businessman for ransom. Below the story about Ponzi's agreement
to suspend business was the front-page announcement he had
promised to buy:

PUBLIC NOTICE

I have made a personal agreement with
District Attorney Pelletier to cease receiving funds
from the public for investment with the
SECURITIES EXCHANGE CO.
27 School St. Boston
and all branches, until after an official audit is made
to determine my solvency and satisfy him that my
methods of financial operation are thoroughly
legitimate. Meantime, I shall pay all maturing
obligations as fast as presented. Further, during the
auditing of the books any persons holding unmatured
notes can receive back their original investment,
without interest, if they desire.
Signed, Charles Ponzi

Hundreds of people had assembled well before the opening hour of eight o'clock. When Ponzi arrived he could see there were no police officers in sight, the first time in weeks School Street had not enjoyed ample protection. Enraged, Ponzi suspected that the officials investigating him were hoping for a melee they could use as a pretext to shut him down for good. In the absence of the police, even the strong-armed Pinkertons seemed helpless to prevent the crowd from becoming a mob. Temperatures were climbing only toward the mid-seventies, but the crush of bodies made School Street the hottest block in Boston.

Ponzi stayed only a short time at his offices, relying on Lucy Meli and a corps of perhaps two dozen clerks and agents to issue the refunds. His workers had nothing better to do now that Ponzi had suspended taking new investments. Ponzi went around the corner to the

Hanover Trust Company, holing up again in Chmielinski's office and plotting his next moves.

He called Eddie Dunn, city editor of the *Post,* to complain about the "Not Likely to Resume" portion of that morning's front-page headline. Neither Ponzi nor the prosecutors had said any such thing. It appeared that the *Post* was trying to speed his demise in order to claim his scalp. Ponzi was agitated. He did not know that Richard Grozier, the acting publisher, was directing the coverage from his father's office, so Ponzi focused on Dunn. The city editor, Ponzi fumed, was "never letting me out of his sight and nothing less than a shower of buckshot would have discouraged him." Ponzi told Dunn that the newspaper should watch its step or else he would "own its presses."

At the moment, though, Ponzi had more urgent concerns. A lawyer for one of his investors had filed a motion in Suffolk County Superior Court seeking the appointment of a temporary receiver to take over Ponzi's business as well as an injunction shutting Ponzi down immediately. The investor, a twenty-one-year-old Boston news dealer, Alton Parker, had deposited $500 on June 14—he was due $750 in just two days. If Parker's motion succeeded, Ponzi would be finished, done in by a $250 debt.

Fearing the worst, Ponzi sent men scouring the city for Parker to pay him early and render the suit moot. But Parker was nowhere to be found. In the meantime, Parker's lawyer, David Stoneman, was granted an appearance before Judge William Cushing Wait. Frantic, Ponzi sent attorney Samuel Bailen, a law partner of Judge Leveroni's, to argue that there was no need for a receiver or an injunction because Ponzi was paying all claims and had more than enough assets to weather any run. To Ponzi's relief, Judge Wait lived up to his name and delayed issuing a ruling. But the motion remained active, so it represented a grave threat.

Later that day, just when Ponzi had given up hope of quietly locating Parker and settling the case, Parker surprised him by dropping by Hanover Trust. The young man had grown upset when he'd seen his name and news of the suit on the bulletin board outside the *Post* building. He told Ponzi that the lawyer, Stoneman, had tricked him into signing the complaint. Delighted, Ponzi dragged Parker to Bailen's office, paid him the full $750, and got Parker to sign an affidavit absolving Ponzi of all claims. Stoneman, whom Ponzi suspected of acting as a straw man for Boston bankers who wanted to crush him, quickly withdrew the lawsuit.

Ponzi had dodged a bullet, but he decided he wanted more protection than Leveroni and Bailen could provide. He thought about strolling over to State Street, the heart of Boston's business elite, and picking out "one of those lawyers with a *Mayflower* pedigree. One of those blue-ribbon Pomeranians." But he remembered how "Ice King" Charles Morse had manipulated the system and gained his release not by complex legal machinations but by well-connected supporters, Clarence Barron among them. Obviously, Ponzi could not hope for help from Barron, so he would get the next best thing. He decided that he needed a lawyer with deep, even intimate knowledge of the men who ran the state. If that lawyer had dirt on the power brokers, even better. Ponzi chose the most connected lawyer in Boston, a friend to the federal and Suffolk County district attorneys, a man who had spent two decades warming the ears of politicians and prosecutors with his whispers: Dan Coakley.

Coakley's boyish face belied a thoroughly grown-up talent for enriching himself at the expense of others. His work helping Curley push Fitzgerald out of the mayor's race and his badger-game exploits with Pelletier and another district attorney, Nathan Tufts, were only part of his repertoire. Born in South Boston in 1865, Coakley had dropped out of Boston College because of illness and become a streetcar conductor on a line that ran from ribald Scollay Square to redoubtable Harvard Square. Fired for inciting a strike for higher wages, he'd found work as a boxing referee and a sports reporter for the *New York Sun* and the *Boston Herald*. He'd later graduated from Boston University Law School and become a personal injury lawyer, specializing in claims against his former trolley-line bosses. Savoring his revenge, Coakley had framed his canceled conductor's license and hung it on his library wall.

As corrupt as he was charming, Coakley saw his own political prospects dampened by voters' lack of trust. He'd spent three terms in the state legislature as the representative from Cambridge before being ousted in his bid for a fourth. Later he'd served in appointed, largely ceremonial posts on the Boston Park Commission and as a trustee of the Boston Public Library. At fifty-four, a married father of five, Coakley had a roguish sense of humor and a stage actor's voice, capable of booming a line to the far seats without losing its rich palette of emotion. Best of all for Ponzi, not only was he in league with Pelletier, he was close with the federal prosecutor, Gallagher, as well.

Ponzi adored Coakley from the moment they met. Confident he had found the ideal advocate, Ponzi agreed to pay Coakley and his partner, former assistant district attorney Daniel McIssac, the extraordinary retainers of twenty-five thousand dollars each, with the promise of more to come. What Ponzi did not fully realize was that although Coakley was a remarkably effective advocate, he came with a boatload of baggage, having made as many enemies as friends in the trench warfare of Boston politics. Moreover, his reach was almost nonexistent when it came to the Brahmins. Coakley held no sway with the attorney general, J. Weston Allen.

Thinking he had shored up his legal defense, Ponzi returned his attention to 27 School Street. It was turning out to be the busiest day yet for the Securities Exchange Company, but unlike earlier big days, all the money was going out the door rather than coming in.

There was no letup from the moment the business opened at eight o'clock. Lucy Meli and the clerks tried desperately to keep up with the relentless tide, but inevitably they fell behind. As they did, pressure rose along with the temperatures in hallways of the Niles Building. Around noon, a throng of men formed themselves into a flying wedge and forced their way into Room 227 to demand their money, only to be repelled by the men in Ponzi's employ. But with no police in sight, the attackers took another run at the Securities Exchange Company offices, this time heading directly into the glass-paneled door. The door shattered, sending shards of glass flying through the air and into the faces and hands of several members of the invading force. The sight of blood excited the men further. A near-panic ensued as they tried to fight their way to the iron gates of the tellers' windows. Ponzi's clerks fought back again. After ten minutes of shouting and shoving, a fragile peace was restored.

The disturbances slowed payments further, and the line of people seeking refunds, along with a small number holding matured notes, snaked through the corridors, down the stairs, and out into School Street, crowding the sidewalk in front of the Elite Shoe store, Burke & Co. Merchant Tailors, and the Tourist Trunk Shop. Newsboys roamed the crowd, and men huddled in small groups reading the afternoon papers. The heat proved too much for some; as many as a half dozen women fainted in line.

Several speculators hovered on the edges of the crowd, offering to buy Ponzi notes at prices based on when they were due. A hundred-dollar note that would reach maturity within a few days might be worth its face value—the speculator expected to collect the 50 percent interest—while the same note with several weeks until maturity might fetch only seventy-five dollars. But at least its owner would be spared having to wait in line any longer. A small number of people in the crowd were neither note holders nor speculators but would-be investors hoping against hope that Ponzi would relent and take their money.

Reporters from all the Boston papers and several out-of-town newspapers were there to document the scene. While most reporters told the story straight, the writer from the *Evening Transcript* seemed most concerned with the rare mix of well-dressed women and businessmen mingling with lowly stenographers, fruit peddlers, mechanics, and teamsters. Perhaps hoping to reassure his blueblood readership that not all of Boston had gone mad, the *Transcript* reporter added dryly, "Foreigners predominate."

Halfway through the day, Ponzi made arrangements to take over the old Bell-in-Hand pub, a bar on the first floor of the Niles Building that had been shuttered by Prohibition. Though located in the same building as Ponzi's office, the entrance to the Bell-in-Hand was around the corner on Williams Court. The narrow street, hemmed in by brick buildings and barely wide enough for ten men standing shoulder to shoulder, was better known as Pi Alley. The name derived from the piles of jumbled type, called pi, dumped there by printers from Newspaper Row.

Soon Pi Alley filled with investors. Ponzi's clerks ushered them inside the old bar in groups of five, then led them up a back stairway to the dingy second-floor offices of the Securities Exchange Company. There they traded their notes for checks drawn on Ponzi's accounts at Hanover Trust. Ponzi preferred paying by check rather than by cash, suspecting that at least some of his customers would deposit their refunds at the bank he controlled. "It was a case of 'heads I win,' and 'tails you lose,' " he chuckled to himself. After receiving their checks, the investors were shown the front way out of the building and disgorged onto School Street, a system that created an assembly line of sorts in which Ponzi notes entered one door and money exited another.

At the end of the day, Ponzi invited the assembled reporters to join him in Henry Chmielinski's office at the bank. He sat with them for an hour, laughing, joking, and announcing plans to establish something he called the Ponzi Foundation as a vehicle for his intended philanthropy. As a first step, Ponzi said, he would donate $100,000 to a new orphanage, the Home for Italian Children, scheduled to open the coming weekend in the city's Jamaica Plain neighborhood.

When the reporters asked him about the run of withdrawals, he said casually that he believed he had paid out more than a million dollars, though that was almost certainly an exaggeration. Some reporters automatically downgraded his estimate to several hundred thousand dollars. Ponzi adopted a more sober tone when using the reporters as a means of asking his customers to remain patient when awaiting their money.

"I wish the public would be orderly in presenting their demands for payment because all obligations will be honored. The lack of police protection, which has been withdrawn from me since I have discontinued receipt of investments, should not be taken advantage of by the public," he said in what amounted to a formal statement to the press. He insisted he was unconcerned by damage to his property, but added, "I do not want any unnecessary crushing, any rioting, or any acts that may be apt to prejudice the welfare of my customers."

Then, with an absolutely straight face, he criticized the predatory tactics of the men buying notes from his investors at a discount. "I feel I should call attention to the public of this attempt to speculate on their holdings and let them see the inconsistency of giving profit to money sharks who are willing to gamble on the nervous tension of the public."

Although Ponzi displayed his devil-may-care self with the reporters, the size of the day's run left him shaken. If it continued at this pace, he might run out of money before he could prove his solvency, end prosecutors' inquiries, and regain the upper hand. When the reporters left, Ponzi quietly took a precaution against that happening. Under the terms of the certificate of deposit he had given Hanover Trust five days earlier, Ponzi was required to give thirty days' notice before withdrawing the $1.5 million it covered. Before leaving the bank this day he did just that, hoping he could hold on until he could claim the money on August 27.

Unknown to Ponzi, the commissioner of banks, Joseph Allen, was thinking the same way. Though his investigation had turned up nothing illegal about Ponzi's banking practices, Allen knew that sudden, massive withdrawals could imperil Hanover Trust or any other bank where Ponzi did significant business. If Ponzi were overwhelmed by investors turning in their notes, he and his clerks might write checks for more than he had on deposit. However, because Ponzi was a powerful board member at Hanover Trust and a valued depositor elsewhere, the banks might continue to honor his checks in the expectation that he would deposit more money as soon as possible. But by the time the accounts were settled, Allen suspected, Ponzi's reserves might be exhausted, and the banks would have to dip into their own reserves to balance the books. Given the amount of money Ponzi was dealing with, a small bank that honored Ponzi's checks after his account was overdrawn might find its own capital fatally depleted. When word got out, depositors would likely descend on the bank demanding their money, but there would be nothing left for them. The run would destroy the bank and potentially trigger panic throughout Boston as nervous depositors elsewhere did the same. The result, Allen knew, could be a complete meltdown of Boston's banking system, with banks failing left and right. Bank regulators love nothing better than orderly, even boring operations. The risk that Allen believed Ponzi posed was nothing short of a bank commissioner's greatest fear.

To allay his concerns and lessen the danger, Allen had notified Chmielinski and the Hanover Trust treasurer, William McNary, that, beginning immediately, they were required to report daily to him on the bank's financial status, including how much it had in reserve, the amount of all deposits, and whether any depositors had overdrawn their accounts. Though Ponzi didn't yet know it, that kind of scrutiny would make it far more difficult, perhaps impossible, for him to pull off his temporary heist from the Hanover Trust vault. He would need another way to prove that his assets exceeded his liabilities.

When he finished speaking with the reporters, Ponzi stepped outside Hanover Trust. He had offered Lucy Meli a ride home on his way to Lexington, and she was already in the back seat when chauffeur John Collins pulled up. It had been the longest, most trying day of Ponzi's financial career, but he would not show it. When Collins parked the Locomobile outside the bank office, Ponzi walked to his shiny limousine, put his foot on the high running board, and pulled open the door with his left hand. With his hat tipped back slightly on his head, his tie perfectly in place, Ponzi turned to a waiting *Post* photographer and flashed his best showman's smile.

Ponzi woke the next morning, Wednesday, July 28, and saw that the run on his office was bigger news in the *Post* than the final triumph of *Resolute* over *Shamrock IV* in the America's Cup race series. He could also see that one of his enemies was looking to score points with the public. Simon Swig had taken a front-page ad in the *Post* that did not mention Ponzi by name but might as well have. "Our dividends are paid out of our earned and collected income, and not out of the other fellow's principal," it read, wooing depositors to Tremont Trust. To drive home the point, the ad continued: "Save and grow rich. Plunge and grow broke."

More ominously, the *Post* printed another cutting attack by Clarence Barron, who had weighed in again on Ponzi in his latest *Boston News Bureau* circular. Barron posed a series of questions designed to undermine trust in Ponzi. His most incisive question was why Ponzi kept large deposits in local banks paying 5 percent interest, or in the stodgy stocks of banks and companies like J. R. Poole, when he supposedly could use the money to turn huge profits quickly and easily with postal coupons. Barron also hit Ponzi on a question of ethics, suggesting that if Ponzi's claims were true, he would be "sticking" the governments where he bought the coupons or, worse, the United States government.

But if Swig and Barron were hoping to sway public opinion, they failed to recognize that Ponzi, despite his fancy clothes and expensive motorcar, had made himself a man of the people. When the Locomobile pulled up in front of 27 School Street and Ponzi stepped out, the swarm of people began to cheer. He wore a freshly laundered, perfectly pressed copy of his outfit of the day before—blue coat and white pants—but this day he spiced it up with a blue-and-white striped silk shirt and a complementing cravat. Many in the crowd still wanted their money, but something about the elegant little financier had captured their hearts. They had doubts, but they were rooting for him. Certainly they preferred him to the bankers and Barrons of the world. Ponzi acknowledged his fans and, feeling flush, granted reporters a moment of his time. He retold his rags-to-riches story, then offered reporters a populist counterattack against his detractors.

"Bankers and businessmen can easily understand how I could make 100 percent for myself," he scoffed. "But simply because no one ever made an added 50 percent for the general public they reason that it can't be. You remember the old rube who saw the giraffe for the first time? He stared at it and remarked, 'There ain't no such animal.' The truth is, bankers and businessmen have been doing plenty for themselves under the present banking system, but they have done little for anybody else." He outlined yet again his plan for a profit-sharing bank, adding with a touch of sarcasm, "Yes, I know that it is a shock to some of these folks who have been hogging it all, but it is fair and right, and the depositor should get a fair return for his money."

Gaining momentum, Ponzi made a bid for sympathy by complaining that the deferral of deposits had already cost him dearly: "I would have cleaned up three-and-a-half million dollars this week if the authorities had not asked me to suspend operations pending the result of their investigations," he said, ignoring the fact that it was he who had volunteered the stoppage. But never fear, he cried—he would not be kept down by the powers that be. "Despite the temporary interference with my business, I intend to continue it on a larger scale than ever. I have opened offices in New York and mean to start branches all over the country. I am in this business to make money. Ethics does not interest me any more than it interests the bankers. They are in the game to make it pay, and I am going to show them up."

Before he was finished, Ponzi upped his estimate of his personal wealth to $24 million and took a shot at the man who was challenging the *Post* for the title of chief nemesis: "Now please don't think that

I'm boasting, but I have forgotten more about foreign exchange than C. W. Barron ever knew."

But Ponzi was not the only one making statements to reporters. "As I told Ponzi the other day," said Daniel Gallagher, the federal prosecutor, "he is either a benefactor deserving of the blessings of the public officials and all alike—or he should be in jail. Investigation may show that Ponzi is solvent theoretically, yet an offender against the federal law. We are going to find out." Still, Gallagher would not confirm whether federal authorities would work with local and state prosecutors or on their own.

The withdrawals continued apace, though with Ponzi's takeover of the Bell-in-Hand the process became more orderly even with the continued absence of the police. On the other hand, the narrow Pi Alley remained uncomfortably crowded and provided fish-in-a-barrel pickings for speculators buying notes below face value. When lunchtime came, Ponzi relieved the tedium, hunger, and thirst by providing free frankfurters, sandwiches, doughnuts, coffee, and cold soda to everyone in line, begging forgiveness for his failure to do so the day before.

"I want to use my customers right," he told a reporter as the meals were served. "I hope they leave their money with me. There is nothing for them to fear. No one can stop my business, and by leaving their money in my hands those people out there will get the profit they were promised."

Ponzi added to the circus atmosphere by hiring a sometime vaudevillian with a mop of black hair that looked suspiciously like an animal pelt. For a salary of fifty dollars a week, James Francis Morelli played the role of court jester and private poet laureate, distributing circulars with doggerel in support of his master:

What is all the excitement folks? Why these speculators?
Ponzi's notes are good as gold, so why, these black-hearted raiders?
If they should ask you to sell your notes, step forward and exclaim:
"No indeed, I'm sorry, lad, 'cause my notes bear Ponzi's name."

Just step in line, and wait with ease, and avoid all sorts of commotion,
For Ponzi has as many dollars, as there are ripples in the ocean.
He will pay you all, and thank you, too, and solicit your funds once more,
And instead of serving you doughnuts and coffee, he'll serve turkeys
   by the score.

Ponzi's efforts at rebuilding confidence began to gain steam. In the afternoon a group of men appeared at the office of Judge Leveroni and announced their intention to form an association called the Ponzi Alliance. They presented Leveroni with a draft of resolutions for establishment of the alliance, including a pledge of unwavering faith in Ponzi and a promise to pool money on his behalf if needed.

By the time the office closed, Ponzi had paid out another half to three-quarters of a million dollars, but the tenor of the crowd had shifted. There were no flying squads of men breaking through the glass doors this day. Before locking up, Ponzi posted a sign written cheerily in crayon on the side of an old egg crate: WILL REOPEN FOR BUSINESS THURSDAY MORNING AT NINE O'CLOCK. But his day was not yet over.

The officers of Hanover Trust had invited Ponzi to join them for a company outing at a resort called the Waters Club. Ponzi eagerly accepted, expecting the same treatment he had received a few days earlier at a bank-sponsored banquet where he was the guest of honor. There, Hanover treasurer William McNary had proposed a toast to the bank's newest director and biggest depositor. "Three cheers for Ponzi, the greatest wizard and financial genius this country has ever known!" said McNary, at fifty-seven a wily veteran of two terms in Congress as well as the rougher precincts of Boston politics and business. The cheers rang in Ponzi's ears, and he basked in the acclaim. He was so tickled he surprised the bankers by picking up the $640 dinner tab.

Each day that he survived the run, Ponzi felt stronger. And each day they failed to put Ponzi out of business, Richard Grozier, Eddie

Dunn, and the *Post* staff grew more frustrated. This night, while Ponzi partied with the Hanover bankers, a *Post* reporter cornered Calvin Coolidge at the State House to get the governor's opinion on what should be done about Ponzi. On the strength of his no-right-to-strike response to the Boston police walkout, Coolidge had been nominated seven weeks earlier to be the Republican vice presidential candidate on a ticket headed by Warren Harding. Coolidge's mind was clearly elsewhere. He gave a politician's answer, vague yet authoritative enough to make it the lead of the *Post*'s front-page story, set in bold type: "I will direct the attorney general to take action for the purpose of enforcing the law. I have not much knowledge of the affair, but according to the prevailing impression, the matter ought to be investigated by the government." Of course, Attorney General J. Weston Allen was already investigating, so Coolidge clarified his answer to say he would direct Allen to join the federal and local investigations already under way.

The *Post*'s young acting publisher wanted to do more than mouth platitudes; he was ready to claim his inheritance. No longer the Harvard layabout, Richard Grozier had quickly grown into the job foisted upon him by his father's illness. He squared his shoulders, cleared his throat, and exercised the right to speak for his family's newspaper. Richard had watched from the sidelines just four months earlier as his father bet the *Post* against Curley. Now, with the stakes even higher, he did the same against Ponzi.

Richard spent the night preparing the *Post*'s first editorial on Ponzi and the frenzy he had caused, topped with the headline IT CANNOT LAST. Careful not to cross the line to libel, yet unmistakable in its intent, the editorial began, "Is Mr. Ponzi the 'wizard' of the foreign exchange market that his alleged profits appear to make him out, or is he running an old game under a new guise? The experience of the ages arouses skepticism that he can do what he claims to have done, and yet all the forces investigating his scheme so far have been unable to prove him guilty of fraud." The editorial gained steam at the end, concluding that even if Ponzi's postal coupon claims were true, "governments are not going to allow themselves to be mulcted [swindled] on this scale indefinitely, and it must be only a question of a few weeks before the golden goose is killed. There is, of course, still the alternative that possibly there never was any such goose."

The battle had been fully joined between Richard Grozier and Charles Ponzi. The stakes were nothing less than their reputations and their livelihoods. Only one could survive.

*Rose, Ponzi, and Imelde pose for a Post photographer outside
their Lexington home on August 1, 1920.*

The Boston Globe

CHAPTER FOURTEEN

"EVEN HIS COWS COULDN'T GIVE MILK."

The door to the Bell-in-Hand remained locked at nine the next morning, Thursday, July 29, and nervous whispers passed through the scores of people gathered in Pi Alley. Had Ponzi taken the money and run? Had the bubble burst? But shortly before ten o'clock one of Ponzi's clerks swung open the door to the old tavern and invited all with Ponzi notes inside. Ponzi arrived around eleven, and the appearance of his Locomobile evoked a throaty roar. He stepped from the car, waved to his fans, and ducked inside.

Soon after, Ponzi left School Street to begin another jam-packed day of interviews and meetings, much of the time with his new lawyer, Dan Coakley. He understood that the public was taking its cues from him. If he wanted to retain its support, he needed to model himself on the mallards that seemed to glide effortlessly across the duck pond in the Public Garden. On the surface, he would appear placid and carefree, but below he would churn furiously to prevent being pulled under.

Throughout the day, depositors continued to seek refunds at the Securities Exchange Company. When they got to the tellers' windows they caught sight of a large revolver lying menacingly on a desk to discourage thoughts of holdups. One young man, sweat dripping down his face, slid a clerk a Ponzi note for ten thousand dollars due to mature into fifteen thousand dollars on Saturday.

"You know," the clerk told him, "this comes due in two days."

"I want my principal!" he yelled. "I want my principal!"

He got it and left.

But as the day wore on, the balance began shifting toward investors who were there not to claim early withdrawals but to cash matured notes. By two in the afternoon the line had thinned to a trickle. Just after the four o'clock closing time, a Ponzi agent poked his head outside the door to ask if anyone else wanted his money. No one was there, so he locked the door.

Meanwhile, Ponzi was taking sporadic breaks to touch base with reporters. Some had yet to hear his rags-to-riches tale, and he was happy to oblige, telling the story from his arrival with two dollars and fifty cents to his receipt of the postal coupon from the correspondent in Spain to his stupendous success. When the inevitable question arose about exchanging postal coupons for dollars, Ponzi always demurred: "My secret is, 'How do I cash the coupons?' That is what I do not tell." No interview was complete without a tribute to Rose. "And then I found my inspiration," he told a New York reporter. "She was Rose Gnecco, daughter of a wholesale fruit merchant of Boston, and the fairest and most wonderful woman in all the world. All I have done is because of Rose. She is not only my right arm, but my heart, as well." Rose herself was dodging the limelight, preferring to support her husband in the privacy of their home.

Occasionally his press agent, William McMasters, would speak for Ponzi, but he fell far short of his employer's deft touch. While Ponzi avoided direct confrontation with authorities, McMasters seemed intent on antagonizing them. He told reporters that Ponzi's rallying cry had become "Let the government probe and be damned." The *Post* used that comment to justify a Ponzi-bashing headline in the Friday morning paper: EXPRESSES CONTEMPT FOR INVESTIGATIONS.

Ponzi took a few missteps of his own in his talks with reporters. This day, they came to haunt him in the person of his old nemesis, furniture dealer Joseph Daniels, whose million-dollar lawsuit was still pending. When the courthouse opened, a lawyer for Daniels amended his case to put a claim on Ponzi's stock in Hanover Trust, J. R. Poole Company, the Napoli Macaroni Manufacturing Company, and several other firms. Ponzi had bought some of the stock in other people's names expressly to avoid attachments by Daniels or anyone else, but he had defeated his financial disguise by describing his holdings to reporters. Daniels's case also came before Judge Wait, who ordered a hearing on the motion the following week.

On another front, the county prosecutor, Joseph Pelletier, announced that he was opening an investigation of Ponzi's rival, the Old Colony Foreign Exchange Company and its president, a forty-five-year-old former court stenographer from Georgia named Charles Brightwell. Ponzi had gotten his wish—his competitors were feeling as much heat as he was—but he was too busy to enjoy it.

When he returned home to Slocum Road, Ponzi found a *Post* reporter staking out his house. Ponzi rewarded him with a tantalizing bit of information: He was thinking about selling the Securities Exchange Company for $10 million. "I was in conference with a big banker from New York today," Ponzi told the *Post* man, "and he made me this offer for my business. I have not decided to accept it or not." Ponzi would not disclose the man's name or affiliation, but he had in fact received just such an inquiry. Whether it would become reality remained to be seen, but at the moment it was useful in his effort to maintain his credibility. Best of all, Ponzi thought, if he could somehow pull it off he might have found a way to cover his liabilities without robbing his bank.

The next morning, Friday, July 30, the *Post* thought it had an even bigger scoop, which it trumpeted in a front-page headline:

EXTRA
COUPON PLAN
IS EXPLODED

**New York Postmaster Says Not
Enough in Whole World to Make
Fortune Ponzi Claims**

The story—printed entirely in bold type—quoted New York Postmaster Thomas G. Patten as declaring that Ponzi's claims were "impossible" because far too few postal reply coupons existed to create an $8 million fortune. Patten either did not know or did not say how many coupons were in existence worldwide, but he said New York kept only twenty-seven thousand on hand at any time—worth about fourteen hundred dollars—because the demand was so small.

A separate front-page story gave the *Post* an opportunity to vent its growing frustrations at Ponzi's continued survival and prosecutors' apparent inaction. "Federal, state, and local investigations of Ponzi's get-rich-quick scheme failed yesterday to bring any tangible results," the story derisively began. The *Post* also turned to ridicule, printing its first editorial cartoon about the situation. The paper's celebrated cartoonist, William Norman Ritchie, caricatured Ponzi as a dashing little moneybags with cash bursting from his pockets and a dollar sign for a tie clasp. Surrounding him were stereotypical European officials begging him in fractured English to solve their financial problems. An Italian cartoon figure, with a silly crown and a sash labeling him "King," implored, "Signor Ponzi, the Old Home Lire Is ina D'Hole. Will You Taka D'Job of Minister of Finance?"

Yet neither the *Post*'s stories to date nor its latest scoop about the New York postmaster's assertion seemed to be having any lasting effect. If anything, Ponzi appeared to be gaining more fans. Fewer than forty people were waiting when the Bell-in-Hand doors opened. Ponzi was still bound by his agreement not to accept new investments, but the bleeding had stopped. The run was over.

The swing in momentum could be read in several of the city's other newspapers, which seemed to delight in the possibility that the *Post* had been wrong and Ponzi was on the level. The *Boston Traveler* ran a sports column that compared Ponzi to Babe Ruth, written as a letter to the Home Run King. "Give half that pedestal to Charlie Ponzi. Great pair, Ruth and Ponzi," it read. "Ponzi is a lot like you, Babe. The bankers are said to be trying to retire him with the banks full. Just like trying to retire you with the bases full, hey Babe?" Even better for Ponzi, the afternoon *Boston American* quoted a North End banker as saying that Ponzi's business "is honorable and it certainly presents no legal objections." A separate story allowed a New York importer to expound at length about how he had figured out Ponzi's secret formula for wealth. "For an expert in foreign exchange, there is not the slightest mystery about the operation by Mr. Ponzi," said the self-proclaimed authority, E. H. Newfield of the importing firm E. Luca Manoussa.

But the *Post* did have at least one important ally: Clarence Barron. In the Friday edition of his *Boston News Bureau* circular and in several public statements, Barron intensified his attack, strongly suggesting that Ponzi was engaged in a Peter-to-Paul scheme. He also criticized the authorities for the slow pace of their investigations. But what burned Ponzi most was Barron's suggestion that Ponzi was exploiting his own people, Italian immigrants. Ponzi was certain he had been libeled. He immediately ordered his lawyers to file a $5 million lawsuit against Barron that included attachments against his home in Boston and his beloved farm on the South Shore. "I tied him up so thoroughly," Ponzi boasted, "even his cows couldn't give milk."

Barron would not back down. Late in the day he intensified his criticism while leaving himself open to charges of condescending bigotry. "If there is anybody in this country requiring protection at the

present time it is the humble Italian immigrant," he said. "These poor
people from Italy, who are children in finance, come to this country,
and many of them take out citizenship papers. They can then be put
into the trenches and made to give up their lives in defence of this
country. Are we to do nothing to protect their savings and their hard-
earned dollars?" He repeated his challenges to prosecutors and scoffed
at Ponzi's lawsuit: "Ponzi or anyone else in his class may pile their attachments on me as high as Bunker Hill Monument and I shall still be
found answering to the best of my ability the financial problems that
are properly put to me."

Ponzi immediately shot back with a measured yet biting response:
"From the several articles published by Mr. Barron, I derive that he
considers himself an authority on international finance, also that he is
prejudiced, and that he is openly hostile to me," Ponzi said in a statement handed to reporters. "His allusion implies a decided contempt
toward the Italian race, which is uncalled for and unjustifiable." After
scolding Barron for forgetting, or never learning, the rules of polite
society, Ponzi raised the banner of immigrant pride, borrowing from
Curley's playbook on ethnic politics. "If his allusion did not offend
millions of my countrymen I would never even have noticed it, but
since the allusion is plainly offensive and misleading, I wish to remind
him that banking had its origin in Italy and that the bill of exchange
was devised by Italians. It is not surprising, therefore, that I, an Italian
by birth and educated in Italy, should have come from Italy with perhaps a deeper knowledge of foreign exchange, foreign customs, and
foreign commerce far superior than the knowledge Mr. Barron has,
ever did have, or ever will have." To demonstrate that his interest was
principle rather than principal, Ponzi promised that if he won the suit,
the $5 million would go to charity.

Proof that Ponzi's man-of-the-people pose was working came that
afternoon. With the temperature approaching eighty degrees, Ponzi
stepped outside the downtown branch of Hanover Trust onto Washington Street, planning to walk a few blocks to the bank's North End
branch. His appearance on the street caused a stir. As he walked to-

ward the market district, several dozen people fell in step behind him. With each block he covered, more followers walked in his wake. By the time the financial pied piper had reached the North End, his entourage numbered more than a hundred. They called his name and hailed him as a hero. They urged him to resume taking investments. The bolder among them grasped his hand for a congratulatory shake. Some shouted "Ponzi for mayor!" But that seemed too modest to others, who cried, "Ponzi for governor!"

The shouts of encouragement rattled around Ponzi's brain. Afterward, he gleefully told reporters he was thinking about using his wealth to support a "wet" candidate who would oppose Prohibition. But Ponzi preferred the role of king to kingmaker, and soon he mused about running for office—once he got citizenship, of course—as a friend to the workingman.

"I am not a Red or an extreme Socialist," he told a reporter for the *New York Times.* "But I do believe that the average man ought to have his chance to live in the right way. I am advocating that so-much-abused term, 'American standard.' I believe every man should have the opportunity to live a decent, wholesome life, and that he should be able by his industry not only to have enough to live comfortably, but to be able to have enough to take care of him during his old age and meanwhile, to give his children enough education so they may avail themselves of the opportunities which present themselves."

Before writing any acceptance speeches, Ponzi still had to contend with the investigations of his business. The number of inquiries fell from three to two this day, however, when District Attorney Joseph Pelletier withdrew from the probe. Attorney General J. Weston Allen had sent Pelletier a letter stressing Governor Coolidge's call for a state investigation and pointing out that Pelletier's jurisdiction extended only within Suffolk County, while Ponzi was operating throughout Massachusetts and beyond. Pelletier acted unruffled about being elbowed aside. He said he stood ready to help the other investigations. He even gave Ponzi a qualified endorsement, when he told a reporter that the business seemed to have been conducted "normally" and remarked that Ponzi seemed generous to charity. For Ponzi, Pelletier's withdrawal meant less opportunity for Dan Coakley to shape the investigation by playing the influence game, though Coakley's friendship with Gallagher might still prove useful.

Having booted Pelletier from the field, Attorney General Allen was eager to get his hands on Ponzi's books. But he was a step too slow. Gallagher had already appointed an accountant to review the finances of the Securities Exchange Company. He was a meek-looking fellow named Edwin L. Pride who, in recent years, had made himself indispensable to state and federal prosecutors as a financial analyst. Pride had helped the government expose and imprison a swindler named Cardenio F. King, who'd sold bogus stock in a Texas mining company.

Ponzi joined Pride for a meeting in Gallagher's office, and then escorted Pride to the Securities Exchange Company to gather up the unusual bookless bookkeeping system of index cards with investors' names, as opposed to traditional ledgers—Roberto de Masellis had not had time to redo the system. Speaking to reporters who watched the procession, Ponzi repeated that he would not reveal his business methods. The only purpose of the voluntary audit, he insisted, was to determine whether his assets exceeded his liabilities. "There can be but one result," Ponzi told a *Post* reporter. "I am solvent, and the probes will not only reveal that, but will prove that I have carried out every promise made to my investors." He took pains to distance himself from the antagonistic comment McMasters had attributed to him the day before. "My attitude towards the investigators is not one of contempt. I wish to assist them in every way I can." Pride expected that auditing Ponzi's "books" would take about four days. He vowed to work straight through the weekend until the job was done.

The next morning, Saturday, July 31, the *Post* continued its drumbeat, this time quoting Washington postal officials as saying it was impossible for Ponzi to have made a fortune with reply coupons. The paper spent the rest of the weekend impatiently cracking the whip to urge the investigations onward. The peak came when a news story scolded Attorney General Allen, declaring, "All initiative in the case thus far has come from Mr. Gallagher's office, with the attorney general's office trailing behind and apparently not quite sure what to do." While criticizing Allen for his evident inaction, the *Post* heaped praise on New Hampshire officials for initiating their own investigation. Alongside the story, a new editorial cartoon by Ritchie pictured a smiling Ponzi with a magic wand and a pot of money, surrounded by jealous price gougers, war profiteers, greedy landlords, and monopolists.

Unknown to Grozier or his reporters, or to Ponzi for that matter, the attorney general had surreptitiously begun his investigation by tapping Ponzi's telephones at his home and office. Allen hoped to hear damaging admissions or clues about the nature of Ponzi's mysterious business. But Ponzi never revealed anything to anyone. Allen's phone minders only heard Ponzi talking about his idea to sell stock to the public, bank presidents and businessmen soliciting Ponzi's business, and calls from various other people—police officials to professionals to newly arrived immigrants—seeking Ponzi's money, time, help, advice, or all four. Allen also sent one of his assistants, Albert Hurwitz, to New York to check on Ponzi's claims that he had sent more than a million dollars abroad via a Milan bank with a branch in Manhattan. Hurwitz's trip was part of an emerging strategy by the attorney general to determine if Ponzi could be charged with "larceny by false pretenses." It was a charge that depended on proving that Ponzi had knowingly made false statements with the intent to deceive. Lying to the attorney general about how and where he did business might fit the bill.

Meanwhile, Barron seconded the *Post*'s conclusion about the dubious profitability of postal coupons. Ignoring the $5 million lawsuit, Barron published an article on Saturday sarcastically suggesting that Ponzi use his incredible powers of financial alchemy to pay the costs of the Great War. "Surely the allies could spare him a million and within three years clean up that debt tangle. Germany might cheaply hire him to wipe out the indemnity within four years."

Still, no crowds turned up that morning on School Street.

If Barron and the *Post* were openly hostile to Ponzi, the other Boston papers generally reported the unvarnished news of the run and the investigations. Although at times they displayed skepticism, for the most part they recounted the day's events impartially. But in a city with so many different, competing voices, perhaps it was inevitable that one or two would root for Ponzi, pandering to the public's embrace of him and maybe hoping that the powerful *Post* would fall on its face.

As newsboys for the *Post* were yelling about the paper's exclusive Washington reporting, the *Boston American* was crowing over a gossamer interview with Rose Ponzi. The paper splashed a huge headline across its front page—WIFE TELLS OF PONZI'S PLANS—and printed a photo of the flattering portrait of Rose that hung in the Ponzis' living room. Rose offered no revelations; she beamed with pride about "my Charles," and the only plan she disclosed was a hoped-for trip to Florida "to idle away our time on a second honeymoon." The story concluded: "A young woman, rarely beautiful, smiled in wifely triumph. For she was the woman married to the man who had made the dream come true."

On the perfect summer day that story appeared, Mr. and Mrs. Charles Ponzi took a ride in their limousine from Lexington to Boston's Jamaica Plain neighborhood. Shortly after noon, the car stopped on Centre Street and the two stepped out, Ponzi in one of his immaculate summer suits and Rose in a loose-fitting white satin gown that fell well below her knees. Not for her the short-short skirts of the flappers.

"Look at Ponzi!" someone yelled, and several hundred people moved toward them. The Ponzis had arrived at a ceremony to dedicate a new orphanage, the Home for Italian Children, for which Ponzi had pledged $100,000 to honor the memory of his wife's mother, Maria Gnecco. Men, women, and children pressed forward, hoping to touch his hand and thank him for his generosity. Carnival booths dotted the grounds of the orphanage, and Ponzi's luck still held. He won a doll for Rose and a box of candy he handed to an awestruck child. He climbed into one of the booths to play a role he was born for: carnival barker. At the urging of the crowd, he agreed to pay cash prizes. Soon dimes were pouring into the booth—it was as if Ponzi had reopened the Securities Exchange Company for investments. "Wait a minute," he merrily called out. "I'll have to figure out my 50 percent before I begin!"

After he inspected the orphanage, Ponzi's greatest fun came when someone brought out a nanny goat with a sign around her neck saying BARRON'S GOAT. Ponzi posed for pictures with the confused animal. He told reporters, with his usual smile, "The weather is lovely. So is the home. The people are fine and the press is fairly good." Narrowing his eyes, he added: "I think that five-million-dollar suit will keep Mr. Barron busy."

The crowd cheered again as the Ponzis were driven away.

Ponzi got more good publicity that day when a *Herald* reporter sat down with four Ponzi agents over "their daily banquet of baked lobster" to discuss the tens of thousands of dollars they had made promoting the Securities Exchange Company. "Ponzi has solved the capitalists' world game," said one, Pete Brisco, a former waiter who claimed to have made $100,000 in Ponzi profits and fees. "They are trembling with fear of what he is going to do for common men, for all who will share in the great day at hand. His heart is with the people. All he does is for them."

Ponzi spent a relatively quiet Sunday, August 1, relaxing and talking briefly with the New York moneymen thinking about buying his business. He posed at length for a still photographer and another crew of movie men, this time from Fox Film Company. With the cameras rolling, Rose and Imelde pretended to wish Ponzi well as he left home for a day of work. They stood close together on the front porch of the house, Ponzi's right arm around Rose, his left arm around his mother. Though the camera could not capture sound, Ponzi improvised a script.

"Well, Mother, it's time for me to go now," he sang out. Rose played along.

"When do you think you'll be home, dear?" she asked. Then she leaned toward him for a good-bye kiss.

"Great!" said the movie man.

When the still photographer was at work, Imelde Ponzi whispered in Italian that it seemed like a dream. She wondered if she would wake up and find the house and their wonderful new life gone.

"That is why we are having the pictures made, mother," Ponzi answered. "So we can look at them if we find that it is a dream."

Rose would not have minded if it had all been a dream. When the photographer, Arthur Marr, asked what she thought of her new life, she answered with a touch of melancholy. "It's a pretty big burden," she said, "and there are a good many hard things that go with wealth. We used to have such a nice family life, but now there is practically no home life—in spite of the beautiful home we have—and no privacy, and my husband is so busy all the time."

For much of the day Slocum Road was jammed with cars filled with passengers hoping for a glimpse of Ponzi. Pinkerton guards shooed away the more insistent ones who approached the house on foot. Ponzi spoke a few words to reporters, telling them he hoped to resume his business within a week.

After the film crew left, Ponzi, Rose, and Imelde went for a drive. As they passed by the Lynnway airfield, Ponzi had an inspiration: He wanted to fly. On a whim, Ponzi clambered into a biplane, hired pilot L. W. Tracy, and told him not to do anything tricky. Once they were airborne an exhilarated Ponzi changed his mind. Tracy jumped at the chance to strut his stuff, putting the plane into two loop-the-loops and an "Immelmann turn," a daring half loop named for a German World War I ace. Tracy also executed a graceful maneuver called a "wingover." It began like Ponzi's business, with a dramatic heavenward climb. As the plane soared skyward, the engine stalled, and it seemed to hang motionless for a moment. Then it fell into a frightening nosedive.

But before they plummeted to the ground in a death spiral, the power returned. Tracy steered the plane onto its normal flight path, level with the ground. If only Ponzi could do the same with the Securities Exchange Company. He had experienced the climb and the stall; now he hoped to regain momentum and level things off without crashing. Ponzi enjoyed the trick so much he asked Tracy to do it again. A half hour later Ponzi returned to earth delighted. He paid Tracy thirty dollars, gave him a ten-dollar tip, and declared that he would return another day.

While Ponzi relaxed and took flight, the *Post* was preparing to publish its biggest and most damaging story yet on the case, from a source Ponzi had never suspected.

William McMasters had been suspicious of his new boss since the previous Monday, when he'd accompanied Ponzi to the meetings with investigators. Several times McMasters had thought he'd heard Ponzi contradict himself from one meeting to the next, as though the fast-talking financier was making it up as he went along. If Ponzi turned out to be a fraud, McMasters feared, his own credibility and career would go down in flames. He was forty-six, with a young wife and a seven-year-old daughter to support. His loyalty was to them, not Ponzi.

McMasters dusted off the skills he had used years earlier as a reporter for the *Post*, before he'd become a mouthpiece for Fitzgerald, Curley, Coolidge, and now Ponzi. He began nosing around the School Street office, searching for clues to determine whether it was a real investment house or a Peter-to-Paul scheme. By late Saturday he had reached his conclusion. He called Richard Grozier and offered the *Post* an inside look at Ponzi's operations that would expose the man and his company as frauds. Grozier had been frustrated for days by the sight of Ponzi's relentlessly smiling face staring out at him from the pages of his own newspaper, refusing to surrender quietly. Newspapers from around the country had picked up on the Ponzi story, and every day the *Post* was in danger of losing its lead position. McMasters's account could be decisive; the *Post* would have an exclusive its competitors would kill for.

If what McMasters said was true, Grozier told the publicity man, the *Post* wanted the story and would pay dearly for it. Grozier offered McMasters the fabulous sum of five thousand dollars, with a thousand-dollar bonus if the story were borne out by later developments. The next day, McMasters drove to the *Post* building on Washington Street and went to work. The story ran the following morning, Monday, August 2, under a headline stripped across the top of page 1, each letter two inches tall:

DECLARES PONZI IS NOW HOPELESSLY INSOLVENT

The subhead explained:

**Publicity Expert Employed by "Wizard" Says
He Has Not Sufficient Funds to Meet His Notes—
States He Has Sent No Money to Europe nor
Received Money from Europe Recently**

The story, under McMasters's byline and copyrighted to prevent its immediate theft by the *Post*'s afternoon competitors, began with a self-congratulatory note: "After this edition of *The Boston Post* is on the street there will be no further mystery about Charles Ponzi. He is unbalanced on one subject: his financial operations. He thinks he is worth millions. He is hopelessly insolvent. Nobody will deny it after reading this story." McMasters went on to assert that Ponzi was at least $2 million in debt, had sent no money recently to Europe, and had never earned a dollar from operations outside the United States. McMasters also claimed that Ponzi had bribed a policeman for a gun permit and paid leg breakers to keep stories out of the newspapers.

He quoted banker Simon Swig as questioning Ponzi's sanity and denounced "Wall Street 'experts' who never did anything like it

themselves offering 'sure-thing' explanations of his 'operations.' "
McMasters made Pelletier out to be something of a hero, claiming that
the district attorney had said at their meeting, "See here, Ponzi, I
think your scheme is crooked." To explain why he had gone to the
newspaper, McMasters raised the banner of altruism: "As a publicity
man, my first duty is to the public." He wrote nothing about the
money Grozier had paid him.

Editorial cartoon by William Norman Ritchie
in The Boston Post, *August 3, 1920.*

CHAPTER FIFTEEN

"YOU DISCOVERED THE MONEY!"

Anxious investors began gathering in Pi Alley at six-thirty Monday morning, more than two hours before the doors would open at the Securities Exchange Company. The wound had reopened. Ponzi's success in restoring confidence had been undone by McMasters's story in the *Post*. More people than any day the previous week clamored for refunds. The alley soon overflowed. People spilled around the corner into Court Square, next to City Hall. A large detail of police turned out to assist the Pinkertons, some of the officers mounted, some on foot, and a couple on a nearby roof with field glasses, watching for pickpockets.

By ten o'clock several thousand men and women stood in line, shoving and swaying and surging and sweating in the rising heat. News-boys with armloads of *Post*s roamed through the horde, doing brisk business. Some onlook-ers loitered in the street just for the spectacle. A few said they were holding on to the notes and their faith in Ponzi. Those who did want their money had to suffer the slow progress to the entrance to the Bell-in-Hand, then through a rear door to a stairway, then through labyrinthine hallways to the Securities Exchange Company. Clerks brought them a dozen at a time through the boarded-up front door—there had been no time to replace the glass that had been shattered the week before—and soon they emerged with checks for their money drawn on Ponzi's Hanover Trust accounts. The wait proved too much for several women, who fainted from exhaustion in the poorly ventilated building and were carried outside to be revived. Soon Ponzi's clerks began pulling women from the line and leading them up a side entrance into 27 School Street.

Speculators returned to work, buying not-yet-matured Ponzi notes at a discount, in most cases paying 90 percent of the original investment. Among them were several Ponzi agents, whose lucrative 10 percent commissions had dried up the moment Ponzi had stopped taking investments. One was Ricardo Bogni, the South End bricklayer who had initially invested after Ponzi had assured his wife that she could bet her shoes on his business. Bogni roamed the alley, eventually buying nineteen notes for a little more than seven thousand dollars before he ran out of cash. He could have made a quick buck standing in line himself and cashing them at a teller's window, but Bogni had complete faith in Ponzi. He was certain he would make a killing once they matured. Several of Ponzi's branches in other cities experienced miniature versions of the Boston run, though most closed and advised investors to travel to School Street for their money.

The uproar and the allegations by McMasters proved too much for Roberto de Masellis, the foreign exchange expert Ponzi had hired a month earlier to improve his accounting system. De Masellis gathered his belongings and walked out. But Lucy Meli and the rest of the Ponzi staff remained at their posts, fighting their own doubts and fatigue, expressing confidence in their boss, and paying claims as fast as they could.

Ponzi arrived shortly before eleven, and his appearance quieted the crowd. The reception was a far cry from the cheers he had grown accustomed to, but it was a sign that although they were frightened, his investors had not lost all faith. He strutted into his office as unruffled as ever, twirling his snappy walking stick like a drum major, as though his biggest concern was where to eat lunch. Reporters trailed him like goslings as he walked through his office offering hearty "good mornings" to his staff. When he reached his desk, Ponzi tossed his straw boater onto it and declared, "My hat is in the ring."

As the reporters fired questions about McMasters, the investigation, and the run, Ponzi responded true to form. "As far as being insolvent, I absolutely deny the allegation," he said, beaming his grin at his inquisitors. "People have admired me for my nerve. My smile, which has become so well known through cartoons and photographs, is prompted by a clear conscience. A run does not affect my serenity because I have the money to back it." He slyly noted that he doubted there was a single bank in the city that could withstand such relentless withdrawals without bleeding to death.

Ponzi said McMasters knew nothing about his business beyond insignificant advertising matters. He suggested that McMasters was motivated by Ponzi's demand that he account for money Ponzi had given him to place newspaper ads announcing the suspension of investments. If not that, Ponzi said, McMasters was the tool of powerful men out to destroy him. "There is a desire to embarrass the investigators, a desire to turn public opinion against me," he continued. "Should I be able to realize my dreams, such a realization would mean the downfall of an autocratic clique which has been able to prey upon the credulity of the people." Casting himself as David against the Goliath of established bankers and business interests, Ponzi declared, "The issue now at stake is an issue between a man who wants to do all he can for the people and men who want to take as much as they can from the people without giving adequate return."

He picked apart McMasters's allegations one by one. Ponzi insisted that Pelletier had never called his business "crooked" and called on the district attorney to dispute McMasters's claim. He branded Swig's comments to McMasters lies, and showed receipts for money orders sent abroad to show he had indeed engaged in foreign transactions. He vehemently denied that he had bribed a police officer for a gun permit. Ponzi scoffed at the suggestion that he had followed McMasters's advice when meeting with investigators, saying, "My dog follows me, never goes ahead." Ponzi downplayed the likelihood of a libel suit against his former publicity agent—"McMasters hasn't got anything"—but said he would talk to his lawyers about suing the *Post*.

He had just one request for his investors: "Come and get your money, but come in an orderly way. I may run out of check books, but I shall not run out of money.

"Let me tell you this," he added. "I am going to meet all my outstanding obligations and meet them with funds which I have in banks right here in Boston. And when that is done, I shall have millions left." With a sweep of his hand, Ponzi signaled that the half-hour interview was over. Afterward, one of the reporters marveled how Ponzi, at the center of a firestorm, could remain "as calm and undisturbed as a mill pond."

Ponzi's line about leading his dog inspired his personal poet, James Francis Morelli, to write an impassioned poem about McMasters titled "Charles Ponzi Says: 'My Dog Never Leads Me.' " It began:

> He bit the hand that fed him so well, the miserable, contemptible cur.
> While with Ponzi he lived on the fat of the land, and returned nothing
>   but a slur.
> "Hopelessly Insolvent" are the words he used to imperil the Ponzi
>   investor.
> "Millions of Dollars" was the immediate reply of the "people's proud
>   protector."

As the day wore on and more investors received their money, Ponzi's popularity began to return. The only disturbance occurred when police and Ponzi's Pinkerton guards shut the doors at two o'clock and told the remaining investors to come back the next day, figuring it would take several more hours to pay the investors already inside the building. Several men grabbed planks from the alley to use as a battering ram, but they were quickly repelled by a flying squad of officers. The only arrest was a notorious West End pickpocket named Harry Dwyer who had been working the crowd.

Ponzi was heartened by scores of telegrams offering support and money. Gary Johnson of Houston wrote: "Recent news dispatches state you will reopen and extend business to other cities. You will remember me as a fellow worker and friend in Wichita Falls. If you are opening in Texas would like to represent you. Are channels now open for further investments? If so, will invest my savings with you. Reply [at] my expense."

Just after four o'clock, Ponzi wandered outside to buy the afternoon papers, generously tipping the first newsboy he came across. As he did, someone in the crowd yelled, "You're the greatest Italian in history!"

"No," Ponzi answered with a laugh. "I am the third greatest. Christopher Columbus discovered America and Marconi discovered the wireless."

The fan cried out "You discovered the money!"

Before Ponzi could respond, a clerk directed his attention to an elderly woman who was crying. Rose Perchek had two notes worth $450, but the lines were too long for her to get inside before the doors closed. Ponzi wrapped an arm around her shoulders and led her through the mob. As they walked into the building a man with a freshly fat lip grabbed Ponzi by the arm.

"Mr. Ponzi," he said, "one of your men is assaulting people outside. He shoved me in the face. Look. You hadn't ought to allow such business. Are you going to let them maul people?"

"I am very, very sorry," Ponzi said. "He hasn't any business to be rough." He calmed the man and continued into his office with Mrs. Perchek.

"Now, madam," he asked, "what will you have, cash or check?"

She asked meekly for cash, so Ponzi pulled a thick roll of bills from his pocket and paid her.

"Now," he told her, winking to the crowd of investors waiting for their money, "you have the money and I'm broke."

Meanwhile, Edwin Pride continued his audit, as he had been doing almost nonstop for three days. Pride caused a small stir when he told reporters that he had so far found nothing to suggest that Ponzi had violated any laws, but his work on the mass of index-card files was far from finished. With no real movement on the probe, Pelletier and Attorney General Allen traded barbs over Allen's takeover of the case, with each suggesting the other had not been cooperative. Another ripple resulted when Boston's chief postal inspector, Hal Mosby, said Ponzi had written a letter telling one of his investors to come get his money. Mosby suggested that the government could immediately suspend Ponzi's operations based on its belief that Ponzi had used the mails in a scheme to defraud. But with Pride's report still pending and Ponzi paying all claims, no investigator wanted to step out on that limb. As a *Globe* reporter wrote that night, it remained an open question whether Ponzi was "wiping Peter's nose with Paul's handkerchief."

While the Boston papers followed Ponzi's every move, one enterprising *New York World* reporter tracked down William "520 Percent" Miller, the Peter-to-Paul champion of two decades past. When the reporter found him, Miller was holding court on a cracker barrel in the country store he owned in Rockville Centre, New York. Shaking his head over what he had read in the papers about Ponzi, Miller said, "I may be rather dense, but I can't understand how Ponzi made so much money in so short a time in foreign exchange." Though he admired Ponzi's fearlessness, he said he would not change places with Ponzi for $10 million. "I would much rather own this grocery store, where I have few worries and breathe God's free, pure country air."

Before night fell, Ponzi accepted an invitation to meet with the attorney general. They met for two hours but largely went over territory previously covered. Afterward Ponzi emerged tired but unbowed.

Outside the State House, he spotted a *Post* reporter and shook his finger at him. "I shall never say anything to a *Post* reporter again," he declared, surely knowing he would soon break that vow. "The *Post* is a rotten paper."

Another reporter asked, "Shall you go on paying claims tomorrow?"

Ponzi shrugged his shoulders, raised an eyebrow, and smiled once more.

"Why not?" he asked before heading home.

Ponzi returned to work the next day, Tuesday, August 3, more chipper than ever. He arrived to a chorus of "Money boy!" and "Million-dollar daddy!" from the assembled throng.

"Well, they didn't break me yesterday," he answered gaily, "and they won't break me today!"

He joked to the reporters who were now his constant companions that he had just enjoyed a breakfast of coffee and doughnuts because it was all he could afford. Lest the reporters get the wrong idea, he quickly added, "Mountains of money available to pay all claims. All the boys and girls have to do is drop in and get it." He needled his interviewers, too: "How are your newspapers selling? I ought to have a commission—I need the money . . . to give to charity!"

Ponzi's combination of sangfroid and spirited defense, described at length on the front pages of all the morning newspapers, had, incredibly, begun rebuilding his support and stanching the flow of money. Sensing the shift, he moved to seize the offensive, suing McMasters for two thousand dollars—the money Ponzi said was left over from the amount entrusted to the publicity agent to buy ads. The sum was insignificant, but Ponzi was delivering a message. McMasters understood the game and snapped back. He sued Ponzi for five thousand dollars and denied that his exposé had been spawned by malice.

Ponzi's spirits were so high, publicly at least, that even another attack by Barron could not dampen them. The sage of State Street published a story stating that in the three years ending June 1919, the Universal Postal Union had printed annually only about $200,000 worth of reply coupons worldwide. The most recent year's figures were expected to be no higher. Barron fairly begged for action: "Is no prompt protection to be afforded by the authorities to the poor people in this country who know nothing of finance except as to the promised interest return on their savings?" Ponzi did not even bother to respond, letting his $5 million lawsuit speak for him.

At midday, Ponzi strolled happily through Boston's Public Garden, walking past the elegant swan boats making their lazy laps around the lagoon. Again he was followed by scores of people drawn to his celebrity. He headed to the grand Hotel Bellevue, in the shadow of the gold dome of the State House, for a luncheon with the Kiwanis Club. Following club custom, each man stood and named his business. "Everybody's but my own!" Ponzi cackled when his turn came. Lapping up the attention, he amended his job description to: "Dealer in postal stamps and banker's goats. I'm no financial wizard. I'm a financial lizard and professional goat-getter!" The Kiwanians ate it up.

In a restaurant on Blackstone Street in the city's North End, a sign appeared that day behind the bar: "God made the world and rested. God made man and rested. Then God made Ponzi. Since then neither God nor man has rested." Longtime saloonkeeper Pasquale di Stasio showed off seventy-five hundred dollars' worth of Ponzi notes, the largest of which was for five thousand dollars, maturing on August 21. He boasted that he would never consider cashing them in early. Though skepticism remained high in some quarters, no one was getting more publicity. The *Boston American* declared that Ponzi was "the most talked of man in America." The tide had turned again.

While his clerks continued to pay claims, Ponzi paid a visit to the government auditor's office. An exhausted Pride told Ponzi he had never seen so much cash in one place and never expected to again. Tickled, Ponzi offered Pride a princely salary to become his chief accountant. Pride demurred, but he might have been tempted. At the moment, the auditor was feeling better about Ponzi than he was about

the attorney general. J. Weston Allen was trying to appoint a second
accountant to speed the process, and Pride was hurt. He told reporters
that Allen should show him more respect, reminding them that his auditing work on an investigation into a seafood monopoly had pro-
pelled Allen from the state legislature to the attorney general's office.
Allen backed down, saying he'd meant no offense.

Although outwardly Ponzi seemed a carefree bon vivant, privately
his fears were mounting and his stomach was churning. The revived
run—more than $400,000 paid on Monday alone—and the continued
suspension of income-generating investments were depleting his bank
accounts. He knew that the moment he could not pay a claim, his enemies would swoop in and seek a court order shutting down his business and declaring him bankrupt. If that happened, his reputation and
his popularity—his two main assets, really—would be destroyed. The
big house, the fancy car, and all the trappings would, as his mother
feared, disappear as if they had all been a dream.

Ponzi had come too far to allow that, so he resolved to take action
on two fronts. In the short term, the lawsuit by furniture dealer Joseph
Daniels had frozen bank accounts containing roughly $700,000.
Needing that money to survive until new money arrived, Ponzi resolved to redouble his efforts to settle the suit. In the longer term, it
was time to speed up plans to launch a huge new company. He would
offer stock to the public in a conglomerate combining all the ideas he
had been tossing around in his mind—from profit sharing to banking,
importing to steamship lines. The Securities Exchange Company
would pass into history, and the Charles Ponzi Steamship Company
would rise from its ashes. He gathered the reporters to explain his
plans.

"After this investigation has shown that I am on the level, if I should
open again, such a tremendous amount of money would blow in that
I doubt if I should be able to accept such a large amount and continue
to pay 50 percent in forty-five days," Ponzi said. "I am planning an organization for an investment syndicate capitalized at one hundred million dollars, and eventually to be capitalized at two hundred million,

in which subscribers would receive conservative monthly interest plus quarterly, semi-annual, or yearly dividends. This capital is to be invested in industrial enterprises by acquiring control, also in a chain of banks throughout the United States and the world, to be operated on a profit-sharing basis, also in an exporting and importing company affiliated with my banks and having under control steamship lines plying between Boston and all foreign countries."

Burnishing his man-of-the-people image, Ponzi insisted that the profit sharing would extend to all aspects of the business and include not just stockholders but also his workers. And lest anyone suspect he was tiring of Boston, he declared that the city would be the company's world headquarters, "as Boston is my city." Ponzi hoped to begin taking investments in the new company by the end of the week, no later than the following Monday. He did not explain his haste, but it was clear that he hoped the torrents of fresh cash from prospective stockholders would be more than enough to cover all the liabilities Pride tallied. Ponzi would use some of the new money to pay the last outstanding notes of the Securities Exchange Company, and with the remaining loot Ponzi could start anew as a millionaire banker, shipping magnate, import-exporter, and perhaps even anti-Prohibition politician. It would take steel nerves and split-second timing, a prison-defying leap from the carousel to the brass ring. But it was Ponzi's big chance. He was determined to take it.

Ponzi's more immediate plan was a very public night out with his family. He took Rose, his mother, Rose's sister Mary, and her husband, Rinaldo Boselli, who worked as a Ponzi agent, to Keith's Theater on Washington Street. In his hired box on the right side of the stage, he nearly burst with pleasure when the lights went down and the screen filled with the movie footage the Fox crew had taken of him, Rose, and Imelde in Lexington. Seeing Ponzi in the box as well as on the screen, the audience cheered.

When the lights came on and a violinist took the stage, Ponzi went for a walk and a cigarette. The theater's assistant manager, Bart Grady, found Ponzi in the lobby and told him that one of the night's performers wanted to meet him: former heavyweight champion "Gentleman Jim" Corbett, who had moved from the ring to the stage with a comedy act.

"The man that licked John L. Sullivan?" Ponzi said. "I want to meet him."

Grady took Ponzi to the big man's dressing room, which Corbett shared with his comedy partner, Billy Van. Ponzi sat on an upturned trunk and looked in awe at Corbett, who stood a foot taller than he.

"Tell us about it, Ponzi," said Corbett as he applied his makeup. "I was a bank clerk six years and you must have stumbled on something the bankers missed."

"Yes," Ponzi agreed. "Maybe it was an accident the bankers didn't want to see. They don't want people to get money. I told people to come and take it, and the newspapers get sore because the people don't come fast enough. I am all alone in this."

"Well, if they pick on you, let me know," Corbett said.

While Ponzi stared at Corbett's meaty arm, Van spoke up: "Sure, Ponzi, sign up with Jim and I. Jim's got the punch, you've got the brains, and I'm me. We'll knock 'em dead with our act."

Ponzi thought about that a minute. "Maybe I will," he said. "I'd like to be an actor. I had a chance to go in the movies. Now I got a chance to go onto the stage. I think pretty soon I'll take a vacation and go with your act." He seemed serious.

Ponzi returned to his family and laughed at Corbett and Van's act. After the show he was mobbed by people hoping for a glimpse of him, and then it was time to go home.

After the excitement of the day before, Ponzi spent much of Wednesday, August 4, quietly laying plans for his new company. Fewer than a hundred people milled about in Pi Alley when the doors opened, and a majority of them were there to collect on matured notes. Ponzi kept up appearances, dressing this day with unmistakable symbolism in clothes fit for an angel: white Palm Beach suit, white cap, white socks, and white shoes.

Ponzi's imperturbable poise impressed some of the *Post*'s competitors, who took glee in rubbing Richard Grozier's nose in Ponzi's relentless survival. Several papers rooted once again for Ponzi, apparently to embarrass the *Post,* especially when Gallagher, the federal prosecutor, and Attorney General Allen were quoted as saying McMasters's story contained little of evidentiary value. Ponzi's only comment for investigators was to publicly decline Allen's suggestion that he reveal his assets to speed the accounting process.

"The exposé by the man who was employed by Ponzi for a few days as publicity agent has fallen into greater discredit," the *Boston Traveler* intoned, "as investigating officials repudiate its value." Ponzi himself had disproved McMasters's claims of insolvency, the *Traveler* said, by continuing to pay claims "with ready cash to refute its assertions."

Although less money was flowing than at the height of the run, the relentless withdrawals continued to drain Ponzi's formerly bulging account. By the time the doors to the Securities Exchange Company closed in the late afternoon, Ponzi had paid out another $313,000, bringing the total for the week to more than $1 million. In the meantime, Ponzi and Lucy Meli realized that at least one of their employees had turned the run to his own advantage. Louis Cassullo, Ponzi's former Montreal cellmate, had capitalized on the chaos by issuing forged Ponzi notes and getting straws to cash them for him. Ponzi and his trusted gal Friday realized what was happening, but Ponzi feared that refusing to cash any notes presented at his tellers' windows would renew the run and cost him more. So he paid the counterfeit notes even as he hastened his plans to open his new business.

That night Ponzi returned to the theater with Rose, accompanied by two of his lawyers, Frank Leveroni and Sam Bailen, and their wives. This time Ponzi took a step closer to a career on stage, joining Corbett and Van in an impromptu skit in which they bantered about the joys of becoming rich. Corbett and Van pretended to buy Ponzi notes; then Ponzi pretended to redeem them, using stage money.

Only fifty-seven people showed up in Pi Alley on Thursday, August 5, and some of them begged to invest before being turned away. Still, $168,000 would go out the door before the day was out. The biggest withdrawal was for forty-five thousand dollars by Ponzi's pals Louis and Charlotte Blass. The Blasses had bought the note on June 24, so it was not due until Sunday. But Ponzi paid it anyway, for the full amount due at maturity. What were a few days among friends?

Meanwhile, Pride's audit continued while Gallagher traveled to Washington to meet with his boss, the lantern-jawed United States attorney general, A. Mitchell Palmer, who took a moment from his hunt for Communists to hear an update on the Boston financier.

With the investigation plodding along and School Street quieting down, the newspapers struggled to find news to satisfy their readers' insatiable interest. The *Globe* won on this score with a front-page story about Ponzi's humble days in Mobile, Alabama. The story was innocuous enough, nothing more damaging than Ponzi had described himself about his rags-to-riches rise. But newspapers delving into his past held a distinct danger. If they dug deeply enough, Ponzi's prison days in Montreal and Alabama might be exposed. Panic would ensue, and collapse would be certain.

The lowlight of Ponzi's day was a long lunch at the Copley Plaza Hotel with the New York moneymen who claimed to be interested in buying his company. Their leaders were John Castwell, who identified himself as director of the Bolivian Wood Company, and Joseph Herman, who claimed to be an associate of the late South African magnate Cecil Rhodes. The longer they talked, the clearer it became that they would not be Ponzi's salvation. The New Yorkers' $10 million offer was contingent on Ponzi revealing his "secret," and the payment would come only after they had taken their profits. Questions also soon began to be raised about whether the men were working a con

of their own. When Herman's and Castwell's names became public, a
Boston banker remembered them as fast operators with whom he had
refused to do business with a year earlier.

While Ponzi wasted time with the New Yorkers, Bank Commissioner Joseph Allen discovered the first sign of weakness in Ponzi's financial armor. A week earlier, Allen had demanded daily reports on
Hanover Trust, with particular attention paid to Ponzi. Contained in
one of those reports was a strange piece of information: Accounts
under Ponzi's control, but established in other people's names, had
been credited with more than a quarter million dollars in loans from
Hanover Trust. Already suspicious of Ponzi, Allen had to wonder: If
Ponzi was as rich as he claimed and as carefree as he appeared, why was
he borrowing money from the bank he controlled? And why was he
doing it in "straw" accounts held in other people's names? Was it possible that he had nowhere near the $7 million in liquid funds he so
often claimed? Was he using straw accounts to mask his true peril? Was
he, as the *Post* story maintained, insolvent and teetering on the brink
of failure? Allen ended the day by dispatching two bank examiners to
Hanover Trust with a mission: Find out what Ponzi is up to, and find
out fast.

When he awoke the next morning, Ponzi knew he could wait no
longer to deal with Joseph Daniels, the furniture dealer whose million-
dollar lawsuit had helped to create his current predicament, for good
and bad. Though Daniels's suit had incited the *Post* and the authorities, it had also drawn investors by the thousands. But it had lingered
unresolved long enough. Ponzi did not mind borrowing money from
his customers to pay other investors, having long since abandoned the
idea of making money on postal coupons. But now he was forced to
borrow from banks, and that was another level of risk entirely. His
biggest remaining asset was the $1.5 million certificate of deposit in
Hanover Trust, but that was still three weeks from coming due. In the

meantime, Ponzi needed immediate access to the bank accounts frozen by Daniels's lawsuit.

Dressed for the role of banker, in a soft, black suit coat with a chalk stripe, Ponzi sent word to Daniels requesting a meeting. No lawyers, just two business acquaintances working out their differences. Ponzi chose his home turf Hanover Trust. Daniels was certain this would be the biggest payday of his life. His suit claiming half ownership of Ponzi's business had no merit, but sometimes it pays to be a nuisance, and this appeared to be one of those times. As for Ponzi, he was willing to pay a high price, but he wanted to limit the damage. Daniels made an opening bid of $100,000, but when Ponzi scoffed he quickly dropped to seventy-five thousand. Ponzi knew he could get him for less, and he offered an even fifty thousand dollars. Daniels leapt at it.

Ponzi ordered Hanover Trust officials to bring him ten thousand dollars in cash and a certified check for the balance. He hustled Daniels around the corner to Water Street, where the Locomobile was rumbling in wait. They drove together to the courthouse, where Daniels obligingly signed the papers withdrawing his suit. From there they drove to the Cosmopolitan Trust Company, where $389,000 in Ponzi's accounts had been locked up for a month. But there was a hitch. Cosmopolitan's president, Max Mitchell, had grown attached to Ponzi's money. He refused to empty the account into Ponzi's hands unless an attorney for Daniels vouched for the settlement.

Frustrated but eager to move things along, Ponzi agreed to call Daniels's lawyer, Isaac Harris. Daniels, however, stopped him. True to form, Daniels wanted to cheat his lawyer out of the deal. But Mitchell held firm: no lawyer, no money. Facing a stalemate, Daniels agreed to involve Harris on one condition: Ponzi would have to support Daniels in a lie to the lawyer—Daniels intended to say the settlement had been for only twenty thousand dollars, thus lowering Harris's share. Fine, Ponzi said, just call him.

Lawyers hate to be the last to know anything, so Harris began yelling the moment he arrived at Cosmopolitan Trust. He thought the

suit was worth at least a half million dollars, and here Daniels had settled for peanuts. Recognizing that the deed was done, Harris calmed
down, mostly after Daniels agreed to pay him ninety-five hundred
dollars and Ponzi kicked in another five thousand. With Harris paci-
fied, Ponzi could finally make his withdrawal. He insisted on cash,
pocketing thirty-eight ten-thousand-dollar bills and assorted smaller
ones. Ponzi walked out of Cosmopolitan like a strapping six-footer.

Daniels claimed victory. "I could have got more if I had presented
my evidence to the court, no doubt," he prevaricated. Seeing an opportunity to needle Harris, Daniels added, "But the lawyers might
have got it all. Now I am happy and can sleep tonight." Best of all,
Daniels said, Ponzi had agreed to involve him in the mammoth new
company being launched next week.

Ponzi's pockets overflowed with cash. "What a nice picking I
would have made for some of the stickup boys," he joked after depositing the money at the Hanover Trust. It could not have come at a
better time: 255 of his investors were massed in Pi Alley. The good
news, from the standpoint of confidence, was that only ten were in
line to withdraw their principal before maturity. But that was also the
bad news. The rest held matured notes on which Ponzi had promised
50 percent interest. Nevertheless, with Daniels's suit settled, Ponzi felt
more in control, more certain of conquest, than he had in two weeks.

"I am now on the offensive," he told the reporters trailing him.

Impressed by his refusal to succumb, the reporters peppered Ponzi
with questions about a recent rumor, spread in part by Clarence Barron, that might explain his uncanny endurance.

"Are you a Bolshevist?" one asked.

"No, certainly not," said an amused Ponzi. "Do I look like it?"

"Are you an agent of the Soviets?" the reporter persisted.

"No, I am not. I am an agent for no man or men. I am for Ponzi
and the people."

"Are you a Socialist?"

"I am not a Socialist," Ponzi insisted. "I am a firm believer in law
and order and [a] hearty endorser of the established government."

"Washington reports you are representing Lenin and Trotsky."

Ponzi had had enough. "Washington is crazy if what you say is true."

Nevertheless, Attorney General Allen was so concerned about the possibility of foreign influence that he sent an assistant, Edwin Abbott, to New York to consult with former secretary of state Robert Lansing. Fanciful as it might seem, the *Post* acknowledged, some authorities feared that Ponzi's operations were part of "a gigantic plan for the financing of Soviet Russia, and a plan which also embraced within its scope a determined effort to disrupt banks and financial institutions of the United States."

Had Ponzi been a Red agent, he'd have been the most beloved Communist in the country. Even Rose drew hundreds of curious women in her wake when she spent the afternoon on a downtown shopping trip. When she presented a check, the department store salesman acted as though he were in the presence of royalty.

"Are you . . . ? Are you . . . ?" he stammered.

"Yes," Rose said, blushing. "I am his wife."

The staid *New York Times* sensed the pendulum of public opinion shifting in Ponzi's favor. "Charles Ponzi retains his cheerfulness as well as his liberty," the paper said in its first editorial on the phenomenon. "In Boston . . . public distrust seems to be shifting from Ponzi to his critics and assailants, and the once long and excited line of those who wanted his notes paid. with or without 50 percent interest for forty-five days, has fallen away to nobody at all." The *Times*'s only caution involved Ponzi's refusal to reveal his methods, warning that "continued concealment on his part must continue to have the unkindest of interpretations."

Most of the Boston papers all but conceded the success of Ponzi's operations without endorsing his methods. The *Globe,* for instance, donned a puritanical and decidedly racist cloak to warn readers about the moral costs of collecting money without working for it. "There may be regions of the tropics where this is possible, but it will be observed that the people who thrive in those latitudes are not very prolific in anything except offspring," wrote the *Globe*'s editorial figurehead, known as Uncle Dudley. "In those parts of the planet which nourish high-grade human stock there is no such thing as living without working. If anyone does so, it simply means that he is living on the labor of someone else."

The *Post,* meanwhile, conceded nothing. Richard Grozier was as certain as ever that Ponzi was a fraud, and he was determined to prove it.

A crowd of Ponzi investors awaiting their money in Pi Alley.

Albin O. Kuhn Library & Gallery, University of Maryland, Baltimore County

CHAPTER SIXTEEN

"I FEEL THE STRAIN— INSIDE."

Ponzi left Slocum Road early on the muggy morning of Saturday, August 7, eager to visit his nemesis Simon Swig at the Tremont Trust Company. With Daniels's suit settled, Ponzi could withdraw the $185,000 that had remained locked in Swig's safe even as the banker had publicly called Ponzi an unbalanced crook. Ponzi wanted to wish Swig a sarcastic "good morning" as he demanded his money.

But Swig was nowhere in sight, so Ponzi had to settle for his son Benjamin, the bank's treasurer. Benjamin Swig counted out eighteen ten-thousand-dollar bills and various smaller ones and dumped them into a bag, which Ponzi jammed into his pocket just as he had done a day earlier at Cosmopolitan Trust. He hurried to Hanover Trust and deposited the cash, which would more than cover the day's payments to the 265 people crammed in Pi Alley. Collectively they held Ponzi notes worth $127,000. After meeting

briefly with Hanover officials, Ponzi slipped upstairs to an empty office to do some thinking.

While Ponzi closeted himself away, investigators held a flurry of
meetings in the offices of Dan Gallagher The federal prosecutor had
so trumped his state counterpart, Attorney General Allen, that the
Post flatly stated that Governor Coolidge "is far from satisfied with
the way in which Mr. Allen has been conducting the case." Allen's
embarrassment increased in the afternoon when he had to traipse
to Gallagher's office to deliver the transcripts of his meetings with
Ponzi.

In the meantime, Ponzi's rival and imitator, the Old Colony Foreign Exchange Company, quietly capitalized on the attention being
paid to Ponzi. Without fanfare, and without drawing attention from
investigators, Old Colony continued to accept deposits from investors
who otherwise would have preferred to deal with Ponzi.

Ponzi's private recess upstairs from the bank gave him a chance to
reflect on his situation. He wanted desperately to launch his new company, but the more he thought about it the more he realized that it
would be impossible until he proved to the world, and particularly to
his investigators, that he could satisfy all the liabilities of the Securities Exchange Company. If he immediately began collecting investments in the Charles Ponzi Company, he would fuel suspicions that
he was robbing Peter to pay Paul, and then the investigations would
only intensify. Also, his resuming business, regardless of whether he
operated under the banner of a new company, might trigger a confrontation with the authorities and prompt them to shut him down
immediately.

Ponzi realized that he needed to begin his new, relatively more conservative venture with a clean slate. And that meant holding off until
he'd answered Pride's audit with dollar-for-dollar evidence of his solvency. The question remained: How to accomplish that? Two weeks of
investors collecting their principal before maturity had certainly lowered his liabilities, and regaining control of the money frozen by

Daniels's attachment had helped as well. But the simple fact remained that his business plan, by design, guaranteed that he would be in the red. Without new investors in either his old or new companies, Ponzi was down to two choices: a fast and highly unlikely sale to the New York financiers, or a raid on the vaults of Hanover Trust.

During the seven hours Ponzi spent alone working out his options, a rumor took hold that he had fled. The story gained momentum when he skipped a two o'clock meeting he had promised to reporters who needed interviews for the Sunday papers. As the dinner hour approached, Ponzi heard his name being yelled by newsboys. "Ponzi is missing!" they cried, repeating the afternoon headlines. Amused, Ponzi wandered downstairs to read for himself about his disappearance. As he stood on the corner of Washington and Water Streets, word spread that the wizard had miraculously reappeared. Swarms of people rushed to see him, and soon more than two hundred surrounded him, pressing him backward against the building. Ponzi spent a few minutes greeting and shaking hands with his relieved fans before ducking into a nearby doorway. He might as well have chosen a lion's den. Ponzi had taken refuge in the *Boston Post* building.

He had already broken his vow never to speak with a *Post* reporter, so why not climb the stairs to the second floor and have a look around? Soon enough he was up to his usual patter, trying to charm the entire newsroom. For a half hour he held court among the paper-strewn desks in the city room, a crowded, messy, poorly ventilated space with the ambience and dimensions of a bowling alley. Then he got down to business.

"Why are you doing this to me?" Ponzi demanded of Eddie Dunn. "Why are you hounding me? Why do you print such lies about me?"

Dunn responded softly. "I'm 'hounding' you, as you call it, because I don't think you're honest."

"I'm not a crook," Ponzi shot back. "I have met all my obligations. My investors have made money as I promised. Stop trying to take bread from other people's mouths."

"We are only trying to get at the truth," Dunn answered. "Let us investigate your affairs in the interest of the public. If you are honest, there is nothing to fear."

"I've been on the level all my life," Ponzi said, his emotions rising.

Settling down, Ponzi gave the *Post* a statement about the conclusions he had reached regarding his new company.

"I have decided that it would not be fair to the public to open my new company to receive money on Monday until after these investigations have finally given me a clean bill of health," he said. "The investigation won't last long, and it will end very happily." To demonstrate his confidence, Ponzi said, he would instruct his network of agents to take applications from investors, to give him a sense of how much money he would raise. He predicted he would have ten to twenty million dollars in a matter of weeks.

After he left the *Post,* Ponzi told other reporters that one of the first actions of his new business would be to bid on the entire fleet of the United States Shipping Board, for reasons of profit as well as patriotism. "I mean to twist the British lion's tail," Ponzi said, "by keeping these steamships from falling into their hands." Investors could expect 1 to 2 percent a month, a far cry from his current deal, and would get only a plain receipt for their money. "This will be all the security the depositors will have," he said. "They must have faith in me."

For all his bravado, the pressure was beginning to wear on Ponzi. That night, he let down his guard with a reporter from one of the papers he considered most friendly toward him, the *Boston Advertiser.* He spoke of the relentless phone calls and requests for donations, advice, and time, and he complained of Attorney General Allen's repeated requests for lengthy interviews.

"They call me the 'Millionaire Kid' and 'The man with the million-dollar smile,'" Ponzi said. "I do smile. I smile at home and I smile downtown. But no one knows what I have been through in this fight. It keeps me at a tense strain all the time, and people make such demands on my time I cannot get time to sleep. I smile, but I feel the strain—inside."

．　．　．

Like a boxer gathering himself between rounds, Ponzi spent Sunday, August 8, inside his house, dressed in a bathrobe, never once venturing outside to feel the ninety-three-degree heat or witness the gawkers' cars on their daily parade along Slocum Road.

That, of course, did not stop him from speaking with reporters, and once again he held court, downplaying his liabilities and waving a telegram from Herman and the other New Yorkers claiming they were ready to pony up $10 million. Ponzi said a deal would occur only if they came to Boston with cash in hand and allowed him to continue to run the company—to protect the public. Neither condition was likely to be met.

While he relaxed, Ponzi spent several hours telling *Post* reporter P. A. Santosuosso the story of his life. He spun a picaresque tale of his boyhood in Italy, his arrival in America, and his travels before finding his fortune. Notably, though, he left several blanks in his chronology and cloaked the empty spaces in mystery. Ponzi told Santosuosso he had been engaged in "confidential investigations" in Canada. Then, "after three years traveling throughout that country, I was sent South." Ponzi had conveniently excised his prison years. As the young *Post* reporter pointed out in the paper, Ponzi's supposed vow of secrecy regarding those years "necessarily leaves out a great deal of Ponzi's activities in the story of his life between 1906 and 1916."

It was no accident that Santosuosso enticed Ponzi to wax poetic about his past. Santosuosso had previously heard portions of Ponzi's life story, and he had noticed the holes in the timeline on those occasions as well. He had begun to suspect that Ponzi was hiding something, and those suspicions had grown more urgent in recent days when a woman Santosuosso knew in the North End had passed along a rumor that Ponzi had spent time in a Montreal jail. Sensing that he was on the verge of a major scoop, Santosuosso had gone to the very top of the *Post* with his suspicions, sharing what he knew with Richard Grozier. They had nowhere near enough information to print a story—not unless they wanted to hand Ponzi the keys to the newspaper—but Grozier told Santosuosso to keep asking Ponzi about his past to see what other clues might shake loose.

As Ponzi regaled Santosuosso on Sunday afternoon with his auto-hagiography, Rose Ponzi walked into the parlor. Her eyes brimmed with tears. Dinner was waiting on the table and here her husband sat, still in his robe, talking to the *Post* reporter. Fiercely private, longing for his attention, Rose had been frustrated for days—she missed their old life, and she abhorred people staring at her in the streets, shops, and theaters of Boston. She turned to Santosuosso and delivered a statement of her own: "I would much rather that he was a bricklayer working eight hours each day and undisturbed by anyone in the evenings and on Sunday than to have all the wealth he has brought to me."

Later that day, a telegram arrived at the *Post* building from the newspaper's correspondent in Montreal with information that seemed to fill one of the gaps Ponzi had left in his story. A man who went by the name "Charles Ponsi, alias Bianchi," had been convicted of forgery while working for the Banco Zarossi in Montreal. Santosuosso called Ponzi's home to ask if he was the same man. Ponzi scoffed—that was ridiculous. Santosuosso persisted: Were you in Canada when this took place? Yes, Ponzi said. But what did that prove? Santosuosso pressed on: Did you work at Banco Zarossi?

"I might have," said Ponzi, ending the conversation.

Grozier, Dunn, and their reporters were tempted to run the story the next morning. But Ponzi had more lives than a cat, surviving the attacks by Barron and the *Post,* the relentless runs, the unceasing in-vestigations, and the McMasters exposé, without breaking a sweat or losing his grin. This time the *Post* was determined to finish the job. Grozier called for his ace reporter, Herb Baldwin, and gave him a mission: Get to Montreal as fast as you can. And bring some pho-tographs of Ponzi. Find out if the forger and the financier are one and the same.

. . .

The moment Santosuosso posed the question, Ponzi knew he could not avoid being revealed as a forger. And he was certain of one thing: "Exposure spelled ruin." By denying he was Bianchi/Ponsi, Ponzi hoped to delay the *Post* story for at least a few days. By then, Pride's audit might be complete and, if he could tap a new vein of luck, somehow he might be able to prove his solvency.

His plans on that front had not progressed much further than an unexpected influx of cash or a scheme to "borrow" whatever he needed from the Hanover Trust. But in light of how long Pride's audit was taking—approaching two weeks—there was a growing possibility that the accountant was stymied by Ponzi's admittedly chaotic system of bookkeeping. The index-card system designed by eighteen-year-old Lucy Meli might be having the unintended bene-fit for Ponzi of frustrating Pride from determining the true extent of his liabilities. If Pride came up with an artificially low figure, Ponzi might have enough money on hand with his $1.5 million certificate of deposit to demonstrate solvency. Or if that was not enough, Ponzi might be able to cobble together cash from several accounts, sell the stock he had accumulated, and secretly "borrow" a bit from Hanover Trust to cover Pride's artificially deflated number. Even without tak-ing money that did not belong to him from the Hanover vaults, Ponzi estimated that his holdings had a collective value of roughly $4 mil-lion.

Success on that front would mean vindication in the eyes of the public and perhaps even the authorities. And that might give him enough of a shield to weather the storm that would surely follow the *Post*'s disclosure of his criminal past.

He arrived in Boston early the next morning, Monday, August 9, seeking to focus attention on the question of solvency and to fuel his public image as a man of the people who would not be defeated by the "big men" who ran the city.

Ponzi gathered the reporters around him and announced that he would "call the bluff of all the public authorities and gossip mongers trying to make out that my liabilities are insurmountable." Specifically, he promised to pay the 50 percent interest on all outstanding notes, regardless of when they would mature, immediately after he proved he had enough cash to cover whatever debts Pride calculated. That would clean the slate completely. Then he turned his fire directly on prosecutors and bankers.

"After I have been proved on the level, I will demand that the public authorities be investigated," Ponzi declared. "I and the public want to know whether the actions of these officials have been instigated by bankers, or not, to try to cross me."

Public support certainly appeared high. Ponzi's clerks had to turn away people hoping for a chance to invest in his new business. Boston barber Joseph Bonina stood at the front of the line with five hundred dollars, hoping to be the first shareholder in the Charles Ponzi Company. He was outdone two hundredfold by pharmacist Louis Mantani of Portsmouth, New Hampshire, who had collected $100,000 of pooled savings from that city's Italian immigrants.

Shortly before noon, Ponzi received an invitation from Gallagher to hear Pride's preliminary accounting and to begin checking the accountant's figures. Ponzi brought along his two newest lawyers, Dan Coakley and his partner, former assistant district attorney Daniel McIsaac, who, he believed, would hold the most sway with the federal prosecutor. For the next three hours they discussed Pride's early totals, which looked as though they would be higher than Ponzi had hoped.

While they met, Ponzi sustained the most direct attack yet on his business, from the public official he least expected to skewer him.

It had been weeks since Ponzi had met with Bank Commissioner Joseph Allen. Ponzi had walked out of that meeting certain he had charmed and bamboozled the banking bureaucrat. But Ponzi had dangerously underestimated this Mr. Allen. While Attorney General

J. Weston Allen had publicly thrashed around with his investigation, the bank commissioner had employed a stealth offensive designed to starve Ponzi of the lifeblood of his company: cash.

Upon concluding that Ponzi's game was fixed, Joseph Allen had been quietly, carefully watching Ponzi's accounts at Hanover Trust, waiting for the opportunity to pounce. Two days earlier, on Saturday, Allen's bank examiners had informed him that Ponzi's main account at the bank, the one opened in the fictitious name Lucy Martelli, had dipped dangerously close to the breaking point. Even after Ponzi had deposited the money he had taken from Cosmopolitan Trust and Tremont Trust, the ceaseless withdrawals of the previous two weeks had left only about thirteen thousand dollars in the Martelli account.

Ponzi had tried over the weekend to replenish the account by transferring money from a bank in Manchester, New Hampshire, but in his haste he had made two mistakes. Ponzi believed the Manchester account held $275,000, so he wrote himself a check for $200,000 and deposited it in the Martelli account. When that check bounced, he wrote a second for $150,000. But Ponzi had only $146,000 in the New Hampshire account. By the time his second check bounced it was too late for him to write a third. Allen had already begun moving against him.

Knowing that Ponzi's Martelli account was on the verge of depletion, Allen had stationed examiners at Hanover Trust on Monday morning with orders to act as his eyes and ears. They watched as several dozen Ponzi investors walked from Pi Alley and School Street around the corner to Washington Street, then into the bank to cash their checks from the Securities Exchange Company. By early afternoon the examiners were certain that Ponzi's Martelli account was deeply overdrawn. They called Allen with the news: The Martelli account is busted.

At fifteen minutes before two in the afternoon, with the temperature approaching ninety-two degrees, Joseph Allen dialed the Hanover Trust Company from his State House office. He ordered the treasurer, William McNary, to immediately stop paying checks drawn on

Ponzi's accounts. Ponzi was the biggest stockholder and depositor in Hanover Trust, a man with a seemingly bottomless pit of money. Even if the Martelli account was overdrawn, Ponzi still had $1.5 million in Hanover Trust, locked in a certificate of deposit. McNary told the bank commissioner he would not comply with his order.

Allen's authority was on the line. He dictated a written order to Hanover Trust insisting that no more Ponzi checks be honored and implying that McNary and the bank's other officers would be held liable for any losses if there were. The order reached Washington Street at two forty-five in the afternoon; this time McNary and bank president Henry Chmielinski complied.

Within minutes of Allen's initial call to Hanover Trust, he had launched the second half of his carefully choreographed attack. Three Ponzi depositors, with combined investments of a mere $750, appeared in court to file an involuntary petition seeking to declare Ponzi bankrupt. Allen denied having orchestrated the bankruptcy filing, but his involvement was unmistakable. Under normal circumstances, Ponzi could laugh at such a petition and quickly pay off the investors. But filed in concert with the bank commissioner's declaration that Ponzi's account was overdrawn, it carried heavy symbolic weight, just as Allen certainly knew it would when he walked into the State House press office to hand a statement to reporters.

"I have directed the Hanover Trust Company not to pay any more checks of Charles Ponzi, the Securities Exchange Company, or any of his agencies, as the account of Lucy Martelli, trustee, against which these checks are charged, is now overdrawn," it read. "As commissioner of banks I have no supervision over the affairs of Charles Ponzi or the Securities Exchange Company. The moment I learn, however, that he is overdrawing his account in a trust company, which is under my supervision, it is my duty to interfere."

The reporters instantly understood: Bank Commissioner Joseph Allen, who neither sought nor liked publicity, had acted decisively while federal, state, and local prosecutors—Daniel Gallagher, J. Weston Allen, and Joseph Pelletier—had spent weeks battling one another and keeping a weather eye on public opinion. Even more than the others, Attorney General Allen, already subject to ridicule and second-guessing over his handling of the case, realized he was watching his political future vanish before his eyes.

Hoping to steal back some thunder, the attorney general immediately issued a statement built on the meager findings of the New York trip taken by his assistant Albert Hurwitz. Hurwitz had gone searching for banks Ponzi used to transfer money to and from Europe. He had learned that the banks that fit the description Ponzi had given had done only token business with him, nothing on the scale that Ponzi had claimed. Hurwitz believed he had cracked the case, though in reality it was small potatoes. Ponzi had not been under oath when he had met with Attorney General Allen, and he'd had no obligation to detail his business methods or his banking relationships. Hurwitz's discovery that Ponzi had apparently misled the attorney general was a slender thread on which to hang a charge of larceny by false pretenses. Ponzi could easily say he had misspoken, set the record straight, and move on. But in his moment of political desperation, the attorney general believed he had something to crow about.

What Attorney General Allen's statement lacked in substance it made up for in length, detailing Hurwitz's work and its tenuous findings. Its strongest line demonstrated its flaws: "Although Mr. Ponzi claims that his dealings in International Reply Coupons have been conducted upon a very large scale, aggregating millions of dollars, the investigation has disclosed nothing to confirm his statement." Allen acknowledged that his investigation was incomplete, but he said he was speaking out because it was in the public interest. What he did not say, of course, was that his statement left open the possibility that his investigation had hit a roadblock or had simply failed. The attorney general's timing was even more suspect because there was no need for urgent disclosure—the public faced no risk, because Ponzi still had not resumed accepting investments.

Attorney General Allen intensified his new offensive by urging Ponzi note holders to visit an office he had set up in the State House to collect their names, addresses, and amounts invested for some undisclosed future use in the investigation.

The moves by the two Allens had their desired effect. By the time Ponzi stepped out of his meeting at Gallagher's office, the presses were already running on the afternoon papers declaring him in crisis. To escape the firestorm, Ponzi rushed to the tenth floor of the Hanover Trust building, where he holed up in the empty offices of the C & R Construction Company, in which he held a controlling interest. By six o'clock, just as the heat of the day had begun to break, Ponzi invited the reporters to join him.

When they arrived, Ponzi sat nibbling on the remnants of a box lunch and sipping ginger ale. A bottle of milk was nearby, no doubt to coat the lining of his ravaged stomach. He was well dressed as always, but reporters noticed something different: His smile had lost its radiance.

"I have played fair with everybody," he began. "I have paid out to date all I could pay out, regardless of the attacks and impediments thrown my way by the state authorities, meaning Attorney General Allen and Bank Commissioner Allen. I do not propose to take issue with either official until after the investigation. But since it has developed that the above two mentioned gentlemen are not working for the interests of the people, but they are rather furthering the plans of the bankers against the people, I think that the time has arrived to make some revelations. Attorney General Allen, to begin with, has shown very little interest in what I was doing up to the time that I invited an investigation. In my opinion, it is the duty of a public official to prevent an alleged criminal from taking money, not from stopping him when he is paying that money out."

Reporters read him the attorney general's statement and Ponzi scoffed: "All I told Attorney General Allen was bull and it has kept him busy. If I see him again I will tell him some more bull which will keep him busy for two months."

When the reporters stopped laughing, Ponzi turned his attention to the bank commissioner, insisting he had more than enough money to cover any overdraft, either from his certificate of deposit or from accounts in other banks. But Ponzi claimed the commissioner's action would force him to stop paying investors at least until he had proved his solvency to Pride.

"That I am solvent there is not the slightest doubt in anybody's mind. Why should then my investors be delayed in receiving payments which are rightfully theirs when I have cash available to pay them?"

Ponzi urged the public to rise up "and demand the removal or dismissal of public officials who not only have proven inefficient in the performance of their duties, but who have also overstepped their authority for reasons which are undoubtedly open to criticism."

"I am sick and tired of the whole mess," he declared flatly.

Several times as he spoke, Ponzi was interrupted by the shouts of newsboys on Washington Street, carried ten floors skyward by the warm breeze: "Ponzi stopped!" they cried. "Ponzi stopped!"

Ponzi had grown to like several of the newspapermen who had followed him around nonstop for two weeks. In his moment of need, he appealed to them as little guys just like him. "Don't you fellows knock me, for I am fighting in a desperate game, and if I win you will be benefited and interested as much as me," he implored them. "I am a fighter and I shall stay with the devils to the end, for I am sure you fellows are no more of the autocracy than I am, and I am fighting the autocracy."

To lighten the mood, one of the reporters asked Ponzi if he had enough money to buy his supper. Ponzi gave a half smile and produced a roll of cash, with a ten-thousand-dollar bill on the outside.

"I am broke," he said sarcastically. "They say I am broke and am a criminal. You boys all know me. If I did not have the money to pay all my notes with I would have stopped paying on the twenty-sixth [of July]. I would have flown the coop."

"Did you have passports?" a reporter asked.

"I don't need passports," Ponzi answered. "I have not got my second papers [for citizenship] out yet."

"If you went away you would have go to in the steerage and you could not come back again," the reporter said.

"Do you think I would care to come back after I had stolen seven or eight million dollars—if I had stolen the money? I could have gone away any time I wished. I did not wish to. I did intend to go to Italy on July Fourth and I bought my tickets three months ahead of that time. But my business was becoming bigger and bigger and I could not afford to leave or get away, so I sent for my dear mother to come over here and she came. I am not going to run away. That is what the officials would like to have me do. I am a fighter and I am going to fight them to the end. And I am going to win my fight."

As the reporters went off to file their stories for the morning, Ponzi returned home to Lexington. After the day he had endured, it was not hard to persuade Rose to break her vow about never again accompanying him to the theater. He needed to be out in public, to show no doubt, no fear. They both dressed in white as if to prove the point.

They sat together in the back of the Locomobile for the return to Boston, where a box was waiting for them at the Park Square Theatre. On stage was a play called *My Lady Friends*. They were the guests of the show's producer, Harry Frazee, a theatrical manager who owned the Boston Red Sox. Frazee apparently hoped to capitalize on Ponzi's popularity, having forfeited his own eight months earlier by selling Babe Ruth to the Yankees. By coincidence, that very day a devoted Red Sox fan had sent Ponzi a letter. "Dear Charlie," it began. "For God's sake, buy the Red Sox." The theater crowd was equally enthusiastic, greeting Mr. and Mrs. Ponzi with sustained cheers.

Between acts, Ponzi ducked outside for a snack in a little fruit store on Eliot Street, where P. A. Santosuossc caught up with him. The smile and the confidence had returned. Asked about the attempt to force him to declare bankruptcy, Ponzi laughed.

"That is foolish. I am solvent absolutely," he said, adding that he would probably keep his offices closed until Friday. "I am very sure I that I will open for business again, and I predict a rush of business that will make financial history in Boston."

.   .   .

With his owlish glasses, receding hairline, and soft jowls, Herb Baldwin looked like a refugee from Edwin Pride's staff of accountants. But "Baldy," as his friends in the newsroom called him, was used to being underestimated. Confident of his abilities, Baldwin had become interested in newspapers while growing up in Everett, a blue-collar city four miles north of Boston. After spending his high school years covering schoolboy sports for the weekly *Everett Herald,* he'd earned admittance to Harvard's class of 1911. He'd worked for two years in the Boston bureau of the Associated Press, then had joined the *Post* and made a name for himself as a no-nonsense reporter with a writer's flair.

On Tuesday, August 10, Baldwin arrived in Montreal armed with a few recent photographs of Ponzi and a determination to get the story. It soon turned into a dream day for Baldy.

Although more than a decade had passed since Ponzi's brief stay in Montreal, he had left an indelible image. As Baldwin moved through the Italian quarter of the city, one person after another looked at the recent pictures of financier Charles Ponzi and exclaimed, "That's Ponsi" or "Why, that's Bianchi." The only question they asked was why he had shaved his mustache. Baldwin's best results came with Eugene Laflamme, who oversaw the rogues' gallery for the Montreal Police Department.

"Positively, that's the same man," Laflamme declared, holding his mug shots of Bianchi/Ponsi beside Baldwin's Ponzi photographs. He showed Baldwin the matches of the earlobes, the pout of the lower lip, and the creases on the forehead. Laflamme went so far as to pull Bianchi/Ponsi's criminal file, which contained details of the forgery that had landed him in prison.

From the police offices Baldwin went searching for victims of Zarossi's bank failure. He soon found several willing to express their anger toward Zarossi's erstwhile manager Bianchi/Ponsi. Baldwin also scored with the notorious Montreal padrone Antonio Cordasco. At first, Cordasco said he did not recognize the photographs, but then he looked closer. "Ah, my fine friend," Cordasco purred. "So I see you again. You are, you are—he's Bianchi, the snake!"

Bank clerk Dominico Defrancesco remembered his fellow clerk Bianchi/Ponsi as "a sporty feller" who always talked of making millions and dressed in fine clothes with white-collared shirts. Further confirmation came from a warden at the Saint Vincent de Paul Penitentiary. The only points for Ponzi were the warden's description of him as a model prisoner, though he weakened that portrait by saying that Ponzi had shifty eyes.

Baldwin had more than he could have hoped for: solid confirmation that the man who had gained the trust of tens of thousands of investors was a convicted forger and the former manager of a bank that had collapsed under a cloud of swindles. Elated, he wired what he had found to Richard Grozier.

"Are you sure?" Grozier wired back, knowing that a mistake of that magnitude could cost his family its newspaper and its fortune.

Annoyed but trying to toe the line of respect for his boss, Baldwin fired back: "Do you think I am making it up?"

That was all Grozier needed to hear. Baldy's got a big one. They'd better make room on page 1.

After being released on bond on August 13, 1920, Ponzi marches through downtown Boston, certain that he has suffered only a temporary setback.

Chapter Seventeen

"I'm not the man."

While Baldwin spent the day linking past to present, Ponzi plotted ways to soften the previous day's blows: the freeze on his accounts, the bankruptcy filing, the attorney general's accusations, and the call for his investors to report to the State House. He ordered the offices of the Securities Exchange Company closed until further notice and spent the morning in Lexington, where he assessed the damage, girded for battle, and listened to a summer thunderstorm. He was determined to make some thunder of his own rather than surrender without a fight.

In the meantime, the officers of Hanover Trust tried desperately to balance their books. They calculated that Ponzi had overdrawn his account by $441,778, a potentially devastating dip into the red that could send the bank to its death. Treasurer McNary decided on the only course of action he thought possible to save the bank: He would use part of Ponzi's $1.5 million certificate of deposit to cover the overdraft. Ponzi would not have gained access to that money until August 27—thirty days after he gave notice that he wanted to withdraw the money—but this was an emergency and McNary made up the rules as he went along. After returning Ponzi's checking account to zero, McNary made out a new certificate of deposit to Ponzi with a balance of $1,058,222, having deducted the amount of the overdraft from the certificate.

Before the latest uproar, Ponzi had agreed to return this day to the weekly luncheon of the Kiwanis Club. This time, though, the club's president had arranged a "battle royal" between Ponzi and a celebrated psychic named Joseph Dunninger, a friend of Harry Houdini's and Thomas Edison's. The club advertised that the mind reader would "throw the X-ray of clairvoyancy on the subtle brain of the little Italian and reveal what he found to the audience." So many people hoped to hear Ponzi's secret formula that the Kiwanians oversold the Hotel Bellevue ballroom and had to feed guests in shifts.

The afternoon was slipping away and still the show had not begun. Ponzi hated to disappoint his public, so at two forty-five he climbed onto a table, cigarette holder dangling from his fingers, and agreed to take questions. Before he could begin, someone called out, "Three cheers for Ponzi!" The crowd answered with gusto. Ponzi then regaled the room with his version of his rise from obscurity and poverty to fame and, apparently, fortune, tailoring his story to fit some of the latest developments. He said he obtained reply coupons directly from foreign governments, and that was why his activities were not reflected on the published tallies of how many coupons were issued in recent years. Ponzi also said those governments had profited from the deals, and that was why he had to keep his overseas contacts confidential. He vowed to reopen by Saturday, smiled incessantly, and needled the attorney general: "He has a good job, but mine is better." The audience roared. Ponzi got the same response when he paid mock respects to "my opponents, the bankers."

Finally it was time to pit Ponzi against Dunninger, wizard against wizard. First, Dunninger agreed to lower the stakes by promising not to reveal Ponzi's business secrets. The mystic asked Ponzi to write a sentence on a piece of paper and place it in his pocket.

"First," said Dunninger, "is the letter 'I.' "

"Correct," agreed Ponzi.

"The next letter is 'P,' " said Dunninger.

"Correct," Ponzi repeated.

Encouraged, Dunninger claimed to have received a vision of the complete sentence in Ponzi's pocket: "I propose to apply to banking the principle of giving the people full value for the use of their money." It was, indeed, what Ponzi had written, and the audience left the ballroom satisfied and enthralled at the magic they had witnessed. It was 1920, and anything seemed possible.

While Ponzi cavorted with the Kiwanians, offers of money flooded his offices. Hundreds of letters arrived at 27 School Street containing checks in amounts from twenty-five to ten thousand dollars, that last sum from a man in Savannah, Georgia. But Ponzi's clerks sent them all back on his orders. Ponzi spoke only briefly with reporters, using them to send a message to his investors: Hang on and do not cooperate with the attorney general. Nevertheless, about a hundred Ponzi note holders turned up at the State House.

Pride continued to refine his calculations, while federal prosecutor Dan Gallagher and Attorney General J. Weston Allen held one meeting after another to plot their next moves. Meanwhile, Bank Commissioner Allen took aim at a more established institution than Ponzi: the Hanover Trust Company.

As midnight approached, Herb Baldwin's copyrighted story rolled off the *Post* presses with a cannon's roar:

CANADIAN "PONSI" SERVED JAIL TERM

**Montreal Police, Jail Warden and Others Declare
That Charles Ponzi of Boston and Charles Ponsi
of Montreal Who Was Sentenced to Two and
Half Years in Jail for Forgery on Italian Bank
Are One and the Same Man**

**State Authorities Now Active and Promise
at Least One Arrest in Case Soon**

The headline writer had nailed it, though in his excitement he'd overstated the "promise" of an impending arrest. The story said only that
one or more arrests were expected "momentarily," and no state officials were quoted, even anonymously, making such a claim. Baldwin
also overstepped a bit, making it seem as though Ponzi's forgery conviction was directly related to Zarossi's scheme of swindling his depositors by stealing money they intended for their relatives in Italy.
Despite those minor missteps, Baldwin's story was as damaging as
Ponzi had feared it would be when Santosuosso had first called to inquire about his Montreal past. For the moment, though, Ponzi refused
to acknowledge it.

An hour after midnight, another *Post* reporter, Harold Wheeler,
rushed to Lexington with a copy of the August 11 *Post* still warm and
redolent of ink. Hours remained before it would hit the streets, and
Grozier and Dunn wanted Ponzi's reaction to Baldy's scoop. Whatever Ponzi said could be added to a later edition; the *Post* was driving
the story forward, and its leaders did not want to cede the next news
break—Ponzi's response—to the afternoon papers.

Wheeler made his way past the guards who surrounded the Slocum
Road house and handed Ponzi the paper. Ponzi read Baldy's story
slowly, deliberately, with a poker face. Wheeler studied him as he read,
but could see no reaction—not a muscle in his face moved, nor did his
eyes betray the gravity of the situation. When he had finished, Ponzi
shrugged his shoulders.

"I'm not the man," he said. "It does not concern me."

"We think this is the truth," Wheeler answered, "and we're going
to print it."

"Then you are going to get the presses ripped out of your building," Ponzi threatened.

If Ponzi imagined that the *Post* would retract its story, by dawn he
knew that any such hope was false. He met reporters again on his front

porch at eight in the morning, dressed in a silk bathrobe with his Colt
.25-caliber in the pocket. Seeming on the verge of coming unglued,
he pulled it out and explained to the startled reporters that he intended to use it for self-protection against two men he had noticed
loitering near his house.

Asked about the *Post* story, Ponzi seemed uncertain about the best
approach. He began with a rambling, awkward statement referring to
himself in the third person that sounded like the start of a confession
about his Montreal past. "If the statements printed in certain morning
papers are true," he said, "I feel that either he is one of many who
have made some mistake and paid for it, or that he paid for some mistake of another, and a perusal of the records there might hide a deeper
motive than it would be expedient to establish at the present time."
Ponzi then took a shot at the *Post:* "It is evident that some of the local
papers are endeavoring to hurt him for purposes which are as clear to
him as they are to the public." Suddenly he interrupted himself and
began a new statement. After starting and stopping two more times,
Ponzi got into the Locomobile and went to Boston to meet with his
lawyers.

By noon, Ponzi was ready to meet the press once again. The reporters were admitted into Daniel McIsaac's imposing law offices on
the tenth floor of the Pemberton Square building known as Barristers'
Hall. They found Ponzi seated behind a large desk, hunched down in
a chair, looking smaller than they had ever seen him. His gold cigarette holder dangled from his hand. The reporters looked for his smile,
but it was gone.

"The statement that I am about to make I should probably have
made before, in view of the notoriety given me by the press," he
began, a stenographer recording his every word. "However, I felt that
my past had no bearing on the present situation. If several years ago I
sinned—if I made a mistake and paid for it—I had every reason to believe that society owed me another chance.

"I am not the first one to commit a sin. I am not the only one, even
in the city of Boston. And when I see others who have been under the

same circumstances years ago and are today occupying prominent positions I do not see why I should be made an exception to the general rule and become an object of persecution on the part of either the authorities, the press or the public."

He paused and turned to McIsaac. They spoke for several minutes about one of Ponzi's former prison mates, not in Montreal but in Atlanta, a man who had enjoyed the support not only of President Taft but also the very same Clarence Barron who had helped lead the charge against Ponzi. To speak of "Ice King" Charles Morse, Ponzi would also have to disclose his own prison term in Atlanta, but at the moment that seemed the least of his concerns. McIsaac gave him the go-ahead.

"Charles W. Morse, at one time a prominent banker, was also convicted in the United States court," Ponzi said, "and sentenced to fifteen years in Atlanta, Georgia. I know it because I was there with him. Released after serving a very small part of his sentence, he has been out occupying for three years a position greater than he occupied before. He is a banker, mingles with bankers, deals with the United States government, and associates with the most respectable men in the United States.

"I do not mean in any way to imply that he is not deserving the respect of the public. But I merely ask, if he is as deserving why shouldn't I be?"

Ponzi paused again to let that sink in. Then, to lighten the mood, he gave a half smile and announced to the reporters surrounding him: "A new paragraph."

"The Montreal records," he continued, "show that a man of my description was convicted of forging in 1908 and sentenced to three years in the penitentiary of Saint Vincent de Paul, and served twenty months. That is all that the public in general cares to know. However, I feel that it is also very important for the people at large to know that, although I am the man who was convicted and sentenced for that crime, I am not the man who perpetrated that crime."

Grasping for a life preserver, Ponzi spun a fanciful tale in which he claimed to have taken the blame for a forgery committed by his former boss Zarossi, who had been enticed into the illegal act by an extortionist. Ponzi said he'd acted to save Zarossi because his boss had a wife and four children. Halfway through the complicated story, Ponzi's lawyer, McIsaac, had heard enough; he put on his coat and hat and said he would be back later.

"I am not trying to pose as a hero," Ponzi insisted even as he did just that. He claimed that at least two other men in Boston could vouch for his story, though he declined to name them.

Having opened the door on his second conviction, Ponzi felt compelled to address it. Again he assumed the pose of a wrong-place-at-the-wrong-time Samaritan.

"My next unfortunate experience," he began, "did not come of my own volition, but happened as a consequence of my first mistake. Released from prison without a friend, without a dollar, and without credentials—they didn't give me anything—I tried to earn a living as best I could. Within ten days of my release I was asked to escort five Italians into the United States. I did not smuggle them in. I crossed the border on a train—openly—and was placed immediately under arrest. I didn't dodge the consequences and I pleaded guilty. I expected leniency in view of the fact that the crime was only a misdemeanor and not a felony and that I didn't resist conviction. Yet I was sentenced to two years at the federal prison at Atlanta, Georgia, and my sentence was the maximum ever imposed for a similar offense.

"There isn't much more to be said. The public knows the facts and whether the same are such to make me unworthy of their confidence is for them to decide."

Ponzi then announced that he would resign, at least temporarily, as a director of the Hanover Trust. He displayed a measure of optimism, however, by insisting that the disclosures about his past would not prevent him from paying off all Ponzi notes "within the course of a few days."

When he had finished his statement, Ponzi waved off the reporters' questions. He slumped back in the chair. The sparkling energy that had made him a star was spent.

Before the reporters left, Ponzi added two codas that in many ways were the truest parts of his confession. First Ponzi told the reporters that he worried that news of his prison record would lead to his deportation. But even that was not his greatest fear.

Not knowing that his mother had secretly told Rose about his prison past before their marriage, Ponzi said his biggest regret, the biggest mistake of his life, was not having told his wife about his time behind bars. His eyes filled with tears at the thought of losing Rose. Somehow, Ponzi said, he hoped to keep his prison record from her at least a little longer. He told the reporters he had ordered all the newspapers kept out of their house. "I want to keep all this news from my wife," Ponzi said. "It would kill her."

"My nerves can't last forever," Ponzi added before the last reporter filed out. "I've got to go rest. I'm not going to give out any more statements for a while. I'm going to keep away from people—not come downtown."

If Ponzi thought the worst part of the day was over, he was mistaken. The next blow came at one forty-five in the afternoon, when Bank Commissioner Joseph Allen posted a notice on the door of the main branch of Hanover Trust. Above his signature, the sign read: "Under the authority vested in me by law, I hereby take possession of the property and Business of the Hanover Trust Company." It was the most dramatic act in the arsenal of a banking regulator, and it was the first time Allen had used the power since taking office six months earlier.

The examination Allen had ordered of the bank's books had revealed problems that went far deeper than Ponzi's overdraft. Under its president, Henry Chmielinski, and its treasurer, William McNary, Hanover Trust had exhausted its reserves and issued unsafe and illegal loans. Loans to companies with connections to bank insiders exceeded legal limits, and in some cases the accounts of those companies carried huge overdrafts. For instance, Chmielinski treated Hanover Trust like a rich relative, secretly borrowing money to finance real estate purchases and a company he ran called the Polish-American Finance and Trading Association. But Ponzi's overdraft was the last straw. Allen described how he had expressly prohibited McNary from tapping into Ponzi's certificate of deposit to cover the overdraft, yet McNary had done it anyway.

Hundreds of people raced to the Washington Street bank. Most came out of curiosity or to catch sight of Ponzi. As word spread a small number of depositors arrived and jostled their way through the horde to rattle the locked doors and demand their money, to no avail. A cordon of police officers surrounded the bank, but the excited mob pushed and pressed against them. After forty-five minutes of shoving, the police regained control and the crowd dispersed.

When Ponzi heard of Allen's move, he issued a statement without his usual vigor. "I learn with regret that the bank commissioner has ordered the Hanover Trust Company to close its doors. I feel that this action on the part of the bank commissioner is merely a new attempt on his part to prevent me from gaining possession of the one-point-five-million dollars which I have in that institution, in the hope that I will not be able to meet my obligations to note holders." Ponzi continued to insist that he had at least $4 million in assets. That would be more than enough, he declared, to meet his liabilities and move on to his new business. Publicly, he estimated that Pride would find no more than $800,000 in liabilities, though privately he certainly knew that the number would be many times higher.

Ponzi left Barristers' Hall at about five o'clock. As usual, a crowd gathered the moment his Locomobile pulled to the curb to carry him home. He flashed his smile and stepped into the car just as a newsboy leapt onto the running board. Amused, Ponzi bought copies of all the evening papers to read on the ride to Lexington.

As night fell, reporters took their places outside the house on Slocum Road. Around eight o'clock, they heard the sound of a woman weeping inside.

A few minutes before midnight, Ponzi paced along the gravel walk-way outside his home. If he could find any solace, it was in knowing that the events of the past twenty-four hours had not disproved his claims about his solvency or demonstrated that he had done anything illegal in building his fortune. Though his credibility was damaged, he still had fervent believers, among them thousands of people who had already profited from the Securities Exchange Company. At that moment, editors of the *Boston Traveler* were preparing an editorial about him, marveling at "the grip which this apostle of rapid finance is able to retain upon thousands of people." The editors even urged that Ponzi "receive the benefit of every doubt" and likened him to Jean Valjean in *Les Misérables*. Ponzi and the fictional Valjean spent their lives "striving to live down some misdeed, and oftentimes society appears to conspire against them."

Ponzi had one last flickering hope: He could preserve the life he had built if he could somehow cover the liabilities counted by Pride's audit, which was scheduled to be revealed at noon on Friday.

As he walked, a thought occurred to him, one he wanted to share with the public. He asked his guards to summon two reporters he knew were keeping vigil nearby. But by the time they'd arrived he had changed his mind and momentarily lost his bearings.

"Get away from here!" Ponzi shouted.

"One of your guards said you wanted to see a reporter," one of the newspapermen said.

"I made two statements today—that's enough," Ponzi answered. He pulled out his blue steel pistol and began waving it in the air.

"My guards' power is limited, but mine is unlimited," he yelled. "When I shoot I hit. Get away or there'll be some tall shooting."

Of all Ponzi's concerns, none had shaken him more than his belief that Rose had been unaware of his prison record and would now think less of him. But early the next morning, Thursday, August 12, he learned the truth: Rose confessed that she had known all along and had loved and married him regardless. Relief swept over him. He regained the composure he had lost the night before.

His personal fears resolved, it was time to confront the rest of his worries. Since Monday, Ponzi had been thinking about the preview he had been given of Pride's audit. Even with the Securities Exchange Company's maddening bookkeeping system, the diligent accountant had calculated that Ponzi's liabilities were about $7 million, maybe more. Ponzi had spoken briefly with Pride again on Wednesday, and it appeared that this would be the figure facing him at the showdown set for Friday in the federal prosecutor's office.

During the two weeks since Pride had begun his tally, Ponzi had done everything possible to marshal his resources. He had closed his far-flung bank accounts, pooled his money in Hanover Trust, and gathered the certificates and titles to the stocks, bonds, and real estate he had purchased during his shopping spree. Repeatedly, he'd tried to cash his certificate of deposit by selling it at a discount to another bank, but there had been no takers. Ponzi had also sought help cashing the certificate from Thomas W. Lawson, a legendary Boston stock speculator and longtime enemy of Clarence Barron's. Lawson's fame derived in part from a book he'd written called *Frenzied Finance,* about stock market abuses. An endorsement from Lawson would go a long way. But Ponzi was too late. Weeks earlier, Simon Swig of Tremont Trust had approached Lawson for his opinion on Ponzi, and Lawson had concluded that it was almost certainly a swindle. Even if Lawson had agreed to help Ponzi turn his certificate of deposit into cash, his assets totaled only $4 million—$3 million shy of Pride's number.

As the Friday deadline approached, Ponzi's slim hopes of closing that gap disappeared. His last chance was his plan to temporarily "borrow" assets in the vaults of Hanover Trust. But the bank commissioner had unwittingly foiled that far-fetched idea by seizing the bank and locking its doors. Time was fast running out.

If Ponzi had any doubts about what would happen next, he needed only to look at the screaming headline atop the front page of that morning's *Post:*

ARREST IN PONZI CASE MAY BE MADE TODAY

Below were four photographs that made Ponzi cringe. Two were twelve years old—the grim-faced mug shots from his Montreal forgery arrest. Below those were two recent photographs of the smiling Ponzi, but a *Post* illustrator had added a mustache on one "for the purpose of comparing it with his Canadian pictures," the caption read. Inside the paper was the latest sketch by Ritchie, titled "Ready to Burst." Cartoon images of four men—Gallagher, Pride, and the two Allens—stood atop the federal building and the State House using spears to poke holes in a balloon labeled "The Ponzi Get-Rich-Quick Bubble."

Ponzi knew what he had to do. He dressed in a somber suit with a chalk stripe, a fashion choice that reflected his decision as much as it fit the cloudy weather. Speaking briefly with the reporters camped out on Slocum Road, Ponzi gave no indication of what he had planned, addressing only suggestions that he might run and the disclosures about his record.

"I am not going to flee," he said, "but will stay here and face the music. I am going to prove that I am on the level now. The past has nothing to do with the present."

He went back inside but a short time later slipped out a back door, ducked into the Locomobile, and pulled down the window shades for the ride to Boston. It was a long enough ride for him to think about how miserable he'd felt in 1908 when two Montreal police detectives had surprised him at his apartment and placed him under arrest. He also had time to recall his shock in 1910 when the immigration inspector had seized him for smuggling aliens. This time, a decade older and wiser, he was determined to change the script. Ponzi wanted to remain as much in control as possible under the circumstances, deciding when, where, and by whom he would be taken into custody.

Attorney General Allen was greedy to do the honors, having spent nearly three weeks battling accusations that he had bungled the investigation. But Ponzi was loath to give him that satisfaction. Federal prosecutor Dan Gallagher had played straight with him and, more important, the federal prosecutor was a friend and ally of Ponzi's lawyer Dan Coakley. If the time came to cut a deal, Ponzi wanted Coakley by his side and Gallagher on the other side of the table. He told his driver to take him to Coakley's office.

With Coakley in tow, Ponzi went glumly to Gallagher's office on Devonshire Street, his walking stick hanging limp on his arm and his jaunty cigarette holder nowhere in sight. When Gallagher received them, Ponzi admitted no wrongdoing and asserted his belief that Pride had overestimated his debts.

"But you have agreed to accept the auditor's figures," Gallagher said.

"Yes," Ponzi acknowledged. "I have agreed to accept his figures."

At that moment, Ponzi knew he was defeated, but he had no intention of remaining that way. He would take his medicine but surely rise again, next time even higher than before. "No man is ever licked, unless he wants to be," Ponzi told himself. "And I didn't intend to stay licked. Not so long as there was a flickering spark of life left in me."

Ponzi told Gallagher he was ready to turn himself in. Gallagher readily accepted. They left Gallagher's office and crossed the street to the federal building. Ponzi walked into the office of U.S. Marshal Patrick J. Duane, an eccentric who was dressed, as usual, as if for a wedding, in a tall silk hat, striped pants, and a long, double-breasted frock coat.

"Mr. Ponzi wishes to surrender," Gallagher said, beaming. They sat around Duane's office while a warrant was hastily drawn up charging Ponzi with using the mails in a scheme to defraud. With Ponzi putting himself at Gallagher's disposal, it made no difference that the charge was almost comical. His only use of the mails had been to send letters to investors urging them to collect their money, which he'd gladly paid when they'd showed up. Gallagher glossed over that fact, focusing the clamoring reporters on Ponzi's admission that he could not meet the debts Pride had counted. Gallagher even borrowed a phrase from turncoat publicity agent William McMasters, declaring that the financier who had gripped the nation was now "hopelessly insolvent."

Ponzi waited quietly in Duane's office for Coakley to summon a bail bondsman named Morris Rudnick, who dutifully put up the twenty-five thousand dollars in cash needed to secure Ponzi's freedom.

Meanwhile, Attorney General Allen continued to collect names and stories from Ponzi note holders who seemed certain to reclaim only a fraction of their investments. They came from all walks of life, young and old, new arrivals and the deeply rooted. Some were on the verge of panic. Others took their expected losses philosophically. A printer from the North End had invested his life savings, four thousand dollars, in the hope of buying a house. "Wife and I were going to buy a real palace if Ponzi doubled my money," he said. "Guess it's a dog house now."

Still others refused to give up. "You bet he's all right," said one man in a North End grocery store. "He could have gotten clean away with it if he'd wanted to. Would he have been fool enough to stick around if he'd been crooked?" Nearby, two children negotiating the sale of a rusty pocketknife spoke the language of Ponzi. "Give you 50 percent," said one.

A reporter found Edwin Pride still sifting through Ponzi's receipts. "Don't you think Ponzi started out all right—with some sort of a coupon scheme?"

"Well, I don't know," Pride said. "Ponzi may have had, and may still have, the best intentions in the world. But I think he 'played the game' from the start."

By the time Ponzi had entered his innocent plea, made bail, and emerged on the street, some of his vigor had returned. He began swinging his walking stick again, and as he promenaded through Post Office Square, scores of onlookers fell into step behind him. They did not cheer as they had in days past, but it was still one last parade for the biggest little man in town. Ponzi's starched white shirt glowed bright against his dark tailored suit, and his shoes shone with high gloss as they clicked against the trolley tracks embedded in the cobblestoned street. Office workers rushed to see him. Soon every window in the square was filled with the faces of the curious and the furious. The procession passed in front of a horse-drawn carriage. Its driver surveyed the scene, peering out from under a hat tipped low on his forehead to block the sun. He kept his hands on the reins and a scowl on his face. A boy wearing knee britches, high socks, and a messenger's cap ran alongside Ponzi's group, smiling and calling out to the famous man. Ponzi shot the boy a crooked half grin. He still had his fans, and they still hoped he would prove the doubters wrong.

Ponzi darted into a car, but before he could get away two Boston police inspectors flashed their badges. They served him with a warrant from Attorney General Allen charging Ponzi with three counts of larceny. Once again, Allen had to settle for second place. Ponzi delayed his return home for another court appearance. He again pleaded innocent and posted an additional ten thousand dollars' bond.

When Ponzi arrived at Lexington, he had little to say to reporters. "I am going to stay home tonight. I am not going away," he said. "If I had planned to run away at any time I certainly would not have done what I did today."

But Rose, who had shunned the limelight her husband had so craved, recognized that this was the moment she needed to speak for them both. Having never told Rose the true nature of his business, Ponzi could not have asked for a more loyal or trusting advocate. They stood together in the garden, her arm linked with his, a brave smile on her face.

"I love him more than ever," she began. "My faith in my husband is as unshaken as it was before. Somehow, I am rather pleased with what happened today, for it gives me a chance to show the world and to give added evidence to my husband that I love him."

"Of course he is innocent," Rose continued. "He has been terribly persecuted. Allow him and he will be able to meet every obligation honorably. I suppose that not everybody has the faith in him that I have. That is because everybody does not know him as well as I. To

meet my husband is to like him—at least. To know him well is to love
him. I would not be able to enjoy life with ill-gotten riches. It is not
in my makeup. Yet at the moment I feel almost perfectly contented for
I am certain that my husband's gains were honorably received. He is a
big man who will face the danger of having his skin grafted on a
woman he did not know, and serve a prison term to absolve a friend.
My husband did both, and he is a bigger and more honorable man
today than he ever was."

Rose capped her speech by calling Ponzi her "ideal." Hearing that,
he pulled her close and kissed her. They went together into the house
and closed the door.

Later that night on Washington Street, the lights were blazing inside
the *Post* newsroom as the staff raced to make the deadline for the next
morning's paper. For nearly three weeks, Richard Grozier and his staff
had pursued Ponzi. Now they were ready to beat their chests and yell
to the heavens.

Cartoonist William Norman Ritchie began work on a new sketch
showing "Ponzi's Pot of Gold" smashed atop caricatured bank officials
and Ponzi note holders, with a smiling Ponzi looking on from behind
bars. That would be followed by a half-biblical, half-puritanical editorial from Richard Grozier urging readers to reflect on the satisfaction
of earning one's keep. The editorial proclaimed that "poverty is not
the curse which many think it is, but the blessing which makes men
strive to attain a higher standard of living."

The most urgent work was the writing and editing of the lead news
story for the next morning's paper, printed under a triumphant banner headline:

**PONZI ARRESTED;
ADMITS NOW HE CANNOT PAY—
$3,000,000 SHORT**

By the time it went to press, the story was polished as brightly as
Ponzi's shoes. Eschewing the usual dividing line between news and

opinion, the story heaped scorn on Ponzi and unleashed pent-up fury that previously would have been potentially libelous. "He was ignorant of business, knew little or nothing of banking, his knowledge of foreign exchange was ludicrous, his statements to newspapers and business men's clubs were grotesque in their absurdity," it sneered. "He painted halos around his head, but the facts have shown only sordid swindles."

Yet even as it condemned Ponzi, fairness demanded that the *Post* concede he was something special. Grudgingly, the story acknowledged "his bubbling vivacity, his boundless imagination, his smooth and ready tongue, coupled with a remarkable and winning charm." Finding a balance between the images of the debonair and the debased, the *Post* gave Ponzi a backhanded compliment for the ages: "Of all the get-rich-quick magnates that have operated, Ponzi is the king."

The day the story appeared, bail bondsman Morris Rudnick got cold feet and withdrew the twenty-five thousand dollars he had put up to secure Ponzi's freedom. At about four o'clock that afternoon, Ponzi returned to the federal building, a dour look on his face. At first, he hoped to quickly find a new bail bondsman, but soon he realized he would have to spend the night in jail. He called Rose in Lexington and told her he needed to stay overnight in Boston "on business."

Ponzi exited the federal building flanked by federal marshals. With his captors at his side Ponzi rushed past reporters and photographers and hopped into a taxicab waiting to take them to the East Cambridge Jail. When the cab pulled up to the jail, Ponzi leapt out and ran to the door to escape the photographers he had once courted.

"You didn't get me, did you?" he called back to them as he rushed inside. "You didn't get me."

Soon his spirits flagged, and as he shuffled toward the jail's receiving desk, a frightened look settled on his face. He looked up at a calendar on the wall and shuddered at the date: Friday the thirteenth. Like a deposed monarch stripped of his scepter, Ponzi surrendered his walking stick. In short order he was booked, bathed, and taken to a cell for a dinner brought from a nearby restaurant: breaded veal chops, fried potatoes, a pot of coffee, a bottle of ginger ale, and a cantaloupe. A jailer brought him a briar pipe and a pouch of tobacco, and he smoked as he read week-old newspapers in his cell before falling asleep.

Ponzi thought he would soon regain his freedom, at least on bail, but it was not to be. Attorney General Allen made it known that if Ponzi were freed again from federal custody, the state would immediately file more charges and ask a judge to set bail so high that no bondsman would bet that heavily on Ponzi.

So Ponzi spent the next three months holed up in the East Cambridge Jail, awaiting trial on the federal charges. Rose was crestfallen by his imprisonment but remained as loyal as ever. She was certain he would satisfy all his investors, beat the charges, and return to her. In the meantime, one of her sisters moved in to keep her and Ponzi's mother company in the big house on Slocum Road.

As the weeks passed, federal and state indictments rained down upon Ponzi. He became the subject of what quickly shaped up as the biggest and most complex bankruptcy proceeding in Massachusetts history. Meanwhile, Pride expanded his work to include a search for hidden assets, but it was a mission doomed to fail. Ponzi had believed that the good times would keep rolling: he had not squirreled away so much as a dime.

In November, Ponzi faced trial in federal court on two lengthy indictments of using the mails to defraud the public. Federal prosecutors had located scores of people who had received Ponzi letters telling them their notes had matured—any use of the postal system in a fraud scheme was potentially a criminal act—so the two indictments contained eighty-six separate counts.

Before the trial began, lawyers Dan Coakley and Daniel McIsaac met with Ponzi and Rose at the jail. For two hours they talked about the best course of action. Time and again, Coakley and McIsaac urged

Ponzi to plead guilty. They had spoken with their good friend Dan Gallagher and cut a deal. Ponzi would enter a guilty plea to one of the eighty-six counts against him, and all the rest would be placed permanently on file. He would receive a prison term of no more than five years, but likely would serve only twenty months with the rest waived for good behavior. Once he had served his federal sentence, Coakley said, the state would almost certainly leave him alone. Coakley had never heard of anyone being prosecuted on essentially the same facts in both the federal and the state court, so Ponzi and Rose would be free to begin life anew. The alternative, Coakley warned, was a high likelihood of a guilty verdict and more time behind bars.

Rose wanted to know if Coakley was making the recommendation because they had no money to pay legal fees. She knew that Coakley and McIsaac had already returned to the bankruptcy trustees the fifty thousand dollars Ponzi had paid them; they would be working for nothing. Coakley and McIsaac pledged to defend Ponzi, fee or no fee, if he decided not to plead. That convinced Rose.

"I think Mr. Coakley is right," she said. But Ponzi would not hear of it. He insisted that he was innocent and wanted to fight to the end. He told Rose and the lawyers that he did not care if he was sentenced to thirty years—he would not plead guilty.

After three months of holding her chin up, Rose could take no more. She gasped, then fainted. When she was revived, tears washed her rounded cheeks. The lawyers left them alone to talk.

"What difference does it make what the world thinks, as long as I know you're innocent?" Rose pleaded. "When you come out we'll start life over again.'

Still Ponzi resisted. He worried that she might think he truly had been guilty if he entered such a plea, and he abhorred the thought of being separated from her. "I might as well be dead as away from you for five years," he told her.

But what if something went wrong, Rose wanted to know, and he was away for twenty years?

They went around and around, neither giving ground, until Ponzi finally said he would spend the night thinking and, uncharacteristically, praying about it.

The next morning, when Rose and the lawyers returned to the jail, Ponzi told them his decision: no plea. Rose shrieked and fell to the ground. Looking up at her husband, she begged him once more to take her feelings into consideration.

When they filed into the fourth-floor federal courtroom on November 30, 1920, reporters noticed that Ponzi appeared to be the same dapper gent they had spent the summer chasing all over town. He wore a brown, double-breasted suit with a dark blue silk handkerchief peeking from the pocket. But something seemed different about him. Then it struck them: He seemed nervous, unsure of himself. Rose, dressed for mourning in a black dress, a black hat, and a gray squirrel wrap, sat in the front row of spectators, sobbing.

Clerk Arthur Brown read the charges against Ponzi and reminded him that he had originally pleaded not guilty. Asked if he now wanted to change that plea, Ponzi remained silent. Standing behind him, Coakley whispered, "Yes." The clerk persisted, asking Ponzi if he wanted to plead guilty or not guilty. Again Coakley prompted him, "Guilty."

Ponzi seemed startled. But in a timorous voice, he said the word: "Guilty."

Coakley dug deep into his rhetorical tool kit and made a plea for leniency. "It is very hard for him to stand in this court and admit it," the lawyer began. "So he has asked me to present certain considerations to your honor. He had seven million dollars in banks that he could have got in half an hour. He had a passport for Italy and he could have taken a boat along with his seven million dollars. So, he said to me: 'Would I, if I had any intent to defraud, and if I did not intend to pay my creditors, have acted as I did? Would I go to the United States district attorney and ask him to put an auditor on my books and also offer not to take any more money?' He did that and he paid out the seven million dollars."

"The auditor says that he is insolvent. It appears that because of poor investments and paying out millions to his creditors, the entire amount Ponzi gained was about twenty-five thousand dollars, or ordinary living expenses."

Judge Clarence Hale interrupted: "Is there anything you can say that the court can conclude this was not a wild scheme?"

"I don't believe the defendant considers it a wild scheme," Coakley answered. "Ponzi absolutely believed that if he was not arrested that he would have paid dollar for dollar and be a millionaire standing here now. . . . He is not a malicious criminal. He is not a criminal of the stamp of 520 Percent Miller. . . . He paid out and today he has not got a dollar and his wife has not a dollar. You must not consider this case as that of a man who got seven million dollars and spent the money in riotous living."

When Gallagher's turn came, the prosecutor came down hard.

"He is a strange mixture of childishness and duplicity," he declared before demanding a lengthy prison term. "He committed the government to the scheme which he must have known was fraudulent. The postal department regards this as the most flagrant case of its kind. Ponzi made the government an acquiescent observer of his scheme. And in view of the fact of the postal department, and widespread losses, I ask you to impose the maximum jail sentence."

Judge Hale considered the opposing lawyers' arguments and made a pronouncement of his own: "The court is impressed with much that Mr. Coakley has said. But the court has a great duty to perform to the public as well as to the person immediately before it. . . . Here was a man with all the duties of seeking large money. He concocted a scheme which, on his counsel's admission, did defraud men and women. It will not do to have the world understand that such a scheme as that can be carried out through the United States instrumentality, without receiving substantial punishment."

With that, Hale agreed with Gallagher and sentenced Ponzi to five years in prison. Rose fainted when she heard it, even though that was what Coakley had told her to expect. She was quickly revived, then fainted again. The judge's one concession was to order Ponzi to serve the sentence in the Plymouth County Jail, near enough for him to assist in the bankruptcy proceedings and for his family to visit.

Rose cried softly. For what seemed like the first time in his life, Ponzi was silent. He sat deflated, shrunken, a little emperor without a shred of clothing. Before a marshal led Ponzi away, he scribbled a note on a legal pad. Reaching over the rail separating him from the crowd of spectators, he passed it to the clutch of reporters in the front row.

It read, "Sic transit gloria mundi." The scholars in the press corps duly translated: "Thus passes worldly glory."

As long as Rose remained by his side, Ponzi kept smiling, even
after his business closed and his legal troubles began.

The Boston Globe

EPILOGUE

Ponzi settled quickly into his new home: Cell 126 at the Plymouth County Jail, a concrete monolith with a million-dollar view of the Pilgrim landing site at Plymouth Harbor and, beyond that, Cape Cod Bay. He returned to the jailhouse routine familiar to him from Montreal and Atlanta: wake at dawn, dress in prison grays, work in the prison library, lights out at 8:30 P.M. Still, he retained his refined tastes, ordering engraved stationery—"Charles Ponzi, Plymouth, Mass."—as if the jail were his summer home by the sea.

A few days after Ponzi's guilty plea, a *New York Times* editorial offered a remarkably balanced epitaph on the affair. First, it poured on the condemnation, decrying him as "an egregious falsifier and a wholesale betrayer of simple confidences." But the *Times* recognized that there was more to Ponzi. "There was something picturesque, something suggestive of the gallant about him, and it is almost possible, though not quite, to believe that he was as credulous as his victims and deceived himself as much as he did them," the *Times* mused. "Perhaps the disinclination for being harsh in characterizing Ponzi is due to lack of any sympathy for those whom he robbed. . . . They showed only greed—the eagerness to get much for nothing—and they had not one of Ponzi's redeeming graces."

When New Yorkers went to the polls a few weeks later, election officials came across the names of two unexpected write-in candidates for state treasurer: John D. Rockefeller and Charles Ponzi. It was the company he had always hoped to keep.

Rose became a regular visitor to the prison, though she needed to get lifts and ride the trolley because authorities confiscated the Locomobile. She filled her lonely days caring for Ponzi's mother and their Lexington home. "The house was never as clean and tidy when we had servants around as it is now," she preened. Soon the job would get easier; bankruptcy trustees moved to seize and sell the elegant house to help defray the losses of thousands of clamoring creditors. The sale included an auction of all furnishings except a bedroom set the Ponzis had brought from their Somerville apartment. Ponzi's erstwhile chauffeur, John Collins, stood among the auction crowd that trampled the lawn on Slocum Road. He won the bidding for the music rolls from the Ponzis' player piano, as a memento of the glory days.

Some of Ponzi's other friends and associates had problems of their own to keep them busy. Several Ponzi agents not only had to worry about customers to whom they had sold notes, they also had to hire defense lawyers. Although Ponzi's guilty plea ended the federal investigation, that did not satisfy Attorney General J. Weston Allen. He insisted that the state seek punishment, too. Allen filed charges against Ponzi and several of his top agents, including his brother-in-law Rinaldo Boselli; cousins John A. and John S. Dondero; Henry Neilson; Harry Mahoney; and Ponzi's old Montreal cellmate, extortionist Louis Cassullo. All but Cassullo turned themselves in.

The last time anyone saw Cassullo, in August 1920, he was cleaning out one of Ponzi's safe-deposit boxes in the midst of the furor. Some said he fled to Italy. Wherever he went, Cassullo was never heard from again. Another of Ponzi's old Montreal pals was not so successful in avoiding prosecution. The attention surrounding Ponzi prompted authorities to renew their search for Antonio Salviati, who had skipped out on larceny charges relating to the Zarossi bank failure. Salviati was arrested in late August 1920 in New York, living in a cheap hotel under the alias Dongello Buccini.

In the aftermath of Ponzi's plunge, furniture dealer Joseph Daniels learned that turnabout is fair play. When the profits were rolling in, Daniels had demanded that he be treated as Ponzi's partner, filing the million-dollar lawsuit that had triggered Ponzi's downfall. After Ponzi's arrest, Daniels sang a different tune: He insisted he was wholly unconnected to the Securities Exchange Company. Eventually he was forced to disgorge the money Ponzi had paid him to settle the lawsuit, leaving him no richer from his Ponzi adventure. Ponzi's imitators fared even worse. The copycats from the Old Colony Foreign Exchange Company were shut down immediately after Ponzi's arrest and soon found themselves behind bars.

The banks where Ponzi did business came under closer scrutiny than ever. In late September, the Cosmopolitan Trust Company followed Hanover Trust into failure. Bank Commissioner Joseph Allen had begun focusing on Cosmopolitan when its panicked depositors had made heavy withdrawals in the wake of Hanover Trust's collapse. When he looked closely, Allen found that Cosmopolitan president Max Mitchell and his cohorts were so reckless with depositors' money that they would have embarrassed even Ponzi. Oddly enough, just a week before Allen seized the bank, Mitchell had publicly hailed the bank commissioner for his "fairness, skill and courage." The Fidelity Trust Company failed three days after Cosmopolitan, in part because of unsound practices but largely because of a run of withdrawals by nervous depositors. Simon Swig's Tremont Trust also suffered a run. Several months later it failed, too. Swig, Mitchell, and Henry

Chmielinski, president of Hanover Trust, not only lost their banks; all
three ended up in bankruptcy court.

Joseph Allen remained bank commissioner until 1925, seeing Massachusetts through the worst banking crisis in decades. He left the
state's financial institutions on solid, solvent footing and took a job as
vice president of the American Trust Company. He returned to
Springfield and resumed the quiet life he craved. Calvin Coolidge,
who by then had ascended to the presidency, remarked that of all the
appointments he'd made as Massachusetts governor, his choice of
Allen made him the most proud.

Ponzi and his former publicity agent, William McMasters, continued their feud in court. Despite the money he was paid for the *Post*
exposé, McMasters sued Ponzi for $4,067.50 he claimed he was still
owed for his publicity work. Outraged, Ponzi pressed forward from
jail with his lawsuit seeking return of fourteen hundred dollars he had
paid McMasters for ads that were never placed. Ponzi gained a small
measure of satisfaction when he won both suits. McMasters went on
to a career writing fiction, including novels and plays, one of which,
The Undercurrent, played on Broadway in 1925. He ran unsuccessfully
for governor in 1936, and taught journalism at Mount Ida College in
Newton, Massachusetts, before his death in 1968.

Clarence Barron continued to revel in his role as a living legend of
financial journalism, though the years after his clash with Ponzi were
marked by a losing battle with his already expansive girth. He became
a regular visitor to the celebrity weight-loss clinic at the Battle Creek
Sanitarium in Michigan, where he died, at age seventy-three, in 1928.
His death deprived him of covering the biggest financial news story of
the century, the stock market crash of 1929.

One year after Ponzi's arrest, his lawyer Dan Coakley and Suffolk
County District Attorney Joseph Pelletier faced the music for their
long-running sexual extortion scheme. Both were disbarred along
with a third member of their ring, Middlesex County District Attorney Nathan Tufts. Pelletier died soon after in what was widely believed to be a suicide triggered by his humiliation. Federal prosecutor

Daniel Gallagher, whose closeness to Pelletier tarred him by association, faded from public view.

Meanwhile, although disbarred, the irrepressible Coakley successfully defended himself against criminal charges related to the extortion scheme. He ran unsuccessfully for mayor of Boston, but bounced back to win election to the Executive Council, which confirmed gubernatorial appointments and performed other vague duties. That cushy job ended in 1941 when Coakley was removed from office for selling pardons to criminals. He died, unrepentant, in 1952.

Attorney General J. Weston Allen never achieved his dream of higher office. He ran for governor as a Republican in 1922 but was defeated by Channing Cox, lieutenant governor under Calvin Coolidge. Allen later served as a special adviser in the trial of Sacco and Vanzetti and in several appointed positions for the U.S. Justice Department. He spent the last days of his life as a psychiatric patient at McLean Hospital, where he died in 1941. His top assistant on the Ponzi case, Albert Hurwitz, was named acting district attorney in Suffolk County after Pelletier's removal. Later, Hurwitz became a leader in Jewish philanthropic circles, and his one hundredth birthday was declared Albert Hurwitz Day in Massachusetts.

In the aftermath of Ponzi's arrest, Boston newspapers told a handful of stories of people who had lost money in the mania, though reporters' interest in individual victims was scant and short-lived. The stories were written without including investors' names, almost certainly to spare them further embarrassment. A veteran who had twice been gassed in the Great War told how he had hoped to parlay his seven hundred dollars of savings into enough to move to Arizona, where the government had opened a health clinic. Instead he was stuck in Boston with a persistent cough. A Revere woman described how she had mortgaged her home for eight thousand dollars and lost it all. A young couple lamented having trusted Ponzi with twenty-six hundred dollars that they had intended to send to relatives in Italy.

After the collapse, hundreds of Ponzi investors swamped the Massachusetts State House, some weeping and others crying out for blood, to register their names with authorities in hopes of getting at least some of their money back. Yet some among them were philosophical. A tailor told a reporter how his hunger for what he called "unearned increment" caused him to give Ponzi eight hundred dollars against his wife's wishes: " 'Jake,' she said, 'you know yourself you never had any luck. Why, if you were to bet on the sun coming up in the morning, it would be just your luck to have Gabriel blow his horn before daylight. You keep your money in the bank.' " He ignored his wife. "I gave it to Ponzi. Of course he failed. It's just my luck."

On the other side of the ledger, a handful of Ponzi winners—those who'd collected their 50 percent interest before the collapse—turned over the money voluntarily. First among them was Joseph Pearlstein, who had learned about the Securities Exchange Company from Rose Ponzi when he'd sold her luggage. "This is dirty money," Pearlstein said. "I don't want it."

For the most part, Ponzi's investors suffered their losses, licked their wounds, and moved on with their lives. For the next ten years they received small reminders of their gullibility and greed each December. Trustees appointed by the bankruptcy court sent small holiday-season payments to Ponzi's creditors until the money ran out and the case closed at the end of 1930. All told, twenty thousand people who had held Ponzi notes at the time of the collapse received refunds equal to 37.5 percent of their investments.

The aftermath of Ponzi's story kept the *Post* and its reporters busy for years, not that there was any shortage of other news. Just a month after Ponzi's fall, the nation learned that players on the Chicago White Sox had taken bribes to lose the 1919 World Series in a scheme hatched by a Boston gambler, Joseph "Sport" Sullivan. The *Post* covered it as closely as any Boston newspaper, though Herb Baldwin was distracted by a series of immensely popular stories he was writing about the fictitious exploits of the newsroom cat, known as Von Hindenburg, "Hindy" for short.

Before moving on to the cat beat, Baldwin had a brief encounter with Ponzi. During an arraignment in federal court, Ponzi caught sight of the reporter who had gone to Montreal in search of his past. "You did a fine job on me," Ponzi admitted to Baldwin. "If it hadn't been for that story in the *Post,* maybe things would have been a lot different for me today." Baldwin eventually rose to night city editor of the *Post* before taking a public relations job with the Boston & Maine Railroad. He died in 1973.

Eddie Dunn remained city editor of the *Post* for thirty-five years. When he left in 1953 to open a public relations firm, the *Boston Herald* hailed him as "one of the ablest editors in his craft." Twice during his *Post* tenure he refused appointment as Boston police commissioner, preferring the city room to the squad room. Though he had helped to engineer Ponzi's downfall, Dunn had a soft spot for his old foe. They exchanged letters now and then, and more than once Ponzi urged Rose to seek out Eddie Dunn if she ran into any problems. When he died in 1961, Dunn was remembered as a friend to three presidents, Theodore Roosevelt, Calvin Coolidge, and John F. Kennedy, and as the city editor who'd overseen the *Post*'s Ponzi coverage.

P. A. Santosuosso left the *Post* a year after the Ponzi story to launch a weekly newspaper called the *Italian News.* He chose a sly location for his new business, one he knew would be available—196 Hanover Street, the empty office of Ponzi's North End branch. On the tenth anniversary of the *Italian News,* Santosuosso was presented with a purse of gold coins by Boston's Italian-American community. He gave the money to the Home for Italian Children, the orphanage that had never received the $100,000 donation promised by Ponzi.

Richard Grozier remained in daily control of the *Post* while his father continued his convalescence. Clear proof that Edwin Grozier had

placed his newspaper in steady hands came in May 1921, when the
Post's investigation of Ponzi was awarded the Pulitzer Prize gold medal
for public service, the highest honor in American journalism. The
occasion marked the first time the Pulitzer—endowed by Edwin
Grozier's mentor at the New York *World*—had gone to a Boston
newspaper.

The *Post* made news of the prize its lead page 1 story on May 30,
1921, under a headline as big and bold as the ones it had used nine
months earlier to assail Ponzi. The story, rich in self-congratulation,
recounted the long odds and lonely road the *Post* had faced at the start
of its campaign, including the support Ponzi enjoyed from public officials, police, other newspapers, and, most of all, readers. The story
told how the paper had been swamped with letters of protest in the
early days of its Ponzi coverage, and how many staffers in the *Post*
newsroom feared that taking on Ponzi would mean the paper's death.
Finally, the story detailed Richard Grozier's unwavering "courage and
fine sense of newspaper honor" and hailed him for having "stuck to
his guns when the outlook was dark indeed."

The young acting editor tried to deflect the attention. He ordered
his reporter to write that, as far as Richard Grozier was concerned, he
"had merely been carrying out the general instructions which had
been given to him by his chief, the editor and publisher, Mr. Edwin
A. Grozier, his father." Richard then heaped praise on *Post* editors and
reporters for "securing evidence of Ponzi's past career in Montreal
and elsewhere which pricked the bubble and exposed the fraud."

In a signed editorial two days later, Edwin Grozier set the record
straight. He bestowed upon his son the approval Richard had long
craved, doing so in the way they both knew best: in black ink on a
newspaper page. Edwin Grozier disclosed that he had been away from
Boston and incommunicado during the entire episode, and that his
managing editor had also been absent the previous summer from
Newspaper Row.

"The entire office, editorial, business, and mechanical, was in the
sole charge and responsibility of my son, Mr. Richard Grozier,"

Edwin Grozier wrote with evident pride. "It is to him personally, assisted by an exceptionally loyal staff, that the entire credit . . . was due." In closing, Edwin Grozier offered a rare, awkward window into his emotions: "We encounter in this life many difficulties and many compensating pleasures, and not the least of the latter in my case is to publicly give credit where credit is fairly due in this important and conspicuous case."

Edwin Grozier's homage to his son was ratified soon after when Richard Grozier was profiled as a newspaper hero on the cover of *Editor & Publisher,* a highly regarded trade magazine. It said the judges of the Pulitzer had honored Richard for "public spirit, courage, and persistence." The deans who had tried to kick him out of Harvard must have been surprised.

Edwin Grozier never regained his health. For the next three years, he was confined to his home while Richard ran the *Post.* When Edwin Grozier died in 1924, his will named Richard as the paper's new owner and offered some final fatherly words of advice: "I urge my son, in whose integrity and ability I have full confidence, to conduct *The Boston Post* . . . not as a mere money-making enterprise, but primarily and zealously in the interests of the people of Boston and New England."

In his first few years as editor and publisher, Richard exceeded his father's high expectations, continuing the *Post*'s aggressive news coverage and driving circulation up above 600,000 copies a day—50 percent more than at the height of his father's reign. In 1929, when he was forty-two, Richard married a beautiful secretary at the *Post,* Margaret "Peggy" Murphy. In quick succession they had two sons, Richard Jr. and David. But in 1933, Peggy Grozier died giving birth to a daughter, Mary. Richard Grozier fell into a paralyzing depression from which he never recovered.

He hired a nurse, Helen Doherty, to care for his children, and he married her the next year. But it did little to mend what his children called his broken heart. He became increasingly housebound, overseeing the *Post* from his Cambridge mansion. He read to his children, taught them chess, and occasionally he would take walks with his sons around the Cambridge reservoir. But as the years passed he ventured out less and withdrew further into his sadness. When depression finally consumed him, his family had him committed to McLean Hospital, where he died in 1946. He was fifty-nine. Of all the tributes he received, it is likely Richard Grozier would have been most touched by a plaque presented to his widow by the printers in the *Post*'s composing room, the very men he was most concerned about losing money during Ponzi's run. Inscribed on the plaque were expressions of sorrow and "deep gratitude for the fairness and generosity of Mr. Grozier as an employer and our admiration for his qualities as a man."

Richard Grozier's long, slow decline took a heavy toll on the newspaper. By the early 1950s, the *Post* was struggling to survive. Joseph P. Kennedy, the father of a young U.S. senator with presidential aspirations, offered to buy the *Post* and the *Globe,* but only if he could own both. The *Globe* was not for sale, and so the *Post* limped further into debt. The paper eventually fell into the hands of an arrogant, shady operator named John Fox, who never paid the Grozier family the $4 million he had promised. By the mid-1950s, nothing was left of the paper Edwin and Richard Grozier had built. The *Post* published its last edition on October 4, 1956.

The *Boston Globe* bought the *Post*'s library and its name, lest someone try to capitalize on the paper's glory days. Indeed, during the thirty-five years between the *Post*'s winning the Pulitzer for the Ponzi story and the paper's demise, it held an enviable distinction: No other Boston newspaper was awarded the gold medal for public service.

While Ponzi was serving his federal prison term, Massachusetts authorities pressed forward with plans to try him on state charges. Ponzi fought the efforts, claiming double jeopardy, but the state prevailed. In October 1922 he was back in court, his small frame thinner and his dark hair grayer than in his heyday. But he still had style, flashing his grin for reporters and sauntering into court in a blue serge suit, a dark tie, and gray spats. His fine clothes notwithstanding, Ponzi was too broke to hire a lawyer, so he acted as his own advocate, in a strange way fulfilling his mother's dream that he would follow their ancestors into the legal profession. To the dismay of his prosecutors, Ponzi proved remarkably able, grilling witnesses for the state and charming the jury. The crux of his defense was simple yet clever: A promise of profits is not larceny, it is merely a promise; when it comes to investments, promises may be broken when circumstances change. Rose was a courtroom fixture, leaning over the rail each morning to kiss her husband and wish him luck.

For six weeks, the all-male jury—a leather sorter, a rubber worker, an engineer, and assorted other workingmen—heard the extraordinary story of Ponzi and the Securities Exchange Company. To hedge their bets, the prosecutors decided to try Ponzi on only a dozen of the indictments against him, six for larceny, five for being an accessory before the fact to larceny, and one for conspiracy to commit larceny. Among the star witnesses were disbarred lawyer Dan Coakley and Ponzi's former bookkeeper Lucy Meli. Ponzi gently guided her through an account that roamed from their early days in the School Street office to the chaos of August 1920. Meli had faced some legal threats as well, but they had been dropped after it became clear that she had suffered investment losses of her own as a result of her blind faith in Ponzi.

Rose took the stand at one point, weeping as she told her version of the meteoric rise and fall. Ponzi testified in his own defense, regaling the jury with his life story and insisting that he had done just what he had advertised, trading in International Reply Coupons purchased in Europe by his agent Lionello Sarti. Under questioning he acknowledged that he had no proof, claiming that he had destroyed all correspondence with Sarti. One of Ponzi's investors, Carmela Ottavi, was called to the stand by prosecutors but ended up benefiting Ponzi. During Ponzi's cross-examination, she declared firmly that she still believed in him, despite her losses. He thanked her.

By the end of the trial, the jury was sold. Ponzi and his codefendants were all found innocent. When the foreman called out the final "not guilty," Ponzi bowed his head and began to sob. Rose rushed to him and threw her arms around his neck. Together they wept for joy. Massachusetts officials dropped the cases against his agents, but they were not finished with Ponzi—with the *Post* egging them on, prosecutors immediately began making plans for trial on the remaining ten indictments.

In the meantime, Ponzi was returned to the Plymouth jail to complete his federal sentence. While there, he faced surgery at Massachusetts General Hospital for the painful ulcers that had tormented him for years. Doctors warned him that he might not survive, so he sat in his cell and wrote Rose a passionate letter to be opened only in case of his death. "I do hope that I may live," he wrote, "because as long as I have you, life seems sweet regardless of our present sorrows. . . . I am leaving you forever, but I am bringing with me a most wonderful recollection of your wonderful self, and I am leaving with you kisses of lips which will close with your name firmly impressed upon them, and with a smile of eternal love for you." Ponzi survived the surgery, and Rose eventually opened the letter. She saved it among her treasures, along with several dozen other letters he wrote to her over the years.

Though Ponzi's health improved after the surgery, even more trouble lay ahead.

In August 1924, Ponzi was released from the Plymouth jail, having served nearly four years of his five-year federal sentence, with the remainder waived for good behavior. He spent several months as a free man, enjoying his reunion with Rose. But by November, the state had him back on trial, this time on five of the remaining indictments. Once again Ponzi acted capably as his own lawyer, and the case ended with the jury hopelessly deadlocked. Still the state was not finished. A third trial on state charges was held in February 1925, and Ponzi's luck ran out. The state prosecutors had learned from their errors at the earlier trials, and they had honed their responses to Ponzi's arguments.

When the jury foreman pronounced the verdict "guilty," Ponzi took the news stoically. Rose burst into tears. As she left the courtroom she collapsed, injuring herself when her head slammed against the stone floor.

Several months later, Ponzi was sentenced to seven to nine years in state prison as "a common and notorious thief." The sentence was stayed pending Ponzi's appeal, and he remained free on bail. Granted that reprieve, Ponzi began plotting his comeback, determined to repay all his creditors and regain his fortune.

For a few months he earned money doing a vaudeville act—a corny reprise of the impromptu stage show he had done at Keith's Theater—but he knew the real money was in large-scale investments. In September 1925 he and Rose headed south to a huckster's version of paradise, joining the tail end of the Florida land boom.

To avoid unwanted scrutiny, he at first adopted the alias Charles Borelli. But his ego could not quite stand the anonymity. He named his company the Charpon Land Syndicate—"Charpon" being an abbreviation of his real name. When Ponzi's true identity was revealed, he decided to make the most of his notoriety. He offered investors a better return than from the Securities Exchange Company: 200 percent in sixty days. The promise of such immense profits was based on Ponzi's far-fetched plan to sell ten million tiny lots of property around Jacksonville.

With money borrowed from his few remaining friends, Ponzi began the scheme by buying a hundred acres of land for forty dollars an acre. The property was in an area Jacksonville officials called "desolate and lonely," and at least some of it was waterlogged. Ponzi named it the Rose Maria tract after his wife. The Oreste and Imelde tracts would follow to honor his parents. He divided each acre into twenty-three puny lots he planned to sell for ten dollars each. That meant every acre would yield a profit of $190, or nearly 500 percent of Ponzi's original investment. Ponzi also intended to sell shares in his new company for investors more focused on profits than land. But his impossible dream was short-lived. Goaded into action by newspaper reports, Florida and Massachusetts officials quickly shut down the Charpon Land Syndicate. Ponzi beat charges of land fraud but was sentenced to a year in jail for violating Florida's securities laws. He was allowed to remain free pending an appeal.

Two months later, in June 1926, a dejected Ponzi decided he could not bear a return to prison. With Massachusetts authorities clamoring to bring him north to begin his seven- to nine-year prison term, and the yearlong Florida sentence looming as well, he disappeared. Eluding a nationwide manhunt, Ponzi made his way to Tampa, where he hoped to land a berth on an Italian freighter at the port. For several days he waited, and then he spotted a ship fittingly called the *Sic Vos Non Vobis*. The ship's name translates from the Latin as "Thus not for yourselves," a phrase used by the poet Virgil to decry those who profit unduly from the labors of others.

Ponzi called himself Andrea Luciana and signed aboard as a waiter and dishwasher, relying on skills he had honed during his early days in America. The ship left Tampa bound for Houston, and during the trip Ponzi disguised himself by shaving his head, growing a mustache, and outfitting himself in overalls and a sailor cap. Before he'd left, he'd

Flanked by authorities, Ponzi prepares for extradition to Boston after his flight from justice and arrest in Texas.

added to the intrigue by faking his suicide, asking friends in Jacksonville to place some of his clothing on a beach with a note apologizing to his wife and mother for taking his life. But Ponzi made the mistake of revealing his identity to a shipmate, and word spread to a deputy sheriff named George Lacy. The deputy followed the ship to Galveston and then New Orleans, where Lacy confirmed Ponzi's identity and placed him under arrest. The only good that came of it for Ponzi was the five hundred dollars he earned by selling an account of his capture to the *Post*.

Ponzi appealed to Calvin Coolidge, sending the president an urgent telegram claiming persecution and proposing his own deportation to avoid more prison time: "May I ask your excellency for official or unofficial intervention in my behalf? The Ponzi case has assumed the proportions of a national scandal fostered by the state of Massachusetts with the forbearance of the federal government. But, for the best interests of all concerned, I am willing to submit to immediate deportation. Will your excellency give his consideration of the eventual wisdom of my compromise?" Coolidge ignored the plea.

Desperate, Ponzi sent a cable to Italy appealing to the dictator Benito Mussolini. No help there either, making Ponzi one of the rare topics on which Coolidge and Mussolini agreed. Ponzi was returned to Texas to await extradition, a process he fought for months. While Ponzi battled, Rose accompanied Imelde Ponzi home to Italy, where she wanted to spend her final years.

Finally Ponzi was returned to Boston in February 1927 to begin his sentence in the Massachusetts State Prison in Charlestown. His prison job was sewing underwear. Ponzi sought a pardon in April 1930 when he learned that his mother was on her deathbed, but the request was denied. Ponzi maintained that Imelde Ponzi died without knowing the trouble he was in, but that was certainly wishful thinking.

When the final payment to Ponzi's creditors was made in December 1930, *Time* magazine took note of it. "Glittering in the archives of financial fraud is the record of Charles Ponzi, duper extraordinary, personification of quick riches," the item began. It went on to recount his aliases and his occupation—"thief"—and to claim that in his prime Ponzi slept in lavender pajamas. Ponzi wrote a lengthy, jocular reply from his cell, which the magazine gleefully printed. First he set the record straight on his sleepwear, insisting that he never wore purple nightclothes, "nor pink ribbons on my night shirt. Fur coat and overshoes on extremely cold nights have been my limit." In his letter, Ponzi mused about challenging the editor of *Time* to a duel, then thought better of it. "You know," he wrote, "I like you in spite of your jabs because you have given me an opportunity of spending an hour writing this letter. If you come over to Boston after I am out, I have a damned good mind to buy you a drink. Two if you can stand the gait. Will you libate with me?"

Ponzi was released on parole in February 1934 with seventy dollars he had earned in prison. He declined the customary free suit of clothes given to departing prisoners. Outside the walls, he stepped into a clutch of reporters. Balding and thicker around the middle, he was still Ponzi. "It's great to see you boys," he said, posing for photos.

After completing his state prison term, Ponzi is escorted up the gangplank of S.S. Vulcania *for his deportation to Italy in 1934.*

Though Ponzi's debt to society was paid, U.S. officials had still not forgiven him.

Ponzi had never obtained citizenship, so federal authorities moved immediately to deport him. Ponzi, Rose, and Dan Coakley pleaded for mercy and a pardon, even enlisting Ponzi's old nemesis publicity man William McMasters. At one point Ponzi went to the *Post,* hoping to persuade his former pursuers that he had suffered enough for his misdeeds. On his way into the newsroom, Ponzi walked past the Pulitzer Prize on display. He strolled over to Eddie Dunn's desk. The two shook hands and talked quietly about the old days. But there was nothing Dunn or anyone else could do. Appeals to the governor for a pardon were denied. Ponzi was deemed an undesirable alien.

On October 7, 1934, Ponzi's three-decade American adventure came to an end. At times crying softly, the fifty-two-year-old Ponzi was escorted to the S.S. *Vulcania* for deportation to Italy. He carried a suitcase filled with newspaper clippings, wore a new brown suit Rose had bought him, and in his pocket carried five hundred dollars she had given him. "I am not bitter," he told reporters. "I have met with much kindness. . . . I'm afraid I'm not a credit to this country but I hope to do better in the future. . . . I went looking for trouble and I got it, more than I expected." Asked what he would do differently if he were just arriving in the United States as a young man, he said ruefully, "I'd cut my hands off. And my head, too, I guess." When a reporter asked about Rose, Ponzi's eyes brimmed with tears. "No, she won't be here," he said. "I saw her for the last time last night."

He spoke of sending for Rose once he got settled, but her home and family were in Boston. Even if she had wanted to join him in Italy, Ponzi could not support her. He barely scraped by doing odd jobs and working occasionally as a guide in Rome. For the next two years they corresponded regularly. Ponzi enlisted Rose in his vigorous, lengthy, unsuccessful attempts to find an American publisher for the autobiography he called *The Rise of Mr. Ponzi.*

The inevitable blow came in 1936, when after eighteen years of marriage, more worse than better, more apart than together, Rose decided she could no longer remain Mrs. Ponzi. Her feelings for him had not changed, but their separation seemed likely to be endless. It was time to move on. "When he was down, when he was in trouble, when he was in prison, I stuck to him," she told a *Post* reporter. "When he had millions, when he had a mansion, when he had cars, I stuck with him. And now I feel that I have proved my loyalty through thick and thin, and I intend to secure a quiet divorce."

Reached in Rome, Ponzi tried to bluff Rose into jealousy by telling a reporter that he had become engaged to an eighteen-year-old girl. Rose would not bite. She said simply that she hoped he was happy. Rose resolved for religious reasons that she would not remarry, and so she would never fulfill her dreams of motherhood. Ponzi sought to return to Boston to oppose the divorce but ultimately fought it in absentia and lost. The marriage ended in December 1936.

In 1939, Ponzi moved to Brazil to take a job with the Italian airline LATI. The job had been arranged by his cousin Attilio Biseo, an Italian air force colonel who commanded the Green Mice Squadron and was friendly with Mussolini's son Bruno. Ponzi did well for a while, but eventually it fell apart. He became enmeshed in what he claimed were efforts to expose a smuggling ring operated within the airline. By 1942 he was out of a job. He made ends meet by running a small rooming house in Rio de Janeiro and teaching English in a private school. Soon the momentary millionaire was living on seventy-five dollars a month, though he optimistically called it "quite a tidy sum here." His eyesight and his health began to fail, and he remained weakened from a heart attack that had struck him seven years to the day after his deportation.

In the meantime, Rose supported herself working as the bookkeeper and de facto manager of the Cocoanut Grove, a Boston nightclub partially owned by her divorce lawyer, Barnett Welansky. Rose found herself thrust unwillingly back into the headlines in November 1942, when a fast-moving fire claimed the lives of 492 people at the nightclub. Tired after a long day of work, Rose had resisted the urgings of friends to remain at the club that night for a party. Instead she'd

gone home early, a decision that probably saved her life. Later, she became a key witness in the hearings to assess blame.

Even after the divorce, Ponzi and Rose corresponded with some
regularity and with obvious affection. Ponzi sent her notes at Christmas and on her birthday, usually addressed to "My dear Rose" and
signed "Your Charlie." Sometimes he sent kisses, and sometimes she
sent photos in return. In one 1941 letter, Rose coyly inquired if Ponzi
was married. "Of course I am, in a way," he answered. "I am married
to you, even if it is a one-sided and long-distance affair." When a
Brazilian friend urged him to marry a forty-five-year-old woman who
could nurse him through his last years, Ponzi scoffed: "If forty-five was
my measure, I would rather take it in three installments of fifteen
each."

The nightclub fire seemed to draw the two closer. When he
learned that Rose had survived, Ponzi poured out his heart. "I have
missed you terribly," he wrote. "I have thought you lost forever, and
under circumstances more horrible than death itself. I don't know
how the shock did not kill me right then and there. I believe it was because somehow there still remained a dim ray of hope at the bottom
of my heart: hope that the gods would not be so unmerciful to you."

"Perhaps I made a mess of your life but it was not for lack of the
necessary sentiment," Ponzi continued. "Here I am, past sixty-one,
thousands of miles away from you, physically separated from you these
past nine years, legally a stranger to you, and yet feeling toward you
the same as I did that night in June when I took you home from the
first movies we saw together in Somerville Avenue."

Their letters continued, and several times each tiptoed around the
possibility of getting back together, either for a visit by Rose to Brazil
or an attempt by Ponzi to return to the United States. "Dear Sweet
Thing," Ponzi wrote in 1947. "Decidedly you have lost all sense of
morals and social behavior! What do you mean by suggesting that I
come up there and make myself at home in your apartment? What
would the people say of you . . . living with a strange man? I am just
joking, dear, so as to forget the tragic side of the thing: the impossibil-

ity of going with it. As to your coming down here, it is entirely out of the question not only for the reasons you mention but also because life here would be unbearable for you." They continued writing to each other, long letters that described daily life and the comings and goings of old friends Ponzi had not seen in decades. Once Ponzi tried to enlist Rose in a moneymaking idea involving the importation of trucks, pens, watches, radios, clocks, and other goods from the United States. But the deals evaporated with Ponzi's diminishing finances and failing health, and their letters became less frequent.

By 1948, Ponzi was almost blind. A brain hemorrhage robbed him of control of his left leg and left arm. He lived in a small apartment with a young family and subsisted on a small pension from the Brazilian government. As his body weakened, he spent increasing amounts of time on the charity ward of a Rio hospital. A photograph of him there shows a man who looks much older than his years, his bald head propped on a pillow, his frail body swimming in an ill-fitting hospital gown. A reporter for the Associated Press found him there. Though the reporter showed no signs of realizing it, Ponzi took the opportunity of a final interview to unburden himself as never before. During

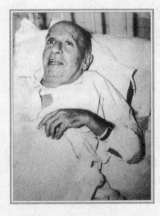

Ponzi in bed in the charity ward of a Rio de Janeiro hospital in 1948.

The Boston Globe

his trials he had claimed innocence, and even in his memoirs Ponzi had danced around the true nature of his investment business. But with the reporter at his hospital bedside, Ponzi came clean.

"Well," he began, smiling his old smile, "how much do you know about me? I was number one in those days before Al Capone. . . . Once I had fifteen million dollars. I used to carry a couple of million in my pockets in certified checks and cash. Look at me now. I guess a lot of people would say I got what I deserved. Well, that was twenty-eight years ago. A lot of water has gone under the bridge since. But I hit the American people where it hurts—in the pocketbook. Those were confused, money-mad days. Everybody wanted to make a killing. I was in it plenty deep, rolling in other people's money."

Then came the confession: "My business was simple. It was the old game of robbing Peter to pay Paul. You would give me one hundred dollars and I would give you a note to pay you one-hundred-and-fifty dollars in three months. Usually I would redeem my note in forty-five days. My notes became more valuable than American money. . . . Then came trouble. The whole thing was broken."

Ponzi recounted the story honestly and without rancor. When he was finished, he told the reporter he was regaining his strength and hoped to have an operation soon to restore his sight.

Ponzi said as much in his final letter to Rose, dictated to a hospital employee: "I am doing fairly well, and in fact I am getting better every day and I expect to go back home for Christmas." It was false hope, but that had always been his strength. Deep within the impoverished old man in the hospital bed remained the optimistic young dandy of 1920.

He was still Ponzi, and he still believed the triumphant words he had used to end his memoirs: "Life, hope, and courage are a combination which knows no defeat. Temporary setbacks, perhaps, but utter and permanent defeat? Never!"

Ponzi never left the hospital's charity ward. He spent his last days flanked on one side by a patient with a hacking cough and on the other by an old man who stared at the ceiling. Ponzi died of a blood clot on the brain on January 17, 1949. He was sixty-six. He had seventy-five dollars to his name, just enough for his burial. Rose would have liked to have had his body returned to Boston for a proper funeral, but she had lacked the money to do so.

Ponzi's death was reported by newspapers and magazines across the country, including a full page in *Life* magazine, giving reporters an opportunity to colorfully revisit the phenomenon he had created. They ran photos of Ponzi at the height of his popularity, and waxed poetic about his charm and moxie. Of course, the Peter-to-Paul scheme did not die with him. In the years that followed, reporters and fraud investigators began using Ponzi's name as shorthand when describing similar investment scams. In 1957, the *Encyclopaedia Britannica* formally acknowledged that his name had become synonymous with swindle. Soon the language sentinels at the *Oxford English Dictionary* followed suit, entering it into the great book as "Ponzi scheme." Its definition: "A form of fraud in which belief in the success of a fictive enterprise is fostered by payment of quick returns to first investors from money invested by others." It was not how Ponzi had hoped to be remembered, but it would have to suffice.

In 1956, Rose was working as a bookkeeper at the Bay State Raceway in Foxboro, Massachusetts, when she married the track's manager, Joseph Ebner. They had a good life together, regularly traveling back and forth between racetracks in Massachusetts and Florida. She died in 1993 at age ninety-seven, happily anonymous and beloved by her many nieces and nephews. After Rose died, her family went through her belongings and found Ponzi's letters. Reading his words, his playful responses to the notes she had sent him over the years, their suspicions were confirmed.

Despite the divorce and the heartaches, despite their dashed dreams and decades apart, the one thing Ponzi had never lost was Rose's love.

ACKNOWLEDGMENTS

Heartfelt thanks to the Gnecco family, especially John and Betty Gnecco, William and Florence Gnecco Hall, and Mary Gnecco Treen, for sharing reminiscences and mementos of their great-aunt Rose Gnecco Ponzi Ebner. I am especially grateful to them for providing me with the letters Ponzi sent Rose during their marriage and after. I'm grateful also to Philip Treen for sharing his theories about his great-great uncle Ponzi.

I owe equal appreciation to Mary M. Grozier for trusting me with her memories and photographs of her father, Richard. Thanks also to Elizabeth and Damian Grozier.

I received generous support and genuine fellowship at the Batten Institute at the Darden Graduate School of Business Administration at the University of Virginia. Special thanks to Bob Bruner and Debbie Fisher. Greg Fairchild sponsored me for the fellowship, and for that and so many other things I thank him, Tierney Temple-Fairchild, and their entire family.

My agent and friend Richard Abate made this book possible, despite the fact that he suspects that a distant relative of his lost money with Ponzi. Thanks to Kate Lee for believing in this idea and saying so. My editor, Jonathan Karp, has the rare gift of knowing precisely what a writer needs to achieve his dreams. He provides it with grace, charm, and a steady hand. I am grateful to the entire Random House team, notably Jonathan Jao, Dennis Ambrose, and Bonnie Thompson.

In Ponzi's hometown of Lugo, Italy, I received invaluable help from Rosanna Rava, who oversees registry documents in city hall. When we met, Rosanna was wearing a T-shirt that said "Boston Celtics," which I interpreted as a grand omen. "Boston! That's where I'm from," I said. Confusion swept across her face; Rosanna's English was as sparse as my Italian. When I looked more closely, I noticed that below the basketball team's name was a sketch of a baseball player in midswing, and below that were the meaningless words "Spring Trophy." Nevertheless, she patiently listened as I explained Ponzi's scheme in pidgin Italian. "Like Al Capone?" she asked. "Not really," I said. "Capone took lives. Ponzi took money." Rosanna smiled. *"Ah. Bene."* Then she unearthed his birth record and census documents.

Genealogist Carolyn Ugolini traced Ponzi's family history and led me to Rosanna. I am grateful for her creativity, persistence, and encouragement.

My friend and former professor Wilbur Doctor was among the journalists whom the *Boston Post* owed money when it failed a half century ago. Now I owe him, too, for the care he took in reading and improving this manuscript. I benefited as well from the insights and efforts of my friends and longtime colleagues Dick Lehr and Gerry O'Neill.

Ofer Gneezy and Christine McLaughlin graciously allowed me to traipse through their beautiful home to get a feel for what it was like when it belonged to Ponzi.

Henry Scannell of the Boston Public Library Microtext Department is a living treasure within a civic treasure. Thanks also to Aaron Schmidt of the library's Print Department; research librarian Frank Wilmot of the Darden Graduate School of Business Administration; John Beck of the Albin O. Kuhn Library at the University of Maryland, Baltimore County; archivists Edouard Desrochers and Shelley Bronk of Phillips Exeter Academy; Michael Moore of the National Archives and Records Administration; Massachusetts judicial archivist

Elizabeth Bouvier; Lisa Tuite of the *Boston Globe* library; John Cronin of the *Boston Herald* library; Evan Ide, curator of the Larz Anderson Auto Museum; Nancy Richard of the Boston Historical Society; Jim Gallagher of the Beebe Library at Boston University; and Millie Teixiera, secretary and resident historian at Saint Anthony's Church in Somerville. Mark Mathosian deserves credit for rescuing Ponzi's autobiography.

Steve Bailey of the *Boston Globe* made me a banking reporter despite my unbalanced checkbook, a job that eventually set the stage for me to tackle this subject. For their enduring support, special thanks to Allan Zuckoff, Jeff Feigelson, Brian McGrory, Naftali Bendavid, Joann Muller, Chris Callahan, Ben Bradlee Jr., Wil Haygood, Jim and Deb Kreiter, Paul Kreiter, Jo Kreiter, Reita Ennis, Helene Atwan, Joe Kahn, Kate Shaplen, Dan Field, Colleen Granahan, Ruth and Bill Weinstein, Jeff Struzenski, Amy Axelrod, Brooke and Eric Meltzer, and all my colleagues, students, and friends at Boston University.

My mother, Gerry Zuckoff, was a bookkeeper, and I suspect she would have seen the flaws in Ponzi's plan her first day on the job. This book is dedicated to my father, Sid Zuckoff, who taught me to appreciate history and to value ideas and ideals. My daughters, Isabel and Eve, kept me happy and grounded in the present when my mind wandered to the past. My wife, Suzanne, is my Rose.

A Note on Sources

This is a work of nonfiction. Though I have tried to bring Ponzi's story to life by writing this book in narrative form, I have invented none of the dialogue, altered none of the chronologies, and imagined none of the scenes described herein. All thoughts and feelings ascribed to persons came from the persons themselves, based on spoken or written comments. Descriptions of what a person experienced through his or her senses came either from the person or from photographs, newsreel footage, detailed street and fire insurance maps, or accounts in newspapers of the day. When I wrote that Rose Ponzi blushed, for instance, it was because a reporter had witnessed and recorded it. Put simply, I employed no fictional devices under the umbrella of literary license.

This approach was important for several reasons. First, given the nature of the subject himself, it seemed essential to draw a bright line between real and fake. Second, the truth was better than anything I could have invented. Third, Ponzi's true story was already at risk of being permanently obscured in misinformation as a result of a "fictionalized biography" and other imaginary tales. One writer referred authoritatively, and erroneously, to Ponzi's brothers and sisters, and then let his fantasies run amok when describing Ponzi's Lexington home: "Interior decorators charged him half-a-million dollars to make the home livable. One hundred thousand dollars went to stock his wine cellar with clarets and brandies from the 1870s. He had a

house staff of fifteen employees including armed guards with orders to
shoot any prowler on sight. The twenty-acre estate was surrounded by
a brick wall topped with barbed wire." And so on.

Important insight into Ponzi, as well as dialogue and certain scenes,
came from his little-noticed autobiography, *The Rise of Mr. Ponzi.*
Portions of his memoirs are, like the man himself, flawed by self-
aggrandizement and unreliability. However, much of Ponzi's account
squares with verifiable facts. I have used Ponzi's version primarily to
illuminate his unique impressions of people and events, and I have
been careful to avoid repeating his errors. Moreover, I have used expanded source notes in several places to sort through the more tangled
or incredible aspects of his account. Finally, newspaper stories without
page numbers came, almost without exception, from the archives of
the *Boston Globe,* where clips were cataloged by date without notations
of the pages on which they appeared.

NOTES

PROLOGUE

xii a gullible newspaper reporter: "Police Bring Back Money Magicians," *Boston Herald,* August 27, 1920, p. 5. Also "Money 'Made' as Victims Looked On," *Boston Daily Globe,* August 27, 1920, p. 1.

xii In 1920, anything seemed possible: David E. Kyvig, *Daily Life in the United States, 1920–1939: Decades of Promise and Pain,* Greenwood Press, 2002. Also Frederick Lewis Allen, *Only Yesterday: An Informal History of the 1920s,* Harper & Row, 1931, and numerous newspaper stories.

CHAPTER ONE: "I'M THE MAN."

3 Locomobile: Information on the Locomobile was provided by Evan Ide, curator of the Larz Anderson Auto Museum in Brookline, Massachusetts, which displays one that belonged to General Pershing.

3 At the wheel: "Receiver for Ponzi Today," *Boston Traveler,* August 17, 1920, p. 1.

5 holding copies of that morning's: "Ponzi Has a Rival Next Door to Him," *Boston Sunday Post,* July 25, 1920, p. 1.

5 On the left side of the front page: "Doubles the Money Within Three Months," *Boston Post,* July 24, 1920, p. 1.

6 eclipsed two previous stories: "Dear Old 'Get Rich Quick' Pops out of Postal Guide," *Boston Traveler,* June 9, 1920, p. 1; "Boston Man Is Sued for $1,000,000," *Boston Post,* July 4, 1920, p. 1.

6   Three weeks earlier: Charles Ponzi, *The Rise of Mr. Ponzi,* originally self-
     published in 1937, republished by Inkwell Publishers, Naples, Florida, 2001.
     Pages cited here are from the Inkwell edition, pp. 105–6.

8   Cost of living figures are from various sources, including newspaper ads;
     JoAnne Olian, *Everyday Fashions 1909–1920* Dover Publications, 1995; Har-
     vard University treasurer's statement, 1919–20, p. 174; and Kyvig.

8   would-be investors had begun assembling: Names of Ponzi investors, along
     with the dates and amounts they invested, as well as quotes from a few, were
     printed in the *Boston Post* during a two-week period in August 1920. Per-
     sonal details about some of the investors were obtained from the 1920 census
     and the 1920 Boston City Directory. Also "Pearlstein Made $500—Now He
     Sets Good Example for All the Others Who Collected in Time," *Boston
     Globe,* August 14, 1920, p. 2. John Collins did, indeed, add another $700 to
     his investment on July 26; his investments were included in the *Post*'s pub-
     lished list of investors on August 26, 1920. Names and dates of depositors
     were also found in numerous court documents, including *Cunningham v.
     Brown,* 265 U.S. 1 (1924), a case involving Ponzi that made it to the U.S.
     Supreme Court.

11   was five foot two: There are differing accounts of Ponzi's height. Most put
     him between five foot two and five foot four. My decision to settle on five
     foot two was based on a detailed physical description contained in a
     "Wanted on Indictment" poster issued in 1926 by the Suffolk County,
     Massachusetts, District Attorney.

12   "the two million inhabitants": Ponzi, p. 148.

12   blue steel pistol: "Ponzi Pays, Smiling, as Pi Alley Rages and Mob Beats
     Door," *Boston Herald,* August 3, 1920, p. 1. Also Ponzi, p. 133.

12   Another pocket: "Ponzi Stops Taking Money, Awaits Audit," *Boston Globe,*
     July 27, 1920, p. 1.

12   he stepped from the car: An account of the scene at Ponzi's office on July 24,
     1920, is contained in "Ponzi Has a Rival Next Door to Him," *Boston Post,*
     July 25, 1920, p. 1. Although the story has no byline, the reporter's knowl-
     edge of Italian and other details makes me suspect that it was written by P. A.
     Santosuosso, who also did significant later reporting on Ponzi for the *Post.*

12   a mellifluous tone: Although the newsreel movies made of him were silent,
     news accounts of the day noted the quality and tone of Ponzi's voice and its
     almost complete lack of an Italian accent.

13   "a swirling, seething": Mary Mahoney, "Ponzi Bothered None at All by Ac-
     counting: His Million-a-Week Business Carried Entirely on Handwritten
     Cards, No Ledgers," *Boston Traveler,* July 29, 1920, p. 3.

14   a man named Frederick J. McCuen: "Agent's Profit Large: McCuen Got
     $10,000 for 2½ Days' Commissions; Has Not Turned Back a Cent to Ponzi
     Estate; Left Ponzi to Engage with Rival Concern," *Boston Evening Transcript,*
     October 26, 1922.

15   "would have made": "Ponzi Has a Rival Next Door to Him," *Boston Sunday
     Post,* July 25, 1920, p. 1.

15   "They had me": Ponzi, pp. 146–47.

15   newly hired officers: Francis Russell, *A City in Terror: 1919, the Boston Police
     Strike.* New York: Viking Press, 1975, pp. 50, 112–13.

15   Several patrolmen even moonlighted: Reports of police acting as agents for
     Ponzi are contained in numerous stories in the *Boston Post* and other news-
     papers, as well as "Bursting Golden Bubble Wins Gold Medal," *Editor &
     Publisher,* June 4, 1921, p. 1.

15   Captain Jeremiah Sullivan: "$100,000 Ponzi Gift to Charity," *Boston Sunday
     Advocate,* August 1, 1920, p. 1.

15   Inspector Joseph Cavagnaro: "Reported Investor Denies Depositing with
     Ponzi," *Boston Herald,* August 24, 1920, p. 8. The story focuses on the denial
     of Richard Engstrom but also mentions Cavagnaro's refusal to comment
     about his investments. The inspector's name was first revealed in a list of in-
     vestors published a day earlier by the *Boston Post.*

16   Providing for his wife and four daughters: 1920 Boston Census, viewed on-
     line at www.ancestry.com.

CHAPTER TWO: "I'M GUILTY."

19   born March 3, 1882, in Lugo: Numerous accounts give Ponzi's birthplace as
     Parma, but in fact he was born in the smaller city of Lugo, where copies of
     his birth records and a certificate of family status and residence were ob-
     tained from the clerk's office. See Comune di Lugo, Situazione di Famiglia
     Originaria, under Oreste Ponzi.

19   a decidedly working-class neighborhood: Author's visit to Lugo in August
     2003 and accounts from city registrar Rosanna Rava.

20   honor his maternal and paternal grandfathers: Pedigree chart based on Italian
     baptismal records, prepared by genealogist Carolyn Ugolini.

20   employed in Lugo as a postman: Registro di Popolazione for Lugo, Italy,
     1882.

20   significantly more prominent stock: Pedigree chart based on Italian baptismal
     records, prepared by genealogist Carolyn Ugolini.

20   "castles in the air": Ponzi is an important source of information on his early

life, and his accounts are consistent enough with verifiable facts to be considered reliable. Among the most complete reports can be found in: Ponzi's autobiography; "Ponzi Tells How He Rose," *Boston American,* August 9, 1920; "Ponzi Relates Story of His Life," *Boston Post,* August 9, 1920, p. 16; and Charles Ponzi, "Ponzi's Own Story of His Life Reads Like a Romance," *Boston Sunday Advertiser,* August 8, 1920, p. 3.

20   settled in Parma: Certifico di Stato di Famiglia Piu' Certificato di Residenza. Lugo, Italy, for Ponzi family.

21   a group of wealthy students: "Ponzi Tells How He Rose," *Boston American,* August 9, 1920.

22   "Poor, uneducated Italian boys": Ibid.

22   "paved with gold": Ponzi, p. 2.

22   the S.S. *Vancouver:* Information on the ship that brought Ponzi to the United States was obtained from the National Archives and Records Administration office in Waltham, Massachusetts. Postcards picturing the ship are held by the Peabody Museum of Salem and can be viewed online at www.greatships.net.

23   conditions for steerage passengers: A description of steerage is contained in a 1911 report to President William H. Taft by the United States Immigration Commission, an excerpt of which was found online at www.americanparknetwork.com/parkinfo/sl/history/journey.html.

23   Most of the *Vancouver*'s passengers: The complete manifest of the November 3, 1903, voyage, including details on passengers, has been preserved on microfiche and was viewed and copied at NARA's Waltham office.

23   A cardsharp: Ponzi, pp. 2–3.

24   Splendor Macaroni Company: Sanborn Fire Insurance maps of Boston, vol. 5, pp. 551–53.

24   "like a million": Ponzi, p. 2.

24   sticky, black mud: Ibid., p. 3.

24   "some fifth cousin": Ibid., p. 3.

24   Ponzi was feeling tricked: "Ponzi Tells How He Rose," *Boston American,* August 9, 1920.

25   into the arms of an Irish policeman: Ponzi, p. 4.

25   Ponzi's series of jobs: Ibid. Also Ponzi, p. 6; "Ponzi's Own Story of His Life Reads Like a Romance," *Boston Sunday Advertiser,* August 8, 1920, p. 3.

25   spree at Coney Island: "Mr. Ponzi and His 'Ponzied Finance,' " *Literary Digest,* August 21, 1920, p. 49.

26   Banco Zarossi: Ponzi, p. 7.

26 Antonio Cordasco: Robert F. Harney, "Montreal's King of Italian Labour: A
Case Study of Padronism," *Labor/Le Travail* vol. 4, (1979), pp. 57–84. Also
Donna R. Gabaccia, *Italy's Many Diasporas,* UCL Press, 2000, pp. 58–80.

27 the full 3 percent, plus: "Montreal Detective Believes Ponzi's Story; Always
Thought Him Guiltless; Cordasco Says Scheme Was That of Zarossi," *Boston
Globe,* August 12, 1920. Also Herbert L. Baldwin, "Canadian 'Ponsi' Served
Jail Term," *Boston Post,* August 11, 1920, p. 1.

27 Zarossi's pretty seventeen-year-old daughter: Ponzi, pp. 10–20.

28 Antonio Salviati: "Old Partner of Ponzi Arrested," *Boston Globe,* datelined
August 19, 1920.

28 the Canadian Warehousing Company: "Ponzi's Canada Career: Stole a Bank
Check and Committed Poor Forgery," *Boston Post,* August 12, 1920. In his
autobiography, Ponzi gives an elaborate account of his Montreal caper, explaining that he took the blame for the forgery to spare Zarossi from prison
because Zarossi had a wife and family. Ponzi's general account was believed
by a Montreal detective, George Sloan, who brought Zarossi back from
Mexico City and was quoted in the *Boston Globe* on August 12, 1920. But
Sloan was not directly involved in Ponzi's arrest, and Ponzi's claims of
chivalry are contradicted by the timing of his actions relative to Zarossi's disappearance and extradition, and also by a court transcript of the case unearthed by the *Post.* Somewhat less believably, Zarossi also disavowed Ponzi's
account with his own self-serving explanation of his bank's demise: "Zarossi
Disputes Ponzi: Blames 'Wizard' for Loss of $10,000 in Montreal Crash,"
Boston Traveler, August 12, 1920, p. 1.

29 vermin-infested jail: Ponzi, p. 12.

30 Saint Vincent de Paul Penitentiary: Ibid., pp. 17–22.

30 a swindler named Louis Cassullo: "Denounces Ponzi . . . as Embodiment of
a Lie," *Boston Globe,* November 30, 1922.

30 Ponzi sized up Cassullo: Ponzi, p. 90.

30 a model prisoner: Herbert L. Baldwin, "Canadian 'Ponsi' Served Jail Term,"
Boston Post, August 11, 1920, p. 1.

30 five dollars in his pocket: Ponzi, p. 22.

CHAPTER THREE: "NEWSPAPER GENIUS"

33 living in his parents' house: Cambridge City Directory, 1917–20.

33 nearly flunking out of college: Numerous letters between E. A. Grozier and
Harvard's Dean Hurlbut between 1905 and 1909 regarding Richard

Grozier's grades, deficiencies, and so on, contained in student files located in the Harvard University Archives.

33   destined to inherit: "Editor of Post Dies," *Boston Post,* May 10, 1924, p. 1.

33   largest-circulation newspaper: *Editor & Publisher,* January 22, 1921, p. 41.

33   largest in the nation: *Editor & Publisher,* March 19, 1921, p. 1.

34   fifteen printed: Herbert A. Kenny, *Newspaper Row: Journalism in the Pre-Television Era,* Globe Pequot Press, 1987, p. 18.

34   "On roof and wall": Oliver Wendell Holmes, "After the Fire," 1872.

34   oceans of water: Kenny, p. 19.

34   The eager buyer was the Reverend Ezra D. Winslow: "The Short Story of a Big Swindle," *Boston Times,* January 30, 1876, p. 1.

35   forged the signatures: "E. D. Winslow: A Partial List of His Forged Endorsements and More of His Guilty Doings," *Boston Post,* from the newspaper files of the Boston Public Library, date missing.

35   fewer than three thousand subscribers: Kenny, p. 20.

35   antiquated printing plant: "Editor of Post Dies," *Boston Post,* May 10, 1924, p. 1.

35   Grozier was born: Ibid.

36   "It was soon raised": Keene Sumner, "A Great Editor Tells What Interests People," *American,* January 1924, p. 37.

36   most profitable and most copied newspaper: "Sensationalism: Joseph Pulitzer and the New York *World*," *Cambridge History of English and American Literature in Eighteen Volumes,* 1907–21, vol. 17, online at www.bartleby.com.

36   "I never saw": Keene Sumner, "A Great Editor Tells What Interests People," *American,* January 1924, p. 117.

37   one thousand dollars in gold coins: Kenny, p. 23.

37   wish was to buy a newspaper: Ibid., p. 119.

37   his meager price range: "Editor of Post Dies," *Boston Post,* May 10, 1924, p. 1.

37   "If you have even the slightest objection": Keene Sumner, "A Great Editor Tells What Interests People," *American,* January 1924, p. 37.

37   crowded with newspapers: Timelines of Massachusetts newspapers prepared by Henry Scannell of the Boston Public Library.

38   "a small, brownish man": Kenneth Roberts, *I Wanted to Write.* Doubleday, 1953.

38   "Of first importance": G. S. MacFarland, "The Owner of the Boston *Post,*" *Hearst's Magazine,* May 2, 1914.

39   "By performance rather than promise": "Editor of Post Dies," *Boston Post,* May 10, 1924, p. 1, excerpt taken from October 14, 1891, editorial.

---

39 dropped the paper's price: Kenny, p. 24.

39 "Most of the time": Keene Sumner, "A Great Editor Tells What Interests People," *American,* January 1924, p. 122.

40 Accounts of *Post* promotional gimmicks, including the *Boston Post* Cane: Kenny, pp. 32–33; Keene Sumner, "A Great Editor Tells What Interests People," *American,* January 1924, p. 121; Laurel Guadazno, "The *Boston Post* Cane," *Provincetown Banner,* January 13, 2000.

43 friend to the little guy: Kenny, p. 53.

43 careful reader of the census: Ibid., pp. 54–55.

43 "identical justice": Ibid., p. 57.

Chapter Four: "A long circle of bad breaks"

45 "Bianchi the Snake": Herbert L. Baldwin, "Canadian 'Ponsi' Served Jail Term," *Boston Post,* August 11, 1920, p. 1.

45 inspector named W. H. Stevenson: Letter of immigration, inspector James Yale to John Clark, commissioner of immigration, Montreal, Canada, viewed online at www.mark-knutson.com.

46 an old schoolmate: Ponzi, pp. 23–24.

46 the old friend was Antonio Salviati: "Receivers Grill Ponzi," *Boston Traveler,* August 21, 1920, p. 1.

46 Ponzi bought the deal and pleaded: Ponzi, pp. 26–28.

46 lounged in the plush seats: Ponzi, p. 29.

47 "might as well be a gilded cage.": Ibid.

47 A. C. Aderhold: "Planned Coup While Prisoner," *Boston Herald,* August 12, 1920, p. 3.

47 F. G. Zerpt: "Arrest in Ponzi Case May Be Made Today," *Boston Post,* August 12, 1920, p. 1.

47 Ignazio "the Wolf" Lupo: Lupo also was known as Ignazio "Lupo the Wolf" Saietta. Jay Maeder, "Pay or Die: Lieutenant Petrosino and the Black Hand, 1909," New York *Daily News,* March 3, 1998, p. 49. Also www.gangrule.com/biography.php?ID=1.

48 kinship with his countryman Lupo: Ponzi, p. 30.

48 Lupo was tough: Ibid.

49 Charles W. Morse: Henry F. Pringle, *The Life and Times of William Howard Taft: A Biography.* Farrar & Rinehart, Inc., 1939, pp. 627–36. Also Ponzi, pp. 31–32.

49 "the most brutal": Ibid., p. 628.

50 false medical claims against coal-mining companies: Ponzi, pp. 33–34.

51   Truman H. Aldrich: Charles E. Adams, "The Great West Blocton Town
      Fire of 1927," *Alabama Heritage,* Summer 1998.

51   "a brotherhood of common interests": Ponzi, p. 35.

52   "Something always happens!": Ibid.

52   Pearl Gossett: The story of Ponzi's donation of skin can be traced to A. C.
      Aderhold, his boss at the Atlanta prison, who shared the newspaper clipping
      of the account with reporters in 1920. See " 'Ponci' of Great Help in Fed-
      eral Prison," *Boston Globe,* August 12, 1920, p. 10. Ponzi provides his own
      account in his autobiography, pp. 36–38.

54   S.S. *Tarpon:* Ponzi, p. 39.

54   "Librarian Wanted at the Medical College": "A Leaf out of Ponzi's Past:
      'Fired' from $30 a Month Mobile Job in 1915," *Boston Globe,* August 5, 1930,
      p. 1. Gus Carlson Jr. is quoted extensively in the story, along with Mrs. T. C.
      White. Also Ponzi, pp. 39–43.

56   New Orleans: In his autobiography, Ponzi tells an interesting but largely un-
      verifiable story about his time in New Orleans (see pp. 44–50). In it, he
      claims the following: Following a string of unsolved murders, he and a min-
      ister took it upon themselves to improve the reputation of the city's Italian
      community. The two men went to the editor of the *New Orleans States*
      newspaper claiming to represent a secret society of prominent Italians that in
      truth existed only in their minds. Insisting on anonymity, they told the edi-
      tor that "the better element of the Italian colony have decided to take mat-
      ters into their own hands and put an end to all these killings." To do so, the
      society would gather information about everyone suspected of involvement,
      and that information would be turned over to the police. They reasoned
      that the public announcement of such a society would slow the killings be-
      cause the killers would fear that "they might be secretly denounced by per-
      sons whose identity they could not establish." The *States* ran a story about
      the society, Ponzi claimed, after which other newspapers poured reporters
      into the city's Italian enclave, hoping to learn more; of course they could
      not, because no such society existed. The upshot of Ponzi's story was that
      the editor of the *States* arranged a secret meeting between Ponzi, the minis-
      ter, the mayor of New Orleans, and the chief of police, at which the mayor
      supposedly offered Ponzi and the minister thirty thousand dollars to help the
      society in its investigation. Ponzi claimed that he and the minister realized
      they had gone too far; had they been identified as the originators of a law-
      and-order society they would have faced danger from the killers. But if their
      society was shown to be a ruse, they might face charges from the authori-
      ties. Their only choice was to leave town, separately, which Ponzi insisted

NOTES

they did. "We were just a couple of madcaps," he wrote. "Not swindlers." Although the story cannot be confirmed and may well be fanciful, it is reasonable to think that there are several grains of truth to it. Mostly, it is consistent with Ponzi's trademark brand of impetuous scheming in which a seemingly clever idea gets him in over his head.

56 Wichita Falls: Historical information found online at www.wichitafalls.org/index.htm. Also Ponzi, pp. 51–52.

56 a sixteen-dollar-a-week clerk: "Arrest in Ponzi Case May Be Made Today," *Boston Post,* August 12, 1920, p. 1.

57 Italy was seeking emigrants as reservists: "Ponzi's Career Is Spectacular," *Boston Globe,* August 13, 1920. Also "Ponzi Relates Story of His Life," *Boston Post,* August 9, 1920, p. 16; "Arrest in Ponzi Case May Be Made Today," *Boston Post,* August 12, 1920, p. 1.

Chapter Five: "As restless as the sea"

59 "There were many times": Keene Sumner, "A Great Editor Tells What Interests People," *American,* January 1924, p. 122.

59 guest at his dinner table: Ibid., p. 120.

59 "The bulk of the work": "Editor of Post Dies," *Boston Post,* May 10, 1924, p. 1.

60 drawing tiny boats and ships: "Reminds of Early Days," letter from Herbert Kenny to Edwin A. Grozier, published in the *Boston Post,* June 1, 1921, p. 25.

60 Edwin often remained in Boston: Interview with Mary Grozier, March 7, 2003.

60 Phillips Exeter Academy: Richard Grozier's transcripts and pages from the 1905 Exeter yearbook, *The Pean,* were obtained through the school with the help of archivist Edouard L. Desrochers and assistant archivist Shelley C. Bronk.

60 Richard was accepted at Harvard: The Harvard University Archive contains an extensive file on the academic history of Richard Grozier, including his complete transcripts and the remarkable letters written by him, his father, E. A. Wells, B. S. Hurlbut, W. G. Howard, and Joseph Ross.

60 Half were from Massachusetts: *First Report of the Harvard Class of 1909,* printed in 1910.

61 fine wine and champagne: Interview with Mary Grozier, March 7, 2003.

62 "Gold Coast": Interview with Marvin Hightower, senior writer and archivist, Harvard news office, March 7, 2003.

64 Vera Rumery: "Romance Disclosed: Newton High School Girl to Wed Harvard Man," *Boston Globe,* November 24, 1907.

68 "One of our teachers": Hans Von Kaltenborn, "The College and the Press," disquisition presented at Class Day 1909, reprinted in *First Report of the Harvard Class of 1909,* printed in 1910, pp. 235–36.

68 "a very routine life": *Harvard Class of 1909, Fiftieth Anniversary Report,* 1959. pp. 452–53.

69 168 Brattle Street: "Mr. J. G. Thorp's House on Brattle Street," *Cambridge Tribune,* February 2, 1889, p. 1; information on the house and the neighborhood is also from the files of the Cambridge Historical Commission and the Cambridge Historical Society.

69 Alice had found the house: Interview with Mary Grozier, March 7, 2003.

69 editorial writer: "Bursting Golden Bubble Wins Gold Medal," *Editor & Publisher,* June 4, 1921, p. 1.

CHAPTER SIX: "AN AMERICAN BEAUTY"

73 James Michael Curley: There is no better source on Boston's rogue mayor than Jack Beatty's *The Rascal King: The Life and Times of James Michael Curley,* Addison-Wesley, 1992. For the period covered here, I relied most heavily on pp. 67–211. For Curley's attack on the *Post,* see p. 209 and also the *Boston Post,* December 2, 1917. Also on Curley and John "Honey Fitz" Fitzgerald: Francis Russell, *The Knave of Boston,* Quinlan Press, 1987, pp. 1–84; Thomas H. O'Connor, *The Boston Irish: A Political History,* Northeastern Press, 1995; pp. 179–217; Doris Kearns Goodwin, *The Fitzgeralds and the Kennedys: An American Saga,* Simon & Schuster, 1989. pp. 244–52; and Kenny, pp. 163–173.

78 Ponzi found himself rooting for Curley: Ponzi, p. 58.

79 "By starving one day": Ibid., p. 53.

79 Meeting Rose: "Ponzi Relates Story of His Life," *Boston Post,* August 9, 1920, p. 16. Also Ponzi, pp. 53–55; "Wife Tells of Ponzi's Plans," *Boston American,* July 31, 1920, p. 1; and Charles Merrill, "His Pretty Girl Wife Sorry When Ponzi Quit $50 Job," *Boston Globe,* August 8, 1920, p. 8. Information about Rose Gnecco Ponzi also was gathered during interviews in April and May 2003 with John Gnecco, Rose's nephew, who cared for her during the years before she died, and his sisters, Florence Gnecco Hall and Mary Gnecco Treen.

79 four foot eleven: Rose's height was confirmed by her nephew. Her pride in her weight comes from " 'Charlie's a Born Aristocrat,' Says Mrs. Rose Ponzi," *Boston Post,* December 3, 1922, Special Feature Section, p. 1.

80   "Time, space, the world": Ponzi, p. 54.

81   nephews and nieces to the beach: Interview with Mary Gnecco Treen, May 5, 2003.

81   Imelde wanted to be sure Rose knew: "Mrs. Ponzi Loyal," *Boston Post,* August 13, 1920, p. 9. Also Clarence White, "Mrs. Ponzi Says, 'We Will Stay Here and Square Debts,' " *Boston Globe,* July 17, 1921.

82   Saint Anthony's Church: marriage license obtained from the Commonwealth of Massachusetts Division of Vital Statistics. Also church records from Saint Anthony's, provided in April 2003 by church secretary Millie Teixiera.

82   dinner and the theater once a week: Margaret Strickland, "Mrs. Ponzi Willing to Surrender All," *Boston Post,* August 17, 1920, p. 1.

82   song on the mandolin: " 'Charlie's a Born Aristocrat,' Says Mrs. Rose Ponzi," *Boston Post,* December 3, 1922, Special Feature Section, p. 1.

83   "tastes of the millionaire": Charles Merrill, "His Pretty Girl Wife Sorry When Ponzi Quit $50 Job," *Boston Globe,* August 8, 1920, p. 8.

83   stamp collection: Ibid.

83   with Roberto de Masellis: "Ponzi Asks Aid . . . Witness Says Foreign Exchange Plan Feasible," *Boston Evening Transcript,* October 27, 1922. The physical description of de Masellis comes from a *Boston Traveler* sketch published on October 28, 1922.

84   "Charlie, for heaven's sake": " 'Charlie's a Born Aristocrat,' Says Mrs. Rose Ponzi," *Boston Post,* December 3, 1922, Special Feature Section, p. 1.

84   "When a man is always a gentleman": Ibid.

84   "An American beauty. My Rose!": Ponzi, p. 55.

84   "I want you to be able to throw away a hundred dollars": Charles Merrill, "His Pretty Girl Wife Sorry When Ponzi Quit $50 Job," *Boston Globe,* August 8, 1920, p. 8.

84   Once she took a photograph of him: Nancy Wrynne, "Ponzi's Home Life Is Simple and Devoid of Ostentation," *Boston Sunday Herald,* August 1, 1920.

84   the world to take notice of him: " 'Charlie's a Born Aristocrat,' Says Mrs. Rose Ponzi," *Boston Post,* December 3, 1922, Special Feature Section, p. 1.

85   Rose's mother died: Margaret Strickland, "Mrs. Ponzi Offers All," *Boston Post,* August 17, 1920, p. 1.

85   Her love for him deepened: Ibid.

85   "tired of working for expectations": Ponzi, p. 59.

85   inherited some money from her mother: Clarence White, "Mrs. Ponzi Says, 'We Will Stay Here and Square Debts,' " *Boston Globe,* July 17, 1921.

86   He sat in the office's lone armchair: Ibid.

86   stealing 5,387 pounds of cheese: "Ponzi's Career Is Spectacular," *Boston Globe,* August 13, 1920, p. 9.

86   kingmaker and blackmailer Dan Coakley: Annual Report of the Massachusetts Commissioner of Banks, 1921, pp. lv–lvi.

87   a deal with the store's owner: The terms of the furniture deal come from multiple sources, including, "Ponzi Sent No Representative to Europe," *Boston Globe,* September 29, 1920.

87   anglicized his name from Giuseppe Danieli: Albert Hurwitz, "The Ponzi Bubble," *Boston Sunday Herald Magazine,* August 30, 1970, p. 13.

88   The ill-fated story of the *Trader's Guide* comes from Ponzi himself. His most complete telling is found at Ponzi, pp. 60–66.

89   "with the same inflection": Ponzi, p. 64.

89   "I cannot approve the loan": Ibid.

89   Sitting alone in the office: Ponzi told the story of how he came up with the idea of speculating in International Reply Coupons on many occasions, each time recounting the same essential facts about the letter from the Spaniard who wanted a copy of the *Trader's Guide.* See Ponzi, pp. 67–70; Charles Ponzi, "Ponzi's Own Story of His Life Reads Like a Romance," *Boston Sunday Advertiser,* August 8, 1920, p. 3; and "Ponzi Tells His Story," *Boston Evening Transcript,* November 27, 1922, p. 1.

CHAPTER SEVEN: "THE ALMIGHTY DOLLAR"

93   Universal Postal Union: A history of the UPU and the advent of International Postal Coupons can be found at www.upu.int. Also Herman Herst Jr., "Charles Ponzi and His International Postal Reply Coupon Scheme," Speaking of Stamps Column, *Stamps,* December 9, 1995, p. 8.

95   cost the Spaniard thirty centavos: Ponzi frequently told the same story of how the idea came to him and how he investigated its likelihood of success by sending three dollars abroad. The most complete account is from Ponzi, pp. 67–70. See also Mabel Abbott, "Ponzi's Profits on $9,522,590 of Investors—$45," New York *World,* November 26, 1924. For details of the Austrian example, see "Mr. Ponzi and His 'Ponzied Finance,'" *Literary Digest,* August 21, 1920, p. 47.

96   Ponzi was deep in the hole: Ponzi, pp. 68–69.

96   fifteen hundred dollars in loans: "Ponzi Sent to Europe No Representative," *Boston Globe,* September 29, 1920.

96   they might steal it: "Ponzi Tells His Story," *Boston Evening Transcript,* November 27, 1922, p. 1.

97   "They could not limit the number of coupons": Ponzi, p. 69.

97   "Environment had made me rather callous": Ibid., p. 70.

98   Uncle Ned's Loan Company: "Ponzi Pawned Watch, Rings to Get Start,"
     Boston Sunday Herald, August 15, 1920. The story does not say the diamond
     rings belonged to Rose, but it is reasonable to infer that they were hers, in
     light of a separate story, "Mrs. Ponzi Would Not Take Gems," *Boston Post,*
     November 22, 1922. In that story, Lillian Mahoney, the wife of one of
     Ponzi's salesmen, testifies that Rose had three diamond rings when she lived
     in Somerville. Also: Rosenberg's first name and background, which were
     not included in the *Herald* story, come from U.S. Census records obtained
     through www.ancestry.com.

98   debts approached three thousand dollars: "Made All His Money in Past
     Seven Months," *Boston Sunday Globe,* August 8, 1920, p. 17.

99   Seeing the angry look on Daniels's face: Ponzi, p. 73. The account of
     Daniels's December 1919 loan, which would play a pivotal role in Ponzi's
     downfall, was pieced together from numerous sources, including: "Ponzi
     Partnership and Receiver Hearings On," *Boston Traveler,* October 1, 1920;
     "Ponzi Criminal Trial to Start Soon, Belief," *Boston Traveler,* October 2,
     1920, p. 1; "Ponzi to Tell More on 'Partnership Deal,' " *Boston Traveler,* Oc-
     tober 5, 1920, p. 1; "Insist Daniels Tell Disposition of $55,000," *Boston Trav-
     eler,* October 9, 1920, p. 1; "Bar Witnesses as Spectators During Trial of
     Ponzi Case," *Boston Traveler,* October 26, 1922, p. 1; "Ponzi Sent No Repre-
     sentative to Europe," *Boston Globe,* September 29, 1920; "Ponzi Tells How
     He Borrowed Millions," *Boston Globe,* September 30, 1920; "Figures of Au-
     ditor Rittenhouse," *Boston Globe,* October 5, 1920.

101 extracting gold from seawater The story of the Reverend Prescott Ford
     Jernegan comes from sources including "Get Rich Quick Schemes of Boston
     Yesterdays: Gold from Sea Water," *Boston Herald,* August 2, 1920. Also Diana
     Ross McCain, "Fortune Sucked from the Sea Was a Golden Scam," *Hartford
     Courant,* November 18, 1998, p. 11, and Shoshana Hoose, "All That Glittered
     in Lubec," *Portland Press Herald,* November 5, 1995, p. 1G.

103 a smooth talker named Ferdinand Borges: "Get Rich Quick Schemes of Bos-
     ton Yesterdays: Rubber, Coffee and Pineapples," *Boston Herald,* August 3, 1920.

104 robbing Peter to pay Paul: John Bartlett, comp. *Familiar Quotations,* 10th ed.,
     rev. and enl. by Nathan Haskell Dole. Boston: Little, Brown, 1919; found at
     Bartleby.com.

104 The ad had been placed by Sarah Howe: "Get Rich Quick Schemes of
     Boston Yesterdays: Mrs. Howe's Bank for Ladies Only," *Boston Herald,* Au-
     gust 7, 1920.

105   William Franklin Miller: Robert Jay Nash, *Hustlers and Con Men*. New
       York: M. Evans and Company, Inc., 1976, pp. 195–203. Also "Get Rich
       Quick Schemes of Boston Yesterdays: 520 Per Cent," *Boston Herald,* August
       3, 1920, and Mary Darby, "In Ponzi We Tru$t," *Smithsonian,* December 1,
       1998, p. 134.

106   C. D. Sheldon: Morgan Marietta, "The Historical Continuum of Financial
       Illusion," *American Economist,* March 1, 1996, p. 79; "Montreal Detective
       Believes Ponzi's Story; Always Thought Him Guiltless; Cordasco Says
       Scheme Was That of Zarossi," *Boston Globe,* August 12, 1920; Herbert Bald-
       win, "Ponzi No Martyr," *Boston Post,* August 13, 1920, p. 10.

107   International Security Company: "Know Today Receiver in Ponzi Case,"
       Boston Post, August 18, 1920, p. 1. On p. 72 of his autobiography, Ponzi mis-
       takenly says he included two other names on the original registration papers,
       when in fact he did not add the names until March. The question of
       whether he had silent partners would become significant months later at his
       trial, but the general consistency between his trial testimony and the ac-
       count in his autobiography suggests that his erroneous statement about
       when he named the partners was an innocent mistake. Indeed, there are sev-
       eral instances in his autobiography where his sequence of events is contra-
       dicted by the record, but in no case do the discrepancies result in significant
       conflicts.

107   He was pleased that the transaction: Ponzi, p. 72.

108   "We are all gamblers": Ponzi, p. 76.

108   a point of never directly soliciting: Ponzi, p. 75.

108   Someone knocked on the door: "Ponzi Wins Avowal of Confidence,"
       Boston Post, November 1, 1922, p. 9. Also Ponzi, pp. 75–76.

CHAPTER EIGHT: "A SMALL SNOWBALL DOWNHILL"

111   thirty-two-year-old Giberti: Information about Giberti's life, including his
       date of immigration and his family, comes largely from the 1930 census; he
       was not counted in 1920.

111   Giberti's net worth: "Ponzi Wins Avowal of Confidence," *Boston Post,* No-
       vember 1, 1922, p. 9.

112   A shiver of panic: Ponzi's feelings during his meeting with Giberti come
       from Ponzi himself; see Ponzi, p. 75. Giberti also offered an account of their
       first meeting in court testimony. See "Seek Flaws in Testimony of Giberti,"
       Boston Traveler, November 2, 1922, p. 1. Also "Ponzi Wins Avowal of Confi-
       dence," *Boston Post,* November 1, 1922, p. 9.

112   "I was selling my dollars at about sixty-six cents": Ponzi, pp. 75–76.

113   a total of $1,770: "Ponzi in Sharp Cross-Examination," *Boston Globe*, November 6, 1922. Also Ponzi, p. 76. An accountant for Ponzi bankruptcy receivers, Charles Rittenhouse, claimed that Ponzi paid only 40 percent interest during his first three months in business. Ponzi, however, maintained that he always paid 50 percent. In those first three months he took in just over seven thousand dollars, or less than one-tenth of 1 percent of the total.

113   Giberti put up only ten dollars: "Seek Flaws in Testimony of Giberti," *Boston Traveler*, November 2, 1922, p. 1.

113   a pivotal moment in the career: This passage might be open to interpretation and dispute, but it is based on a careful reading of Ponzi's actions before, during, and after his scheme. Among the significant elements in considering him overly impetuous and ethically challenged but not a premeditated swindler are small yet telling details such as his claiming only his watch at the pawnshop (see below). Later, he makes even clearer the absence of intent to follow the fly-by-night path of William Franklin Miller by purchasing his Lexington home, canceling his planned visit to Italy, and bringing his mother to the United States.

114   returned to Uncle Ned's pawnshop: "Ponzi Pawned Watch, Rings to Get Start," *Boston Sunday Herald*, August 15, 1920, p. 1.

115   just four hundred dollars: "Ponzi Tells His Story," *Boston Evening Transcript*, November 27, 1922, p. 1.

115   a Massachusetts bureaucrat named Frank Pope: "Ponzi Has a Rival Next Door to Him," *Boston Sunday Post*, July 25, 1920, p. 1.

116   skeptics would doubt Sarti's existence: Ponzi first mentioned Sarti during his 1922 trial, and his existence was never proved. Indeed, prosecutors at Ponzi's 1925 trial informed the jury that no evidence could be found that a Lionello Sarti had entered the United States in Boston, Portland, or Philadelphia, though Ponzi objected that the search was far from exhaustive and should not be limited to those ports. See "McIsaacs to Testify for Ponzi," *Boston Traveler*, November 28, 1922, p. 1. Also "Coakley on Stand, Believes Ponzi Was Solvent," *Boston Globe*, November 28, 1922, p. 1; "Denounces Ponzi . . . as Embodiment of a Lie," *Boston Globe*, November 30, 1922; "State Rests in Ponzi Case," *Boston Globe*, February 21, 1925. Ponzi does not name Sarti in his autobiography but provides a description of his supposed deeds that fits with trial testimony. See Ponzi, p. 81.

116   "Each satisfied customer": Ponzi, p. 76.

116     $5,290 in new investments: Monthly investment totals come from the federal audit that led to the closure of the Securities Exchange Company and were

evidence at Ponzi's 1922 trial. Also "How the Bubble Grew," *Boston Evening Transcript,* November 6, 1922, p. 24.

116   sum came from the life savings: *In re Ponzi,* 268 F. 997 (District Court, Massachusetts, November 12, 1920). Also "Ponzi Named Dead Man as Partner," *Boston Globe,* September 30, 1920.

117   Ponzi returned to Uncle Ned's: "Ponzi Pawned Watch, Rings to Get Start," *Boston Sunday Herald,* August 15, 1920, p. 1.

117   He died on February 13, 1920: Interview with his great-grandson John Gnecco, April 22, 2003.

117   On March 9 he wired ten thousand lire: "Receipts Produced by Ponzi," *Boston Post,* August 3, 1920, page 2.

118   He assigned John A. Dondero: "Ponzi Liberal with Bonuses," *Boston Herald,* September 23, 1920.

118   To further satisfy Daniels: *In re Ponzi,* 268 E 997 (District Court, Massachusetts, November 12, 1920).

118   afraid that the Fidelity Trust Company: *In re Ponzi,* 268 F. 997 (District Court, Massachusetts, November 12, 1920). Also "Ponzi Named Dead Man as Partner," *Boston Globe,* September 30, 1920.

118   Fidelity Trust brought a lawsuit: *In re Ponzi,* 268 F. 997 (District Court, Massachusetts, November 12, 1920).

119   "Does anyone accept funds": "Police Relief Ass'n May Return Ponzi's $250 Gift," *Boston Daily Globe,* August 27, 1920, p. 5.

119   five Boston police inspectors and a lieutenant: "Five Police Inspectors and One Lieutenant Caught in Ponzi Net," *Boston Herald,* August 29, 1920, p. 1; "Ponzi's Records in Girl's Home," *Boston Post,* August 15, 1920, p. 1; "Four Inspectors Are Named," *Boston American,* August 28, 1920, p. 1; "Creditors to Grill Ponzi," *Boston Herald,* September 8, 1920, p. 3.; "Ponzi Evidence Laid Before Grand Jury," *Boston Globe,* September 30, 1920.

120   Acid was drilling: "Charles Ponzi Now Patient 'De Luxe,' " *Boston Globe,* November 10, 1921; "Ponzi in Surgeons' Care," *New York Times,* November 12, 1921, p. 23.

120   On March 24, three months: "Ponzi Was Warned in April Not to Speculate," *Boston Globe,* August 11, 1920, p. 8. See also "Closing of Bank Ruffles Ponzi's Accustomed Calm," *Boston Herald,* August 12, 1920, p. 1, and "Post Office Authorities, Fearing Ponzi's Escape, Chafed at Inaction Here," *Boston Herald,* August 13, 1920, p. 14. In his autobiography, Ponzi recounts a visit by a postal inspector accompanied by police. In it, he describes how he spun an elaborate, fanciful financial story about how he could take $1 mil-

lion and buy coupons in France, sell them in the United States, and turn profits for himself, his agents, the United States, France, French bond buyers, and the Universal Postal Union. He concluded the story by claiming to have told his supposedly awestruck visitors, "If you can show me where the entire transaction results in a loss to anyone, I'll buy each one of you a Stetson hat." Ponzi, pp. 82–88.

121   Clementi Viscarello ran into cook: "Clash over Woman at Ponzi Trial," *Boston Traveler,* October 21, 1922, p. 1.

121   Canal Street butcher Amarco Cataldo: "Ponzi on Trial in State Court," *Boston Globe,* January 19, 1925.

121   South End bricklayer Ricardo Bogni: "Sub-Agent Is Sure State Ruined Ponzi," *Boston Traveler,* November 2, 1922, p. 2; "Defence to View Ponzi Documents," *Boston Post,* November 2, 1922.

122   Rose came by . . . Abe Rhodes . . . Antonio D'Avanzo: "Ponzi Winners Include Coupon Wizard's Wife," *Boston Traveler,* August 24, 1920, p. 1.

122   More than ten thousand dollars a week: "Says Ponzi Kept No Record of Receipts," *Boston Globe,* September 21, 1920, p. 1.

122   The agency sent him a doe-eyed eighteen-year-old: "Well-Known Men Got Big Hauls from Ponzi," *Boston Post,* August 25, 1920, p. 1; "Ponzi Clerk Still Hopeful," *Boston Traveler,* August 16, 1920, p. 4. Lucy Meli's feelings toward Ponzi were never expressed publicly, but they can be gleaned from her extensive testimony at his trials, where she consistently supported him and expressed her belief in his honesty.

123   April receipts would exceed $140,000: Monthly investment totals come from the federal audit that led to the closure of the Securities Exchange Company and were evidence at Ponzi's 1922 trial. "How the Bubble Grew," *Boston Evening Transcript,* November 6, 1922, p. 24.

123   Lamb, a thirty-three-year-old English immigrant: "Lawrence Man Backs Ponzi," *Boston Sunday American,* August 8, 1920, p. 2; "Ponzi Criminal Trial to Start Soon, Belief," *Boston Traveler,* October 2, 1920, p. 1; "One Ponzi Agent Got $200,000 Commissions," *Boston Globe,* October 1, 1920; "Lamb Testifies as Ponzi Witness," *Boston Globe,* November 24, 1920.

123   chronic thief and con man Louis Cassullo: "Swell Ponzi's Assets $15,500," *Boston Post,* September 6, 1920, p. 18; "Two Witnesses Sought in Ponzi Case Disappear," *Boston Herald,* September 12, 1920, p. 1; Ponzi, pp. 89–95.

123   "And he was my most": Ponzi, p. 90.

124   Soon Ponzi had Massachusetts branch offices: "Attacks Testimony of His Former Secretary," *Boston Traveler,* October 25, 1922, p. 1. Also, Kenny, p. 193.

125   suspended sales of reply coupons: "Questions the Motives Behind Ponzi
       Scheme," *Boston Post,* July 26, 1920, p. 1; "Federal Officials Scout Ponzi
       Claim," *Boston Post,* July 31, 1920, p. 1.

Chapter Nine: "Always reaching for the moon"

128   the Supreme Court took: Leonard Levy, *Emergence of a Free Press,* Oxford
       University Press, 1985.
128   "protect a man in falsely": *Schenck v. United States,* 249 U.S. 47 (1919).
129   one that would take a heavy toll: The story of Curley's feud with Edwin
       Grozier and the *Post* is told in Kenny, pp. 165–75 and in Beatty, p. 414. Valu-
       able information also came from a March 7, 2003, interview with Mary
       Grozier.
131   Louis and Charlotte Blass: "Ponzi Winners Include Coupon Wizard's Wife,"
       Boston Traveler, August 24, 1920, p. 1; "Two Witnesses Sought in Ponzi Case
       Disappear," *Boston Herald,* September 12, 1920, p. 1; "Sued for $90,000 by
       Ponzi Trustee," *Boston Globe,* March 8, 1925; "Blass Denies He Was an
       Agent for Ponzi," *Boston Globe,* November 9, 1920; 1920 U.S. Census
       records.
132   Henry Neilson: "Many Attend Ponzi Hearings," *Boston Traveler,* August 19,
       1920, p. 1; "To Quiz Other 'Stars' of Ponzi Sales Force," *Boston Traveler,*
       September 17, 1920; "Reported Investor Denies Depositing with Ponzi,"
       Boston Herald, August 24, 1920, p. 8; "Neilsen [sic], Ponzi Agent, a Witness
       Today," *Boston Globe,* September 17, 1920, p. 1.
133   Charles Ritucci, who ran the Plymouth office: "South Shore Invests in
       Ponzi's Coupon Scheme," *Boston American,* July 31, 1920, p. 2.
133   the North End branch: *Cunningham v. Commissioner of Banks,* 144 N.E. 447;
       "History of Hanover Trust Company and Ponzi," *Boston Evening Globe,* Au-
       gust 31, 1920, p. 1.
133   index-card system: "Ponzi to Be Called in Federal Hearing," *Boston Globe,*
       September 22, 1920.
134   In May alone, 1,525 investors: Monthly investment totals come from the fed-
       eral audit that led to the closure of the Securities Exchange Company and
       were evidence at Ponzi's 1922 trial. "How The Bubble Grew," *Boston
       Evening Transcript,* November 6, 1922, p. 24.
134   "A little dollar could start on a journey": Ponzi, p. 93.
134   If flight or surrender crossed his mind: Only much later would he recognize
       his hubris, writing of this time period, "But I lacked judgment and caution.
       I thought I'd reach for more. It was there in plain sight. I did not look be-

yond it. If I did, I did not see. I must have been blinded by ambition and conceit." Ibid., p. 89.

134 "The average man is never satisfied": Ibid., p. 89.

134 Gneccos and the Donderos had poured: List of Unsecured Creditors, in Summary of Debts and Assets of Charles Ponzi in Bankruptcy, Schedule A, Case 28063, on file at the National Archives and Records Administration in Waltham, Massachusetts.

135 a tentative step toward flight: Nancy Wrynne, "Ponzi's Home Life Is Simple and Devoid of Ostentation," *Boston Sunday Herald,* August 1, 1920.

135 "What was I going to do?": Ponzi, p. 109.

135 He consoled himself with a story: Ibid., p. 114.

136 a vacant house on Slocum Road: Details of the house come in part from a June 3, 2003, tour of the home and property records found at Lexington Town Hall. The amount and method of Ponzi's purchase of the house was long subject to dispute, but the figure of thirty-nine thousand dollars was ultimately deemed most credible by the bankruptcy trustees. For purchase and decoration details, see "Understood He Paid $29,000 for Home," *Boston Globe,* January 7, 1925, p. 1; "*Post* Prints Ponzi List of Investors," *Boston Post,* August 23, 1920, p. 1; "Well-Known Men Got Big Hauls from Ponzi," *Boston Post,* August 25, 1920, p. 1;, " 'Charlie's a Born Aristocrat,' Says Mrs. Rose Ponzi," *Boston Post,* December 3, 1922, Special Feature Section, p. 1; "Ponzi Won't Admit Giving Note for Home," *Boston Globe,* June 9, 1921; "Dispose of Ponzi Mansion," *New York Times,* June 10, 1921, p. 24; "His Pretty Girl Wife Sorry When Ponzi Quit $50 Job," *Boston Globe,* August 8, 1920, p. 8; and Nancy Wrynne, "Ponzi's Home Life Is Simple and Devoid of Ostentation," *Boston Sunday Herald,* August 1, 1920.

138 Ponzi received his first notice: "Dear Old 'Get Rich Quick' Pops out of Postal Guide," *Boston Traveler,* June 9, 1920, p. 1.

139 Ponzi mollified Cassullo: "Swell Ponzi's Assets $15,500," *Boston Post,* September 6, 1920, p. 18; "Two Witnesses Sought in Ponzi Case Disappear," *Boston Herald,* September 12, 1920, p. 1; "Ponzi, Defiant, Balks Efforts of Receivers," *Boston Post,* August 23, 1920, p. 1; "Sale of Home Ponzi Bought Restrained," *Boston Globe,* September 7, 1920.

139 Cassullo was not satisfied: "Says Three-Fourths of Police Ponzi Investors," *Boston Globe,* November 22, 1922.

140 June was on track: Monthly investment totals come from the federal audit that led to the closure of the Securities Exchange Company and were evidence at Ponzi's 1922 trial. "How the Bubble Grew," *Boston Evening Transcript,* November 6, 1922, p. 24.

140 Daniel Desmond: "Desmond Resigns from Lawrence Trust Company," *Boston Globe,* August 24, 1920, p. 8; "Grill Ponzi Again Today," *Boston Post,* August 24, 1920.

140 Blasses spun the wheel of fortune: "Ponzi Winners Include Coupon Wizard's Wife," *Boston Traveler,* August 24, 1920, p. 1; "Two Witnesses Sought in Ponzi Case Disappear," *Boston Herald,* September 12, 1920, p. 1; "Sued for $90,000 by Ponzi Trustee," *Boston Globe,* March 8, 1925; "Blass Denies He Was an Agent for Ponzi," *Boston Globe,* November 9, 1920.

CHAPTER TEN: "I NEVER BLUFF."

143 Napoli Macaroni Manufacturing Company "Well-Known Men Got Big Hauls from Ponzi," *Boston Post,* August 25, 1920, p. 1; Summary of Debts and Assets of Charles Ponzi in Bankruptcy, Schedule B(2), Case 28063, on file at the National Archives and Records Administration in Waltham, Massachusetts; Ponzi, p. 104.

144 Ponzi walked unannounced: Ponzi, pp. 106–8. Although Ponzi is the only source of the exchange between himself and Poole, his account is supported by verifiable facts about his purchase of the company. See Summary of Debts and Assets of Charles Ponzi in Bankruptcy, Schedule B(2), Case 28063, on file at the National Archives and Records Administration in Waltham, Massachusetts; "Ponzi Creditors May Get Back 47 Percent," *Boston Globe,* October 6, 1920.

145 He bought a small tenement house: Summary of Debts and Assets of Charles Ponzi in Bankruptcy, Schedule B(2), Case 28063, on file at the National Archives and Records Administration in Waltham, Massachusetts; "Ponzi Creditors May Get Back 47 Percent," *Boston Globe,* October 6, 1920; Ponzi, p. 104.

145 forty thousand dollars to Charles Pizzi: "Bank Cashed Ponzi Notes for $240,000," *Boston Globe,* September 1, 1920, p. 1. Pizzi's notes were not included in the schedule of Ponzi's bankruptcy assets because Pizzi took responsibility for repaying them.

145 The smallest, for five hundred dollars: Summary of Debts and Assets of Charles Ponzi in Bankruptcy, Schedule B(2), Case 28063, on file at the National Archives and Records Administration in Waltham, Massachusetts; "Well-Known Men Got Big Hauls from Ponzi," *Boston Post,* August 25, 1920, p. 1; Ponzi, p. 123.

145 He bought fifty shares: Summary of Debts and Assets of Charles Ponzi in

Bankruptcy, Schedule B(2), Case 28063, on file at the National Archives and Records Administration in Waltham, Massachusetts.

145 Hanover Trust, a bank with about $5 million: Annual Report of the Massachusetts Commissioner of Banks, 1920, p. vi, and 1921, pp. vi–xv.

146 The largest mortgage loan Ponzi made: Summary of Debts and Assets of Charles Ponzi in Bankruptcy, Schedule B(2), Case 28063, on file at the National Archives and Records Administration in Waltham, Massachusetts.

146 he controlled about six hundred: Ponzi, p. 100.

146 issue another two thousand shares: Cunningham v. Commissioner of Banks, 144 N.E. 447.

146 Ponzi was depositing more: Ibid. Also "Story of Hanover Trust Company and Ponzi," Boston Globe, August 31, 1920, p. 1.

147 One afternoon in early June: The narrative account of Ponzi's effective takeover of the Hanover Trust Company comes from Ponzi himself; see Ponzi, pp. 100–103. Ponzi engages in a certain amount of self-aggrandizement on the subject of Hanover Trust, but his version fits with the findings of the Massachusetts bank commissioner, the testimony of Hanover Trust officials in Ponzi's bankruptcy and criminal court cases, and the rulings of several judges, including the Supreme Judicial Court of Massachusetts, in Cunningham v. Commissioner of Banks, 144 N.E. 447.

147 Chmielinski was a bull of a man: "Polish Industrial Association Was Closed Up Today," Boston Evening Globe, August 14, 1920, p. 1; census data on Henry Chmielinski from 1930; photographs of Chmielinski from the files of the Boston Globe.

148 bank's annual meeting of stockholders: Cunningham v. Commissioner of Banks, 144 N.E. 447.

148 The more he bought: Ponzi, p. 105: "The more I bought, the more I wanted to buy."

149 a latter-day Count of Monte Cristo: Ibid., p. 106; Alexandre Dumas, The Count of Monte Cristo, trans. Robin Buss, Penguin, 1997.

149 he wanted to "test its power": Ibid., p. 99.

149 "Wrap it up, please": Ibid., p. 106.

150 "The more servants, the less freedom": "Ponzi Long Had Plan for Riches, Says Wife," Boston Globe, July 30, 1920.

150 a glittering diamond bracelet: "Mrs. Ponzi Would Not Take Gems," Boston Post, November 22, 1922.

150 a string of lustrous pearls: Clarence White, "Mrs. Ponzi Says, 'We Will Stay Here and Square Debts,' " Boston Globe, July 17, 1921.

151 a Boston terrier puppy: "Ponzi Pursued," *Boston Post,* August 13, 1920, p. 9.

151 Ponzi was dealing with: The colloquy between Ponzi and the inspectors comes from his autobiography, pp. 109–11. Confirmation comes, in part, from court testimony by Al Ciullo, who confirmed that he had received a package of reply coupons from Italy and brought them to Ponzi. "Hope to End Ponzi Case by Wednesday," *Boston Globe,* November 25, 1922; "Affecting Meeting of Ponzi and His Mother," *Boston Globe,* November 24, 1922.

152 John Elbye of Everett: "*Post* Prints List of Ponzi Investors," *Boston Post,* August 23, 1920, p. 1. It took two weeks for the newspaper to print the complete list, and some names are taken from later entries. Information on some of the depositors was supplemented by 1920 and 1930 U.S. Census data.

152 an unassuming man with a prominent nose: The Securities Exchange Company note issued to Principio Santosuosso was reproduced in "Mr. Ponzi and His Ponzied Finance," *Literary Digest,* August 21, 1920, p. 49. Details of his life come from U.S. Census data and from Edward Martin, "Retiring Editor of Italian Newspaper Proud of 30-Year Record of Service to North End Folk," *Boston Post,* June 22, 1952, found in the newspaper files of the Boston Public Library.

153 J. Rufus Wallingford: George Randolph Chester, *Get-Rich-Quick Wallingford: The Cheerful Account of the Rise and Fall of an American Business Buccaneer,* Curtis Publishing Company, 1907. Ponzi certainly read the book. He titled the introduction to his autobiography "Meet Mr. Ponzi, the Champion Get-Rich-Quick Wallingford of America." His tone and chapter titles also strongly echo Chester's. For instance, Ponzi's chapter 12 is titled "Mr. Ponzi Finally Discovers an Untrodden Path to Fabulous Wealth and Takes It." Chester's chapter 3 is titled "Mr. Wallingford's Lamb Is Carefully Inspired with a Flash of Creative Genius."

154 wired more than five thousand dollars: Nancy Wrynne, "Ponzi's Home Life Is Simple and Devoid of Ostentation," *Boston Sunday Herald,* August 1, 1920; "Receipts Produced by Ponzi: Sent $7,500 to Italy Since Sept. 5, 1919," *Boston Post,* August 3, 1920, p. 2.

154 Rose worried: Charles Merrill, "His Pretty Girl Wife Sorry When Ponzi Quit $50 Job," *Boston Globe,* August 8, 1920, p. 8.

154 Roberto de Masellis: "Reporters Convinced of De Masellis' Honesty," *Boston Evening Globe,* August 26, 1920, p. 8; "Ponzi Asks Aid . . . Witness Says Foreign Exchange Plan Feasible," *Boston Transcript,* October 27, 1922.

155 "Mr. Ponzi bears a favorable": A copy of the credit report, which describes the June 30, 1920, visit and was dated July 26, 1920, was found among the oldest stories on Ponzi in the *Boston Globe* clippings library.

155 obtain coupons from Poland: Ponzi, pp. 111–13.

155 "I was left high and dry": Ibid., p. 113.

155 clerks had filled wastebaskets with greenbacks: Ponzi, p. 99.

155 In June alone: Monthly investment totals come from the federal audit that led to the closure of the Securities Exchange Company and were evidence at Ponzi's 1922 trial. "How the Bubble Grew," *Boston Evening Transcript,* November 6, 1922, p. 24.

155 prohibiting post offices from redeeming: "Seeking Source of Big Profits," *Boston Post,* July 28, 1920, p. 20.

156 a ten-thousand-dollar loan: *Cunningham v. Commissioner of Banks,* 144 N.E. 447.

156 He paid all Gnecco Brothers' creditors: The Bradstreet Company credit report dated July 26, 1920.

CHAPTER ELEVEN: "LIKE STEALING CANDY FROM A BABY"

159 Joseph Daniels had watched streams of people: The account of Daniels's suit against Ponzi and Ponzi's response comes from *In re Ponzi,* 263 F. 997 (District Court, Massachusetts, November 12, 1920); "Ponzi Partnership and Receiver Hearings On," *Boston Traveler,* October 1, 1920; "Ponzi Criminal Trial to Start Soon, Belief," *Boston Traveler,* October 2, 1920, p. 1; "Ponzi to Tell More on 'Partnership Deal,' " *Boston Traveler,* October 5, 1920, p. 1; "Insist Daniels Tell Disposition of $55,000," *Boston Traveler,* October 9, 1920, p. 1; "Bar Witnesses as Spectators During Trial of Ponzi Case," *Boston Traveler,* October 26, 1922, p. 1; "Ponzi Sent No Representative to Europe," *Boston Globe,* September 29, 1920; "Ponzi Tells How He Borrowed Millions," *Boston Globe,* September 30, 1920; "Figures of Auditor Rittenhouse," *Boston Globe,* October 1, 1920.

161 Frank Leveroni: Obituary of Judge Frank Leveroni found in the library files of the *Boston Globe;* clip is undated but is hand-stamped August 2, 1948. Information on Leveroni and his family also was obtained from the 1920 U.S. Census.

161 Leveroni had invested five thousand dollars: "Creditors of the Ponzi Enterprise," *Boston Post,* August 27, 1920, p. 8.

161 his Lucy Martelli account at Hanover Trust: *Cunningham v. Commissioner of Banks,* 144 N.E. 447; "Questions Ex-Secretary," *Boston Globe,* October 25, 1922.

161 Ponzi emptied his account: Annual Report of the Massachusetts Commissioner of Banks, 1921, p. 20.

162   Grozier stopped at the desk: Interview with Mary Grozier, March 7, 2003.
      Also "Bursting Golden Bubble Wins Gold Medal," *Editor & Publisher,* June
      4, 1921, p. 1; Kenny, p. 194; "Pulitzer Prize Is Awarded to *Post,*" *Boston Post,*
      May 30, 1921, p. 1.

162   A Boston native: "Post Executive E. J. Dunn Dies," *Boston Herald,* May 6,
      1961, p. 1.

163   Much more creative ideas were percolating: Ponzi's ideas to transform
      the Securities Exchange Company into a less speculative and more legiti-
      mate operation come largely from Ponzi himself; see Ponzi, pp. 127–34 and
      139–43. Elements of his ideas are confirmed elsewhere, notably by the fact
      that publicity man William McMasters, who would play an instrumental
      role in helping the *Boston Post* build its case against Ponzi, was initially
      hired to promote Ponzi's deposit contest idea. See "All Demands Met by
      Ponzi: Investigators Still at Sea," *Boston Daily Globe,* August 3, 1920, p. 1.

163   Over their initial dinner at the Copley: "Reporters Convinced of De Masel-
      lis' Honesty," *Boston Evening Globe,* August 26, 1920, p. 8; "Ponzi Asks
      Aid . . . Witness Says Foreign Exchange Plan Feasible," *Boston Transcript,*
      October 27, 1922.

164   To get the ball rolling: "Ponzi Halts Loans at 50 Per Cent till Books Are
      Checked," *Boston Herald,* July 27, 1920, p. 1.

164   he quietly paid his debt: *In re Ponzi,* 268 F 997 (District Court, Massachu-
      setts, November 12, 1920).

164   "There was absolutely nothing to it": Ponzi, p. 128.

165   "floating sample rooms for American products": Ibid., p. 142.

166   S.S. *Cretic:* A copy of the first-class manifest of the S.S. *Cretic* upon its arrival
      in Boston on July 9, 1920, was obtained from microfiche at the National
      Archives and Records Administration office in Waltham, Massachusetts.
      Also "Ask the *Globe,*" *Boston Globe,* September 14, 1991, p. 60.

166   "castles in the air": "Ponzi Tells How He Rose," *Boston American,* August 9,
      1920.

166   Joseph Merenda: Merenda invested two hundred dollars on June 21, 1920;
      "Creditors of the Ponzi Enterprise," *Boston Post,* August 27, 1920, p. 8.

166   Ponzi opened his wallet: "Affecting Meeting of Ponzi and His Mother,"
      Boston Globe, November 24, 1922.

167   "seventeen years since I have seen you": "Grills Merenda at Ponzi Trial,"
      Boston Traveler, November 24, 1922, p. 1.

167   "I made up my mind": "Hope to End Ponzi Case Wednesday," *Boston
      Globe,* November 25, 1922.

167 rot undermining the roots: "J. C. Allen, Bank Commissioner, ' undated clip from the library files of the *Boston Globe;* Wendell Howie "Joseph C. Allen Resigns as Bank Commissioner," *Boston Transcript,* May 11, 1925. Information about Allen was also taken from 1920 and 1930 U.S. Census data.

168 a candidate far from the cloistered world: "Mirrors of Beacon Hill," *Boston News Bureau,* September 30, 1922.

168 pince-nez glasses perched on a handsome nose: The description of Allen comes from photographs in the library files of the *Boston Globe.*

168 "quiet, dignified, immaculate, kind": "Mirrors of Beacon Hill," *Boston News Bureau,* September 30, 1922.

168 a lousy golf game: Ibid.

169 "I am new to this game": Ibid.

169 Allen called for an opinion: Annual Report of the Massachusetts Commissioner of Banks, 1921, p. vii

169 a classic Boston pedigree: "J. Weston Allen Dies at Age of 69," *Boston Post,* January 1, 1942, p. 1; "J. Weston Allen Funeral Today at Mt. Auburn," *Boston Globe,* January 2, 1942; Mason Ham, "People You Ought to Know," *Boston Herald,* October 23, 1929.

169 He answered the bank commissioner's inquiry: Annual Report of the Massachusetts Commissioner of Banks, 1921, p. vii.

170 On July 15, Hanover Trust officials reported: Ibid.

170 The two Allens agreed: Ibid. Albert Hurwitz, "The Ponzi Bubble," *Boston Herald Sunday Magazine,* August 30, 1970, p. 15.

170 meeting at the State House: Albert Hurwitz, "The Ponzi Bubble," *Boston Herald Sunday Magazine,* August 30, 1970, p. 15; Ponzi, pp. 119–20.

170 "I couldn't very well stay away": Ponzi, p. 119.

170 his standard speech about International Reply Coupons: Albert Hurwitz, "The Ponzi Bubble," *Boston Herald Sunday Magazine,* August 30, 1970, p. 15.

170 "I was almost ashamed": Ponzi, p. 119.

171 Hurwitz was an immigrant: "For the Common Council," *Boston Transcript,* December 9, 1905, pp. 5–7; Harry Schneiderman, and I. J. Carmin Karpman, editors, *Who's Who in World Jewry,* David McKay Company, 1965, p. 434. Information about Hurwitz also was taken from 1930 U.S. Census data.

171 Hurwitz respected the confidence and ease: Albert Hurwitz, "The Ponzi Bubble," *Boston Herald Sunday Magazine,* August 30, 1970, p. 15.

171 Ponzi's impeccable fashion sense: Ibid.

171   Hurwitz mildly challenged Ponzi: Ibid.

172   declared they were satisfied: Ibid. In his description of the meeting, Hurwitz
        did not identify Abbott as his fellow assistant attorney general. However, it is
        reasonable to conclude that Abbott was his partner that day because the two
        were the only investigators from the attorney general's office on the Ponzi
        matter at the time.

172   Unknown to Hurwitz: Ponzi, pp. 119–20. Ponzi also did not name Abbott,
        but his account echoes Hurwitz's throughout.

172   Since arriving in Boston from Lithuania: Information about Simon Swig
        was obtained from the 1920 U.S. Census.

172   he had alienated a large portion: "Action Taken to Protect Depositors,
        Shareholders," Boston Globe, February 18, 1921, p. 1.

172   Swig had tended to ignore laws: Annual Report of the Massachusetts Com-
        missioner of Banks 1921, pp. xlv–lix.

173   Swig's house was a prime example: Ibid.

173   Ponzi thought Swig looked down: Ponzi, p. 97.

173   Swig wrote Ponzi a caustic letter: "Ponzi Closes; Not Likely to Resume,"
        Boston Post, July 27, 1920, p. 1.

173   Ponzi did as Swig asked: Ponzi, p. 129. Ponzi does not name Tremont Trust
        here, but his account generally fits with the information contained in Swig's
        letter.

174   Ponzi took the first step: "All Demands Met by Ponzi: Investigators Still
        at Sea," Boston Daily Globe, August 3, 1920, p. 1. The date Ponzi hired
        McMasters is significant because McMasters has often been incorrectly
        credited, or blamed, for the story in the Post on July 24. In one of their rare
        agreements, Ponzi and McMasters both said McMasters had nothing to do
        with initiating that story, a claim made more plausible by the fact that Mc-
        Masters would have had to arrange for a Post reporter to spend the day at
        Ponzi's office and his Lexington home virtually within minutes of his hir-
        ing. Far more likely is that Richard Grozier and Edward Dunn had already
        assigned a feature story about Ponzi as a follow-up to the item about
        Daniels's lawsuit.

174   publicity man William McMasters: Obituary for William McMasters, Boston
        Globe, March 1, 1968; "Ponzi and McMasters Sue Each Other—Run Con-
        tinued Today," Boston Evening Globe, August 3, 1920, p. 1; Kenny, pp.
        191–95; Beatty, p. 418.

175   The remarkable result appeared: "Doubles the Money Within Three
        Months," Boston Post, July 24, 1920, p. 1.

Chapter Twelve: "Money madness"

179 The clear goal for Grozier and Dunn: "Ponzi Has a Rival Next Door to Him," *Boston Sunday Post*, July 25, 1920, p. 1.

180 A few pages past the report: Marguerite Mooers Marshall, "To Make Old Women Young," *Boston Sunday Post*, July 25, 1920, p. 8.

181 an item buried in the *Boston Sunday Herald:* Elizabeth Ellam, "Lawrence Mill Workers Have Money to Invest," *Boston Sunday Herald*, July 25, 1920, p. 4.

181 dashing undertaker Byron M. Pettibone: "Wife Took Overdose, Pettibone Defense," *Boston Daily Globe*, July 27, 1920, p. 1.

181 "a wizard of finance": "Questions the Motive Behind Ponzi Scheme," *Boston Post*, July 26, 1920, p. 1.

181 The telephone began ringing: Ponzi, p. 148.

181 "Every one of them": Ibid., p. 148.

182 "As a judge of the Juvenile Court": "Questions the Motive Behind Ponzi Scheme," *Boston Post*, July 26, 1920, p. 1.

182 "Will you pose for us?": Ibid.

182 Ponzi and Leveroni strategized: "Questions the Motive Behind Ponzi Scheme," *Boston Post*, July 26, 1920, p. 1.

182 "none of them had either the courage": Ponzi, p. 147.

182 Perhaps my activities": Ibid. p. 147.

183 "Follow them everywhere": Ibid., p. 147.

183 he made arrangements to move: "Ponzi Closes; Not Likely to Resume," *Boston Post*, July 27, 1920, p. 1

183 "That Sunday was the busiest day": Ponzi, p. 148.

184 Clarence Walker Barron: Information about Barron was taken largely from a biographical sketch printed as a preface to the book *They Told Barron: Conversations and Revelations of an American Pepys in Wall Street*, Harper & Brothers, 1930, pp. xv–xxxiii. Also "Clarence W. Barron Could Dictate Four Letters at the Same Time," *Boston Post*, October 7, 1928; "Boston News Bureau in New Building," *Boston Post*, September 3, 1912, p. 14; "C. W. Barron, Publisher, and Associates Thus Celebrate 25th Anniversary," undated newspaper clipping found in the files of the Boston Public Library

185 "No man of wide financial": "Questions the Motive Behind Ponzi Scheme," *Boston Post*, July 26. 1920, p. 1. All of Barron's comments from the night of July 26, 1920, are taken from this story.

186 only two cars were allowed: Ponzi, p. 149.

186   A conga line of would-be investors: Ponzi, p. 149; "Ponzi Closes; Not Likely to Resume," *Boston Post,* July 27, 1920, p. 1.

186   "And three groans for the *Post!*": Kenny, p. 197.

187   "The air was tense": Ponzi, p. 149.

187   The new office he opened that morning: "Mrs. Ponzi Would Not Take Gems," *Boston Post,* November 22, 1922.

187   in July alone, Ponzi had taken in: Monthly investment totals come from the federal audit that led to the closure of the Securities Exchange Company and were evidence at Ponzi's 1922 trial. "How the Bubble Grew," *Boston Evening Transcript,* November 6, 1922, p. 24.

188   Ponzi picked up a copy: Ponzi, p. 151.

188   "The situation was especially dangerous": Ibid., p. 151.

188   Ponzi reached for the phone: Ibid., p. 152.

188   Gallagher was an undistinguished lawyer: http://politicalgraveyard.com/bio/gallagher.html; 1920 and 1930 U.S. Census data; Knights of Columbus, Massachusetts State Officers, at http://massachusettsstatekofc.org/StateOfficers.htm.

189   Pelletier was forty-eight: "Decision of Five Justices for Pelletier's Removal," *Boston Sunday Post,* November 5, 1922; "Summary of the Trial of the District Attorney," unidentified newspaper clipping, dated February 21, 1922, from the files of the Boston Public Library; "Blackmail Victims Revealed," *Boston American,* September 30, 1921, p. 1; Michael Kenney, "Beneath Boston's Catholic Subculture," *Boston Globe,* June 18, 1994, p. 29. Also see Beatty, pp. 195–98.

190   Pelletier and Coakley had even enlisted: "Decision of Five Justices for Pelletier's Removal," *Boston Sunday Post,* November 5, 1922.

190   With his publicity man, William McMasters: "Ponzi Closes; Not Likely to Resume," *Boston Post,* July 27, 1920, p. 1; William McMasters, "Declares Ponzi Is Now Hopelessly Insolvent," *Boston Post,* August 2, 1920, p. 1; Ponzi, pp. 153–55. It is worth noting that in their separate accounts of these events, Ponzi and McMasters agreed on general points and certain key details about the conversations with Pelletier, Gallagher, and Allen. However, each framed his account to place himself in the best possible light. Ponzi, for instance, did not mention in his autobiography that McMasters accompanied him to the meetings, which is not surprising considering the animosity that had developed between the two men. As for McMasters, he wrote, "The resumed confidence of his note-holders was due to my own personal efforts. I issued the statements. I directed the stories." And so on. McMas-

ters's August 2, 1920, account, which he elaborated upon during several later court hearings, is also suspect because of timing: It was written in the midst of his most fierce effort to discredit Ponzi to the public through the *Post*. It was almost certainly too flattering not only to himself but also to Pelletier. And Pelletier was no great help, saying only that McMasters's generous account of his actions "is true as far as my memory serves me" (Wilton Vaugh, "M'Masters in Reply to 'The Wizard,' " *Boston Post*, August 2, 1920, p. 1). I have relied on demonstrable facts, areas where they were in agreement, and my own logic to sift through the more tortured elements of their accounts.

190   a man going to a cotillion: "Ponzi Closes; Not Likely to Resume," *Boston Post*, July 27, 1920, p. 1; "Ponzi Stops Taking Money, Awaits Audit," *Boston Daily Globe*, July 27, 1920, p. 1.

192   "Mr. District Attorney": Fonzi, pp. 154–55.

192   Gallagher agreed to consider Ponzi's offer: "Ponzi Closes; Not Likely to Resume," *Boston Post*, July 27, 1920, p. 1.

193   "I don't need the money": Transcript of meeting between Gallagher and Ponzi, read into evidence at Ponzi's 1922 trial; "Ponzi's Political Aims, as Told to the Officials," *Boston Globe*, November 16, 1922; "Million Is Paid Back by Ponzi," *Boston Post*, July 28, 1920, p. 1.

193   they headed toward the State House: "Ponzi Closes; Not Likely to Resume," *Boston Post*, July 27, 1920, p. 1; Ponzi, p. 156.

194   He merrily waved a slip of paper: "Ponzi Stops Taking Money, Awaits Audit," *Boston Globe*, July 27, 1920, p. 1.

194   "He was the same Ponzi": "Ponzi Closes; Not Likely to Resume," *Boston Post*, July 27, 1920, p. 1.

194   "I can't say anything now": Ibid.

Chapter Thirteen: "Master of the situation"

197   refining a daring survival plan: Ponzi, pp. 157–58. In his autobiography, Ponzi says he came up with the idea to "borrow" Hanover Trust's assets on the ride home the night before. He no doubt was still refining the plan en route to work that morning.

197   "master of the situation": Ibid., p. 157.

197   "Every time I refunded the principal": Ibid.

198   "He wasn't likely to make any trouble": Ibid.

198   "unless I happened to have": Ibid.

199 "The investigation would have ended right there": Ponzi, p. 158.

199 its lead headline triumphantly predicting: "Ponzi Closes; Not Likely to Resume," *Boston Post*, July 27, 1920, p. 1.

200 PUBLIC NOTICE: Paid notice on page 1 of the *Boston Post*, July 27, 1920.

200 Ponzi suspected that the officials: Ponzi, p. 156. Ponzi's chronology is slightly compressed on this point. He places the withdrawal of the police as occurring the afternoon of July 26, immediately after he struck his deal with Pelletier. The *Post* more credibly reported that the police disappeared the next day. See "Million Is Paid Back by Ponzi," *Boston Post*, July 28, 1920, p. 1.

201 Ponzi told Dunn that the newspaper: Kenny, p. 196, and Ponzi, pp. 160–61. Neither Kenny nor Ponzi specifies when Ponzi made his threat to Dunn, but it stands to reason Ponzi would have done so immediately upon seeing the story as he marshaled his resources to confront the run of withdrawals.

201 A lawyer for one of his investors: "Suit Filed Against Ponzi, but Quickly Withdrawn," *Boston Evening Globe*, July 27, 1920, p. 2; "Withdraws Bill to Enjoin," *Boston Evening Transcript*, July 27, 1920, p. 5; "Million Is Paid Back by Ponzi," *Boston Post*, July 28, 1920, p. 1; Ponzi, pp. 159–60. Biographical information on Alton Parker from 1920 U.S. Census.

202 "one of those lawyers": Ponzi, p. 160.

202 Dan Coakley: Beatty, pp. 100, 137–39, 265; "Daniel H. Coakley, Dead at 87; Long Political Figure," *Boston Herald*, September 19, 1952; "Dan Coakley Has Been Teamster, Conductor, Reporter and Politician," *Boston Traveler*, September 30, 1921; Albert Hurwitz, "The Ponzi Bubble," *Boston Sunday Herald Magazine*, August 30, 1970, p. 13.

203 Ponzi adored Coakley: Ponzi, p. 160.

203 There was no letup: The scene at Ponzi's office on July 27, 1920, was taken from multiple sources, including: "Million Is Paid Back by Ponzi," *Boston Post*, July 28, 1920, p. 1; "Ponzi Has World Scheme," *Boston Evening Transcript*, July 27, 1920, p. 1; "Exchange 'Wizard' Is Paying Claims," *New York Times*, July 28, 1920, p. 13; "Ponzi Pays Money Back to Hundreds," *Boston Globe*, July 28, 1920, p. 1; and "Six Women Faint in Crowd at School St. Building Seeking to Redeem Notes," *Boston Herald*, July 28, 1920, p. 1. Elements of the scene also came from a photograph found in the files of the *Boston Globe* stamped July 27, 1920, and captioned "Crowd Outside of Ponzi's Office, 27 School Street." A note written in red pencil ordered that the photo be saved for Ponzi's eventual obituary.

204 Perhaps hoping to reassure: "Ponzi Has World Scheme," *Boston Evening Transcript*, July 27, 1920, p. 1.

204 arrangements to take over: "Exchange 'Wizard' Is Paying Claims," *New York Times,* July 28, 1920, p. 13.

205 "a case of 'heads I win': Ponzi, p. 160.

205 At the end of the day: "Million Is Paid Back by Ponzi," *Boston Post,* July 28, 1920, p. 1.

206 Ponzi quietly took a precaution: Annual Report of the Massachusetts Commissioner of Banks, 1921, pp. vii–viii.

207 To allay his concerns: Ibid.

208 Ponzi turned to a waiting *Post* photographer: Photo captioned "Charles Ponzi as He Appeared Yesterday," *Boston Post,* July 28, 1920, p. 20.

208 bigger news in the *Post:* Front page of the *Boston Post,* July 28, 1920.

208 another cutting attack by Clarence Barron: "Seeking Source of Big Profits," *Boston Post,* reprinted from the *Boston News Bureau,* July 28, 1920, p. 20.

208 the swarm of people: "Ponzi Puts Wealth at $24,000,000; Pays Out $750,000 More," *Boston Herald,* July 29, 1920, p. 1.

209 "Bankers and businessmen can easily understand: "Exchange 'Wizard' to Fight Bankers," *New York Times,* July 29, 1920, p. 15.

209 Ponzi upped his estimate: "Ponzi Puts Wealth at $24,000,000; Pays Out $750,000 More," *Boston Herald,* July 29, 1920, p. 1.

209 "Now please don't think that I'm boasting": "Exchange 'Wizard' to Fight Bankers," *New York Times,* July 29, 1920, p. 15.

210 "As I told Ponzi the other day": "Uncle Sam to Get the Facts of Ponzi's Case," *Boston Post,* July 29, 1920, p. 1.

210 Ponzi relieved the tedium, hunger, and thirst: "Exchange 'Wizard' to Fight Bankers," *New York Times,* July 29, 1920, p. 15.

210 James Francis Morelli: "Receivers Searched Bank Officers' Boxes," *Boston Globe,* September 4, 1920. Also, copies of several of Morelli's poems were preserved in the library files of the *Boston Globe.*

211 an association called the Ponzi Alliance: "Exchange 'Wizard' to Fight Bankers," *New York Times,* July 29, 1920, p. 15.

211 half to three-quarters of a million dollars: "Uncle Sam to Get the Facts of Ponzi's Case," *Boston Post,* July 29, 1920, p. 1.

211 sign written cheerily in crayon: "Ponzi Makes Big Profits from 'Run,' " *Boston Daily Globe,* July 29, 1920, p. 1.

211 company outing at a resort: "Mass of Ponzi's Papers Found on Junk Heap May Give New Clue to Assets," *Boston Herald,* September 2, 1920, p. 1.

211 banquet where he was the guest of honor: "McNary Hailed Ponzi as 'Financial Genius,' " *Boston Post,* August 15, 1920, p. 12.

211   William McNary: Congressional biography, found online at http://biogu-
ide.congress.gov/scripts/biodisplay.pl?index=M000584.

212   Calvin Coolidge: "Uncle Sam to Get the Facts of Ponzi's Case," *Boston Post,*
July 29, 1920, p. 1.

212   the *Post*'s first editorial on Ponzi: "It Cannot Last," *Boston Post,* July 29,
1920, editorial page. Editorials were unsigned, but this was clearly the work
of Richard Grozier, who wrote it either himself or in collaboration with another writer. Regardless, it was fully his responsibility as the paper's acting
editor and publisher, and he certainly knew that any resulting cost would be
borne by him.

CHAPTER FOURTEEN: "EVEN HIS COWS COULDN'T GIVE MILK."

215   The door to the Bell-in-Hand: "Ponzi to Start 'Bank' in New York," *New
York Times,* July 30, 1920, p. 1.

215   time with his new lawyer: "Pelletier Begins to Audit Ponzi's Books," *Boston
Herald,* July 30, 1920, p. 1.

216   a large revolver lying menacingly: Ibid.

216   One young man, sweat dripping: Ibid.

216   Just after the four o'clock closing time: "Ponzi to Start 'Bank' in New
York," *New York Times,* July 30, 1920, p. 1.

216   When the inevitable question arose: Ibid.

216   "And then I found my inspiration": "Exchange 'Wizard' to Fight Bankers,"
New York Times, July 29, 1920, p. 1.

217   McMasters seemed intent on antagonizing them: "Officials Balked by Ponzi
Puzzle," *Boston Post,* July 30, 1920, p. 1.

217   his old nemesis: "Governor Acts in Ponzi Case," *Boston Evening Globe,* July
29, 1920, p. 1.

217   an investigation of Ponzi's rival: "Officials Balked by Ponzi Puzzle," *Boston
Post,* July 30, 1920, p. 1.

217   a tantalizing bit of information: Ibid. Ponzi, pp. 161–62.

218   *EXTRA:* "Coupon Plan Is Exploded," *Boston Post,* July 30, 1920, p. 1.

218   The *Post* also turned to ridicule: "Plenty of Opportunity," editorial cartoon
printed in the *Boston Post,* July 30, 1920, p. 11.

219   The *Boston Traveler* ran a sports column: "Old Scout Jim Compares Babe
Ruth with Financier Ponzi," *Boston Traveler,* July 30, 1920.

219   quoted a North End banker: "Ponzi Pays $1,450,000 in 3 Days," *Boston
American,* July 30, 1920, p. 1.

219 Ponzi's secret formula for wealth: "N.Y. Man Tells How Ponzi May Get His
     Millions," *Boston American*, July 30, 1920, p. 2.

219 In the Friday edition: "Both Barron and Ponzi Give Talk," *Boston Post*,
     July 31, 1920, p. 5.

220 "Ponzi or anyone else": Ibid.

220 "From the several articles": Ibid.

220 the temperature approaching eighty degrees; Ponzi stepped outside: "May
     Enter Politics," *Boston Post*, July 31, 1920, p. 5; "Ponzi Gives Aid to Federal
     Agents," *New York Times*, August 1, 1920, p. 10. The temperature comes
     from a chart on the front page of the *Boston Post*, July 31, 1920.

221 gleefully told reporters: "Federal Officials Begin Ponzi Inquiry," *New York
     Times*, July 31, 1920, p. 2; "May Enter Politics," *Boston Post*, July 31, 1920, p. 5.

221 "I am not a Red": "Ponzi Gives Aid to Federal Agents," *New York Times*,
     August 1, 1920, p. 10.

221 Pelletier withdrew from the probe: "Allen Guiding Ponzi Inquiry," *Boston
     Daily Globe*, July 31, 1920, p. 1; "Federal Officials Scout Ponzi Claims,"
     Boston Post, July 31, 1920, p. 1; "Ponzi Sues C. W. Barron for $5,000,000;
     Pelletier Drops Case; U.S. Audit Begins," *Boston Herald*, July 31, 1920, p. 1;
     "Federal Officials Begin Ponzi Inquiry," *New York Times*, July 31, 1920, p. 2;
     "Ponzi Gives Aid to Federal Agents," *New York Times*, August 1, 1920, p. 10.

222 a meek-looking fellow named Edwin L. Pride: "Starts Audit of Ponzi's
     Books," *Boston Evening Globe*, July 30, 1920, p. 1; "Audit on Ponzi Ac-
     counts," *Boston Traveler*, July 31, 1920, p. 1; "Federal Officials Scout Ponzi
     Claims," *Boston Post*, July 31, 1920, p. 1.

222 Ponzi joined Pride for a meeting: "Federal Officials Scout Ponzi Claims,"
     Boston Post, July 31, 1920, p. 1.

222 "There can be but one result.": Ibid.

222 impossible for Ponzi to have made a fortune: "Washington Authorities State
     He Could Not Possibly Have Made Huge Fortune Dealing in Reply
     Coupons," *Boston Post*, July 31, 1920, p. 1.

223 scolded Attorney General Allen: "New Hampshire Taking a Hand in Ponzi
     Case," *Boston Sunday Post*, August 1, 1920, p. 1.

223 tapping Ponzi's telephones: Albert Hurwitz, "The Ponzi Bubble," *Boston Sun-
     day Herald Magazine*, August 30, 1970, p. 13. As an assistant attorney general on
     the Ponzi case, Hurwitz had firsthand knowledge of the telephone taps.

223 Allen also sent one of his assistants: "Atty Gen Allen Trying to Get Inter-
     view with Ponzi," *Boston Globe*, August 2, 1920, p. 2; Albert Hurwitz, "The
     Ponzi Bubble," *Boston Sunday Herald Magazine*, August 30, 1970, p. 13.

223   Barron seconded the *Post's* conclusion: "Dazzling Future with Limousines Rolling on Coupon Carpet," *Boston Herald*, August 1, 1920, p. 8. Reprinted from the *Boston News Bureau*, which used the headline " 'Ponzied' Finance."

224   *Boston American* was crowing: "Wife Tells of Ponzi's Plans," *Boston American*, July 1, 1920, p. 1.

224   Mr. and Mrs. Charles Ponzi: "Ponzi Promises $100,000 to Home for Children," *Boston Herald*, August 1, 1920, p. 1; "New Hampshire Taking a Hand in Ponzi Probe," *Boston Sunday Post*, August 1, 1920, p. 1.

225   Ponzi got more good publicity: "Ponzi the New Emancipator," *Boston Herald*, August 1, 1920, p. 8.

225   Ponzi spent a relatively quiet Sunday: "Ponzi Investigation Goes on Day and Night," *New York Times*, August 2, 1920, p. 3; "Film Men Keep Ponzi Busy; Ponzi Home Mecca of Curious; Ponzi Takes Flight," *Boston Post*, August 2, 1920, p. 6.

225   With the cameras rolling: Muriel Caswall, "Ponzi Enjoys Himself Before the Camera," *Boston Sunday Post*, August 8, 1920, p. 39. Although the story was published on August 8, it describes a scene that took place a week earlier.

226   Ponzi had an inspiration: "Film Men Keep Ponzi Busy; Ponzi Home Mecca of Curious; Ponzi Takes Flight," *Boston Post*, August 2, 1920, p. 6.

227   He was forty-six, with a young wife: 1920 U.S. Census data on William McMasters and family.

227   He called Richard Grozier: "McMasters Loses Both the Ponzi Suits," *Boston Globe*, February 11, 1921.

228   Grozier offered McMasters the fabulous sum: Kenny, p. 196; "McMasters Loses Both the Ponzi Suits," *Boston Globe*, February 11, 1921.

228   The story, under McMasters's byline: "Declares Ponzi Is Now Hopelessly Insolvent," *Boston Post*, August 2, 1920, p. 1.

CHAPTER FIFTEEN: "YOU DISCOVERED THE MONEY!"

231   Anxious investors began gathering in Pi Alley: "Great Run on Ponzi Continues Until Office Is Closed for Day," *Boston Post*, August 3, 1920, p. 1; "Mobs Flock to Ponzi's Office," *Boston Post*, August 3, 1920, p. 2; "Ponzi Absolutely Denies He Is Insolvent—Alleges Malice," *Boston Evening Globe*, August 2, 1920, p. 1; "All Demands Met by Ponzi, Investigators Still at Sea," *Boston Daily Globe*, August 3, 1920, p. 1; "Big Run on Ponzi, but All Get Cash," *New York Times*, August 3, 1920, p. 15; Hundreds Paid by Ponzi," *Boston American*, August 2, 1920, p. 1; "Ponzi Pays, Smiling, as Pi Alley Rages and Mob Beats Door," *Boston Herald*, August 3, 1920, p. 1.

232   Ricardo Bogni: "Sub-Agent Is Sure State Ruined Ponzi," *Boston Traveler,* November 2, 1922; "Defence to View Ponzi Documents," *Boston Post,* November 2, 1922.

232   De Masellis gathered his belongings: "Ponzi Manager Returns $10,000," *Boston Post,* August 26, 1920, p. 1; "Coakley to Testify in Ponzi Court Fight," *Boston Traveler,* August 26, 1920, p. 1.

233   twirling his snappy walking stick: "Ponzi Absolutely Denies He Is Insolvent—Alleges Malice," *Boston Evening Globe,* August 2, 1920, p. 1.

233   "My hat is in the ring": "Great Run on Ponzi Continues Until Office Is Closed for Day," *Boston Post,* August 3, 1920, p. 1.

233   Ponzi responded true to form: Ponzi's response to reporters on August 2, 1920, was pieced together from the following: "Great Run on Ponzi Continues Until Office Is Closed for Day," *Boston Post,* August 3, 1920, p. 1; "Mobs Flock to Ponzi's Office," *Boston Post,* August 3, 1920, p. 2; "Ponzi Absolutely Denies He Is Insolvent—Alleges Malice," *Boston Evening Globe,* August 2, 1920, p. 1; "All Demands Met by Ponzi, Investigators Still at Sea," *Boston Daily Globe,* August 3, 1920, p. 1; "Big Run on Ponzi, but All Get Cash," *New York Times,* August 3, 1920, p. 15; "Hundreds Paid by Ponzi," *Boston American,* August 2, 1920, p. 1; "Ponzi Pays, Smiling, as Pi Alley Rages and Mob Beats Door," *Boston Herald,* August 3, 1920, p. 1; "Storm Ponzi for Money," *Boston Traveler,* August 2, 1920, p. 1.

234   "as calm and undisturbed as a mill pond": "Ponzi Absolutely Denies He Is Insolvent—Alleges Malice," *Boston Evening Globe,* August 2, 1920, p. 1.

234   an impassioned poem: James Francis Morelli, "Chas. Ponzi Says: 'My Dog Never Leads Me.' Who Is the Dog?" An undated copy of the poem was found in the Ponzi clip files of the *Boston Globe.*

235   Gary Johnson of Houston wrote: "All Demands Met by Ponzi, Investigators Still at Sea," *Boston Daily Globe,* August 3, 1920, p. 1.

235   Ponzi wandered outside: The scene is told in several papers, but the best version is in "All Demands Met by Ponzi, Investigators Still at Sea," *Boston Daily Globe,* August 3, 1920, p. 1. The *Globe* spells her name Percheck, but that is almost certainly a phonetic spelling, as Mrs. Perchek, according to the reporter, was illiterate. When asked to sign her name, she could only make a mark, which Ponzi had one of his clerks cosign as a witness.

235   "You're the greatest Italian in history!": Ibid. There are numerous versions of this exchange, all essentially the same but with minor variations. The *Globe* account seems the most reliable because it is told in context, strongly suggesting that the unnamed reporter witnessed the scene firsthand in close proximity to Ponzi.

236   Edwin Pride continued his audit: "Ponzi Absolutely Denies He Is Insolvent—Alleges Malice," *Boston Evening Globe,* August 2, 1920, p. 1.

236   Pelletier and Attorney General Allen traded barbs: "Great Run on Ponzi Continues Until Office Is Closed for Day," *Boston Post,* August 3, 1920, p. 1.

236   "wiping Peter's nose with Paul's handkerchief": "All Demands Met by Ponzi, Investigators Still at Sea," *Boston Daily Globe,* August 3, 1920, p. 1.

236   William "520 Percent" Miller: George Boothby, "Reformed Wizard Discusses Ponzi," New York *World,* August 3, 1920. Reprinted in the *Boston Post,* August 3, 1920, p. 2.

237   "I shall never say anything": "Great Run on Ponzi Continues Until Office Is Closed for Day," *Boston Post,* August 3, 1920, p. 1.

237   "Shall you go on paying claims tomorrow?": "All Demands Met by Ponzi, Investigators Still at Sea," *Boston Daily Globe,* August 3, 1920, p. 1.

237   "Money boy!": "Ponzi and McMasters Sue Each Other—Run Continued Today," *Boston Evening Globe,* August 3, 1920, p. 1.

237   "Well, they didn't break me yesterday": "Department of Justice Joins in Probe of Ponzi's Business," *Boston Post,* August 4, 1920, p. 1.

237   "Mountains of money available": "Another Day's Run Sees Ponzi Smiling," *New York Times,* August 4, 1920, p. 6.

237   "How are your newspapers selling?": "Ponzi and McMasters Sue Each Other—Run Continued Today," *Boston Evening Globe,* August 3, 1920, p. 1.

237   suing McMasters for two thousand dollars: "Department of Justice Joins in Probe of Ponzi's Business," *Boston Post,* August 4, 1920, p. 1; "Ponzi Sues Agent, $2,000; Agent Sues Ponzi, $5,000," *Boston Herald,* August 4, 1920, p. 4.

237   McMasters understood the game: Ibid.; Wilton Vaugh, "M'Masters in Reply to 'The Wizard,' " *Boston Post,* August 3, 1920, p. 1.

237   even another attack by Barron: "Entire Issue of Coupons Last Year Only $60,000," *Boston Post,* August 4, 1920, p. 6, reprinted from the previous day's *Boston News Bureau.*

238   "Everybody's but my own!": "Mounted Police Rout Ponzi Clients; Frantic Thousands Mob Defender; Federal Agents to Speed Up Inquiry," *Boston Herald,* August 4, 1920, p. 1.

238   a sign appeared that day: "Ponzi Greatest Man in Country, North End View," *Boston Daily Globe,* August 4, 1920, p. 1.

238   "the most talked of man in America": Photo caption alongside story "Crisis for Ponzi," *Boston American,* August 3, 1920, p. 1.

238   Ponzi paid a visit: "Another Day's Run Sees Ponzi Smiling," *New York Times,* August 4, 1920, p. 6.

239 more than $400,000: "Crisis for Ponzi," *Boston American,* August 3, 1920, p. 1.

239 "After this investigation": "Department of Justice Joins in Probe of Ponzi's Business," *Boston Post,* August 4, 1920, p. 1; "Another Day's Run Sees Ponzi Smiling," *New York Times,* August 4, 1920, p. 6.

240 a very public night out: "Ponzi Wants to Be an Actor," *Boston Post,* August 4, 1920, p. 2; "Ponzi Pays All Comers; Federal Agent Arrives," *Boston Daily Globe,* August 4, 1920, p. 1.

241 Fewer than a hundred people: "Ponzi Baffles Probers," *Boston American,* August 4, 1920, p. 1.

242 clothes fit for an angel: Floyd Gibbons, "Ponzi Pays as Probers Work," *Boston Post,* August 5, 1920, p. 1.

242 Ponzi's only comment for investigators: "Ponzi Refuses Inquiry to Show His Assets; Run on His Boston Office Practically Ended," *New York Times,* August 5, 1920, p. 15.

242 "The exposé by the man: "Run on Ponzi Dwindles," *Boston Traveler,* August 4, 1920, p. 1.

242 Ponzi had paid out another $313,000: Floyd Gibbons, "Ponzi Pays as Probers Work," *Boston Post,* August 5, 1920, p. 1.

242 capitalized on the chaos: Ponzi, p. 165; "Questions Ex-Secretary," *Boston Globe,* October 25, 1922. Ponzi's autobiography and the newspaper articles about Lucy Meli's testimony do not name Cassullo, but both provide enough detail to allow one to conclude that he was the culprit. Also, given his criminal past, his blackmailing of Ponzi, and his eventual disappearance, the shoe fits.

242 Ponzi returned to the theater: "Ponzi Poses for Movies on Boston Theatre Stage," *Boston Daily Globe,* August 5, 1920, p. 10.

243 Only fifty-seven people showed up: "Palmer Takes Up the Ponzi Case," *Boston Daily Globe,* August 6, 1920, p. 1.

243 $168,000: "Ponzi Case Probe Shifts to Capital," *Boston Post,* August 6, 1920, p. 1.

243 Ponzi's pals Louis and Charlotte Blass: "Ponzi Winners Include Coupon Wizard's Wife," *Boston Traveler,* August 24, 1920, p. 1; "Two Witnesses Sought in Ponzi Case Disappear," *Boston Herald,* September 12, 1920, p. 1; "Sued for $90,000 by Ponzi Trustee," *Boston Globe,* March 8, 1925; "Blass Denies He Was an Agent for Ponzi," *Boston Globe,* November 9, 1920.

243 Ponzi's humble days in Mobile, Alabama: "A Leaf out of Ponzi's Past," *Boston Daily Globe,* August 5, 1920, p. 1.

243 The lowlight of Ponzi's day: "Ponzi Case Probe Shifts to Capital," *Boston Post,* August 6, 1920, p. 1; "Four New Yorkers Ask Ponzi Backing," *New*

York Times, August 6, 1920, p. 6; "Ponzi Joins New York Promoters, Forming $200,000,000 Concern" *Boston Herald,* August 6, 1920, p. 1. Also see Ponzi, pp. 161–71. In his autobiography, Ponzi suggests that Herman and his partners might well have invested in his business and at one point even displayed a $10 million check. Ponzi's point appears to be to suggest that if he had only been given a little more time he could have weathered the storm and righted his ship. However, it is more plausible to believe that even if Herman did wave a check before Ponzi's face, it could never have saved him. Ponzi had no secret to sell Herman, and although Herman might have been willing to become partners in an operation based purely on Ponzi's charisma, it is difficult to imagine he would pay $10 million for that privilege.

244 Joseph Allen discovered the first sign: Annual Report of the Massachusetts Commissioner of Banks, 1921, p. vii–viii.

244 Ponzi knew he could wait no longer: "Call Lansing in Ponzi Case," *Boston Post,* August 7, 1920, p. 1; "Ponzi Agents Tell of Receipts," *Boston Globe,* October 27, 1922; "Refuses to Tell Where Money Went," *Boston Post,* October 5, 1920; *In re Ponzi,* 268 F. 997 (District Court, Massachusetts, November 12, 1920); "Daniels Withdraws Suit Against Ponzi," *Boston Evening Globe,* August 6, 1920, p. 1; "Ponzi Settles Claim for Million, Taking Daniels as Partner," *Boston Herald,* August 7, 1920, p. 1; Ponzi, pp. 132–33.

246 "I am now on the offensive": "Ponzi Settles Claim for Million, Taking Daniels as Partner," *Boston Herald,* August 7, 1920, p. 1.

246 "Are you a Bolshevist?": "Daniels Withdraws Suit Against Ponzi," *Boston Evening Globe,* August 6, 1920, p. 1.

247 "the financing of Soviet Russia": "Call Lansing in Ponzi Case," *Boston Post,* August 7, 1920, p. 1.

247 "Are you . . . ? Are you . . . ?": Ibid.

247 *New York Times* sensed the pendulum: "One Record at Least Is Broken," *New York Times,* editorial, August 6, 1920, p. 8.

247 a puritanical and decidedly racist cloak: "Something for Nothing," *Boston Evening Globe,* editorial, August 6, 1920, p. 10.

CHAPTER SIXTEEN: "I FEEL THE STRAIN—INSIDE."

251 Ponzi could withdraw the $185,000: "Unite upon Ponzi Case," *Boston Post,* August 8, 1920, p. 1; "Ponzi Defies Arrest," *Boston American,* August 7, 1920, p. 1; "Consulted Lansing on Ponzi's Operations; Return of Assistant Attorney General Abbott," *Boston Evening Globe,* August 7, 1920, p. 1.

251   a sarcastic "good morning": "Ponzi Defies Arrest," *Boston American,* August
      7, 1920, p. 1.

251   Ponzi had to settle for his son: "Consulted Lansing on Ponzi's Operations;
      Return of Assistant Attorney General Abbott," *Boston Evening Globe,* Au-
      gust 7, 1920, p. 1.

252   investigators held a flurry of meetings: "Unite upon Ponzi Case," *Boston
      Post,* August 8, 1920, p. 1; "Ponzi Starts Scare by Seven-Hour Absence,"
      Boston Sunday Globe, August 8, 1920, p. 1; "Ponzi Defies State or Nation to
      Stop Him from Opening Tomorrow," *Boston Sunday Herald,* August 8, 1920,
      p. 1.

252   Governor Coolidge "is far from satisfied": "Unite upon Ponzi Case," *Boston
      Post,* August 8, 1920, p. 1.

252   Old Colony continued to accept deposits: "Ponzi Starts Scare by Seven-
      Hour Absence," *Boston Sunday Globe,* August 8, 1920, p. 1.

252   a chance to reflect on his situation: Ponzi does not specifically detail his true
      reasons for his about-face regarding collecting money for his new company.
      When he announced his decision immediately upon emerging from
      Hanover Trust, he spoke only of doing what was best for his investors.
      However, the more complete rationale suggested here is more plausible,
      given the intensity of the investigations and even some newspapers' sugges-
      tions that his new company might be viewed as repaying the debts of the
      Securities Exchange Company. See "Ponzi Opens Offices in His New
      Company," *Boston Traveler,* August 9, 1920, p. 1.

253   a rumor took hold: "Unite upon Ponzi Case," *Boston Post,* August 8, 1920,
      p. 1; "Ponzi Starts Scare by Seven-Hour Absence," *Boston Sunday Globe,*
      August 8, 1920, p. 1; "Ponzi Defies State or Nation to Stop Him from
      Opening Tomorrow," *Boston Sunday Herald,* August 8, 1920, p. 1; "Ponzi to
      Refuse Money in His New Venture," *New York Times,* August 9, 1920, p. 6.

253   his name being yelled by newsboys: "Unite upon Ponzi Case," *Boston Post,*
      August 8, 1920, p. 1.

253   trying to charm the entire newsroom: "Unite upon Ponzi Case," *Boston
      Post,* August 8, 1920, p. 1; "Ponzi Starts Scare by Seven-Hour Absence,"
      Boston Sunday Globe, August 8, 1920, p. 1.

253   "Why are you doing this to me?": Curt Norris, "Ponzi," *Yankee,* November
      1975, p. 115.

254   "I have decided": "Ponzi Will Wait," *Boston Post,* August 8, 1920, p. 14.

254   bid on the entire fleet: "Ponzi Defies Arrest," *Boston American,* August 7,
      1920, p. 1.

254   "This will be all the security": Ibid.

254   "They call me the 'Millionaire Kid' ": "Ponzi to Resume Monday," *Boston
       Sunday Advertiser*, August 8, 1920, p. 1.

255   dressed in a bathrobe: "Ponzi's Debts Known Today," *Boston Post*, August 9,
       1920, p. 1.

255   the ninety-three-degree heat: "Relief from Heat Today," *Boston Post*, August
       10, 1920, p. 1.

255   waving a telegram from Herman: Ibid.

255   telling *Post* reporter P. A. Santosuosso: "Ponzi Relates Story of His Life,"
       Boston Post, August 9, 1920, p. 16. The story does not carry a byline, but
       there are several reasons to believe it was the work of Santosuosso. He was
       responsible for day-to-day coverage of the case (see Kenny, p. 197) and he
       had also heard the rumor about Ponzi spending time in jail in Montreal
       (Kenny, p. 197), which would explain why the story explicitly pointed out
       the lengthy gaps in Ponzi's account of his life.

255   a rumor that Ponzi had spent time: Kenny, p. 197.

255   sharing what he knew with Richard Grozier: Ibid.

256   Her eyes brimmed with tears: "Ponzi Relates Story of His Life," *Boston Post*,
       August 9, 1920, p. 16.

256   she abhorred people staring at her: Charles Merrill, "His Pretty Girl Wife
       Sorry When Ponzi Quit $50 Job," *Boston Globe*, August 8, 1920, p. 8.

256   "I would much rather that he was a bricklayer": "Ponzi Relates Story of His
       Life," *Boston Post*, August 9, 1920, p. 16.

256   Later that day, a telegram arrived: "Ponzi Shown Dispatch," *Boston Post*, Au-
       gust 11, 1920, p. 18. This brief story details how and when the *Post* got wind
       of Ponzi's Montreal conviction and also describes the phone call to Ponzi
       asking for comment or confirmation. Again, as described above, it is reason-
       able to deduce that the phone call was made by Santosuosso. Also see Ponzi,
       pp. 165–67, for his account of this episode. Separately, on p. 169, Ponzi de-
       scribes another version of the event in which he says "a city editor came up
       to my house in Lexington about midnight. Flashing a telegram from Mon-
       treal." Based on the *Post*'s account and other elements of the chronology,
       there is strong reason to believe that Ponzi was confusing this event with a
       later one, in which he was shown a copy of the *Post* shortly after midnight
       on the day the story broke.

256   Grozier called for his ace: Kenny, p. 197.

257   Ponzi knew he could not avoid: Ponzi, p. 166. See "It was vital for me to
       delay the exposure until after the show-down [with Pride]."

257   Ponzi estimated that his holdings: "Register, but Keep Money," *Boston
       American*, August 9, 1920, p. 1.

258 "call the bluff of all the public authorities" Ibid.

258 "After I have been proved on the level": Ibid.

258 Joseph Bonina: "Register, but Keep Money," *Boston American*, August 9, 1920, p. 1; Also 1930 U.S. Census data.

258 pharmacist Louis Mantani: "Ponzi Funds Tied Up; Bankruptcy Petition Filed by 3 Clients," *Boston Herald*, August 10, 1920, p. 1; "Stop Ponzi Checks: Say He's Bankrupt," *New York Times*, August 10, 1920, p. 1.

258 Ponzi received an invitation from Gallagher: "Ponzi Stops Payment—Not to Take Up Any Notes upon Loans," *Boston Post*, August 10, 1920, p. 1; "Ponzi Account Overdrawn; All Checks Ordered Stopped," *Boston Evening Globe*, August 9, 1920, p. 1; "Ponzi Funds Tied Up; Bankruptcy Petition Filed by 3 Clients," *Boston Herald*, August 10, 1920, p. 1.

259 Ponzi's main account at the bank: *Cunningham v. Commissioner of Banks,* 144 N.E. 447; Annual Report of the Massachusetts Commissioner of Banks, 1921, p. vii–viii.

259 thirteen thousand dollars in the Martelli account: Ibid.

259 tried over the weekend to replenish: *Cunningham v. Commissioner of Banks,* 144 N.E. 447; Annual Report of the Massachusetts Commissioner of Banks, 1921, p. vii–viii; "Ponzi Assails 'Bank Ring,'" *Boston Traveler*, August 10, 1920, p. 1; Ponzi Stops Payment—Not to Take Up Any Notes upon Loans," *Boston Post*, August 10, 1920, p. 1. For a brief time Ponzi claimed, erroneously, that New Hampshire officials had illegally transferred the money in his Manchester account to an account controlled by his Manchester agent, Joseph Bruno. There was no evidence to support that claim, which was strongly and convincingly denied by New Hampshire officials. Far more likely was that Ponzi had simply overestimated the amount of money in the account and had bounced his checks.

259 Joseph Allen dialed the Hanover Trust Company: *Cunningham v. Commissioner of Banks,* 144 N.E. 447; Annual Report of the Massachusetts Commissioner of Banks, 1921, pp. vii–viii.

260 his carefully choreographed attack: "Ponzi Stops Payment—Not to Take Up Any Notes upon Loans," *Boston Post*, August 10, 1920, p. 1; *Cunningham v. Commissioner of Banks* 144 N.E. 447; "Stop Ponzi Checks: Say He's Bankrupt," *New York Times*, August 10, 1920, p. 1; "Ponzi Funds Tied Up; Bankruptcy Petition Filed by 3 Clients," *Boston Herald*, August 10, 1920, p. 1; "Ponzi Account Overdrawn; All Checks Ordered Stopped," *Boston Evening Globe*, August 9, 1920, p. 1. Joseph Allen never took responsibility for the bankruptcy filing, but it is impossible to believe its timing was a coincidence. Indeed, Allen's efforts to distance himself from the filing only serve

to tie him more closely. In his annual report and in court testimony, Allen
or his assistants maintained that the bankruptcy filing was made at 1:40 P.M.
on August 9, or five minutes before the order to stop paying Ponzi checks.
Newspaper reports from that day, however, say the filing actually came
closer to 3:00 P.M., which is more credible because the claim of bankruptcy
would have been credible only after the commissioner's stop-payment order.

260   "I have directed the Hanover Trust Company": "Ponzi Stops Payment—Not
      to Take Up Any Notes upon Loans," *Boston Post,* August 10, 1920, p. 1.

261   attorney general immediately issued a statement: "Allen Finds Discrepancy
      in Ponzi's Statement of His Financial Operations," *Boston Herald,* August 10,
      1920, p. 2.

261   an office he had set up in the State House: Allen bought space to run the
      announcement on the front page of the *Post* on August 10, 1920.

262   Ponzi rushed to the tenth floor: "What He Told Allen Was Bull, Says
      Ponzi," *Boston Daily Globe,* August 10, 1920, p. 1.

262   nibbling on the remnants of a box lunch: Ibid.

262   "I have played fair": "Ponzi Stops Payment—Not to Take Up Any Notes
      upon Loans," *Boston Post,* August 10, 1920, p. 1.

262   "All I told Attorney General Allen": "What He Told Allen Was Bull, Says
      Ponzi," *Boston Daily Globe,* August 10, 1920, p. 1.

263   "That I am solvent": "Ponzi Stops Payment—Not to Take Up Any Notes
      upon Loans," *Boston Post,* August 10, 1920, p. 1.

263   the shouts of newsboys: Ibid.

263   "Don't you fellows knock me": "What He Told Allen Was Bull, Says
      Ponzi," *Boston Daily Globe,* August 10, 1920, p. 1.

263   "I am broke": Ibid.

264   Harry Frazee: "Ponzi Very Sore over Treatment," *Boston Post,* August 10,
      1920, p. 2.

264   a devoted Red Sox fan: "Ponzi Helped Himself to $1,000 Deposits," *Boston
      Herald,* Sept. 6, 1920, p. 1.

264   Ponzi ducked outside for a snack: "Ponzi Very Sore over Treatment," *Boston
      Post,* August 10, 1920, p. 2. Although the story is unbylined, the candor and
      comfort Ponzi displays with the reporter make it reasonable to conclude that
      it was the work of Santosuosso.

265   owlish glasses, receding hairline, and soft jowls: Photograph of Herbert
      Baldwin accompanying undated story found in library files of the *Boston
      Herald,* headlined "Baldwin Joins B & M Staff."

265   "Baldy," as his friends in the newsroom " 'Baldy' Quits B & M Post,"
      Boston Herald, October 13, 1949.

265 while growing up in Everett: Biographical details on Baldwin came from 1920 and 1930 U.S. Census data, and also from an obituary, "Herbert L. Baldwin, 79, Former Boston Newsman," *Boston Herald,* January 23, 1973.

265 "That's Ponsi": Herbert L. Baldwin, "Canadian 'Ponsi' Served Jail Term," *Boston Post,* August 11, 1920, p. 1.

265 "Positively, that's the same man": Ibid.

265 notorious Montreal padrone Antonio Cordasco: Ibid. Other details from Baldwin's trip to Montreal also come from his August 11, 1920, story.

266 "Are you sure?": Kenny, p. 198.

Chapter Seventeen: "I'm not the man."

269 spent the morning in Lexington: "Ponzi's Talk Leaves Club Still Puzzled," *New York Times,* August 11. 1920, p. 15.

269 a summer thunderstorm: "Relief from Heat Today," *Boston Post,* August 10, 1920, p. 1.

269 overdrawn his account by $441,778: *Cunningham v. Commissioner of Banks,* 144 N.E. 447; Annual Report of the Massachusetts Commissioner of Banks, 1920, p. vii.

270 a "battle royal": "Ponzi Tells Kiwanis Club How He Got His Millions," *Boston Evening Globe,* August 10, 1920, p. 1; "Nobody Loses by Ponzi's Transactions, He Says," *Boston Daily Globe,* August 11, 1920, p. 8; Herbert L. Baldwin, "Canadian 'Ponsi' Served Jail Term," *Boston Post,* August 11, 1920, p. 1.

270 "He has a good job": "Ponzi Tells Kiwanis Club How He Got His Millions," *Boston Evening Globe,* August 10, 1920, p. 1.

271 write a sentence on a piece of paper: "Nobody Loses by Ponzi's Transactions, He Says," *Boston Daily Globe,* August 11, 1920, p. 8.

271 Hundreds of letters arrived: "Ponzi Tells Kiwanis Club How He Got His Millions," *Boston Evening Globe,* August 10, 1920, p. 1.

271 Ponzi note holders turned up: Herbert L. Baldwin, "Canadian 'Ponsi' Served Jail Term," *Boston Post,* August 11, 1920, p. 1.

271 Herb Baldwin's copyrighted story: Ibid.

272 An hour after midnight: "Arrest in Ponzi Case May Be Made Today," *Boston Post,* August 12, 1920, p. 1; Curt Norris, "Ponzi," *Yankee,* November 1975, p. 115.

272 "I'm not the man": "Crisis Looms for Ponzi," *Boston Herald,* August 13, 1920, p. 1.

272 "We think this is the truth": Curt Norris, "Ponzi," *Yankee,* November 1975, p. 115.

272   He met reporters again: "Crisis Looms for Ponzi," *Boston Herald,* August 12,
      1920, p. 1.

273   They found Ponzi seated: "Arrests Near in Ponzi Case; Audit Almost Com-
      pleted," *Boston Daily Globe,* August 12, 1920, p. 1; "Arrest in Ponzi Case
      May Be Made Today," *Boston Post,* August 12, 1920, p. 1; "Ponzi Confesses
      Record in Prisons; Pleads for a Chance," *New York Times,* August 12, 1920,
      p. 1; "Bank Commissioner Takes Possession of Hanover Trust," *Boston
      Evening Globe,* August 11, 1920, p. 1; "Crisis Looms for Ponzi," *Boston Her-
      ald,* August 12, 1920, p. 1; "Confessed to Forgery to Protect His Friend,"
      Boston American, August 11, 1920, p. 1; "Sleuths to View Ponzi," *Boston Trav-
      eler,* August 11, 1920, p. 1.

273   "The statement that I am about to make": A stenographer was present when
      Ponzi made his statement, which was then shared with all the newspapers.
      Several printed it verbatim or nearly so, including: "Arrest in Ponzi Case
      May Be Made Today," *Boston Post,* August 12, 1920, p. 1, and "Took Blame
      to Shield Employer, Says Ponzi," *Boston Daily Globe,* August 12, 1920, p. 1.

274   He paused and turned to McIsaac: "Arrest in Ponzi Case May Be Made
      Today," *Boston Post,* August 12, 1920, p. 1.

275   he'd acted to save Zarossi: "Crisis Loom for Ponzi," *Boston Herald,* August
      12, 1920, p. 1.

276   When he had finished his statement: "Arrest in Ponzi Case May Be Made
      Today," *Boston Post,* August 12, 1920, p.1.

276   prison record would lead to his deportation: "Ponzi Confesses Record in
      Prisons; Pleads for a Chance," *New York Times,* August 12, 1920, p. 1.

276   His eyes filled with tears: Ibid.

276   "I want to keep all this news": "Arrests Near in Ponzi Case; Audit Almost
      Completed," *Boston Daily Globe,* August 12, 1920, p. 1.

276   "My nerves can't last forever": "Arrest in Ponzi Case May Be Made Today,"
      Boston Post, August 12, 1920, p. 1.

276   at one forty-five in the afternoon: "Arrests Near in Ponzi Case; Audit Al-
      most Completed," *Boston Daily Globe,* August 12, 1920, p. 1; "Arrest in
      Ponzi Case May Be Made Today," *Boston Post,*" August 12, 1920, p. 1;
      "Ponzi Confesses Record in Prisons; Pleads for a Chance," *New York Times,*
      August 12, 1920, p. 1; "Bank Commissioner Takes Possession of Hanover
      Trust," *Boston Evening Globe,* August 11, 1920, p. 1; "Crisis Looms for
      Ponzi," *Boston Herald,* August 12, 1920, p. 1; "Confessed to Forgery to Pro-
      tect His Friend," *Boston American,* August 11, 1920, p. 1; "Sleuths to View
      Ponzi," *Boston Traveler,* August 11, 1920, p. 1.

277   Chmielinski treated Hanover Trust: Annual Report of the Massachusetts
       Commissioner of Banks, 1921, pp. ix–xv.

277   Hundreds of people raced: "Crowd Gathered at Bank in Record Time,"
       Boston Evening Globe, August 11, 1920, p. 1; "Arrests Near in Ponzi Case;
       Audit Almost Completed," *Boston Daily Globe,* August 12, 1920, p. 1.

277   "I learn with regret": "Arrest in Ponzi Case May Be Made Today," *Boston
       Post,* August 12, 1920, p. 1.

277   no more than $800,000 in liabilities: "Confessed to Forgery to Protect His
       Friend," *Boston American,* August 11, 1920, p. 1.

277   Ponzi left Barristers' Hall at about five o'clock: "Accuses Allen of Closing
       Bank to Tie Up $1,500,000," *Boston Traveler,* August 12, 1920, p. 7.

277   the sound of a woman weeping: "Ponzi Draws Pistol," *Boston Herald,* Au-
       gust 12, 1920, p. 3.

278   A few minutes before midnight: "Accuses Allen of Closing Bank to Tie Up
       $1,500,000," *Boston Traveler,* August 12, 1920, p. 7.

278   he still had fervent believers: "Ponzi Confesses Record in Prisons; Pleads for
       a Chance," *New York Times,* August 12, 1920, p. 1.

278   marveling at "the grip": "Things Look Black for Charles Ponzi," *Boston
       Traveler,* August 12, 1920, editorial page.

278   "Get away from here!": "Arrest in Ponzi Case May Be Made Today," *Boston
       Post,* August 12, 1920, p. 1.

278   he learned the truth: "Ponzi Arrested; Affairs 'Hopeless'; Bank Involved,"
       Boston Herald, August 13, 1920, p. 1.

279   Thomas W. Lawson: "Supposed Ponzi Tried to Get Lawson's Aid," *Boston
       Evening Globe,* August 12, 1920, p. 1.

279   front page of that morning's *Post:* "Arrest in Ponzi Case May Be Made
       Today," *Boston Post,* August 12, 1920, p. 1.

280   made Ponzi cringe: "Ponzi Under Arrest," *Boston Evening Globe,* August 12,
       1920, p. 1.

280   "I am not going to flee": "Ponzi Arrested," *Boston American,* August 12,
       1920, p. 1.

280   pulled down the window shades: "Ponzi Under Arrest," *Boston Evening
       Globe,* August 12, 1920, p. 1. Additional narrative details about this day come
       from Harold Wheeler, "Ponzi Arrested: Admits Now He Cannot Pay—
       $3,000,000 Short," *Boston Post,* August 13, 1920, p. 1; "Ponzi Under Ar-
       rest," *Boston Evening Globe,* August 12, 1920, p. 1; "Ponzi Freed on $35,000
       Bail on Federal and State Charges," *Boston Daily Globe,* August 13, 1920,
       p. 1; "Ponzi Arrested; Liabilities Put at $7,000,000," *New York Times,* August

13, 1920, p. 1; "Ponzi Arrested," *Boston American,* August 12, 1920, p. 1; "Ponzi Arrested; Affairs 'Hopeless'; Bank Involved," *Boston Herald,* August 13, 1920, p. 1.

281 "But you have agreed": Ponzi, p. 172.

281 "No man is ever licked": Ibid.

281 as if for a wedding: Kenny, p. 200.

282 "Mr. Ponzi wishes to surrender.": "Ponzi Arrested," *Boston American,* August 12, 1920, p. 1.

282 "hopelessly insolvent": "Ponzi Arrested; Liabilities Put at $7,000,000," *New York Times,* August 13, 1920, p. 1.

282 "Wife and I were going to buy": "Ponzi Lodged in Cambridge Jail," *Boston Post,* August 14, 1920, p. 1.

282 "You bet he's all right": "Little Italy Still Believes in Ponzi," *Boston Daily Globe,* August 13, 1920, p. 9.

282 "Give you 50 percent": Ibid.

282 "Don't you think": "Ponzi Arrested; Affairs 'Hopeless'; Bank Involved," *Boston Herald,* August 13, 1920, p. 1.

282 he promenaded through Post Office Square: Details of this scene come from a remarkable photograph originally printed on the front page of the *Boston Herald* and now held in the print collection of the Boston Public Library.

283 police inspectors flashed their badges: "Ponzi Arrested; Affairs 'Hopeless'; Bank Involved," *Boston Herald,* August 13, 1920, p. 1.

283 "I am going to stay home": "Ponzi Pursued," *Boston Post,* August 13, p. 9.

283 "I love him more than ever": "Mrs. Ponzi Loyal," *Boston Post,* August 13, 1920, p. 13; "Ponzis Happy at Day's End," *Boston Herald,* August 13, 1920, p. 14; "Mrs. Ponzi Still Has Faith in Husband," *Boston American,* August 13, 1920, p. 2.

284 Ritchie began work: "Viewing the Ruins," *Boston Post,* August 14, 1920, p. 4.

284 half-biblical, half-puritanical editorial: "By the Sweat of Thy Brow," *Boston Sunday Post,* editorial page, August 15, 1920, p. 39.

284 the lead news story: Harold Wheeler, "Ponzi Arrested: Admits Now He Cannot Pay—$3,000,000 Short," *Boston Post,* August 13, 1920, p. 1.

285 bail bondsman Morris Rudnick: "Ponzi Lodged in Cambridge Jail," *Boston Post,* August 14, 1920, p. 1.

285 At about four o'clock that afternoon: Ibid.

285 He looked up at a calendar: Ibid. Additional details of Ponzi's surrender and jailing come from "Ponzi Spends Night in Jail; Surrendered by Bondsman," *Boston Herald,* August 14, 1920, p. 1, and "Ponzi Wearing His Smile Even in East Cambridge Jail," *Boston Evening Globe,* August 14, 1920, p. 1.

286 For two hours they talked: "Testimony of State Officer," *Boston Globe,* November 28, 1922, p. 1. Similar accounts of the meeting between the lawyers and the Ponzis in the East Cambridge Jail come from coverage of Ponzi's 1922 state trial, including: "Thinks Ponzi Honest Man," *Boston Post,* November 28, 1922, p. 1; "Coakley on Stand," *Boston Globe,* November 28, 1922; and "Ponzi Evidence Ends," *Boston Transcript,* November 28, 1922.

287 "I think Mr. Coakley is right": "Thinks Ponzi Honest Man," *Boston Post,* November 28, 1922, p. 1.

287 "What difference does it make": "Testimony of State Officer," *Boston Globe,* November 28, 1922, p. 1.

287 "I might as well be dead": Ibid.

288 When they filed: "State Still After Ponzi," *Boston Post,* December 1, 1920, p. 1; "Ponzi Sentenced to 5 Years in Jail," *New York Times,* December 1, 1920, p. 9; "Ponzi Gets Five Years," *Boston Globe,* December 1, 1920, p. 1; "To Serve Term in Plymouth," *Boston Evening Globe,* November 30, 1920, p. 1.

288 Coakley dug deep into his rhetorical tool kit: The account of Coakley's argument and the court appearance is taken from several sources, largely because of small differences between the accounts in different newspapers. Among the best are: "State Still After Ponzi," *Boston Post,* December 1, 1920, p. 1; "Ponzi Sentenced to 5 Years in Jail," *New York Times,* December 1, 1920, p. 9; and "Ponzi Gets Five Years," *Boston Globe,* December 1, 1920, p. 1.

290 "Sic transit gloria mundi": "Ponzi Sentenced to 5 Years in Jail," *New York Times,* December 1, 1920, p. 9.

EPILOGUE

293 new home: "Ponzi in Cell 126 Looking Out to Sea," *Boston Globe,* December 12, 1920, p. 1.

293 jailhouse routine: "No Chauffeur's Job for Ponzi," *Boston Sunday Globe,* December 5, 1920, p. 1.

293 a remarkably balanced epitaph: "His Victims Much Like Himself," *New York Times,* editorial, December 2, 1920, p. 10.

294 two unexpected write-in candidates: "End Election Canvass in Manhattan-Bronx," *New York Times,* December 29, 1920, p. 14.

294 authorities confiscated the Locomobile: "Mrs. Ponzi, Shorn of Money, Finds Joy in Simple Household Tasks," *Boston Globe,* October 17, 1920.

294 "The house was never as clean": Ibid.

294 John Collins: "Crowd Too Big to Be Allowed in House," *Boston Globe,* October 26, 1921.

294   his top agents: "Ponzi Agents Surrendering," *Boston Herald*, September 15, 1920.

294   All but Cassullo: "Two Witnesses Sought in Ponzi Case Disappear," *Boston Herald*, September 12, 1920, p. 1.

295   renew their search for Antonio Salviati: "Grill Ponzi on Assets," *Boston Traveler*, August 21, 1920, p. 1; "Ex-Partner of Ponzi Taken," *Boston Daily Globe*, August 20, 1920, p. 1.

295   forced to disgorge the money: "Settlement Made by Joseph Daniels," *Boston Globe*, October 28, 1920.

295   copycats from the Old Colony Foreign Exchange Company: "Ponzi Indicted by Grand Jury; Charles M. Brightwell, Head of Rival Get-Rich-Quick Scheme, Also Under Indictment," *Boston Post*, September 12, 1920.

295   banks where Ponzi did business: "Allen Declares the Banking Situation in Boston Is Now Clearer," *Boston Globe*, September 28, 1920, p. 1; "Tremont Trust Company Closed," *Boston Globe*, February 18, 1921, p. 1.

295   "fairness, skill and courage": "Extols Bank Commissioner," *Boston Herald*, September 19, 1920.

296   his choice of Allen: "Joseph C. Allen Resigns as Bank Commissioner," *Boston Transcript*, May 11, 1925.

296   he won both suits: "McMasters Loses Both the Ponzi Suits," *Boston Globe*, February 11, 1921.

296   a career writing fiction: "William H. McMasters Rites Set; Journalist, 94," *Boston Globe*, March 1, 1968, obituary.

296   Clarence Barron: "Clarence W. Barron Could Dictate Four Letters at the Same Time," *Boston Post*, October 7, 1928; *They Told Barron: Conversations and Revelations of an American Pepys in Wall Street*, Harper & Brothers, 1930, pp. xv–xxxiii.

296   their long-running sexual extortion scheme: "Unanimous Decision of 5 Justices for Pelletier's Removal," *Boston Sunday Post*, November 5, 1922, p. 58.

296   suicide triggered by his humiliation: Beatty, p. 247.

297   the irrepressible Coakley: "Daniel H. Coakley Dead at 87; Long Political Figure," *Boston Herald*, September 19, 1952.

297   J. Weston Allen: "J. Weston Allen Dies at Age of 69," *Boston Post*, January 1, 1942, p. 1; "J. Weston Allen Funeral Today at Mt. Auburn," *Boston Globe*, January 2, 1942.

297   Albert Hurwitz: "Albert Hurwitz," *Jewish Advocate*, August 8, 1985, obituary, p. 19.

297   people who had lost money: Katharine Bartlett, "Holders of Ponzi Notes Flock to State House as Last Hope," *Boston Globe*, August 14, 1920, p. 3.

298 Joseph Pearlstein: "Pearlstein Made $500—Now He Sets Good Example," *Boston Globe,* August 14, 1920, p. 2.

298 refunds equal to 37.5 percent: "Estate of Ponzi Now Cleared Up," *Boston Post,* December 17, 1930.

298 Joseph "Sport" Sullivan: "Gambler Indicted for Bribery of White Sox Players," *Boston Herald,* September 30, 1920, p. 1.

298 Herb Baldwin was distracted: Kenny, p. 161; "Store Cat Challenges Hindy to Catnip Meet," *Boston Sunday Post,* October 5, 1920.

299 a brief encounter with Ponzi: "More Arrests Are Coming in Ponzi Case," *Boston Post,* August 20, 1920, p. 1.

299 public relations job: "Herbert L. Baldwin, 79, Former Boston Newsman," *Boston Herald,* January 23, 1973.

299 Eddie Dunn: Caption under a photograph printed in the *Boston Herald,* March 20, 1953.

299 Twice during his *Post* tenure: "Post Executive E. J. Dunn Dies," *Boston Herald,* May 6, 1961, p. 1.

299 P. A. Santosuosso: Edward T. Martin, "Retiring Editor of Italian Newspaper Proud of 30-Year Record of Service to North End Folk," *Boston Post,* June 22, 1952; "Pay Tribute to Santosuosso," *Boston Post,* March 11, 1931.

300 *Post*'s investigation of Ponzi was awarded the Pulitzer Prize: "Bursting Golden Bubble Wins Gold Medal," *Editor & Publisher,* June 4, 1921, p. 1.

300 The *Post* made news of the prize: "Pulitzer Prize Is Awarded to Post," *Boston Post,* May 30, 1921, p. 1.

300 Edwin Grozier set the record straight: Edwin A. Grozier, "The Ponzi Award of Merit," *Boston Post,* editorial page, p. 14, June 1, 1921.

301 "public spirit, courage, and persistence": Photo caption in the *Boston Post,* October 20, 1921, upon presentation of the Pulitzer gold medal.

301 final fatherly words of advice: "Edwin A. Grozier's Will Is Filed," *Boston Post,* June 14, 1924.

301 Margaret "Peggy" Murphy: "Richard Grozier Weds in New York," *Boston Globe,* October 29, 1929.

301 died giving birth: Interview with Mary Grozier, March 7, 2003; "Mrs. Richard Grozier Passes Away Suddenly," *Boston Post,* June 28, 1933.

301 Helen Doherty: "Richard Grozier Marries Nurse," *Boston Traveler,* January 19, 1934.

302 committed to McLean Hospital: Interview with Mary Grozier, March 7, 2003.

302 Inscribed on the plaque: "Tribute Paid to Post Publisher," *Boston Post,* September 23, 1946.

302   struggling to survive: The decline of the *Post* is best told by Kenny, pp. 218–29.

302   In October 1922 he was back in court: "Jury Is Ready to Try Ponzi," *Boston Globe,* October 24, 1922, p. 1.

303   a dozen of the indictments against him: "Ponzi Own Lawyer in Trial for Larceny," *Boston Globe,* October 23, 1920, p. 1.

303   Lucy Meli: "Questions Ex-Secretary," *Boston Globe,* October 25, 1922, p. 1.

303   regaling the jury with his life story: "Coakley on Stand," *Boston Globe,* November 28, 1922, p. 1.

303   Carmela Ottavi: "Ponzi Wins Avowal of Confidence," *Boston Post,* November 1, 1922, p. 9.

304   all found innocent: "Find Ponzi Not Guilty," *Boston Post,* December 2, 1920, p. 1; "Ponzi Is Acquitted of Larceny Charge," *New York Times,* December 2, 1922, p. 9; "Ponzi Verdict Arouses Allen," *Boston Globe,* December 3, 1922, p. 1; "Ponzi Is Freed; Goes to Jail All Smiles," *Boston Traveler,* December 2, 1922, p. 1.

304   the painful ulcers: "Ponzi Will Be Brought to This City for Operation," *Boston Globe,* January 14, 1923; "Ponzi Doing Well After Operation," *Boston Globe,* undated clip, marked "1923."

304   "I do hope that I may live": Letter from Ponzi to Rose, postmarked January 1, 1923; generously provided by the Gnecco family.

304   back on trial: "Ponzi Goes on Trial," *Boston Globe,* November 5, 1924.

304   Ponzi's luck ran out: "Guilty on 14 Counts," *Boston Globe,* February 26, 1925, p. 1; "Charles Ponzi Is Sentenced," *Boston Globe,* July 11, 1925, p. 1.

306   Charpon Land Syndicate: "Florida Lot Plan Opens," *Boston Traveler,* January 12, 1926, p. 1; Robert Norton, "U.S. Keeping One Eye on Mr. Ponzi," *Boston Post,* December 8, 1925, p. 1; "Faithful Rose Squeezes Pennies in Florida to Aid Ponzi in 'Come-Back.' " *Boston Traveler,* December 18, 1925, p. 15; "Ponzi's Friends Declare Wizard Will Give Self Up," *Boston Globe,* February 9, 1926; "Find Water over Ponzi's $10 Lots," *Boston Post,* February 10, 1926, p. 1.

306   violating Florida's securities laws: "Charles Ponzi Sentenced to Year in Prison," *Boston Globe,* April 21, 1926.

306   *Sic Vos Non Vobis:* Charles Ponzi, "Lay Off and I'll Get Out," *Boston Post,* June 30, 1926, p. 1; "Inspector Mitchell Tells Inside of Ponzi's Capture," *Boston Herald,* February 27, 1927, p. 1; Alfred Shrigley, "The Extradition of Charles Ponzi," *City Club Life,* February 17, 1931, p. 3.

307   selling an account of his capture: "Ponzi Appeals to Mussolini for Aid," *Boston Globe,* July 2, 1926.

307 appealed to Calvin Coolidge: "Ponzi Asks Help from President," *Boston
     Globe,* July 4, 1920, p. 1. A copy of the telegram was found on the Web site
     www.mark-knutsen.com.

307 Benito Mussolini: "Ponzi Appeals to Mussolini for Aid," *Boston Globe,* July
     2, 1926.

307 Rose accompanied Imelde Ponzi: "Ponzi Begins 7 to 9 Years Prison Term,"
     Boston Globe, February 16, 1927, p. 1.

307 sewing underwear: "Ponzi Given Prison Work," *Boston Globe,* February 21,
     1927.

307 mother was on her deathbed: "Ponzi's Parent Dies in Italy," *Boston Post,*
     April 18, 1930.

308 the item began: "Ponzi Payment," *Time* magazine, January 5, 1931, p. 42;
     Ponzi's reply was printed January 26, 1931, under the headline "Ponzi from
     Prison."

308 "It's great to see you boys": "Ponzi Unable to Raise $1,000 Bail," *Boston
     Globe,* February 15, 1934, p. 1.

308 Ponzi's old nemesis: "Decided Soon After Hearing," *Boston Globe,* July 10,
     1934, p. 1.

308 Ponzi went to the *Post:* Kenny, p. 202.

308 "I am not bitter": "Ponzi Leaves Boston in Brig of Liner *Vulcania,*" *Boston
     Herald,* October 8, 1934, p. 1; "Ponzi Deported, Leaves in Tears," *Boston
     Globe,* October 8, 1934, p. 1.

310 she could no longer remain Mrs. Ponzi: "Wife of Ponzi Seeks Divorce,"
     Boston Globe, June 27, 1936; "Wife's Divorce Suit 'Tragic,' Says Ponzi,"
     Boston Globe, June 27, 1936.

310 "When he was down": "Mrs. Ponzi Files for Divorce," *Boston Post,* June 27,
     1936.

310 tried to bluff Rose into jealousy: Letter from Ponzi to Rose, dated July 29,
     1941.

310 his cousin Attilio Biseo: James Alan Coogan, "Spy Plot Shown Up by
     Ponzi," *Boston Post,* April 27, 1942, p. 1; Also, Ponzi wrote frequently about
     Biseo in his letters to Rose. Ponzi often called Biseo his nephew, but it ap-
     pears more likely they were cousins; Ponzi's references to him as a nephew
     might have been because of the difference in their ages.

310 efforts to expose a smuggling ring: "Spy Plot Shown Up by Ponzi," *Boston
     Post,* April 27, 1942, p. 1.

310 "quite a tidy sum here": Letter from Ponzi to Rose, dated August 18, 1943.

310 a heart attack: James Alan Coogan, "Spy Plot Shown Up by Ponzi," *Boston
     Post,* April 27, 1942, p. 1.

310   manager of the Cocoanut Grove: Lester Allen. "Club Finances in Name of
      'Straw,' " *Boston Post,* December 8, 1942, p. 1; "Welansky Deposited Funds
      in the Name of Rose Gnecco," *Boston Globe,* December 8, 1942, p. 1.

311   "Of course I am": Letter from Ponzi to Rose, dated July 29, 1941.

311   "I have missed you terribly": Letter from Ponzi to Rose, dated June 26,
      1943.

312   A reporter for the Associated Press: Hoyt Ware, "Ponzi, Once Wizard, Now
      Broken Old Man in a Charity Hospital," *Boston Globe,* May 4, 1948. Ware's
      story received wide attention, appearing in numerous newspapers across the
      country.

312   "Life, hope, and courage": Ponzi, p. 172.

313   died of a blood clot: "Ponzi Dies in Rio in Charity Ward," *New York Times,*
      January 19, 1949.

313   his body returned to Boston: "Won't Try to Return Ponzi Body," *Boston
      Post,* January 19, 1949, p. 1.

313   a full page in *Life* magazine: "Ponzi Dies in Brazil," *Life,* January 31, 1949,
      p. 63.

314   the one thing Ponzi had never lost: Interviews in April and May 2003 with
      John Gnecco, Florence Gnecco Hall, and Mary Gnecco Treen.

Select Bibliography

Allen, Frederick Lewis. *Only Yesterday: An Informal History of the 1920s.* New York: Harper & Row, 1931.

Andros, Howard S. *Buildings and Landmarks of Old Boston: A Guide to the Colonial, Provincial, Federal, and Greek Revival Periods, 1630–1850.* Lebanon, N.H.: University Press of New England, 2001.

Barron, Clarence W. *They Told Barron: Conversations and Revelations of an American Pepys in Wall Street.* New York: Harper & Brothers, 1930.

Beatty, Jack. *The Rascal King: The Life and Times of James Michael Curley (1874–1958).* New York: Perseus Publishing, 1992.

Bulgatz, Joseph. *Ponzi Schemes, Invaders from Mars and More: Extraordinary Popular Delusions and the Madness of Crowds.* New York: Three Rivers Press, 1992.

Chester, George Randolph. *Get-Rich-Quick Wallingford: The Cheerful Account of the Rise and Fall of an American Business Buccaneer.* New York: Curtis Publishing Company, 1907.

Churchill, Allen. *Park Row.* New York: Greenwood Publishing, 1973.

Cooper, John Milton. *Pivotal Decades: The United States, 1900–1920.* Reprint, New York: W. W. Norton & Co., 1992.

Dunn, Donald. *Ponzi: The Boston Swindler.* New York: McGraw-Hill, 1975.

Galbraith, John Kenneth. *The Great Crash, 1929.* Reprint, New York: Mariner Books, 1997.

Goodwin, Doris Kearns. *The Fitzgeralds and the Kennedys: An American Saga.* New York: Simon & Schuster, 1989.

Handlin, Oscar. *Boston's Immigrants, 1790–1880: A Study in Acculturation.* Boston: Harvard University Press, 1991.

Kenny, Herbert. *Newspaper Row: Journalism in the Pre-Television Era.* Boston: Globe Pequot Press, 1987.

Kindleberger, Charles P. *Manias, Panics, and Crashes: A History of Financial Crises.* 4th ed. New York: John Wiley & Sons, 2001.

Kruh, David S. *Always Something Doing: A History of Boston's Infamous Scollay Square.* New York: Faber & Faber, 1990.

Kyvig, David E. *Daily Life in the United States, 1920–1939: Decades of Promise and Pain.* Westport, Conn.: Greenwood Press, 2002.

Mackay, Charles. *Extraordinary Popular Delusions and the Madness of Crowds.* Reprint, New York: Three Rivers Press, 1995.

Maurer, David W. *The Big Con: The Story of the Confidence Man.* New York: Anchor Books, 1999.

Murray, Robert K. *Red Scare: A Study in National Hysteria, 1919–1920.* New York: McGraw-Hill, 1955.

Nash, Robert Jay. *Hustlers and Con Men.* New York: M. Evans and Company, Inc., 1976.

O'Connor, Thomas H. *Bibles, Brahmins, and Bosses: A Short History of Boston.* Boston: Boston Public Library, 1991.

————. *The Boston Irish: A Political History.* Boston: Northeastern University Press, 1995.

————. *The Hub: Past and Present.* Boston: Northeastern University Press, 2001.

Olian, JoAnne. *Everyday Fashions 1909–1920.* Mineola, N.Y.: Dover Publications, 1995.

Ponzi, Charles. *The Rise of Mr. Ponzi.* 1937. Reprint, Naples, Fla.: Inkwell Publishers, 2001.

Pringle, Henry F. *The Life and Times of William Howard Taft: A Biography.* New York: Farrar & Rinehart, 1939.

Puleo, Stephen. *Dark Tide: The Great Boston Molasses Flood of 1919*. Boston: Beacon Press, 2003.

Rayner, Richard. *Drake's Fortune: The Fabulous True Story of the World's Greatest Confidence Artist*. New York: Doubleday, 2002.

Russell, Francis. *A City in Terror 1919, the Boston Police Strike*. New York: Viking Press, 1975.

———. *The Knave of Boston: And Other Ambiguous Massachusetts Characters*. Boston: Quinlan Press, 1987.

Sobel, Robert. *The Great Bull Market: Wall Street in the 1920s*. New York: W. W. Norton & Co., 1968.

INDEX

Page numbers in *italics* refer to illustrations.

A

Abbott, Edwin, Jr., 170, 171–72, 247
Aderhold, A. C., 47, 54
Alabama, 50–56, 243
Albano, Giuseppe, 152
Aldrich, Truman H., 51
Allen, J. Weston, 11, 169, 170, *178*, 190,
    193–94, 197, 198, 203, 212,
    221–23, 236, 239, 242, 247, 252,
    259, 260–61, 271, 280, 282, 283,
    286, 294, 297
Allen, Joseph C., 11, 168–72, 176. *178*,
    198, 206–7, 244, 258–62, 271,
    276–78, 295, 296
American Trust Company, 296
Associated Press, 265, 312
Atlanta Federal Penitentiary, Ponzi in,
    46–50, 274, 275
Austria, 96
  krone, 96
Authoir, Alfred, 9
Avanzino, Lawrence, 82

B

badger game, 189–90
Bailen, Samuel, 201, 202, 242
Baldwin, Herbert L., 183–84, 256,
    265–66, 271–72, 298–99
Banco Zarossi, Ponzi and, 26–28, 30,
    34, 81, 256, 265–66, 272, 275
Bangor, Maine, 124
banking, 49, 56, 145–48, 163–64, 209
  bank commissioner's investigation of
    Ponzi, 170–76, 198, 206–7, 244,
    258–62, 276–78
  Boston, 164–76
  failures after Ponzi's arrest, 276–78,
    295–96
  fraud, 28
  Ponzi's investments in, 143, 145–48,
    161, 163–64, 170, 173, 208,
    239–40, 279
  press and, 168–69, 173, 175–76,
    179–83
  regulation, 167–76, 207, 276–77, 296

banking (*cont'd*):
   Zarossi scheme, 26–28, 30, 45, 81,
     256, 265–66, 272, 275
   see also specific banks
Bank of Hochelaga, 29
Barron, Clarence W., 50, *178,* 184–88,
   202, 208, 210, 219–20, 237–38,
   246, 256, 274, 279, 296
   Ponzi's lawsuit against, 219–20, 223,
    225, 238
Barrows, W. J., 120
Bayonne, New Jersey, 124
Bell-in-Hand pub, Ponzi's operations
   in, 205, 210, 215, 219, 232
Bertoldi, George, 156
Bertoldi, Theresa, 156
Bertollotti, Guglielmo, 118
Bevilacqua, Fiori, 10
Birmingham, Alabama, 50–51, 55–56
Biseo, Attilio, 310
Black and Tans, 129
Black Hand, 47–48
Blass, Louis and Charlotte, 131–32, 140,
   243
Blocton, Alabama, 51–54
Bogni, Ricardo, 121–22, 232
Bologna, 20
Bonina, Joseph, 258
Borden, Lizzie, 42, 74
Borges, Ferdinand, 103–4
Boselli, Mary, 240
Boselli, Ronaldo, 132, 240, 294
Boston, 4–17, 22, 24, 33–43, 57, 73–78,
   96, 105, 106–7, 121, 189, 240
   banking industry, 164–76
   banking regulation, 167–76, 207,
    276–77, 296
   caste system, 149, 173, 203

Curley as mayor of, 76–78
fire of 1872, 34
Irish population, 43, 74–76, 171
newspaper industry, 33–43, 59,
   77–78, 127–31
politics, 74–78, 129–31, 168–71, 203,
   297
Ponzi's arrival in, 24
Ponzi's deportation from, 308, 309
Ponzi's return to, 57, 78
real estate, 145
Securities Exchange Company of-
   fices, 124, 133, 159, 187
State Street, 184–85
Boston Advertiser, 169, 254
Boston American, 37, 219, 224, 238
Boston Board of Aldermen, 75
Boston City Council, 75–76
Boston Common Council, 74, 75, 76,
   171
Boston Daily Advertiser, 37
Boston Daily News, 184
Boston Evening Transcript, 184, 204–5
Boston Globe, 36, 37, 43, 59, 64, 181,
   236, 243, 247–48, 302
Boston Guardian, 43
Boston Herald, 36, 37, 104, 181, 202, 225,
   299
Boston News Bureau, 184, 208, 219
Boston Park Commission, 203
Boston Police Department, 15, 115, 119,
   299
   Securities Exchange Company and,
    119, 127, 145, 200, 206, 231
   strike, 128, 167, 212
Boston Pops, 79
Boston Post, 5–11, 17, 32, 33–43, 69,
   128, 153, 265, 307

cartoons about Ponzi, 218, 223, *230,*
    280, 284
Curley and, 77–78, 129–32
decline of, 302
Edwin Grozier as publisher of,
    37–43, 59–60, 62, 66, 69, 77,
    128–31, 163, 301
Richard Grozier as publisher of,
    162–63, 179–80, 201, 212, 266,
    299–302
history of, 34–43, 59–60
McMasters story on Ponzi, 227–29,
    231–34, 296
Ponzi investigation and stories, 5–11,
    160–63, 169, 175–76, 179–88, 194,
    199–201, 208, 211–13, 217–29,
    231–48, 253–57, 266, 271–76,
    279–80, 284, 298–302, 309
promotions and gimmicks, 40–42,
    69–70
Pulitzer Prize won by, 300, 301, 302,
    309
Boston Public Library, 203
Boston Red Sox, 40, 264
Boston Sunday Herald, 181
Boston Sunday Post, 180
Boston Transcript, 37
Boston Traveler, 6, 37, 138–39, 151, 219,
    242, 278
Bradstreet Company, 155
Brazil, 310, 311, 312, 313
Bridgeport, Connecticut, 124
Brightwell, Charles, 217
Brisco, Peter, 225
Brockton, Massachusetts, 124
Brown, Arthur, 288
Brown, Benjamin, 9
Burlington, Vermont, 124

C

Cahaba Coal Mining Company, 51
Callahan, Catherine, 152
Canada, 26–30, 45, 256, 265–66,
    271–72, 280
Canadian Warehousing Company,
    28–29
C & R Construction Company, 143,
    262
Carberry, Clifton B., 129, 162
Carlson, Gus, 55
Carnegie, Andrew, 54
Case, Arthur, 9
Cassullo, Louis, 13, 123–24, 139–40,
    242, 294–95
Castwell, John, 243–44
Catholicism, 43
Cavagnaro, Joseph, 15–17
Charles Ponzi Steamship
    Company, 165, 239, 252,
    254, 258
Charles River, 185
Charpon Land Syndicate, 305–6
Chester, George Randolph, *Get-*
    Rich-Quick Wallingford: The Cheer-
    ful Account of the Rise and Fall of
    an American Business Buccaneer,
    153–54
Chicago White Sox, 298
Chmielinski, Father John, 147
Chmielinski, Henry, 89, 146–48, 155,
    173–74, 188, 201, 205, 207, 260,
    276–77, 295–96
Ciullo, Alphonso, 151–52
Clifton, New Jersey, 124
Clinton, Massachusetts, 124

Coakley, Daniel, 75, 76, 77, 86, 190, 202–3, 296, 297, 303, 309
  as Ponzi's lawyer, 202–3, 215, 222, 258, 281, 286–89
coal mining, 50–52
Cocoanut Grove fire (Boston), 310–11
Cohan, George M., 153
Collins, John, 3–5, 10, 11, 207, 294
Columbus, Christopher, 135, 235
Communism, 246–47
Congress, U.S., 76
Connecticut, Securities Exchange Company offices in, 124
Consolidated Ubero Plantation Company, 103
Coolidge, Calvin, 11, 15, 128, 167–68, 174, 227, 297, 299
  Ponzi and, 212, 221, 252, 307
  as president, 296, 307
copper, 49
Corbett, "Gentleman Jim," 241, 242–43
Cordasco, Antonio, 26–27, 30, 45, 265–66
Cosmopolitan Trust Company, 8, 161–62, 245–46, 251, 259
  failure of, 295
Cox, Channing, 297
Cretic, S.S., 166
Croker, Richard, 49
Curley, James Michael, 73–78, 129–31, 174, 190, 202, 212, 220, 227
  attacks on Edwin Grozier, 129–31, 163
  as Boston mayor, 76–78
  house scandal, 73–74, 77–78
currency values, exploiting fluctuations in, 97, 113–16, 154–55, 170, 185–86; see also specific currencies

D

Daniels, Joseph, 87, 98–100, 118, 159–62, 295
  lawsuit against Ponzi, 160–63, 169, 173, 175, 217, 239, 244–46, 295
Defrancesco, Dominico, 266
de Masellis, Roberto, 83, 90, 95, 154–55, 222, 232
Democratic Party, 43, 74, 75, 77
Desmond, Daniel, 140, 145
DiPietro, Enrico, 146
Dodge, Lucius, 184
Doherty, Helen, 301
Dondero, John A., 13, 117, 118, 122, 134, 139, 294
Dondero, John S., 116–18, 134, 294
Donovan, Timothy, 9
Dow Jones & Company, 185
Drener, Fred, 152
Drinkwater, Frank, 10
Duane, Patrick J., 281
Dumas, Alexandre, The Count of Monte Cristo, 149
Dunn, Edward J., 162–63, 179, 183, 186, 187, 201, 211–12, 253–54, 299, 309
Dunninger, Joseph, 270, 271
Dwyer, Harry, 235

E

East Cambridge Jail, 285–86
Ebner, Joseph, 314
economy, post–World War I, 83, 94, 95–96
Editor & Publisher, 301

Elbye, John, 152
Electrolytic Marine Salts Company, 102
Eliot, T. S., 61
Engstrom, Richard, 136–37

F

Fall River, Massachusetts, 124
Faneuil Hall, 79, 85, 118, 143
Feinstein, Philip, 9
Fenway Park, 40
Fernandez, Bijou, 40
Fidelity Trust Company, 83, 95, 96, 118, 145, 154, 164
  failure of, 295
Finkel, Sam, 132
First Amendment, 128
Fisher, Charles E., 102–3
Fitzgerald, John "Honey Fitz," 76–77, 78, 174, 190, 202, 227
Florida, 54, 305
  Ponzi's land scheme in, 305–6
Ford, Henry, 4
foreign currencies, 100, 113, 170
  exploiting fluctuations in, 97, 113–16, 154–55, 170, 185–86
  post–World War I devaluation of, 94–96
  see also specific currencies
Fournier, Damien, 28–29
Fox, John, 302
Fox Film Company, 225–26
Framingham, Massachusetts, 124
France, 94, 97, 151
Franklin Syndicate, 105–6
Frazee, Harry, 264

G

Gallagher, Daniel J., 11, 178, 180, 188–89, 190–94, 197, 199, 210, 222, 242, 243, 252, 258, 260, 271, 281–82, 287, 289, 297
Gallivan, James A., 78
gambling, 23
Get Rich Quick promoters, 101–6
Giberti, Ettore, 111–14
  as Securities Exchange Company salesman, 111–15
Giovino, Ernesto, 152
Gish, Lillian, 80
Gnecco, Charlie, 10
Gnecco, John, 83, 85, 117, 156
Gnecco, Maria, 83, 85, 224
Gnecco, Rose, see Ponzi, Rose Gnecco
Gnecco Brothers, 85, 134, 156
Goldstein, Samuel, 152
Gossett, Pearl, 52–54, 81–82
Grady, Bart, 240–41
Grant, Ulysses S., 34
Great Britain, 129, 130
Greene, Colonel Charles G., 34–35, 36
Grozier, Alice, 38, 59–60, 68–69
Grozier, David, 301
Grozier, Edwin Atkins, 32, 33–34, 35–43, 59–69, 162
  background of, 35–37
  as Boston Post publisher, 37–43, 59–60, 62, 66, 69, 77, 128–31, 163, 301
  Curley and, 77–78, 129–31, 163
  physical collapse, 131, 163, 212, 299–300, 301

Grozier, Helen, 59
Grozier, Peggy, 301
Grozier, Richard, 10–11, 33–34, 38, *58,*
    59–70, 131, *158*
    background of, 59–60
    as *Boston Post* publisher, 162–63,
        179–80, 201, 212, 266, 299–302
    death of his wife, 301
    declining health of, 301–2
    at Harvard, 60–68, 69
    Ponzi vs., 179–80, 183, 186, 201,
        211–13, 227–29, 242, 248, 255–56,
        266, 284, 300
    Post apprenticeship, 69–70
Grozier, Richard, Jr., 301

H

Hale, Clarence, 289
Hanover Trust Company, 88–89, 96,
    133, 145, 161, 188
    failure of, 276–78, 295–96
    Ponzi's ties to, 145–48, 163–64, 170,
        172–76, 194, 198–208, 211, 217,
        232, 244, 251, 259–62, 269–70,
        275–78
    Ponzi's vault heist plan, 198–99, 207,
        253, 257, 279
Harding, Warren, 212
Harris, Isaac, 160, 245–46
Hartford, Connecticut, 124
Harvard University, 60–68, 69
Hearst, William Randolph, 36
Herman, Joseph, 243–44
Hoff, William, 9
Holmes, Oliver Wendell, 34, 128
Home for Italian Children, 205,
    224–25, 299

Horan, Patrick, 9
Houdini, Harry, 270
Howe, Sarah, 104–5
Hurlbut, Byron Satterlee, 63–68
Hurwitz, Albert, 11, 170–72, 223, 261,
    297

I

ice business, 49
International Reply Coupons, 6–7,
    89
    Ponzi's trafficking in, 93–101,
        106–8, 112–25, 152–56, 165,
        170–72, 174, 180, 191–94, 218,
        238, 261, 270, 303
International Shipping & Mercantile
    Company, 165
International Trust Company, 154
Ireland, 129–30
Irish-Americans, 43, 74–76, 129–30,
    171
Italian News, 299
Italy, 19–20, 83, 97, 166, 220, 307
    lira, 95
    Ponzi's deportation to, *308,* 309
    Ponzi's early life in, 19–22
    postwar, 83, 95
    sales of reply coupons, 95, 97, 125,
        151–52
    World War I, 57

J

Jacksonville, Florida, 305–6, 307
Jernegan, Prescott Ford, 101–3
Jews, 172, 173, 297
Johnson, Gary, 235

K

Keith's Theater, Boston, 240–41, 242–43
Kell, Frank, 56
Kemp, Joseph, 56
Kennedy, John Fitzgerald, 76, 299, 302
Kennedy, Joseph P., 76, 302
Kennedy, Michael, 152
Kennedy, Rose, 76
King, Cardenio F., 222
Kiwanis Club, 238, 270
Knights of Columbus, 189
Knowles, Joe, 41
krone, 96

L

labor, 26, 42
  immigrant, 26–27
  movement, 42–43
  padrone system, 26–27, 265–66
Lacy, George, 307
Laflamme, Eugene, 265
Lamb, Percy, 123
Langone, Bessie, 13
Lansing, Robert, 247
Larsen, Anders, 132
LATI, 310
Lawrence Trust Company, 140, 145
Lawson, Thomas W., 279
  Frenzied Finance, 279
legal system, 50
  treatment of the rich, 50
Leveroni, Frank, 161, 174, 182, 201, 202, 211, 242

Lexington, Massachusetts, 4, 5–6, 17, 136
  Fonzi's home in, 126, 136–38, 150, 176, 180, 181–82, 214, 226, 255, 278, 294
Life magazine, 313
Lippmann, Walter, 61
lira, 95
Locarno, Angela, 13
Locarno, Marie, 13
Locomobile, 3–4, 8, 11, 150, 180, 186, 207, 280, 294
Locomobile Company of America, 4
Lombard, Myrtle, 79, 80
Lugo, Italy, 19–20
Lupo, Ignazo "the Wolf," 47–48, 49
Lynn, Massachusetts, 124

M

Mafia, 47–48
Mahoney, Harry, 132, 150, 294
Mahoney, Lillian, 150
Maine, Securities Exchange Company offices in, 124
Manchester, New Hampshire, 124
Mancani, Louis, 258
Marie-Louise, Princess, 20
Marr, Arthur, 226
Martelli account, 259–60
Massachusetts State Prison, 307
McCall, John, 29, 30
McCuen, Frederick J., 14
McIsaac, Daniel, 203, 258, 273, 274, 275, 286–88

McMasters, William, 6, 174–75, 190–92, 216–17, 222, 227–29, 281–82, 296, 309
  Ponzi lawsuits, 237, 296
  Post story on Ponzi, 227–29, 231–34, 296
McNary, William, 174, 207, 211, 259–60, 269–70, 276–77
McTiernan, James, 145
Meli, Lucy, 14, 122–23, 133, *142,* 155, 161, 192, 200, 203, 207, 232, 242, 257, 303
Merenda, Joseph, 166–67
Milan, 20, 223
Miller, William Franklin, 105–6, 113, 236, 289
mining, 50–52
Mitchell, Max, 245, 295
Mobile, Alabama, 54–56, 243
Model T, 4, 40
Montreal, 26–30, 45, 256, 265–66, 271–72
Morelli, James Francis, 210–11, 234
Morgan, J. P., 174
Morse, Charles W., 49–50, 52, 185, 202, 274
Mosby, Hal, 236
Mussolini, Benito, 307, 310

N

Naples, 83, 166
Napoleon Bonaparte, 20
Napoli Macaroni Manufacturing Company, 143, 145, 217
Neilson, Henry, 132–33, 294
Newfield, E. H., 219

New Hampshire, 223, 259
  Securities Exchange Company offices in, 124, 258
New Haven, Connecticut, 124
New Jersey, Securities Exchange Company offices in, 124
New Orleans, 56, 307
New York, 25, 36, 49, 57, 74, 93, 94, 105, 209, 218, 223, 243, 294
  Wall Street, 184–85
New York Herald, 106
New York *Journal,* 36
New York Sun, 202
New York Times, 194, 221, 247, 293–94
New York *World,* 36, 37, 43, 236, 300

O

Old Colony Foreign Exchange Company, 14–17, 180, 182–83, 217, 252, 295
  federal investigation of, 217
Old South Trust, 145
Olmsted, Frederick Law, 73
Omati, Elena, 166
Ottavi, Carmela, 10, 303

P

Pawtucket, Rhode Island, 124
padrone system, 26–27, 265–66
Palmer, A. Mitchell, 243
Palmer, Cornelius, 137
Palmer, Teresa, 137
Parker, Alton, 201–2
Park Square Theatre, 264

Parma, 20

Patten, Thomas G., 218

pawnshops, 98, 114

Pearlstein, Joseph, 9–10, 298

Pelletier, Joseph, 11, 77, *178*, 182,
    189–94, 197, 199, 202, 203, 217,
    221–22, 229, 233, 236, 260,
    296–97

Perchek, Rose, 235

Pershing, John T. "Black Jack," 4

peseta, 95

Peters, Andrew J., 78

Peter-to-Paul scams, 104–6, 113–16,
    155, 182, 219, 227, 236, 252, 313,
    314; *see also specific scams*

Petrosino, Giuseppe, 48

Pettibone, Byron M., 181

Phillips Exeter Academy, 60

Pi Alley (Boston), 205, 210, 215, *250*,
    251

Pinkerton National Detective Agency,
    Ponzi protected by, 12, 15, 17, 183,
    193, 200, 204, 226, 231, 234

Pittsburgh, 24–25

Pizzi, Charles, 133, 145

Plymouth, Massachusetts, 124

Plymouth County Jail, 290, 293–94,
    302, 304

Poland, 147, 155

police, *see* Boston Police Department

Polish-American Finance and Trading
    Association, 277

Polish Industrial Association, 147

Ponzi, Charles, *2, 44, 196, 214, 268, 292,
    306, 312*
    aftermath of arrest, 293–99
    in Alabama, 51–56, 243
    in Atlanta prison, 46–50, 274, 275

attempts to go legitimate, 163–65,
    182, 188, 192, 239–40, 252

audits of, 191–94, 198–201, 222, 236,
    238–39, 243, 252, 257–58, 271,
    277, 278, 279, 281

bail, 282, 285, 286

bank commissioner's investigation of,
    170–76, 198, 206–7, 244, 258–62,
    276–78

bankruptcy proceedings, 260–61,
    264–65, 269, 286, 290, 294, 298

Barron lawsuit, 219–20, 223, 225,
    238

birth of, 19

bluff of investors, 134–35, 143–56

Boston Post investigation of, 5–11,
    160–63, 169, 175–76, 179–88, 194,
    199–201, 208, 211, 212–13, 217–29,
    231–48, 253–57, 266, 271–76,
    279–80, 284, 298–302, 309

in Brazil, 310–13

in Canada, 26–30, 45, 256, 265–66,
    271–72, 280

caricatures of, 218, 223, *230*, 280, 284

cheese incident, 86

childhood in Italy, 19–21

confession of, 313

courtship of Rose Gnecco, 79–82

Daniels lawsuit, 160–63, 169, 173,
    175, 217, 239, 244–46, 295

death of, 313–14

death of his father, 21, 85

death of his mother, 307

declining health of, 310, 312, 313

deportation to Italy, *308*, 309

divorce of, 309–10, 311, 314

early money-making schemes, 84–90,
    93–101, 106–8

Ponzi, Charles (*cont'd*):
early years and jobs in America.
24–30
in East Cambridge Jail, 285–86
education of, 20–22
emigration to America, 22–24
as ex-convict, 81–82, 86, 123, 149,
193, 243, 255–57, 265–66, 271–76,
280
federal investigation of, 180, 189–94,
198–201, 210–13, 221–27, 236–48,
252–58, 260–61, 271–88, 294
flight from justice, 306–7
Florida land scheme, 305–6
forgery arrest, 29–30, *44*, 45, 81,
123, 255–57, 265–66, 271–76,
280
growing success of, 112–25, 134,
152–56, 172, 187
Richard Grozier vs., 189–70, 183,
186, 201, 211–13, 227–29, 242,
248, 255–56, 266, 284, 300
guilty plea, 288, 294
Hanover Trust ties, 145–48, 163–64,
170, 172–76, 194, 198–208, 211,
217, 232, 244, 251, 259–62,
269–70, 275–78
Hanover Trust vault heist plan,
198–99, 207, 253, 257, 279
import-export business, 87
investments of, 143–48, 153, 161,
163–64, 170, 173, 208, 239–40,
279, 305–6
larceny charge, 283, 303
lawsuits against, 6, 11, 160–62, 201–2,
217, 237, 244–46, 296
Lexington home of, *126*, 136–38, 150,
176, 180, 181–82, *214*, 226, 255,
278, 294

man-of-the-people image, 208–11,
219–21, 224–25, 233, 239–40, 278,
282, 285
marriage of, 82–85, 98, 100, 114, 117,
134, 150–51, 190, 216, 224–26,
247, 256, 264, 276, 278–84,
287–88, 304, 309, 311
Martelli account, 259–60
in Massachusetts State Prison, 307
McMasters's story on, 227–29,
231–34, 296
names of, 25, 26, 30
physical appearance of, 11–12, 24, 25,
29, 117, 171, 190–91, 208–9, 242,
280, 282–83, 288, 302–3
in Plymouth County Jail, 293–94,
302, 304
"Ponzi scheme" legacy, 314
Poole job, 78–79, 81, 82, 85
postal coupon business, 93–101,
106–8, 112–25, 152–56, 165,
170–72, 174, 180, 191–94, 218,
238, 261, 270, 303
postal officials suspicious of, 124–25,
127, 139, 145, 151–52, 156, 161
press and, 5–11, 17, 127–28, 138–40,
160–63, 169, 175–76, 179–88, 194,
199–201, 204–8, 216–29, 231–48,
253–57, 262–66, 271–85, 293,
297–302, 307–9, 312–13
prison record, 29–30, 45, 46–51,
81–82, 86, 123, 149, 193, 243,
255–57, 265–66, 271–76, 280,
293–94, 302–8
real estate holdings, 143, 145, 305
relationship with his mother, 20, 22,
25, 81, 82, 117, 152, 154, 166–67,
225–26, 307
return to Boston, 57, 78

Securities Exchange Company created by, 106–8

security of, 12, 183, 193, 200, 204, 226, 231, 234

ship scheme, 165, 239, 254, 258

skin donation to Pearl Gossett, 52–54, 81–82

smuggling aliens arrest, 46–48, 81, 274, 275, 280

stamp collection of, 83, 90

surrenders to authorities, 281–82

Trader's Guide idea, 87–89, 95, 96, 146

trials of, 286–90, 302–6

ulcers of, 120, 139, 304

voice of, 12–13

wealth of, 7, 149–56, 162, 187, 193, 209

Ponzi, Imelde, 20–22, 25, 81, 82, 117, 152, 153, 154, 180, 182, *214,* 240, 276, 286, 294, 307

in America, 154, 166–67, 225–26

death of, 307

Ponzi, Oreste, 20–21, 22, 90

death of, 21, 83

Ponzi, Rose Gnecco, 9, 10, *72,* 79–80, 156, 180, 182, *214,* 240, *292,* 307

background of, 80

Cocoanut Grove fire and, 310–11

courted by Ponzi, 79–82

death of, 314

divorce from Ponzi, 309–10, 311, 314

Lexington home of, *126,* 136–38, 150

marriage to Ponzi, 82–85, 98, 100, 114, 117, 134, 150–51, 190, 216, 224–26, 247, 256, 264, 276, 278–84, 287–88, 304, 309, 311

physical appearance of, 79–80, 224, 288

Ponzi's deceptions, arrests, and imprisonments, 276–79, 283–90, 294, 303–5, 310

Ponzi's deportation to Italy, 309

press and, 224–26, 256

remarriage of, 314

Ponzi Alliance, 211

"Ponzi scheme" (term), 314

Poole, John R., 78, 144–45

Poole (J. R.) Company, Boston, 57, 78–79, 81, 82, 85, 144–45, 208, 217

Pope, Frank, 115, 119

Portland, Maine, 124

Portsmouth, New Hampshire, 124

postal coupon scheme, 93–101, 106–8, 112–25, 152–56, 165, 170–72, 174, 180, 191–94, 218, 238, 261, 270, 303; *see also* Securities Exchange Company

postal exchange regulations, 93–94, 97, 100, 116, 120, 124–25, 156, 286

press, 168–69

banking industry and, 168–69, 173, 175–76, 179–83

Ponzi and, 5–11, 17, 127–28, 138–40, 160–63, 169, 175–76, 179–88, 194, 199–201, 204–8, 216–29, 231–48, 253–57, 262–66, 271–85, 293, 297–302, 308–9, 312–13

see also specific publications

Pride, Edwin L., Ponzi audited by, 222, 236, 238–39, 257, 258, 265, 271, 277, 279, 279, 281, 282

Prohibition, 116, 128, 205, 221
Properzi, Reverend Nazareno, 82
Providence, Rhode Island, 124
Pulitzer, Joseph, 36–37, 39, 43, 131
Pulitzer Prize, 300, 301, 302, 309

Q

Quincy, Massachusetts, 124

R

Republican Party, 212
Rhode Island, Securities Exchange
    Company offices in, 124
Rio de Janeiro, 310, 312, 313
Ritchie, William Norman, 218
    cartoons of Ponzi by, 218, 223, 230,
    280, 284
Ritucci, Charles, 133
Riverview, 69
Roberts, Kenneth, 38
Rockefeller, John D., 294
Rome, 20, 21–22, 93, 94, 309
Roosevelt, Theodore, 61, 299
Roosevelt, Theodore, Jr., 61
Ross, Joseph W., 67–68
Rudnick, Morris, 282, 285
Rumania, 151
Rumery, Vera, 64, 68
Ruth, Babe, 128–29, 219, 264
Ryan, Elizabeth "Toodles," 76

S

Sacco and Vanzetti, 128, 297
Saint Vincent de Paul Penitentiary, 30,
    274
Salviati, Antonio, 28, 46, 295

Santosuosso, Principio, 153, 183,
    255–57, 264, 272, 299
    Ponzi note issued to, 92
Sarti, Lionello, 115–16, 117, 303
Securities Exchange Company, 5–17,
    107–8, 110, 305
    audit of, 191–94, 198–201, 222,
        236, 238–39, 243, 252,
        257–58, 271, 277, 278,
        279, 281
    bankruptcy proceedings,
        260–61, 264–65, 269, 286,
        290, 294, 298
    beginnings of, 107–8, 112–16
    counterfeit notes, 242
    deposits suspended, 192–93, 197–98,
        200, 209
    federal investigation of, 180,
        189–94, 198–201, 210–13,
        221–27, 236–48, 251–58,
        260–61, 271–88, 294
    growing success of, 112–25, 134,
        152–56, 172, 187
    imitators and competitors, 14–17,
        180, 182–83, 217, 252, 295
    initial investors, 112–16
    investors, 112–16, 131–34, 143–56,
        161, 186–88, 198, 201–7, 231–36,
        243, 250, 260, 282
    investors' losses, 282, 297–98
    notes, 92, 152–53
    offices and branches, 13–14, 108, 118,
        124, 142, 159, 183, 186, 187, 196,
        200, 209
    "partnership," 118
    police and, 119, 127, 145, 200, 206,
        231
    Ponzi's attempt to legitimize, 163–65,
        182, 188, 192, 239

postal officials suspicious of,
124–25, 127, 139, 145, 151–52,
156, 161
press on, 5–11, 17, 127–28, 138–40,
160–63, 169, 175–76, 179–88, 194,
199–201, 204–8, 216–29, 231–48,
253–57, 262–66, 271–85, 293,
297–302
publicity, 6, 17, 127, 137, 138–40,
190, 216–17, 227–29, 237
run of withdrawals, 201–7, 210–11,
216, 219, 231–36, 239, 243, 246,
250, 298
salesmanship, 111–16, 118, 123–24,
132–34
Sheldon, C. D., 106
Sinn Fein, 43
Socialism, 164, 221, 246
Soviet Union, 246–47
Spain, 89, 95, 97
peseta, 95
postwar economy, 95
Stevenson, W. H., 45–46
Stoneman, David, 201–2
Stott, Percy, 9
Sullivan, Jeremiah, 15
Sullivan, John L., 74, 130, 241
Sullivan, Joseph "Sport," 298
Supreme Court, U.S., 128
Swig, Benjamin, 251
Swig, Simon, 86, 172–73, 208, 228,
234, 251, 279, 295

T

Taft, William, 50, 274
Tammany Club, 74–75
Tammany Hall, 49, 74
Tampa, 306

Tarpon, S.S., 54
Taylor, General Charles H., 36, 37, 59
Texas, 56–57, 235
Ponzi's arrest in, 306, 306, 307
Thomas, Frank, 10, 182
Thompson, J. C., 137
Thorndike, Augustus L., 168
Time magazine, 307–8
Tracy, L. W., 226–27
Trader's Guide, 87–89, 95, 96, 146
Tremont Trust Company, 86, 137, 145,
172–73, 208, 251, 259, 279
Trotter, William Monroe, 43
Tufts, Nathan, 202, 296

U

Union Trust Company, 168
Universal Postal Union, 93, 94, 100,
124, 125, 238
University of Rome, 21, 61

V

Van, Billy, 241, 242–43
Vancouver, S.S., 18, 22–24
Van Wyck, Robert, 49
Vanzetti, Bartolomeo, 181
Vermont, Securities Exchange Com-
pany offices in, 124
Veronoff, Dr. Serge, 180–81
Vulcania, S.S., Ponzi deported on, 308,
309

W

Wait, William Cushing, 201–2, 217
Wall Street Journal, 50, 185
Walsh, David I., 43

Waters Club, 211
Welansky, Barnett, 310
Wells, Edgar H., 61
Wheeler, Harold, 272
White, Mrs. T. C., 55
Winslow, Reverend Ezra D., 35
Wichita Falls, 56–57
Wichita Falls Motor Company, 56
Wilson, Woodrow, 188
women's suffrage, 128

Woonsocket, Rhode Island, 124
Worcester, Massachusetts, 124
World War I, 4, 57, 83, 223
    postwar economy, 83, 94, 95–96
    surplus ships, 165

Z

Zarossi, Luigi "Louis," 26–28, 30, 45,
    81, 265, 272, 275

PHOTO: © SUZANNE KREITER

MITCHELL ZUCKOFF is a professor of journalism at Boston University. He is co-author of *Judgment Ridge,* which was a finalist for the Edgar Award, and author of *Choosing Naia,* a *Boston Globe* bestseller and winner of the Christopher Award. As a reporter with *The Boston Globe,* he was a Pulitzer Prize finalist and winner of numerous national honors, including the 2000 Distinguished Writing Award from the American Society of Newspaper Editors. He lives outside Boston with his wife and two daughters. For more information, please visit www.zuckoff.com.

ABOUT THE TYPE

This book was set in Bembo, a typeface based on an old-style Roman face that was used for Cardinal Bembo's tract *De Aetna* in 1495. Bembo was cut by Francisco Griffo in the early sixteenth century. The Lanston Monotype Company of Philadelphia brought the well-proportioned letterforms of Bembo to the United States in the 1930s.